The Deaf Child in the Family and at School

Essays in Honor of Kathryn P. Meadow-Orlans

The Deaf Child in the Family and at School

Essays in Honor of Kathryn P. Meadow-Orlans

Edited by

Patricia Elizabeth Spencer
Carol J. Erting
Gallaudet University

Marc Marschark
National Technical Institute for the Deaf,
Rochester Institute of Technology

 LAWRENCE ERLBAUM ASSOCIATES, PUBLISHERS
2000   Mahwah, New Jersey   London

Lawrence Erlbaum Associates, Inc., Publishers
10 Industrial Avenue
Mahwah, NJ 07430

Cover design by Kathryn Houghtaling Lacey

Library of Congress Cataloging-in-Publication Data

The deaf child in the family and at school : essays in honor of
Kathryn P. Meadow-Orlans / [edited by] Patricia Elizabeth
Spencer, Carol J. Erting, Marc Marschark.
     p.   cm.
Includes bibliographical references and index.
ISBN 0-8058-3220-3 (cloth : alk. paper). — ISBN 0-8058-3221-1
(pbk. : alk. paper)
1. Deaf children—Family relationships. 2. Deaf chil-
dren—Language. 3. Deaf children—Education. 4. Parents of
deaf children. 5. Child development. 6. Socialization. I.
Meadow-Orlans, Kathryn P. II. Spencer, Patricia Elizabeth. III.
Erting, Carol. IV. Marschark, Marc.
HV2392.2.D43   1999
362.4'23—dc21
                                                99-34490
                                                   CIP

Books published by Lawrence Erlbaum Associates are printed on
acid-free paper, and their bindings are chosen for strength and
durability.

Printed in the United States of America
10   9   8   7   6   5   4   3   2   1

This book is dedicated to Dr. Kathryn P. Meadow-Orlans: researcher, educator, mentor, and friend. For more than 30 years, she has enriched the lives of deaf and hard of hearing children, their parents, and the professionals who work with them. We celebrate her contributions and anticipate those yet to come.

Contents

$\mathbb{F}$oreword

Donald F. Moores
Gallaudet University

It is a pleasure to have the opportunity to write the foreword to a book celebrating the accomplishments of Kathryn Meadow-Orlans and her contributions to the field of deafness over the last third of the 20th century. Her past, present, and future work will influence the field well into the 21st century. Very briefly, I discuss her research and writing and her unique contributions to the knowledge base and attitudes toward deafness within the context of developments in the field since the appearance of her dissertation in 1967.

I imagine I was asked to write this foreword because of my professional interactions with Dr. Meadow-Orlans over several decades. It seemed as if our paths were always crossing and that it was inevitable that sooner or later we would work together. I first became aware of her research when we were both freshly minted PhDs, and people were talking about the dissertation of a sociologist at the University of California, Berkeley, on the effects of early manual communication and family climate on a deaf child's environment. Clearly, this was a fresh voice—it was Kay's. We communicated with each other and first met in 1968 in San Francisco at a meeting of the Alexander Graham Bell Association, where we both made presentations. The fact that we met in an environment that was hostile to the use of any type of manual communication, and that we were among a handful of participants who supported manual communication, probably helped to quickly cement a friendship and professional relationship that continues to this day.

Over the next decade or so, we communicated mostly by print, although we came together for presentations or for the development of books. Memorably, we were both on a panel about total communication and deafness at an annual conference of the American Speech and Hearing Association, another organization that, at the time, had little knowledge of the importance of the use of signs and finger spelling with deaf children. We also collaborated in the writing and development of two texts in the field: *Psycholinguistics and Total Communication: The State of the Art* (O'Rourke, 1972) and *Deaf Children: Developmental Perspective* (Liben, 1978).

When we came together in 1980 at Gallaudet to help establish a structure for the Gallaudet Research Institute, it seemed like a natural culmination of a professional relationship. We worked together closely on the development of the Center for Studies in Education and Human Development that existed from 1981 to 1996; it was there that Dr. Meadow-Orlans took the leadership in establishing a program of research on young deaf children and their families. She and her team of gifted colleagues achieved breakthroughs in research in areas such as motivation, cognition, communication, and family relationships.

In 1990, Dr. Meadow-Orlans and I were coeditors of *Educational and Developmental Aspects of Deafness* (Moores & Meadow-Orlans, 1990), which primarily concentrated on work by professionals affiliated with the Center for Studies in Education and Human Development and that, in many ways, was an adumbration of this text. She took responsibility for the portion of the text on development, and the topics addressed reflect the range of her impact on our field. The chapter titles illustrate this forcefully: *Research on Developmental Aspects of Deafness* (Meadow-Orlans); *Parenting a Deaf Child: Stress, Strength and Support* (Koester & Meadow-Orlans); *The Impact of Childhood Hearing Loss on the Family* (Meadow-Orlans); *Expressions of Affect by Deaf and Hearing Infants* (MacTurk); *Directiveness in Mother–Infant Interactions* (Spencer & Gutfreund); *Mastery Motivation in Deaf and Hearing Infants* (MacTurk); *Attachment Behavior of Deaf Children with Deaf Parents* (Meadow-Orlans, Greenberg, & Erting); *Symbolic Play Behavior of Deaf and Hearing Babies* (Spencer, Deyo, & Grindstaff); *A Comparison of Deaf Students in Israel, Denmark and the United States* (Zwiebel, Meadow-Orlans, & Dyssegaard).

Finally, I had the honor of serving as a discussant at a conference in April 1997 at Gallaudet in honor of Dr. Meadow-Orlans: "Developmental Perspectives on Deaf Individuals." The leadership provided by Dr. Meadow-Orlans during the 15 year existence of the Center established the foundation for work that should continue for decades. It is because of her leadership that so much of the work reported in this book is by contributors to the aforementioned text.

In order to appreciate the contributions of Dr. Meadow-Orlans, it is helpful to understand the changing Zeitgeist throughout her career and the ways she helped shape perspectives on deafness for the better. Her dissertation comparing communication and academic and social skills of deaf children of deaf parents with deaf children of hearing parents appeared at a time when the accepted wisdom was far different from what it is today. In 1967, the dominant philosophy in education of the deaf was oralism. In fact, that year celebrated 100 years of oralism in U.S. education of the deaf as symbolized by the establishment of the Clarke School for the Deaf and the Lexington School for the Deaf in 1867. Almost all deaf children in the United States were instructed through oral-only means, at least through age 12. Manual communication, signs, and fingerspelling were permitted in some schools, but only for older children who were labeled *oral failures*. It was believed that children should have the opportunity to live in the hearing world, and this demanded good speech and speechreading skills. There was also a firmly held belief that any kind of manual communication prevented the development of oral skills and mastery of the English language. Thus, signing was prohibited with young deaf children, and most of the school day was devoted to speech and language (meaning English—most educators at the time did not consider Sign a language).

The impact of Dr. Meadow-Orlans' dissertation, along with a seminal study by Stuckless and Birch (1966) on the influence of early manual communication on the linguistic development of deaf children, helped shatter some of the most dearly held, cherished myths of oral-only educators. Research conducted on two different coasts with different instruments came to very similar conclusions: Deaf children with deaf parents who used American Sign Language (ASL) with them from birth seemed to function at higher academic, communicative, and social levels than deaf children with hearing parents who did not sign with them.

If it were true that the use of ASL inhibited the development of speech and speechreading skills, English mastery, academic achievement, and social adjustment, then deaf children of nonsigning hearing parents would be superior in these areas to deaf children of signing deaf parents. The English skills, speechreading, academic achievement, and social adjustment of deaf children of deaf parents was superior, with no apparent difference in speech intelligibility. It was significant that the older the children were, the greater the gap in achievement in favor of deaf children with deaf parents. The entire theoretical framework of oral-only education was thus called into question. These findings contributed to a fundamental shift in instructional mode over a short period of time to the effect that by 1975 approximately two thirds of deaf children in the United States were being taught, to some extent, through a manual communication mode.

Dr. Meadow-Orlans' subsequent work in California with Dr. Hilde Schlesinger and later in Washington, DC helped bring a different paradigm to research in the area of deafness. In the last half of the 20th century, most researchers in the field have been trained in psychology, education, or linguistics, especially structural linguistics. As a trained sociologist, she brought the tools of a different discipline to bear on the issues. Sometimes these differences were subtle, and sometimes they were pronounced. The outcome was a broadening of perspective to look at the deaf individual within an environmental context, whether it be a family, classroom, or broader social grouping. This, of course, is consistent with the evolution of the Education for All Handicapped Children Act of 1975, with a focus on the individual child, to the Individuals With Disabilities Act of 1990 (IDEA), which expands the emphasis to include the entire family.

Any enumeration of the contributions of Dr. Meadow-Orlans must include the development of the Meadow/Kendall Social-Emotional Assessment Instrument (SEAI; Meadow, 1983). One of the very few instruments of its type, it was originally normed on U.S. deaf children. The SEAI is designed for teacher use and consists of 59 items comprising three scales: social adjustment, self-image, and emotional adjustment. The SEAI has been translated into several languages (I hesitate to provide a number because new translations appear regularly) and has been widely applied to research in various countries. The best known of these studies is probably the comparison of deaf students in Israel, Denmark, and the United States by Zwiebel, Meadow-Orlans, and Dyssegaard (1990).

There is an emphasis on social aspects of deafness throughout Meadow-Orlans' writings and presentations. Other themes can also be identified through an analysis of her numerous publications. Due to space limitations here, I refer to three of her books: *Sound and Sign: Mental Health and Deafness* (Schlesinger & Meadow, 1972), *Deafness and Child Development* (Meadow, 1980), *Educational and Developmental Aspects of Deafness* (Moores & Meadow-Orlans, 1990) without going into detail. The most striking theme in these works is that of possibilities, of the potential for growth that all children possess. Such a statement does not appear to say anything unusual today, but at one time it was considered radical.

People heard and read for generations that the deaf child must learn to live in a hearing world and must be normal or normalized. The key was that the standard for normalcy for a deaf child was that he or she function as much as possible as a hearing child. Because the most obvious outward indication of hearing status was speech, the deaf child had to master speech at all costs. This orientation was detrimental to the deaf child in many ways. First, it distracted attention from the fact that the real difference between a deaf child and a hearing child is the lack of hearing, not the lack of speech. Second, the concentration on speech alone detracted from the development of important social, emotional, linguistic, and cognitive skills. Third was the implication that the deaf child could not be normal as a deaf child. Normalcy, by definition, involved the development of the external trappings of a hearing child—speech. This perversion of the concept of normalcy rejected any type of variation. There was only one standard, and any differences were considered to be deficiencies.

Using this pathological model of deafness, a deaf person without good speech cannot be considered successful academically, socially, or emotionally. It would be a contradiction in terms. Within this context, Meadow-Orlans pointed out that one thing difficult for many hearing parents to accept is the irreversibility of deafness. Despite the promises of improved hearing aids and cochlear implants, most deaf children will grow up to be deaf adults. Parents must be helped to understand this and also to understand that deaf people can do anything that hearing people can. This is a message that Dr. Meadow-Orlans has been delivering for decades. Too often, the outside world puts pressure on deaf children to adjust when it should be encouraging them to grow.

Schlesinger, in her 1972 book with Meadow-Orlans, applied the work of Erik Erikson and his model of eight stages of the human life cycle to issues affecting the development of deaf children. Each stage, or crisis, offers both the opportunity for growth and the danger of failure. The stages have been characterized as basic trust versus mistrust, autonomy versus shame and doubt, initiative versus guilt, industry versus inferiority, identity versus identity diffusion, intimacy versus isolation, generativity versus stagnation, and integrity versus despair.

Each of us negotiates these eight stages with varying degrees of success, and none of us is completely successful. To a large extent success depends not only on our own resources, but also on the actions of family members and other significant members of our environment. In 1972, Schlesinger and Meadow wrote:

> We are fully aware from our contact with deaf individuals that the eight stages can be traversed more productively, more joyfully, and with a more adequate resolution of each developmental crisis. This more successful passage through the life cycle we have found most frequently (although not exclusively) in the deaf children of deaf parents. We hope that our account has helped to explain this higher achievement. We also hope it will help hearing parents to ponder, to increase acceptance of deafness in their children, and with this acceptance help their children to meet and master the challenges of each life crisis. (p. 29)

Those words are as significant today as they were when they were written.

REFERENCES

Liben, L. S. (1978). *Deaf children: Developmental perspectives.* New York: Academic Press.

Meadow, K. P. (1980). *Deafness and child development.* Berkeley: University of California Press.

Meadow, K. P. (1983). *The revised SEAI manual (forms for school age and pre-school students).* Washington, DC: Gallaudet University.

Moores, D., & Meadow-Orlans, K. P. (1990). *Educational and developmental aspects of deafness.* Washington, DC: Gallaudet University Press.

O'Rourke, T. (1972). *Psycholinguistics and total communication: The state of the art.* Silver Spring, MD: American Annals of the Deaf.

Schlesinger, H., & Meadow, K. P. (1972). *Sound and sign: Childhood deafness and mental health.* Berkeley: University of California Press.

Stuckless, E., & Birch, J. (1966). The Influence of early manual communication on the linguistic development of deaf children. *American Annals of the Deaf, 111,* 452–469, 499–504.

Zwiebel, A., Meadow-Orlans, K., & Dyssegaard, B. (1990). A comparison of deaf students in Israel, Denmark and the United States. In D. Moores & K. Meadow-Orlans (Eds.), *Educational and developmental aspects of deafness* (pp. 407–416). Washington, DC: Gallaudet University Press.

Introduction to the Book

Researchers studying the growth of deaf[1] children have made significant and impressive strides since the mid-1970s. Indeed, attitudes have evolved from a time when deaf children were seen essentially as broken hearing children to a time when there is an understanding and appreciation of both their special qualities and the many characteristics they share with hearing children. Researchers now are able to provide teachers, lawmakers, and other professionals with sound advice concerning the needs and challenges of deaf children and their families, and to contribute to optimizing their educational and personal growth. This progress notwithstanding, it is rare that basic research and application, family and school, are considered in a single venue.

This volume brings together chapters from an international group of researchers, educators, and clinicians, whose work focuses on the development of deaf and hard of hearing children and adolescents. The ideas presented here have been influenced in various ways by the groundbreaking work of Kathryn P. Meadow-Orlans, who, with her colleague Hilde Schlesinger, promoted the application of developmental theories and approaches to the study of deaf and hard of hearing children (Schlesinger & Meadow, 1972).

---

[1]Variation will be noted throughout this book on the capitalization of the first letter of the word "deaf." Beginning the word with a capital letter is a convention typically used to signify persons who participate in and identify with a specific Deaf cultural group. In contrast, uncapitalized use of the word deaf tends to be used more inclusively and more often describes persons based on audiological status instead of participation in a cultural group. Because interpretation and use of these conventions is not universal, capitalization usage differs across chapters.

A central theme of this book is the ecological nature of development (Bronfrenbrenner, 1979). Characteristics of the child (e.g., temperament, hearing status) interact with characteristics of the environment to produce a unique system that influences, and is influenced by, interactions in ever-broadening, hierarchically layered contexts. These contexts include family, friendship and peer groups, educational and therapeutic service providers, and larger social and political entities. These are all areas that have been touched by Meadow-Orlans' work and must be considered holistically in order to optimize the development and education of deaf children.

The book is organized into three sections. The first focuses on deaf and hard of hearing children in the context of the family. Interactions between family and school are addressed in the second section. The third section considers issues related to design of, and contexts for, educational interventions and programs. Chapters in this last section address ways that special characteristics of deaf and hard of hearing learners, as well as societal expectations for their achievement, affect services provided for and development attained by those students.

The complexity of the individual and societal factors influencing development of deaf and hard of hearing children calls for integration of diverse perspectives and areas of expertise if that development is to be understood. This book provides such a variety of perspectives. To that end, chapters represent the views of authors with backgrounds in a number of professional fields, including anthropology, sociology, psychology, education, medicine, and social work. In addition, chapters represent the perspectives of deaf as well as hearing professionals. Authors of several chapters provide first person descriptions by deaf children and their parents of the systems in which they participate.

Despite the diversity of perspectives provided, a number of basic generalizations about the development of deaf and hard of hearing children can be drawn from the chapters in this book. These include recognition of the following:

- Deaf and hard of hearing children as visual learners and communicators.
- Strengths of both deaf and hearing families in supporting their children's development, especially with early intervention support.
- Continued gaps in the quality of services provided to families of deaf and hard of hearing children.
- Impact of programming and placement variations on personal as well as academic development of deaf and hard of hearing students.
- Continued need for improved educational methods and curricula to better accommodate diverse characteristics of deaf and hard of hearing children and promote their development.

- Need for participation and interaction of children, parents, educators, and researchers in designing more effective interventions and supports.

Taken together, these chapters provide both a broad context for understanding the educational development of deaf children and an outline for fostering their growth. Although not originally intended to tell a single story, the research and observations provided by the various authors weave themselves into a single, multicolored fabric covering an entire community. The families, teachers, and others who seek to expand the opportunities for deaf children will find here a wealth of information and clear direction. Whether dealing with communication between hearing mothers and their deaf children, behavior in suburban classrooms, or the challenges of providing literacy to deaf children in difficult settings, this book provides perspective and understanding. It is only through such collaborations that we can truly succeed and only through such cooperation that we can help deaf children achieve their potentials. We, the editors, therefore thank the authors of these chapters for their contributions and Kay Meadow-Orlans for her years of leadership.

—*Patricia Elizabeth Spencer*
—*Carol J. Erting*
—*Marc Marschark*

REFERENCES

Bronfenbrenner, U. (1979). *The ecology of human development: Experiments by nature and design.* Cambridge, MA: Harvard University Press.

Schlesinger, H., & Meadow, K. (1972). *Sound and sign: Childhood deafness and mental health.* Berkeley, CA: University of California Press.

The Deaf Child in the Family

A child's development is integrally related to the ecology of the family. This is as true for deaf and hard of hearing children as for other children. In this section, a unique set of chapters explores the development of deaf and hard of hearing children within the family. Together, the chapters describe the ways deaf children and those around them develop or fail to develop synchronous and reciprocal relationships. These relationships form the ever-changing matrix for social, language, and cognitive growth as children become, perhaps paradoxically, increasingly independent but increasingly interdependent with their environments. Each in its own way, the following chapters provide insights into the ways deaf children and those around them see themselves and each other, the way their behaviors and those of their parents are intertwined, and the increasing complexity of development in context.

In the first chapter, Sheridan explores deaf children's understanding of who they are and their relations to other deaf and hearing individuals in the family and beyond. Researchers are accustomed to using definitions in research to place children and concepts into various categories. Here, Sheridan discovers the categories in which deaf children place themselves. Thus, she provides a glimpse of the social matrix from the perspective of those who are usually categorized. Sheridan's analysis points out the importance of modes of communication in the children's view of those who are like and unlike themselves. Despite this theme, the children's responses to Sheridan's questions suggest that they are not always sure where they fit—a personal challenge that can continue, often throughout their lives, for deaf individuals.

The five chapters that follow provide a comprehensive, integrative view of the early developmental ecologies of deaf and hard of hearing children within the family. Early research of investigators like Kathryn

Meadow-Orlans, David Wood, Margaret Harris, and others has demonstrated how understanding ways that deaf mothers interact with their deaf children can enrich efforts to support hearing families of deaf and hard of hearing children. In her chapter, Swisher provides an essential primer about the ways deaf mothers support and encourage the development of visual attention and the concomitant foundations for language development in deaf children. She reviews studies of early changes in maternal and child attention-related behaviors and provides new data concerning ways that mother–child dyads share attention with each other and with objects in the environment. The data reveal the complex nature of mothers' sensitive support for the development of communication and a visual language.

Erting, Thumann-Prezioso, and Benedict expand this perspective on dyads of deaf mothers and deaf children. They describe ways these mothers employ visual communication and especially fingerspelling to provide a basis for developing literacy as well as language skills. Together, this chapter and the one before it point out strengths in the model of interaction and communication provided by deaf mothers as well as the presence of natural variations in their behaviors.

Koester, Papoušek, and Smith-Gray broaden the perspective to report on ways that both deaf and hearing mothers maintain behavioral dialogues with deaf and hard of hearing infants, as well as ways the channel of communication (voice, touch, signs, etc.) affects those interactions. The authors employ the concept of *intuitive parenting* to describe interactive behaviors that parents use to support and encourage development. This concept also is used to provide insight into the complex nature of the social–communication interaction and to suggest ways in which reciprocal parent–child interaction can be optimized.

Lederberg and Prezbindowski deal with similar issues in their examination of interactions between hearing mothers and their deaf toddlers. Comparing earlier findings from Lederberg's laboratory and Meadow-Orlans' group, the authors argue the importance of understanding positive aspects of interactions between hearing mothers and their deaf children as well as identifying areas in which they experience problems. The reanalysis of these data, especially as they relate to attachment, communication, and play, suggests that apparent discrepancies between studies are explained in part by educational and socioeconomic differences between the groups of mothers. Again, the complex mosaic of developmentally relevant variables is revealed in the search for those factors affecting the early development of deaf and hard of hearing children.

Steinberg provides yet a different perspective. Based on retrospective interviews and clinical interactions with deaf adolescents and adults, she reports poignant examples of experiences of deaf children who did not grow up in families, schools, and neighborhoods where they had full access to communication. These reports of confusion, isolation, and loneliness give ample evidence of the need to assist hearing families in their quest to provide communication and language access for the deaf and hard of hearing children they love.

Images of Self and Others:
Stories From the Children

Martha A. Sheridan
Gallaudet University

Seven-year-old "Alex" is profoundly deaf and attends a residential school for the deaf. His parents are both hearing, and he has one hard of hearing and one hearing sibling. Alex draws a picture of his family for me. After showing me where he is in the picture, I am curious about the rest of his drawing.

I: Great. Okay. And this is the deaf boy. Who's this?

A: His sister.

I: Who's this?

A: His mom and dad.

I: OK. Are they deaf or hearing?

A: Ummmm, she signs and talks both. She can sign, and she can speak … the sister. And the mom can sign and speak both, and the dad can sign and speak. All of …

I: So are they hearing?

A: Well, hearing and deaf both, because they, they sign and speak. Both. (Sheridan, 1996, pp. 65–66)

This dialogue is an excerpt from a research interview conducted as part of a study of deaf children. The purpose of this research was to explore and describe how deaf children experience and interpret their lifeworlds.

Researchers in deafness have attempted to define who is deaf using cultural (Meadow, 1972; Padden, 1980; Padden & Humphries 1988) or medical (Myklebust, 1954) definitions. However, as will become apparent, the children interviewed in this study have their own voice on the matter. Their definitions of who is deaf, hearing, and hard of hearing are not based on cultural or medical perspectives discussed in the literature on deafness. Instead, they are based on overt visual indicators such as signing, mouth movements, use of speech, hearing aids, or telecommunication devices for the deaf (TTYs). The children's stories in this study have much to tell us about who they see as similar to or different from themselves, where they feel a sense of belonging, and where they feel alienated. Their stories tell us how important it is to listen to the voices of the children, something that few researchers have actually done.

This chapter may be different from others in this book in that it presents children's perspectives, addressing questions that have been largely ignored in the literature and research on deafness. Some of the images that deaf children shared with me during phenomenological interviews will be described (Sheridan, 1996). Although several themes emerged from the study, this chapter focuses on three themes that reflect the children's views of their relationships with others, the similarities and differences they see between themselves and others (acceptance and domesticated others, alienation and disparate others), and how deaf children determine who is deaf, hearing, and hard of hearing (covert and overt identity).

BACKGROUND OF THE STUDY

I came to this study with nearly 20 years of professional experience as a social worker with people who are deaf and hard of hearing, their families, and communities. My clinical social work education and my experiences as a person who is deaf taught me to value diversity and participatory relationships. My regard for collaborative interactive knowledge is congruent with acknowledging the voices of the children in this study pertaining to their lifeworlds.

My life commitment to my work with deaf and hard of hearing people requires me to be familiar with the literature and research on deaf children. My orientation to recent critical perspectives of the literature on deafness influenced my decision to explore the lifeworlds of deaf children using qualitative methods.

The scope of this chapter does not allow for a full review and critique of the literature on deaf children. Briefly, however, there is much discussion of the social experiences and development of the deaf child. Topics include development and the influence of the social environment, as well as parental and family reactions to and acceptance of a child's deafness (e.g., Harvey, 1989; Maher, 1989; Meadow, 1969; Schlesinger & Meadow, 1972; Sloman, Springer, & Vachon, 1993; Vernon & Andrews, 1990); social stigma, social alienation, and institutional discrimination in various sectors of society (e.g., Humphries, 1977; Lane, 1992); issues of identity, self-esteem, and self-concept (e.g., Bat-Chava, 1993; Coyner, 1993; Desselle, 1994; Desselle & Pearlmutter, 1997; Meadow, 1968; Meadow-Orlans, 1983; Schlesinger & Meadow, 1972; Searls, 1993); and belonging (e.g., Becker, 1987; Maxon, Brackett, & van den Berg, 1991; Meadow-Orlans, 1983; Nash & Nash, 1981). The majority of these authors also discuss issues of communication, which is viewed as a predominant factor in deaf children's lives.

Several authors discuss problems in research with deaf persons. These include the failure of researchers to define deafness (Lane, 1992; Lane, Hoffmeister, & Behan, 1996; Moores, 1987; Schein & Delk, 1974), developing knowledge of people who are deaf based on the subjective perceptions of hearing others such as parents and teachers (Lane, 1992; Lane et al., 1996), the inability of hearing researchers to communicate with their deaf subjects (Lane, 1992; Lane et al., 1996; Levine, 1960), and culturally biased instrumentation, which is typically based on English language skills and norms for hearing people (Lane, 1992; Schroedel, 1984). Akamatsu (1993/1994), Foster (1993/1994), Hauser (1993/1994), Pollard (1993/1994), and Stinson (1993/1994) discussed cross cultural issues inherent in research with deaf people and the deaf community. Lane et al. critique the literature so strongly as to propose that it should be ignored because of these flaws and suggest that the observations of professionals who work closely with people who are deaf differ from those reported in much of the research. Moores suggested "complex social contexts" (p. 167) need to be considered in evaluation of deaf people.

In addition to the clinical (Myklebust, 1954) and cultural (Padden, 1980) perspectives on deafness, Foster (1996) introduces the political model to deafness. Research from this perspective can reflect the voices of people who are deaf.

Taking the above into consideration, I was interested in applying a research paradigm that would allow me to generate data from the voices of the children themselves, in the context of their natural environments.

METHODOLOGY

Qualitative researchers are interested in developing knowledge from the perspectives of the participants within the context of the study. The value of an inductive qualitative research method for understanding children who are deaf and hard of hearing lies in the emergence of themes and theory through the inductive analysis of stories told by the children themselves. Advocates of the rights of people who are deaf and hard of hearing have long been saying, "Let us speak for ourselves." This methodology allowed for that through in-depth interviews with children who are deaf.

Naturalistic inquiry (Lincoln & Guba, 1985), which focuses on the meanings that people have of their interactions with the environment, is a viable approach to exploring deaf and hard of hearing children's perspectives of their lifeworlds. The literature discussing the complex problems of conventional research methodology in generating data from such a diverse population supports this (Akamatsu, 1993/1994; Foster, 1993/1994; Hauser, 1993/1994; Lane, 1992; Lane et al., 1996; Levine, 1960; Moores, 1987; Schein & Delk, 1974; Stinson, 1993/1994). Naturalism respects the unique reality of the child who is deaf, allowing the researcher to consider cultural, ethnic, linguistic, communication, and physical differences through detailed documentation. This phenomenological study explores and describes what deaf children see, think, and experience in the context of their subjective lifeworlds.

Selection of Study Participants

Purposeful sampling techniques were used in this study to identify informants able to provide rich information and to document unique variations among the children. The purposive techniques of maximum variation and snowball sampling allowed me to include boys and girls from a variety of cultural, educational, familial, biological, racial, and linguistic backgrounds. Profiles were developed for each child describing his or her unique characteristics. The final sample of seven school children between the ages of 7 and 10 included four boys and three girls. Four of the children were mainstreamed and three were residential school students. Unique characteristics of each child are described in this chapter as the stories unfold.

Data Collection Procedures

An interview guide and open ended questions were used to learn about the perceptions the children had of themselves and others, their social experiences, and the meanings they gave to those experiences. Depth probing (Glesne & Peshkin, 1992) was also used to collect data in video taped interviews. In addition, data was obtained from field journal documentations of observations of the children at home and school. The researcher communicated in ASL with ASL-using children and used simultaneous communication with children who communicated in English. As a precaution, in the event that the signing was not clearly visible on the video tapes, a sign language interpreter was employed to voice the taped interviews. The sign language interpreter also transcribed the interviews to text. Once transcriptions were completed by the interpreter, I checked them for accuracy through repeated review of the tapes and transcriptions.

Trustworthiness of qualitative methods is described by Lincoln and Guba (1985) as the credibility, dependability, transferability, and confirmability of a study. Methods employed in this study to establish trustworthiness of qualitative data analysis include member checking, peer debriefing, triangulation, and reflexive journaling.

Direct and projective interview techniques were used. Projective techniques included the children's drawings of themselves and others and storytelling. Storytelling was encouraged through questions by the interviewer such as, "Can you draw a picture of a deaf boy (or girl) for me?" and, "Tell me a story about that deaf boy (or girl)." Storytelling was also elicited with pictures cut out from magazines.

Data Analysis

In naturalistic inquiry, findings are grounded in the specific context of the study. Themes and theory are discovered through an inductive process that involves the coding and categorizing of data. The constant comparative method (Strauss, 1987) was used to analyze data in this study as it was discovered, comparing new data with concepts emerging from the inquiry. This process involved ongoing reshaping and refining of the interpretations of the words, stories, behavioral observations, and nonverbal communications of the children. Thus, the findings presented in this chapter are themes common to the children that emerged from this process of coding and categorizing of the data within and across cases. The findings are restricted to the particular cases, times, and settings in this study and should not be generalized to the total population of deaf and hard of hearing children.

Findings

The children's stories in the following sections illustrate the themes of attachment and domesticated others, alienation and disparate others, and covert and overt identity. The scope of this chapter does not permit all of the stories to be presented here, and the reader is referred to the original research (Sheridan, 1996) for more details.

ATTACHMENT AND DOMESTICATED OTHERS

The children's feelings about themselves and in the presence of others were indicated by affectual reports (Sheridan, 1996). These affectual reports, or interpretations and stories the children expressed in the interviews about their feelings and experiences, included situations where the children experienced a sense of attachment. Their sense of attachment occurred primarily in the company of domesticated others (Sheridan, 1996). There were, however, situations where the children reported a sense of comfort and attachment in the company of others who were unlike themselves in hearing status, language, or communication mode.

Some of the children's stories tell us that how a person communicates is an important factor in their sense of belonging and their acceptance of others as similar to or different from themselves. Some of the children also expressed feelings of comfort and acceptance in the company of hearing others regardless of how the hearing people communicated. People who the deaf child sees as similar to him or herself, regardless of their hearing status, are called *domesticated others.* Domesticated others is a classification of others based on the children's judgments. Two examples of domesticated others include hearing people that the deaf child sees as deaf or as similar to him or herself because of their ability to sign (e.g. Alex's family members) and other deaf or hard of hearing people that the child sees as similar to him or herself. The children may or may not be aware of the hearing status of the person they are observing.

"Danny" was 9-years-old at the time of the study and was profoundly deaf from birth. His parents both signed. His mother was hard of hearing and active at his residential school. His father and one sibling were both hearing. Danny had no additional disabilities and reported he was happy in the company of his deaf peers. Danny communicated in ASL. As Danny drew a picture of a deaf boy at his residential school, the comfort he felt in this environment was apparent.

I: If the deaf boy was playing with other deaf kids, how would he feel?

D: Happy.

D: (Later) Deaf. Deaf. He has many friends, many friends. Well, his friends are (signs several names of deaf friends at school). He has lots of friends they play "It." You know, where you tag somebody and they're it, and then you run? It's also called "tag" ... and they go on the swing set together.

I: And is the boy happy at his school? Is he happy?

D: Yes, the boy likes to learn. He likes to learn things, lots of things.

I: You like that boy?

D: Mmm hmm.

I: ... That boy's friends, are they deaf or hearing or ... ?

D: Oh, they're deaf. All of them. They're in the other hall, and sometimes there are hearing friends, but very few of them. But most of them are pure deaf.

Danny also discussed a play situation with hearing children where a communication barrier existed. Danny reported a sense of relief when he met a hearing child who signs:

D: ... like if there's hearing people on a team or something like that and there's somebody that's shy, well, hearing people, they can just talk, you know, talk with their mouths. And then they might say, "You can ..." and then they find out this boy's deaf and it's like, "Oh you can sign?" And then the boy might go "Yeah, I can sign. I can sign. I'm hearing but I can sign." And then the deaf boy would, well, they would become friends, and they could be on a football team to-gether or a baseball team together or a basketball team 'cause they could sign together. 'Cause they could learn.

I: So how's the boy feel?

D: Oh, the boy would feel really good and be surprised too.

"Angie" was a ten-year-old profoundly deaf child who was mainstreamed in a total communication program for deaf children. She used ASL. Her parents were both hearing. She had no brothers or sisters. Angie had atten-tion deficit hyperactivity disorder (ADHD). The cause of her deafness and age of onset was unknown. Angie's parents communicated with her in Signed English. It was clear that Angie had domesticated others in her re-port that deaf children are not shy in the company of other deaf children:

A: Deaf kids go to school and have deaf friends and they're not shy.

The aforementioned stories indicate the children's sense of attach-ment, belonging, self-assurance, and fulfillment in relationships with do-mesticated others where communication was accessible regardless of hearing status. These domesticated others included both deaf and hearing children, deaf and hearing parents, teachers, and siblings.

A theme common to most children in this study was comfort in the pres-ence of peers who are deaf. Their comfort level with hearing peers was ev-ident for most if the hearing peers could sign. Data from stories in this study that are not presented in this chapter, in addition to those that are, tell us that communication, not hearing status, appears to be the primary factor in determining the children's comfort level and sense of attachment to others.

A child's sense of attachment occurred primarily in the company of do-mesticated others. However, some of the children's stories also showed situations where the children reported a sense of belonging and attach-ment in the company of others who were unlike them in hearing status, language, or communication mode. Eight-year-old "Mary," a profoundly deaf child of deaf parents whose siblings were also deaf, attended a main-stream total communication program and used both ASL and Signed Eng-lish. Although Mary's family was deaf, she reflected a positive attitude and comfort in her school environment where she was mainstreamed with both deaf and hearing peers. She reported she makes friends very easily and that it is no problem for deaf and hearing children to get along. Mary's response indicated that she felt attached in the company of both deaf and hearing children and makes no mention of communication.

> I: Now suppose there's a hearing family and there's a deaf family. Are there going to be any differences?
>
> M: No, you can still be friends. It doesn't make any difference, you can be friends ... I have lots of friends ... there's lots.
>
> I: Your school now has a mixture, but if you were the only deaf person ...
>
> M: I'd make friends with hearing people, I'd make friends.

After Mary explained how she was mainstreamed for some classes and at other times she attended a self-contained class with other deaf students, I asked if she felt different in the two groups.

> M: You just switch. No. You just go into one or the other. They're both comfortable because I have friends in both. I have a lot of friends.

ALIENATION AND DISPARATE OTHERS

Although the children had stories to tell about feelings of attachment in relationships with domesticated others, they also told of situations where they felt alienated in relationships with disparate others. These feelings of alienation included boredom in communicatively inaccessible situations, awareness of potential rejection by hearing peers, shyness, nervousness, discomfort in the presence of hearing children who did not sign, discomfort with teasing by hearing peers, and frustration.

Disparate others are people that the child sees and judges as different from him or herself regardless of the individual's hearing status. The children were sometimes not aware of the hearing status of the person they were observing.

Three examples of disparate others that arose from this study are a hard of hearing child who was seen by a deaf child from a deaf family as different from her, a deaf child from a deaf family who was perceived by a hard of hearing child from a hearing family as different from him, and hearing children and adults who were portrayed in several of the deaf children's stories as different from themselves.

Danny drew a picture of a deaf boy for me. I asked him to tell me stories about the deaf boy and about playing with hearing children:

> D: Well, he (the deaf boy) might be kind of nervous and ... yeah, a little unsure. Because they're hearing and they might not know ... He might not know how to use his voice, so they might not understand

... Maybe not comfortable ... Kind of shy and kind of embarrassed and kind of hesitant. A little bit afraid if no one signs.

In the second interview with Danny, as I showed him some pictures cut out from magazines and asked him to tell me stories about the characters in the pictures, he told me about a group of hearing children playing together. I wanted to know what he thought would happen if a deaf boy tried to join them.

I: Ok, they're all hearing right? (referring to his story) If a deaf boy should happen along and say, "I want to play with you," what would they do? How would they react?

D: Well, they'd be puzzled and they'd say, "Go away, Go away."

I: Well, that's not very nice. How does the deaf boy feel?

D: Kind of sad. Because they don't want him around. And he might be kind of mad and kind of lonely. That's how he might feel.

While looking at a picture of two children, one talking on the phone and the other sitting close by, several children perceived the one talking on the phone as hearing and identified the other as deaf. They also reported that the deaf child was bored in that situation. Ten-year-old Angie's story is typical of the children's responses:

A: This person's deaf. ... This person's hearing.

I: That person's hearing? How do you know?

A: Talking on the phone. And this person's getting really bored. And waiting and waiting. The friend's chatting on the phone. He wants to play a game with him. But he's bored, his friend's bored. And he's making faces maybe at his friend or something. And the other one's just ignoring him.

"Joe," who was ten years old at the time of the study, had a severe hearing loss and considered himself hard of hearing. He became deaf at approximately 5 months of age from an unknown cause. Joe lived with his mother and was mainstreamed in a total communication program for deaf children. All his family members were hearing, and they communicated primarily through speech but also knew sign language. Joe is African American and had the most hearing of the seven children in the study. He had no additional disabilities. Joe reported being teased by hearing children. He also saw himself as different from a classmate who had a deaf family. To Joe, this family represented another group of disparate others. He spoke and signed as he shared his stories with me.

J: I have this one friend, Thomas and Catherine (he voices and gives name signs). They're all from the same family. And all of his family, their whole family, the parents and everybody else is deaf. They're all deaf. And they have a lot of deaf kids in their family. This one family, they're all deaf. I was really surprised when, when Thomas' mom had the baby and then Catherine was born deaf. Well, when they all came one time, and I said, when I talked they didn't understand. I tried talking, and I talked, and I had to sign. And then they signed back to me, and I thought, "Whoa!" ... Yeah, but when I talked, I just thought they were hearing, but they looked at me funny, and then I started signing and then they signed back ... they don't have hearing aids because in their family everybody's deaf. All of them.

Whereas Joe, who considers himself hard of hearing, saw himself as different from a classmate who had a deaf family, "Mary," who was from an all deaf family, gave an example of how she saw hard of hearing people as different from her. Mary attributed this difference to signing ability and use of speech by hard of hearing people. Mary was the only participant in the study with deaf parents. Mary discussed some visual indicators pertaining to hard of hearing children that the children with hearing parents did not. This passage shows the difference Mary saw between herself and children whom she viewed as hard of hearing. After Mary indicated that one of the children in the picture may be hard of hearing, I asked how she knew when a person is hard of hearing.

M: (Picture is propped in front of her) Because they look like this ... Because they talk, that means they're in an all hearing family ... Maybe they're talking or not clear signing ... They wouldn't sign.

COVERT AND OVERT IDENTITY

One of the themes that emerged out of this inductive study, covert and overt identity, illustrates how the children determined who is deaf, who is hearing, and who is hard of hearing. The children were shown magazine cutouts of individuals and groups. They were asked to tell stories about what they saw happening in the pictures. Often, the children indicated what they believed to be the hearing status of people in the pictures. When this information was not volunteered, I asked for their impressions.

These children specified visual indicators as determinants of a person's hearing status including the use of sign language, hearing aids, TTYs, mouth movements, and speech. Only the mainstreamed children indicated hearing aids as a symbol of a person's hearing status. Use of speech, sign language, or both, and TTYs as indicators of hearing status were recognized by informants from both mainstream and residential settings.

These visual indicators represented the overt identity that the deaf children in the study assigned to those they saw in the pictures. The covert identity of the person the deaf child observed is the actual identity that the observed adopts for himself or herself, which is not visible. Thus, the overt identity that deaf children give to others based on the visual indicators they recognize (signing, hearing aids, TTYs, speech, or mouth movement) may not match the covert identity adopted by the person they are observing. For example, "Lisa," a mainstreamed child of hearing parents, attended a total communication educational program but communicated orally at home. As Lisa observed a picture of a woman and a baby interacting, she stated they were both hearing because no hearing aids were shown in the picture. Not all people who are deaf wear hearing aids, and the possibility still existed that one of the two could have been deaf and not a hearing aid user.

I: Why do you think they're both hearing?

L: 'Cause they're not deaf.

I: How do you know?

L: 'Cause there's no hearing aids.

I: Oh, I see. If they have hearing aids, then that means they're deaf. Do all deaf people wear hearing aids?

L: (long pause) I think so.

L: (another picture) He's hearing ... I see there's no hearing aid, I don't see a hearing aid ... (and yet another picture) hearing, hearing. 'Cause there's no hearing aids.

Danny identified deaf people in pictures based on visible signing or use of TTYs in the following three passages. Each passage reflected his interpretation of a different picture.

I: Do you think they're deaf or hearing?

D: I think they're deaf. I think they're deaf, both of them, they're deaf ... It kind of looks like they might be signing. I think they're signing.

D: It's a mom. It's a mom, and she's calling a friend, and she's typing on the TTY, on the TTY. That means she's deaf ... and she takes the phone and puts it on the TTY and there's an on–off switch. She turns it on, and then she sits and waits, and then she starts typing. And that's her way of chatting, of talking with a friend.

D: Oh, hearing ... I don't know, maybe mom's deaf. No, I don't know, maybe because they're talking or something ... Uh, I think the dad's hearing and the mom's hearing. But I don't know.

I: Well, how might you know?

D: Because I think mom and dad are hearing. Because the baby's got its mouth open, so he's probably hearing.

As can be seen from the passages presented thus far, the children's identification of others as deaf, hearing, or hard of hearing was dependent on the overt visual indicators they recognized. The visible act of signing, mouth movement, use of TTYs, hearing aids, or speech were presented as clues to an individual's hearing status. Alex accepted hearing members of his family who were fluent signers as deaf. Alternatively, in Lisa's story, when she observed a picture of a person without a hearing aid she identified them as hearing (overt), when in fact this non-hearing-aid user may be deaf (audiologically) and adopting a deaf self-identity (covert).

Discrepancies in overt and covert identity may cause incongruent images between the observed and the observer. These have the potential to either delay or facilitate the achievement of harmony in relationships. When hearing aids are observed prior to the action of signing, a person may initially be perceived by other deaf individuals as hard of hearing (overt) and later accepted as deaf, an identity that they hold for themselves (covert), when they are seen skillfully using ASL and are more familiar to the observer. Thus, time and experience play a part in the process of determining an individual's overt identity, as well as his or her covert identity. Experience with another person, even over the course of a single interaction, may result in a reidentification of the person.

SUMMARY

Naturalistic inquiry, an inductive qualitative research method, is a viable approach to understanding what deaf children have to say about their lifeworlds. The stories in this chapter help us clarify the importance of listening to the voices of the children as researchers attempt to respond to issues of importance to them.

This chapter presents three themes that emerged from a study that explored the perceptions deaf children have of their worlds. The three themes are attachment and domesticated others, alienation and disparate others, and overt and covert identity.

Related to attachment and domesticated others, the children experience positive relationships and feelings of attachment or belonging. These feelings of attachment occur primarily in relationships with domesticated others and where communication is not a barrier. Domesticated others are described as people the child sees as like himself or herself regardless of their hearing status. Domesticated others include deaf teachers, classmates, other deaf children, and parents and siblings (both deaf and hearing) who communicate in the same way as the deaf child.

Although the children shared many positive stories of attachment and domesticated others, they also shared the alienation they experience in inaccessible interactions or with disparate others. Affectual reports related to alienation included boredom in inaccessible interactions; awareness of potential rejection by hearing peers; shyness, anger, nervousness, and discomfort in the presence of hearing children who do not sign; discomfort with teasing by hearing peers; frustration in some communicative interactions; and for one child, association of deafness with illness and fear of becoming ill or developing disabling conditions (Sheridan, 1996).

A third theme that emerged from this study is overt and covert identity. This theme describes who children see as similar to and different from themselves and how they make those distinctions. The children in the study were able to tell us through phenomenological interviews how they determine who is deaf, hearing, and hard of hearing.

With domesticated and disparate others, the children may or may not be aware of the actual hearing status of the person they are observing. The child's judgment of a person as similar to or different from him or herself is related to observations of the person's communication, whether the person uses assistive devices, and acceptance of and sense of belonging with the person.

REFERENCES

Akamatsu, C. T. (1993/1994, Winter) The view from within and without: Conducting research on deaf Asian Americans. *Journal of the American Deafness and Rehabilitation Association, 27*(3), 12–16.

Bat-Chava, Y. (1993). Antecedents of self esteem in deaf people: A meta-analytic review. *Rehabilitation Psychology, 38*(4), 221–234.

Becker, G. (1987). Lifelong socialization and adaptive behavior of deaf people. In P. C. Higgins & J. E. Nash (Eds.), *Understanding deafness socially* (pp. 59–79). Springfield, IL: Charles G. Thomas.

Coyner, L. (1993). Academic success, self concept, social acceptance and perceived social acceptance for hearing, hard of hearing and deaf students in a mainstream setting. *Journal of the American Deafness and Rehabilitation Association, 27*(2), 13–20.

Desselle, D. D. (1994). Self esteem, family climate, and communication patterns in relation to deafness. *American Annals of the Deaf, 139*(3), 322–328.

Desselle, D. D., & Pearlmutter, L. (1997, January). Navigating two cultures: Deaf children, self esteem, and parents' communication patterns. *Social Work in Education, 19*(1), 23–30.

Foster, S. (1993/1994, Winter). Outsider in the deaf world; reflections of an ethnographic researcher. *Journal of the American Deafness and Rehabilitation Association, 27*(3), 1–11.

Foster, S. (1996). Doing research in deafness: Some considerations and strategies. In P. C. Higgins and J. E. Nash (Eds.), *Understanding deafness socially: Continuities in research and theory* (2nd ed., pp. 3–20). Springfield, IL: Charles C. Thomas.

Glesne, C., & Peshkin, A. (1992). *Becoming qualitative researchers: An introduction.* White Plains, NY: Longman.

Harvey, M. (1989). *Psychotherapy with deaf and hard of hearing persons: A systemic model.* Hillsdale, NJ: Lawrence Erlbaum Associates.

Hauser, M. E. (1993/1994, Winter). Researchers doing research in their own (or others) backyards: Reflective comments. *Journal of the American Deafness and Rehabilitation Association, 27*(3), 22–28.

Humphries, T. (1977). *Communicating across cultures (deaf/hearing) and language learning.* Unpublished doctoral dissertation, Union Graduate School, Cincinnati.

Lane, H. (1992). *The mask of benevolence; Disabling the deaf community.* New York: Knopf.

Lane, H., Hoffmeister, R., & Behan, B. (1996). *A journey into the deaf-world.* San Diego, CA: DawnSignPress.

Levine, E. S. (1960). *The psychology of deafness.* New York: Columbia University Press.

Lincoln, Y. S., & Guba, E. G. (1985). *Naturalistic inquiry.* Newbury Park, CA: Sage.

Maher, T. M. (1989). The psychological development of prelinguistic deaf infants. *Clinical Social Work Journal, 17*(3), 209–222.

Maxon, A. B., Brackett, D., & van den Berg, A. A. (1991). Self-perception of socialization: The effects of hearing status, age and gender. *Volta Review, 93,* 7–18.

Meadow, K. P. (1968). Parental response to the medical ambiguities of congenital deafness. *Journal of Health & Social Behavior, 9,* 299–308.

Meadow, K. P. (1969). Self-image, family climate and deafness. *Social Forces, 47,* 428–438.

Meadow, K. P. (1972). Sociolinguistics, sign language and the deaf sub-culture. In T. J. O'Rourke (Ed.), *Psycholinguistics and total communication: The state of the art* (pp. 19–33). Washington, DC: American Annals of the Deaf.

Meadow-Orlans, K. P. (1983). *Meadow-Kendall social-emotional assessment inventory for deaf and hearing-impaired students manual.* Washington, DC: Gallaudet College.

Moores, D. F. (1987). *Educating the deaf: Psychology, principles and practices* (3rd ed.). Boston: Houghton Mifflin.

Myklebust, H. R. (1954). *Auditory disorders in children; A manual for differential diagnosis.* New York: Grune & Stratton.

Nash, J. E., & Nash, A. (1981). *Deafness in society.* Lexington, MA: Lexington Books.

Padden, C. (1980). The deaf community and the culture of deaf people. In C. Baker & R. Battison (Eds.), *Sign language and the deaf community* (pp. 89–103). Silver Spring, MD: National Association of the Deaf.

Padden, C. & Humphries, T. (1988). *Deaf in America: Voices from a culture.* Cambridge, MA: Harvard University Press.

Pollard, R. Q. (1993/1994, Winter). Cross cultural ethics in the conduct of deafness research. *Journal of the American Deafness and Rehabilitation Association, 27*(3), 29–41.

Schein, J. F., & Delk, M. T. (1974). *The deaf population of the United States.* Silver Spring, MD: National Association of the Deaf.

Schlesinger, H. S., & Meadow, K. P. (1972). *Sound and sign: Childhood deafness and mental health.* Berkley: University of California Press.

Schroedel, J. G. (1984). Analyzing surveys on deaf adults: Implications for survey research on persons with disabilities. *Social Science Medicine, 19*(6), 619–627.

Searls, M. (1993). Self-concept among deaf and hearing children of deaf parents. *Journal of the American Deafness and Rehabilitation Association, 27*(1), 25–37.

Sheridan, M. A. (1996). Emerging themes in the study of deaf children (Doctoral dissertation, Ohio State University, 1996). *Dissertation Asbtracts International,*

Sloman, L., Springer, S., & Vachon, M. L. S. (1993). Disordered communication and grieving in deaf member families. *Family Process, 32,* 117–183.

Stinson, M. S. (1993/1994, Winter). Research on deaf individuals by hearing persons: One deaf researcher's perspective. *Journal of the American Deafness and Rehabilitation Association, 27*(3), 7–21.

Strauss, A. L. (1987). *Qualitative analysis for social scientists.* New York: Cambridge University Press.

Vernon, M., & Andrews, J. F. (1990). *The psychology of deafness: Understanding deaf and hard-of-hearing people.* New York: Longman.

Learning to Converse: How Deaf Mothers Support the Development of Attention and Conversational Skills in Their Young Deaf Children

M. Virginia Swisher
University of Pittsburgh

Kay Meadow-Orlans has been a pioneer in affirming the competence of deaf mothers (Meadow, Greenberg, Erting, & Carmichael, 1981). She has also had a long-standing interest in the question of maternal sensitivity and has documented the problems that can occur when there is a mismatch of hearing status between parent and child (Meadow-Orlans & Spencer, 1996; Meadow-Orlans & Steinberg, 1993). One way deaf mothers are well equipped to be sensitive to the needs of their deaf children is that they are skilled in communicating in the visual mode, in general terms, as well as fluent in a visual language, which allows them to provide accessible language input to their children from the beginning of life.

Many in the profession have looked eagerly to the gradually accumulating body of research with deaf mothers for models and information that can be used to help hearing parents of deaf children who need guidance in interacting in the visual mode. Now that a number of aspects of deaf mothers' behavior have been identified that show great promise as a basis for assisting hearing parents (see Mohay, chap. 9, this volume), it may be worth asking whether there is any variation in what deaf mothers do. In other words, how much leeway do professionals have in advising hearing mothers? Do the requirements of communicating in the visual mode strongly shape deaf mothers' ways of handling interaction with their infants, leading to a great degree of similarity between them? Do all deaf mothers—or even all deaf mothers who are clearly skilled in interacting with their children—proceed in the same way to foster turn taking? Or, is there a range of behavior that can nurture this development? These questions led to this study of mother–child interaction in deaf mothers whose interactions with their infants were rated positively and whose infants had learned to share attention between their mothers and objects. This investigation was made possible by the major contribution of Dr. Meadow-Orlans and her colleagues, namely the longitudinal study of mother–infant interaction conducted at Gallaudet University and the wealth of information contained in its videotaped data (Meadow-Orlans, MacTurk, Spencer, & Koester, 1991).

THE REQUIREMENTS OF VISUAL COMMUNICATION

For deaf people, the visual channel must be used both to take in language and to inspect objects and events in the environment. Given this constraint, helping a deaf child develop conversational turn-taking skills is something of a hurdle, even for a deaf parent. The problem is heightened because at 5 or 6 months of age all children start to focus on objects and may go through a period when they actually avoid looking at their mothers (Adamson & Chance, 1998; Trevarthen, 1979). The new interest in objects changes and complicates interaction for any mother, but the stakes are particularly high when the mother and child are deaf because mature communication relies to a great extent on attention to the face. For deaf people, having eye contact with those they are talking to is also very important emotionally. Thus, as Kyle and Ackerman (1990) put it, when the child becomes focused on objects, "The deaf mother ... has to contend with a child who is not 'attending' and who is psychologically limiting the nature and extent of her utterances" (p. 209).

Another basic problem for the mother to contend with is that young children do not have long visual attention spans. The duration of visual fixations normally decreases sharply with development, with older infants' fixations being three to four times shorter than those of younger infants (Colombo, Mitchell, Coldren, & Freeseman, 1991). Deaf children must learn to sustain visual attention if they are to receive linguistic input and be able to participate in signed conversations of any length.

Despite these complications, Spencer found that deaf infants from deaf families, observed at 9, 12, and 18 months, spent at least as much time in coordinated joint attention (sharing attention between caregiver and objects) as hearing children and significantly more than deaf children from hearing families (Spencer & Waxman, 1995, cited in Spencer & Lederberg, 1997). Moreover, anecdotal evidence suggests that by the time the child is 2 or 3 years old, interaction between deaf children and deaf mothers is often characterized by a remarkable synchrony and fluidity of turn taking, even in the presence of objects or books. The fact that this synchrony is not typically seen in hearing mother–deaf child dyads tells us that it does not just arise naturally, as a by-product of a deaf child's development. What is it that deaf mothers do to foster such fluency of turn taking in their children?

CHARACTERISTICS OF DEAF MOTHERS

A number of characteristic behaviors of deaf mothers interacting with their young children have been identified, all of which, in concert, may contribute to the successful acquisition of turn taking. In addition to their ability to provide accessible linguistic input from birth, noted earlier, deaf mothers instinctively accommodate their children's perceptual abilities by communicating in a Motherese register, namely signing larger and more slowly than in conversation with adults and employing more repetition (Launer, 1982; Masataka, 1992). They also use a great deal of positive facial expression (Erting, Prezioso, & Hynes, 1990; Meadow-Orlans, MacTurk, Prezioso, Erting, & Day, 1987), as well as touch, and modify the placement of their signs; for example, by signing on the child's body (Maestas y Moores, 1980), directly in the child's line of sight, or in the peripheral field (Harris, Clibbens, Chasin, & Tibbitts, 1989; Prendergast & McCollum, 1996) until the child acquires the habit of shifting visual attention back to the mother's face.

Maternal Responsiveness

Another dimension that may be important in supporting turn-taking development is maternal responsiveness. For example, differences have been found in deaf and hearing mothers' responses to spontaneous looks from their children. Koester, Brooks, and Traci (1996) examined face-to-face interaction when infants were 9 months old and found that "deaf mothers were significantly more likely than hearing mothers to respond in the visual modality when the infant directed eye gaze toward the mother ..." (p. 5). The mothers' responses were "exaggerated facial expression, head-nodding or looming, finger play, gestures, etc." (p. 4), as well as sign language. Prendergast and McCollum (1996), studying mothers' interactions with 18- to 28-month-old deaf infants, also found that deaf mothers responded to significantly more of the child's looks than hearing mothers. Kyle, Woll, and Ackerman (1989) observed that deaf mothers treat their child's eye contact almost as a request and suggested that for hearing mothers "the idea that requests from the child come through eye contact is rather alien" (p. 46), which may cause them to miss many of the child's early bids for communication.

Deaf mothers have also been found to be responsive to their children's attention focus in communicative interaction. A study of the language of randomly selected deaf mothers in the Gallaudet sample showed that the majority of the mothers' comments were related to what the child was looking at or holding, and that responsiveness was in turn positively related to the number of signs the child produced (Wilson & Spencer, 1997).

Another sort of responsiveness is seen in deaf mothers' ability to wait for their children's attention without intervening when the child is looking at something else. Examinations of mothers' behavior when their infants looked away from them revealed that at both 9 months (Koester, Karkowski, & Traci, 1998) and 12 months (Spencer, Bodner-Johnson, & Gutfreund, 1992) deaf mothers often simply waited for the child to look back at them. At the 12-month observation, comments were made related to the child's previous focus of attention after his or her gaze returned to the mother (Spencer et al., 1992). (This waiting behavior may be specifically geared to the early developmental period: It was not found with the older children in Prendergast and McCollum's 1996 study. Waxman and Spencer, 1997, found that as children get older, there is also an increase in the number of times that mothers simply begin signing without a prior signal.)

Overt Attention Getting

Responsiveness notwithstanding, deaf mothers are often very active in seeking their children's attention. Kyle and Ackerman (1990) noted that deaf mothers of deaf infants will "break the child's gaze overtly by moving into the line of sight" (p. 209) in order to try to get their visual attention. They observed that "the 'game' seems to become 'how to get the child to look at me' rather than how to get the child engaged in long interaction" (p. 209). They also observed that whereas hearing mothers of hearing 9-month-olds tend to play far–near games of moving toys closer and closer to a child with simultaneous "gonna get you" commentary, these games are "almost completely missing in the deaf mothers at the same age" and commented that the "same games for the deaf mother seem to exploit the visual space allowing the child's eyes to track the object with less opportunity for linguistic intervention by the mother" (p. 209). Deaf mothers, however, do manage to get their children beyond a focus on the objects alone and to bridge the gap between nonlinguistic and linguistic interaction around objects.

One of the most salient features of deaf mothers' behavior is the use of overt attention getting, for example, tapping the child or waving, which is part of the communication repertoire for deaf adults. Spencer (1998) found that for dyads with deaf infants, mothers' attention getting at 18 months was moderately correlated with both coordinated joint attention and language level.

It is worth remembering that the ability to respond to a tap as a signal for attention to another person is not present from birth and is in fact a cognitive skill. Even learning to achieve joint attention by following another person's gaze or pointing gesture is not always straightforward. For example, a study by Grover (1982; cited in Butterworth & Grover, 1990) of children's visual responses to adult pointing found that at 6 and 9 months the children were as likely to look at the adult's hand as to follow the point. But at least other people's gaze or pointing gestures are potentially focusing attention in the actual direction of a present object or location. By contrast, a tap on the body is not meant to direct the child's attention to his or her own body, but to the person doing the tapping and usually to their communication. There is thus a kind of disjunction between the place where physical contact occurs and what the contact represents, and in that sense a tap is arbitrary and symbolic.[1]

The available information confirms that tapping in the early months of a deaf infant's life is not very effective for attention getting. Harris et al. (1989) reported that in the earliest observations of the deaf children of deaf parents they studied, namely 7, 10, and 16 months, the mothers' attempts to direct the children's attention by tapping—or even by physically moving them—were "usually unsuccessful" (p. 94). In short, the child must learn that such a signal means "look at me" or "pay attention to what is going to come next."

Waxman and Spencer (1997) looked at maternal attention-getting strategies in mother–child dyads of the four possible combinations of hearing and deafness, in groups of approximately 20 dyads. The behaviors coded were presenting or moving objects, tapping objects, tapping the child, and waving or hitting the floor. Using the movement of objects to attract attention was far and away the most frequently used strategy for all groups at all ages, though it declined significantly between the 9- and 12-month and the 12- and 18-month sessions. The strategy of tapping the child directly was used significantly more by deaf mothers of deaf children than by mothers in the other three groups during the 9- and 12-month sessions; by the 18-month session, the deaf mothers of hearing children had increased their use of tapping so that both groups exceeded the two groups with hearing mothers. Tapping in deaf mothers of deaf children did not change significantly over time. For the forty 15-second time segments sampled (10 minutes of interaction), the deaf mothers tapped their deaf infants in an average of 8.4 segments in the 9-month session, 10.7 segments in the 12-month session, and 8.7 segments in the 18-month session. (Note: van

---

[1]My thanks to Dr. George Butterworth for his assistance in thinking about these matters.

den Bogaerde, 1994, also found no change in the overall quantity of deaf mothers' attention getting at 11 months and 23 months.)

Both Waxman and Spencer (1997) and Prendergast and McCollum (1996) found considerable variability in the amount of attention getting that deaf mothers did, which suggests that examination of individual dyads' behavior over time might reveal information that is lost in group data. Waxman and Spencer also noted their impression that the "nature" or "degree of insistence" (p. 113) of deaf mothers' attention getting changed over time and urged further, qualitative investigation of the phenomenon. The purpose of the investigation described here was to look at skilled deaf mothers' attention-getting behavior in individual dyads over time in order to examine individual patterns of attention-getting.

A DESCRIPTIVE STUDY OF DEAF MOTHERS' ATTENTION GETTING

This study looked at the communication of nine deaf mother–deaf child dyads selected from a sample that was part of the Gallaudet longitudinal study ($n = 19$; Waxman & Spencer, 1997). The dyads were chosen on the basis of the children's communication development as indicated by their ability to share attention between their mother and objects, a state referred to as coordinated joint attention (Bakeman & Adamson, 1984; Spencer & Waxman, 1995, cited in Spencer & Lederberg, 1997). In this state, the child actively divides attention between an object and a communication partner as evidenced by shifting gaze between the two. The nine children studied were in the upper half of the sample on this measure at 18 months. Out of a possible 600 seconds of interaction (10 minutes), the amount of time spent in coordinated joint attention at 18 months ranged from 248 to 488 seconds, with a mean of 333 seconds (Spencer, 1995, unpublished data). Five of the nine children were already spending some time in coordinated joint attention with their mothers at 9 months.

The mothers in the sample also had high global ratings (3.3 or better on a 5-point scale) on a composite measure of maternal behavior that included sensitivity and flexibility (Meadow-Orlans & Steinberg, 1993), when the child was 18 months of age. The mean rating for the mothers was 4.3 ($SD = 0.5$).

Demographic characteristics of the subjects are presented in Table 2.1. All children had been identified before 9 months of age, were in parent–infant programs by 12 months of age or earlier, and were functioning within the normal range. Four of the children had profound hearing losses, three had severe-profound losses, and one had a moderate-severe loss. Information about hearing loss was not available for one of the children.

Eight of the nine mothers used ASL with their children, primarily without voice. One mother whose child had a moderate-severe loss signed and spoke with her child. This child was observed in one instance orienting to voice plus tap at 9 months (the only tap she responded to at that age).

TABLE 2.1

Demographic Characteristics of Dyads

Dyad	Sex	Child Hearing Loss	Etiology	Maternal Hearing Status	Maternal Education
1	F	Moderate–severe	Heredity	Deaf	16 yrs.
2	M	Profound	Heredity	Deaf	18 yrs.
3	F	Severe–profound	Heredity	Deaf	20 yrs.
4	M	Unavailable	Heredity	Deaf	18 yrs.
5	F	Profound	Heredity	Deaf	18 yrs.
6	M	Profound	Heredity	Deaf	18 yrs.
7	F	Profound	Heredity	Deaf	18 yrs.
8	M	Severe–profound	Heredity	Deaf	14 yrs.
9	M	Severe–profound	Heredity	Deaf	15 yrs.

The mothers' education ranged from 14 to 20 years, with six of the nine mothers having at least 18 years of education. Clearly, then, this was a privileged group of mothers and children.

The Context of Data Collection

The source of the data was videotaped interactions of mother–infant play with toys, recorded at 9, 12, and 18 months in a laboratory setting with one-way mirrors on two sides of the room. Interaction between mothers and children was taped for approximately 15 minutes at 9 and 12 months and for 20 minutes at 18 months. (One child, Subject 8, was taped for only 10 minutes at 9 months, and two others, Subjects 4 and 7, were taped for 12–13 minutes for the same session.) Parent and child sat on a mat on the floor with toys. Mothers were asked to interact with their children as they normally would at home. (For detailed descriptions of the contexts and procedures, see Spencer and Meadow-Orlans, 1996, and Waxman and Spencer, 1997.)

Coding and Analysis of the Data

For the purposes of this investigation, 15 minutes of interaction were transcribed for each of the sessions. For the sake of comparability with data from other studies, 10 minutes of interaction were coded for maternal use of attention getting (e.g., tapping the child, waving, wiggling fingers in peripheral vision, patting a surface near the child, such as a mat or table).

For the count of maternal attention getting, instances were recorded and totaled. In the case of tapping, an instance was a tap or multiple taps bounded by a pause. The most common pattern of signaling was a two-beat tap, which was counted as one instance. On rare occasions, a mother tapped as many as 9 or 10 times in quick succession until a child finally turned; like the two-beat taps, this was counted as one instance. However, if a mother tapped, stopped, and then tapped again, it was counted as two. Jiggling or shaking the child to get attention was not counted, nor was tickling, with or without a toy in hand. In a few instances a mother used an object to tap a child to get attention, and this was included in the count.

The entire 15 minutes of interaction was used in order to obtain more data on which to base percentages of the children's responses to attention getting, as well as for qualitative description. Instances of attention getting were coded as *child responds after tap,* (meaning the child oriented visually either to the mother's face or signing hand, or to an object she was holding), *no response,* and *other* (including cases where the mother tapped the child when he or she was already oriented in the mother's direction, and no clear response could be seen; taps occurring when the child's back was to the camera, and a response could not be observed; etc.). In order to compute percentages reflecting the children's tendency to respond to a signal, instances of attention getting in the *other* category in which the child's response could not be observed were eliminated. The percentages of child responses to attention getting thus reflect the number of instances of clear responses (orientation to face, hand, or object) divided by the total instances of attention getting for which a judgment about the response was possible.

It should be noted that the mothers typically tapped the child and then signed or pointed, or tapped the child and then presented an object. It was not practicable to determine what the child was responding to, that is whether to the tap, the following sign or presentation of the object, or some combination of the two.

For three of the taped segments (one each of the 9-, 12-, and 18-month sessions), intrarater reliability for the coding of occurrences of the mother's signals and of the child's response to those signals was 90%, 100%, and 89%.

MOTHERS' USE OF ATTENTION GETTING

Frequencies of mothers' attention-getting behaviors in a 10 minute period appear in Table 2.2. The mean frequency of instances of maternal attention getting was approximately 15 in the 9-month session, 17 in the

TABLE 2.2

Number of Instances of Attention-Getting by Deaf Mothers in 10 Minutes

Mother	9 Months	12 Months	18 Months
		Session	
1	3	11	44
2	9	15	11
3	30	27	8
4	7	11	14
5	4	15	11
6	5	9	39
7	35	9	15
8	20	30	21
9	24	27	16
M	15.2	17.1	19.9
SD	12.2	8.5	12.8

12-month session, and 20 in the 18-month session. The high variability of this behavior is reflected in the fact that standard deviations approached the mean for the 9-month and 18-month sessions. Only at 12 months was maternal behavior somewhat more consistent across the group.

Looking at the nine dyads individually across the sessions reveals three distinctly different patterns of maternal behavior. Two mothers in the sample (Subjects 1 and 6) used attention getting infrequently (3–5 taps) during the 12-month session and increased it dramatically in the 18-month session (with 44 and 39 taps respectively). By contrast, three mothers (Subjects 3, 7, and 9) engaged in frequent attention getting in the first session (24–35 taps) when the child was 9 months of age, with less signaling in the 18-month session. Three of the mothers (Subjects 2, 4, and 5) used attention getting more evenly across the three sessions without a high rate of signaling at either 9 or 18 months. Subject 8 was also fairly consistent across the three sessions but with a higher rate of signaling.

CHILDREN'S RESPONSES TO ATTENTION GETTING

Percentages of responses to attention-getting signals (based on approximately 15 minutes of interaction, with the exception of Subjects 4, 7, and 8 at 9 months) are shown in Table 2.3. The mean percentage for the number of attention-getting signals the child responded to was approximately 23% at 9 months, 50% at 12 months, and 78% at 18 months. (As noted earlier,

TABLE 2.3

**Percentages of Attention-Getting Signals to Which Child Responded
(In 15 Minutes of Interaction)**

Child	Age		
	9 Months	12 Months	18 Months
1	14	45	64
2	17	33	69
3	33	69	64
4	43[a]	31	87
5	0	60	77
6	17	36	93
7	31[a]	67	88
8	32[b]	64	81
9	19	43	82
M	22.9	49.8	78.3
SD	13	15.3	10.6

[a]12–13 mins., [b]10 mins.

these responses may have been to either the signal, the following presentation of an object or sign, or the pairing of the two.)

The children's responses to attention getting were much less variable than the mothers' use of signals, particularly at 12 and 18 months. In most cases, the percentage of the individual children's responses to attention getting increased from 9 to 12 months and from 12 to 18 months. One exception was Subject 4, who had his own agenda in the 12-month session (discussed later) and consequently resisted responding to his mother. There was also a slight drop in responding for Subject 3 in the 18-month session; however, this was based on responses to only eight taps by her mother and, given her overall attentiveness to her mother's communication, may well be a result of sampling error.

QUALITATIVE OBSERVATIONS

It should be noted that the nature and intensity of the mothers' attention-getting signaling changed somewhat over time as the children became more responsive and tuned in to communication (as Waxman and Spencer, 1997, suggested). In the 9-month session, the children were not yet visually tuned in to their mothers for the most part. The children's spontaneous looks to their mothers consisted primarily of brief glances, though three of the children were already exhibiting some clear shifting of visual attention to their mothers (e.g., turning around in the midst of crawling or after pulling to stand). A fourth child was still producing only very brief looks, but she often tossed toys in an uncontrolled way and then immediately looked at her mother as if startled. If the mothers wanted to use the children's glances as an opportunity to communicate, they had to rush to sign, and often the infants looked away immediately.

During this first session (and, for dyad number 4, the 12-month session), the mothers were obviously working, to a greater or lesser extent, to get their children's visual attention. In addition to the adult forms of attention getting, two of the mothers (Subjects 3 and 7) produced noncanonical attention-getting waves, or gently wiggled the fingers in peripheral vision to try to get attention. In the 9-month session in particular (though this occurred later as well), there were also more instances of a tap accompanied by other kinds of touch, for example, taking the child by the shoulder or arm and trying to get him or her to turn, jiggling, and so forth. Occasionally there were prolonged attempts to get attention where the mother tapped repeatedly on various parts of the body, jiggled an arm or leg in between, and sometimes finished with a hug or tickling as she gave up the struggle. (The children did not respond even to tapping directly under the chin.)

While communicating, mothers often leaned close to the child and angled their heads around to try to get eye contact. Between these features and the signs themselves, there were multiple cues for the children to respond to. There was also a great deal of (sometimes very artful) use of toys. Mothers exploited their child's ability to notice and track moving objects in order to get his or her attention to their faces or to the toy beside their faces. In sum, the mothers adapted in various ways to the fact that their children were not yet responsive to taps as signals in themselves.

By the 12-month session, all nine children were producing at least some clear shifts of visual attention to their mothers, some of them very frequently. These spontaneous looks had become longer and more obviously communicative. For example, children often accompanied looks to the mother with smiles, or picked up something and then looked at her, or signed and then looked at her. All but one of the children produced some signs in the 12-month session, though for two the only sign noted was clapping. Subject 4 was the child for whom visual attention to his mother was comparatively rare at 12 months. For part of the session, he was determined to look at something on a table in the corner of the observation room, and she was trying to reengage him and get him back to the play interaction. In a brilliant stroke, after a long period of tapping him, tugging at him, patting the table, and signing NO in his line of sight, she put a block on the table in front of him and a line of blocks on the floor leading back to the mat, then removed the blocks one by one so that his attention was led back to her and the toys.

By the 18-month session, mothers could typically use the conventional two-beat gesture and get the child's visual attention without additional efforts (unless the child was resisting looking or was absorbed in a toy). In that session, we begin to see some of the smoothness of turn taking that characterizes slightly older children. Turn taking appeared to be more rapid, with children more often responding quickly and crisply to taps as well as shifting gaze frequently to their mothers. However, even at this age there were instances of mothers making repeated efforts to get the child's visual attention and finally giving up.

DISCUSSION

The data confirm that there are strong individual differences in the attention-getting behaviors that skilled deaf mothers use with their children and that there is indeed a range of attention-getting behavior that can be used to support the deaf child's development of joint attention and turn taking, even in this highly select sample of a select population. The mothers of the children varied both in how much signaling (i.e., tapping, waving) they did and at what child age they chose to do the most signaling. Despite these differences, all three patterns of maternal attention getting were associated with children's success in coordinating attention between persons and objects, as measured at 18 months, and, by extension, in the development of turn taking.

A question of interest is what caused the differences in the mothers' approaches. One possibility is that they may have had different philosophies or beliefs about infants' cognitive capacities and about the best way to get them to adult-like turn-taking behavior. Another possibility is that they were responding to individual differences in their children's development.

Unfortunately, no information is available about the mothers' beliefs and philosophies specifically related to the development of turn taking. The efforts that some mothers made to get their children's visual attention in the 9-month session suggest that they were attempting to teach their children to attend visually, though a lean interpretation might be that they were just trying to get their children to look at them. On the other hand, the variation in the mothers' performance tells us that they did not all treat attention getting, particularly tapping, as a way to train the children visually.

One possible explanation for individual differences in attention getting is differences in maternal directiveness. However, Wilson and Spencer's (1997) study, conducted with many of the same subjects, found that deaf mothers' language was related to the child's attention focus a majority of the time. The study also found that this topic responsiveness and the number of attention-getting attempts by the mother were not related to one another, either positively or negatively. Inspection of the interactions of the present sample reveals that the mothers often used attention getting before making comments related to the child's attention focus as well as before initiating a new topic or activity. Thus, though attention getting involves directing attention, it does not necessarily mean that the mother is being directive, or unresponsive to the child's focus.

When the relationship between the actual amount of time the children spent in joint attention at 18 months and the mothers' signaling patterns at different ages is examined, the results again suggest that attention getting is not the only important factor. The two children highest in coordinated joint attention at 18 months were Subjects 6 and 1 (488 seconds and 387 seconds out of a possible 600, respectively). Both of their mothers signaled infrequently at 9 months and increased their signaling dramatically at 18 months. However, before jumping to the conclusion that it is best to refrain from much signaling early on, consider that Subject 3 was almost identical to Subject 1 in time spent in joint attention at 18 months (386 seconds), yet her mother's pattern was the opposite: frequent signaling at 9 and 12 months, which decreased markedly by 18 months.

When we attempt to assess the virtues of frequent early signaling, we find that there were 3 other children besides Subject 3 whose mothers signaled frequently at 9 months (Subjects 7, 8, and 9), and all of them spent approximately 100 seconds less in coordinated joint attention than she did. Such variability suggests that there is no direct, simple relationship between amount and type of attention getting and joint attention for this subgroup of the larger sample. The lack of such a relationship also suggests that attention getting is only one component in a larger constellation of maternal behaviors—and hence of the children's communicative experience—that foster the children's coordinated joint attention and turn-taking abilities.

One way to consider the relation between attention getting and developmental factors in the children is to look at the individual differences in performance in the 9- and 18-month sessions. In the 9-month session, none of the children was signing, and though some of them exhibited occasional shifting of visual attention toward the mother, it was not with any degree of fluency or automaticity. By 18 months, all the children were carrying on signed conversations with varying degrees of sophistication, and all were attention switching. Despite this comparative consistency with regard to the children's behavior, there was a high degree of variability in the mothers in both sessions. Mothers' attention getting ranged from 3 to 35 instances in the 9-month session, and from 8 to 44 instances in the 18-month session.

The children in dyads 1 and 6 may be taken as counterevidence for a relationship between attention getting and spontaneous attention-switching ability. In both cases, their mothers signaled infrequently during the 9- and 12-month sessions, yet the children were very clear attention switchers by 12 months, suggesting that the latter ability does not depend on mothers' use of signaling. Then, in the 18-month session, with attention switching already well established, we see the dramatic jump in the amount of signaling by the mothers. In the case of these children, it may be that the mothers were using the tapping to speed up the conversational exchange, or to further train the children in adult turn-taking behavior. At that stage, using tapping frequently was evidently a choice for those two mothers, not a necessity. Their tapping had the character of a conventional signal, as opposed to an attempt to teach the children to look.

UNANSWERED QUESTIONS

Some interesting questions are what determines a mother's decision to use an attention signal, and why she does or does not persist until the child looks. There were some indications that the mothers were careful about the signaling they did. At times mothers prepared to tap their child, but stopped when they saw that the child was about to do something else, or held their hands poised in position for a tap for several seconds before tapping the child, or tapped the child once or twice but then gave up when they saw that the child was absorbed in something else. As noted earlier, the cases where a mother persisted and produced many rapid taps in succession until the child finally turned were comparatively rare. The mothers were also not heavy handed, in a literal sense; for the most part, the tapping appeared to be light and delicate (though there were exceptions in the early sessions at moments when the mother apparently really wanted the child to look and used a series of taps on various parts of the body interspersed with more emphatic jiggling.)

It is evident that the use of signaling also depends partly on context. For the mother of Subject 3, once turn taking had been well established, by the 18-month session, there was infrequent tapping while mother and child were in face-to-face mode (partly because the child was walking around); however, in a later segment where they were looking at a book together, and the child was on the mother's lap (facing away, with the possibility of the mother signing in front of the child and not requiring visual attention), she tapped the child frequently to get her to turn and look at her. Another example is the sixth dyad in which 35 of the 39 signals in the 18-month session occurred in approximately 7.25 minutes of the interaction, while the mother and child were sitting together interacting around toys. After that, the child got up to pull a toy cart around the room, and the mother waved only infrequently during the rest of the 15 minutes coded.

Another question is what response mothers are actually seeking when they tap the child. In most cases, it appears that it is visual attention: Mothers tap and then present an object for the child to orient to, or tap and then sign, or both. However, the notions of attention and visual attention can be separated, in principle, and it is possible that some taps are meant just as a general alerting signal as opposed to a signal to turn and look—particularly in the early sessions when the mother was still signing in the child's peripheral field. (Certainly the mothers often accepted the child's not looking in response to a tap.) At times mothers also tapped the children when the children were already oriented in their direction or were oriented toward an object that the mothers then commented on. Occasionally a mother tapped a child lightly, without looking at him or her, while reaching for an object to present. In such cases, the subjective impression is that the purpose of the tap was to alert the child to an upcoming change of activity or topic similar to the function of "hey!" in speech. At any rate, taps of the more conventional sort were often used to signal an upcoming activity (e.g., first the mother tapped the child, then held up a block, then began to build).

HOW DO DEAF MOTHERS SUPPORT TURN TAKING?
SOME FURTHER SPECULATIONS

As the study shows, mothers' signaling behavior does not appear to determine whether children acquire either spontaneous attention-switching behavior or turn taking (given that children whose mothers did not signal much when they were 9 months old had acquired attention switching by 12 months and that some mothers did not tap frequently until 18 months, when both attention switching and turn taking were very well established). If this is true, how do children learn these things? Possible contributors include physical rhythms of interaction, experienced very frequently over time, which may create unconscious expectations about the occurrences of turns and responses, and sources of information in peripheral vision, such as the mother looming in, or changing her position in small but marked ways as she focuses her own visual attention on the child. (In some of the cases in which the child turned before the mother's hand actually reached him or her, the child may have been cued by arm or body movement seen in the periphery.) Presumably the redundancy of these cues helps the child learn what to expect and to anticipate the handing back and forth of turns.

As noted earlier, the interactions include a great deal of tactile activity in addition to the use of taps, particularly in the first two sessions. In addition to hugging or patting the child, this included things like tickling or jiggling or running a wooden car over the child's body, as well as signing on the child. Also, in contrast to Kyle and Ackerman's (1990) findings for their British sample, far–near games were used by seven out of nine of the Gallaudet mothers in the 9-month session. In these routines, which combined visual and tactile aspects, mothers sometimes held toys (a doll or monkey) high in the air and brought them wiggling down to the child's face or hopped a toy toward the child at varying rates of speed ending with tickling the child. Both the physical contact and the games might be thought of as an attention-maintaining device or one of many means of maintaining a certain level of stimulation and activity that the mother may feel is necessary for communication (Erting et al., 1990; Koester et al., 1998).

In addition, it is obvious that both the mothers and children were sensitive to visual events of various kinds, and these things became incorporated into quasi-conversations, that is turn taking. For example, when the children happened to notice themselves or some movement in the mirrors in the room, the mothers often bounced or moved their heads jauntily in response, looking at the mirror, sometimes engaging in a kind of movement dialogue with the child. Some mothers used their child's name sign while they looked in the mirror together, labeling the child and themselves. Occasionally, though by no means always, mothers imitated an involuntary flapping arm movement by the child or made a movement corresponding to "boom!" after an object fell. Likewise, if the child did something, such as take the lid off a bucket, and then turned to the mother, she generally responded in the visual mode even if she did not sign: often with a wide open mouth and wide eyes, sometimes a large two-handed gesture, or a sudden movement forward, and so forth (cf. the results of Koester et al., 1996, for a different condition at 9 months). Finally, peekaboo games (though oddly infrequent, considering the visual nature of this routine) were accompanied by very positive, engaging facial animation.

Attracting and maintaining the child's visual and cognitive attention with toys is clearly also an important part of the story. As noted earlier, Waxman and Spencer (1997), examining the various modes of attention getting in infancy, found that the movement of objects was by far the most common for deaf as well as hearing parents, even when the child was 18 months of age. Whereas attention to an object without accompanying communication can be a dead end, as Harris and Mohay (1997) observed, deaf mothers use objects to attract the child's attention for purposes that seem both interactive and linguistic (i.e., in many instances, the mother apparently got the child's attention in order to label something but it also seems as if one purpose of the interaction was for the child to learn the mechanics of interacting). Researchers need to pin down how deaf parents use objects to draw children into communication.

Finally, it should not be forgotten that the child's attention to the mother is supported by the language the mother produces around their joint experiences, as well as by her nonverbal communicative responses. As communication develops, both mother and child are rewarded by increasing amounts of verbal (signed) communication.

In summary, skilled deaf mothers support the development of communication in their children through a multifaceted complex of behaviors, which include active attention getting to varying extents, depending on the mother and the age of the child. Though the visual mode creates certain constraints in terms of interacting around objects, there is in fact more than one way to help the child learn the process of visual turn taking.

In addition to the substantial variability found even among deaf parents who are skilled communicators, close investigation of the phenomena of interaction can help professionals retain a degree of latitude and flexibility in what they recommend to hearing parents. It seems clear, viewing the interactions, that the mothers respond to the states of their children on a moment to moment basis as they make decisions about when to signal and that these decisions may relate to their knowledge of the child's temperament and capabilities, as well as their own preferred styles of interacting.

ACKNOWLEDGMENTS

I am very grateful to Kay Meadow-Orlans, Rob MacTurk, Patricia Spencer, and Lynne Koester for the opportunity to have access to data collected under the grant and for a variety of different kinds of assistance "above and beyond." My particular thanks go to Patricia Spencer for her rare generosity in sharing her play data and for the pleasure of many stimulating discussions surrounding our joint interests.

REFERENCES

Adamson, L., & Chance, S. E. (1998). Coordinating attention to people, objects, and language. In A.M. Wetherby, S.F. Warren, & J. Reichle (Eds.), *Transitions in prelinguistic communication* (pp. 15–37). Baltimore: Paul Brookes.

Bakeman, R., & Adamson, L. (1984). Coordinating attention to people and objects in mother–infant and peer–infant interaction. *Child Development, 55,* 1278–1289.

van den Bogaerde, B. (1994). Attentional strategies used by deaf mothers. In I. Ahlgren, B. Bergman, & M. Brennan (Eds.), *Perspectives on sign language usage* (pp. 305–317). Papers of the Fifth International Symposium on Sign Language Research (Vol. 2). Durham, England: University of Durham.

Butterworth, G., & Grover, L. (1990). Joint visual attention, manual pointing, and preverbal communication in human infancy. In M. Jeannerod (Ed.), *Attention and performance XIII: Motor representation and control* (pp. 605–624). Hillsdale, NJ: Lawrence Erlbaum Associates.

Colombo, J., Mitchell, D. W., Coldren, J. T., & Freeseman, L. J. (1991). Individual differences in infant visual attention: Are shorter lookers faster processors or feature processors? *Child Development, 62,* 1247–1257.

Erting, C. J., Prezioso, C., & Hynes, M. O'Grady (1990/1994). The interactional context of deaf mother–infant communication. In V. Volterra & C. J. Erting (Eds.), *From gesture to language in hearing and deaf children* (pp. 97–106). Berlin, Germany: Springer Verlag (1990); Washington, DC: Gallaudet University Press (1994).

Harris, M., Clibbens, J., Chasin, J., & Tibbitts, R. (1989). The social context of early sign language development. *First Language, 9,* 81–97.

Harris, M., & Mohay, H. (1997). Learning to look in the right place: A comparison of attentional behavior in deaf children with deaf and hearing mothers. *Journal of Deaf Studies and Deaf Education, 2,* 95–103.

Koester, L. S., Brooks, L. R., & Traci, M. A. (1996). *Mutual responsiveness in deaf and hearing mother–infant dyads.* Poster session presented at the biennial meeting of the International Conference on Infant Studies, Providence, RI.

Koester, L. S., Karkowski, A. M., & Traci, M. A. (1998). How do deaf and hearing mothers regain eye contact when their infants look away? *American Annals of the Deaf, 143,* 5–13.

Kyle, J., & Ackerman, J. (1990). Signing for infants: Deaf mothers using BSL in the early stages of development. In W. H. Edmondson & F. Karlsson (Eds.), *SLR '87: Papers from the fourth International Symposium on Sign Language Research* (pp. 200–211). Hamburg, Germany: Signum.

Kyle, J., Woll, B., & Ackerman, J. (1989). *Gesture to sign and speech: Final report to ESRC.* Project No: C 00 23 2327. Centre for Deaf Studies, University of Bristol.

Launer, P. (1982, November). *Early signs of motherhood: Motherese in American Sign Language.* Paper presented at the American Speech-Language-Hearing Association convention, Toronto, Canada.

Maestas y Moores, J. (1980). Early linguistic environment: Interactions of deaf parents with their infants. *Sign Language Studies, 26,* 1–13.

Masataka, N. (1992). Motherese in a signed language. *Infant Behavior and Development, 15,* 453–460.

Meadow, K. P., Greenberg, M. T., Erting, C., & Carmichael, H. (1981). Interactions of deaf mothers and deaf preschool children: Comparisons with three other groups of deaf and hearing dyads. *American Annals of the Deaf, 126,* 454–468.

Meadow-Orlans, K. P., MacTurk, R. H., Prezioso, C., Erting, C., & Day, P. S. (1987, April). *Interactions of deaf and hearing mothers with three- and six-month-old infants.* Paper presented at the biennial meeting of the Society for Research in Child Development, Baltimore, MD.

Meadow-Orlans, K. P., MacTurk, R. H., Spencer, P. E., & Koester, L. S. (1991). *Interaction and support: Mothers and deaf infants* (Final Report, Grant No. MCJ-110563). Washington, DC: Gallaudet Research Institute.

Meadow-Orlans, K. P., & Spencer, P. E. (1996, April). *Maternal sensitivity to the visual needs of deaf children.* Paper presented at the 10th Biennial International Conference on Infant Studies, Providence, RI.

Meadow-Orlans, K. P., & Steinberg, A. (1993). Effects of infant hearing loss and maternal support on mother–infant interactions at 18 months. *Journal of Applied Developmental Psychology, 14,* 407–426.

Prendergast, S. G., & McCollum, J. A. (1996). Let's talk: The effect of maternal hearing status on interactions with toddlers who are deaf. *American Annals of the Deaf, 141,* 11–18.

Spencer, P. (1995). [Joint attention of deaf children of deaf parents at 9, 12, and 18 months]. Unpublished raw data.

Spencer, P. E. (1998, July). *Communication, attention, and symbolic development: Mothers and infants as an interactive system.* Poster session presented at the 15th Biennial Meeting of the International Society for the Study of Behavioral Development, Bern, Switzerland.

Spencer, P. E., Bodner-Johnson, B., & Gutfreund, M. (1992). Interacting with infants with a hearing loss: What can we learn from mothers who are deaf? *Journal of Early Intervention, 16,* 64–78.

Spencer, P. E., & Lederberg, A. R. (1997). Different modes, different models: Communication and language of young deaf children and their mothers. In L. B. Adamson & M. A. Romski (Eds.), *Communication and language acquisition: Discoveries from atypical development* (pp. 203–230). Baltimore: Paul Brookes.

Spencer, P. E., & Meadow-Orlans, K. P. (1996). Play, language, and maternal responsiveness: A longitudinal study of deaf and hearing infants. *Child Development, 67,* 3176–3191.

Trevarthen, C. (1979). Instincts for human understanding and for cultural cooperation: Their development in infancy. In M. von Cranach, K. Foppa, W. Lepenics, & D. Ploog (Eds.), *Human ethology: Claims and limits of a new discipline* (pp. 530–594). Cambridge, England: Cambridge University Press.

Waxman, R., & Spencer, P. E. (1997). What mothers do to support infant visual attention: Sensitivities to age and hearing status. *Journal of Deaf Studies and Deaf Education, 2,* 104–114.

Wilson, S. J., & Spencer, P. E. (1997, April). *Maternal topic responsiveness and child language: A cross-cultural, cross-modality replication.* Poster session presented at the biennial meeting of the Society for Research in Child Development, Washington, DC.

Bilingualism in a Deaf Family: Fingerspelling in Early Childhood

Carol J. Erting
Carlene Thumann-Prezioso
Beth Sonnenstrahl Benedict
Gallaudet University

Teachers and children in an increasing number of educational programs in the United States and Canada are using ASL in the classroom (ASL in Schools, 1993; Ramsey, 1997; Strong, 1995). Although most of these programs aim to provide bilingual and bicultural or bilingual and multicultural education for deaf and hard of hearing students, some also serve hearing children (Evans, Zimmer, & Murray, 1994; Supalla, Wix, & McKee, in press). Many of these classrooms adopted a model of bilingual education that considers ASL the first language of the students and English the second language, accessible primarily through its written form (Johnson, Liddell, & Erting, 1989). It is not self-evident, however, how a first language in a visual, gestural modality might facilitate the acquisition of the written form of a spoken language. In fact, the argument has been made that competence in a sign language can be of no direct benefit to the acquisition of literacy based on a spoken language (Mayer & Wells, 1996). Nevertheless, Padden (1996) and her colleagues, studying Deaf children acquiring ASL and educated at a residential school, reported that parents introduce English print to children by 3 years of age and that by the time these children are 4 years old they are productively using both fingerspelling and written English. Furthermore, Padden argued, their linguistic productions are often complex, interactive episodes wherein they move back and forth between ASL and English repeatedly within the same activity. Where might researchers look to begin to investigate the relationship between these two languages and the processes whereby ASL literacy supports and assists the acquisition of English literacy? One logical place to start is the everyday interactions among parents and children in bilingual Deaf homes. As Tharp and Gallimore (1988) suggested, educators have much to learn from "an examination of how language is taught and learned in the natural environments of home, community, and culture" (p. 94).

Deaf people have been living bilingual lives for generations, discovering the ways in which ASL and English are similar and different, and using that knowledge to teach their children (Grosjean, 1992; Padden & Humphries, 1988). As Padden (1996) pointed out, Deaf people in the United States are constantly moving between languages and worlds—ASL and English, Deaf and Hearing—yet researchers know little about how they acquire this cultural knowledge. Speculating about the ways in which the process of acquiring ASL might directly promote the acquisition of English literacy, Johnson (1994) theorized that one of the connections between the two languages might be found in the natural acquisition of fingerspelling:

> a set of ASL signs that refer to written alphabetic characters ... typically used to represent the forms of words of spoken languages in ASL sentences or to provide exact representations of the spelling of written words from English or other spoken languages that use the Roman alphabet. (p. 6)

ACQUISITION OF FINGERSPELLING

Several researchers have examined the acquisition of fingerspelling by Deaf and hearing children of Deaf signing parents (eg., Akamatsu, 1985; Akamatsu & Andrews, 1993; Blumenthal-Kelly, 1995; Maxwell, 1980, 1984, 1988; Mayberry & Waters, 1991; Padden, 1991, 1996; Padden & LeMaster, 1985). With the exception of Blumenthal-Kelly's study that began when the child was a few weeks of age, these investigations report on children aged 2 years and older. Based on this earlier work as well as their own research on deaf children between the ages of 7 and 15 years old, Mayberry and Waters proposed three stages in the development of children's word production skills in fingerspelling. First, children produce sign-like attempts to fingerspell whole words. At this stage, it is the movement envelope that is salient (Akamatsu, 1985), and, while the productions preserve some visual and temporal aspects of fingerspelling, sequences of individual fingerspelled letters cannot be discerned. In the second stage of acquisition, children discover that fingerspelled words consist of individual hand configurations in a specific sequence. Productions are no longer sign-like; instead, each letter of the fingerspelled word is articulated separately. The final stage of acquisition is what Mayberry and Waters termed *fingerspelling synthesis*, when the fingerspelled word is no longer produced as a sequence of separate elements but is reconstructed and appears as a whole entity.

Fingerspelling, a fluent sequence of movement units having one or more handshapes linked to them, has been distinguished from *spelling*, the presentation of individual letters of a word in a list-like manner (Maxwell 1980, 1988; Padden, 1991, 1996). Fingerspelling also contrasts with a category of signs known as loan signs (e.g., #CAR, #BUS, #OR) first described by Battison (1978). These signs are created when fingerspelled words undergo phonological and morphological change to become lexicalized. Deaf parents report first attempts at fingerspelling at about 2 years of age, the same age children are typically producing three to four sign strings (Padden & LeMaster, 1985), and researchers describe these early attempts (2;4-2;7) as movement units or loan signs such as #ICE, #TV, #OK, and #OFF (Maxwell, 1988; Padden & LeMaster, 1985). By the end of the third year (2;9-2;11), children recognize fingerspelling as a special form of language used to name a thing or person. At this age, they also attempt to spell, that is, to articulate a series of hand configurations to produce a name (Maxwell, 1988; Padden, 1991). Padden (1996) reported that children's early fingerspelling attempts include their own names, siblings' names, and labels for colors, foods, and common objects. Because these initial efforts are more like signs with internal movements than a sequential ordering of distinct hand configurations, and because they are produced before the children can read and write, Padden concluded that early fingerspellers are not acquiring English, they are acquiring fingerspelling, a "special manual system with its own organizational properties which has links with English alphabetic characters" (p. 106). Children are unaware of the relationship between the two systems, although it appears obvious and transparent to adult ASL-English bilinguals. The challenge is to discover how Deaf children's competence in fingerspelling emerges and how they subsequently come to understand that it is a system used to represent English.

Relating Fingerspelling to English

Padden (1996) argued that one step in the process by which young Deaf children come to understand the connection between fingerspelling and English is learning about the relationships between fingerspelling and ASL. That is, parents help their children link symbols meaningful to them in one representational system, ASL, with those symbols as they are organized and used in a different representational system, fingerspelling.

Blumenthal-Kelly (1995) identified one strategy she called *sandwiching* wherein ASL signs and their fingerspelled translations are presented together in the same phrase. For example, in Blumenthal-Kelly's study, when D was 10 months old, she pointed to the ceiling, and her mother responded by pointing at the ceiling, signing WHITE, fingerspelling C-E-I-L-I-N-G, and pointing to the ceiling again. At 41 months, D's father signed WANT PONYTAIL and then fingerspelled P-O-N-Y-T-A-I-L. Padden and Ramsey (1998), reporting on a classroom study, described a similar strategy used with older children. Teachers, especially Deaf teachers in residential schools, produce chaining structures that serve to highlight correspondences between representations in different symbolic systems. For example, a teacher might fingerspell a word, point to that word in print, and fingerspell the word again.

Previous research has shown that one parental strategy for teaching the relationship between ASL signs and fingerspelling involves the use of initialized ASL signs: a category of signs articulated with a hand configuration that represents the first letter of the English translation of the sign. Fingerspelling the child's own name as well as the names of family members, relatives, and friends whose name signs are initialized plays a prominent role in this process (Maxwell, 1988; Padden, 1991, 1996). In Maxwell's case study, Alice used initialized signs to refer to herself and her four older siblings at 2;0 to 2;1 and she imitated the letters of her name by 2;4. This spelling of the child's name was the first recorded example of Alice's parents providing her with a fingerspelled label for a concept that she could already express in another form, that is, her name sign. Padden (1996) too reported children as young as 2;3 attempting to fingerspell their names and the names of their siblings. Children also employ the strategy of using the hand configuration of the sign in their early attempts to spell (Padden, 1991, 1996; Padden & LeMaster, 1985). In one case, a child 2;6 identified her brother by his initialized name sign and began to spell his name with the correct hand configuration, but was unable to complete the spelling. An older child, at 4;7, utilized initialized signs as a source of information about the first letter of the fingerspelled translation when presented with a list of signs and asked to fingerspell the corresponding names (Padden, 1991). However, the percentage of initialized ASL signs is quite small, and, when young children inevitably overgeneralize this rule, they provide their parents with the opportunity to assist them in extending their analysis of the relationship between ASL and fingerspelling to include the understanding that the hand configuration used to execute most signs does not correspond to the hand configuration that begins the fingerspelled translation of the sign.

Children acquiring ASL, fingerspelling, and English literacy also need to understand the relations between the hand configurations of signs, fingerspelled letters, and English letters and words in print. Previous studies in bilingual Deaf homes revealed that the child's early experiences with the fingerspelled alphabet were closely linked to environmental print, usually in the form of educational toys such as plastic letters, alphabet blocks, and books. Akamatsu and Andrews (1993) identified letter calling as a strategy parents use to help children recognize that words are made up of individual letters of the alphabet, and it is prevalent throughout their data, from the first videotape of K at 2 years until the final tape at 5 years of age. Similarly, Maxwell (1984, 1988) found in her study that fingerspelling for Alice was closely associated with print. As early as 2;8 Alice's parents called her attention to the titles of books, encouraging her to spell them out as well as sign them. The evidence suggests, then, that while children are acquiring fingerspelling without understanding its relationship to English, they are also being taught the correspondence between individual hand configurations and the English alphabet. As Akamatsu and Andrews (1993) emphasized, in order to understand the literacy development of deaf children, it is essential to document and describe the dialogues involving fingerspelling in which they participate, with and without print.

THE STUDY

The research reported here builds on Blumenthal-Kelly's analysis and contributes to the knowledge about the role of fingerspelling during the first three years of parent–child interaction and language and literacy acquisition. Our team independently reanalyzed videotapes of the same child, D, in Blumenthal-Kelly's study and expanded the analysis to include videotapes of her younger sister, A. We asked the following questions: What is the timing and the nature of the Deaf infant's earliest exposure to fingerspelling; what are the linguistic and interactional contexts within which Deaf parents use fingerspelling with their infants, toddlers, and preschoolers; and how is emerging fingerspelling related to other representational systems the child is acquiring (ASL and written English).

The data consist of monthly videotapes made in the home of one white, middle-class Deaf family, supplemented by tapes made at 3, 6, 9, 12, and 18 months in the research lab. Two fourth-generation Deaf infants, D and A, and their Deaf parents were videotaped by Deaf researchers from shortly after birth until the ages of 4;3 and 2;10 respectively. Thirty-one videotaped home sessions averaging 45 minutes each and ten studio tapes were analyzed, as were parental diaries, video journals, and interviews collected over this four-year period of time.

Parental Beliefs and the Home Environment

The parents of these two children were both college educated, had Deaf parents themselves, identified themselves as culturally Deaf, and placed a high value on their bilingualism in ASL and English. They stated that it was important to them that their children understand that they value English as much as they value ASL. Their goal was to create an environment in which their children had full access to language "just like a hearing child would have."

Most often the videotaping occurred in the family room, which had been designated as the children's room, with numerous toys and books at hand. Mom often described new toys to the researcher, explaining how they helped expose the children to a new activity or could be utilized to develop a specific skill. Educational toys included those with the letters of the alphabet displayed, for example, wooden alphabet blocks, and others that incorporated English print, such as the large plastic map of a town with key features prominently labeled (e.g., hospital, post office, etc.). An activity included in almost every videotaped session involved parent–child interaction around books. When the children were infants, they were provided with plastic or cloth books they could hold and examine themselves. As they grew older, Mom explained that they had favorite books and authors and she capitalized on that interest by finding additional books written by those authors to add to their collection.

Both parents regarded ASL as their primary language and believed fingerspelling plays a crucial role in language development for two reasons. First, it allowed them to expose the children to English words that do not correspond to single signs. Second, fingerspelling promoted literacy and contributed to the development of good spelling skills. Reflecting on their earliest interactions with their daughters involving fingerspelling, these parents emphasized that, as with other aspects of their children's development, they followed the principle that their daughters were their teachers, and they were their children's playmates. Determining when to fingerspell, then, often felt as if it "came naturally." They explained that they began by fingerspelling short words that did not have signs, such as rice, ice, bus, and truck. In addition, they sometimes fingerspelled words for emphasis as is common among ASL users. They never sacrificed meaning, however. Mom used an example to explain. When D was an infant she loved ice, and they had a homemade sign they used for it drawn from Mom's own childhood. They decided to use that sign, rather than fingerspell the word, because they wanted D to know how to ask for ice when she wanted some. However, by 1;2 they were fingerspelling the word to her. When we examined our data we saw that there was a developmental context for this change. At 10 months, when D's parents were only using the sign for ice with her, Mom told the researcher that D was pointing a lot and could sign two or three signs, although Mom was not sure of the meaning. Only a few months later, videotapes showed D spontaneously producing the sign for ice, and her parents reported a marked increase in her sign vocabulary. At 1;2 Mom described D's developmental advances remarking that she realized she should not underestimate her daughter. For example, when Mom asked D if she wanted to read a book, she was able to select a book to read, turn the pages until she came to her favorite page showing pictures of cats, and sign CAT repeatedly. At 1;3 her parents reported that she was using more than 100 signs. They also described her as capable of carrying on a conversation and noted her fascination with handshapes for numbers. Our data suggest, then, that D's parents introduced the fingerspelled word for ICE at 1;2 in response to noticeable changes in D's linguistic and communicative behavior.

The Early Linguistic Environment

Elsewhere, we described the earliest interactional environment Deaf parents in our study created with their infants (Erting, Prezioso, & Hynes, 1994). Like other researchers, we found Deaf parents and infants engage in reciprocal, mutually enjoyable, finely tuned interactions in the visual, gestural, and tactile modalities (see Koester, Papoušek, & Smith-Gray, chap. 4, this volume). Both mother and father position themselves in the infant's line of vision and are keenly aware of his or her state of attention and direction of gaze. Establishing eye contact with the infant and confirming that the ability to attend visually is developing are parental concerns during the early weeks and months of life. Parents play games with their infants, often involving exaggerated facial expressions, rhythmic and patterned physical contact, and signing modified for the infant. This child-directed signing, referred to in the literature more generally as Adult Child Language (ACL; Haslett & Samter, 1997), has been described as slower, formationally different, and grammatically less complex than the signing produced during adult-directed discourse (Erting, Prezioso, & Hynes, 1994; Kantor, 1982; Launer, 1982). It also includes fingerspelling, even in the early weeks of the child's life (Blumenthal-Kelly, 1995; Maestas y Moores, 1980).

We analyzed the early linguistic environment, as represented in our videotapes and interviews, with special attention to the quantity of fingerspelled items, the role of fingerspelling in the interaction, and the developmental context within which the use and acquisition of fingerspelling occurred. Our analysis revealed that in the first videotape of D at 5 weeks 3 days of age, Mom and Dad fingerspelled one word, A-T, and the loan sign #OR during communication directed at the infant, but there were 125 fingerspelled productions of 85 different words that took place during communication among the Deaf adults present and within the infant's visual field. This pattern proved to be consistent throughout our data and supports Padden's (1996) observation in her study of parents interacting with their older preschool children, 2;9 to 4;9, that parents use fingerspelling less often with their young children than with adult signers. The parents in our study produced six or fewer fingerspelled words with their infants per 45-minute video session during the first two and one half years of life while continuing to expose the children to fingerspelling as it occurred in adult-directed signing. The preponderance of these fingerspelled words were nouns (one half to two thirds), as in Padden's studies, with very few instances of fingerspelled verbs. Most of these occurred within the context of a signed sentence rather than in isolation, as Blumenthal-Kelly (1995) reported.

Most of the earliest fingerspelled words these parents used with their children at this age comprised the following categories: names of common foods (cake, rice, pizza, ice); common objects, animals, places, and body parts (toy, bat, car, fly, dog, zoo, towel, leg, fingers, feet, wig, fork, hair, jeep, rice cereal, ceiling); proper names (the children's own names, Joey, Nana, Mom, Dad, Minnie); and function words and pronouns (at, it, her, or, of, up, to, but). The words were between two and seven letters, with most three to four letters in length. During our second home visit, when D was 8 weeks old, the second example of fingerspelling to an infant occurred. At this time, D's parents reported that she was able to hold her head up and turn it from side to side. She was laughing more often, sometimes on her own and sometimes in response to someone making funny faces, and she was making better eye contact. Mom believed that D knew her then. She also noticed that the infant moved her fingers in front of her face, sucked on her hand, and engaged in cooing behavior. As reported in Blumenthal-Kelly (1995), one of the words Mom fingerspelled to D on this videotape was C-A-M-E-R-A. The infant was on her father's lap, looking toward the camera, and Mom stated that she thought D was looking at the red light on the camera. Mom and D made eye contact and they exchanged smiles. After tapping D twice on the arm, with the infant's eyes focused on her, Mom told D: IX:YOU SHOULD SMILE FOR T-H-E C-A-M-E-R-A (You should smile for the camera). Mom signed and fingerspelled directly in D's line of vision, near her face, spelling each letter clearly and quickly. When Mom stopped signing, D broke eye contact. On reviewing this videotape, Mom commented that she had no expectation for D to understand the fingerspelling but rather was interested in her learning to focus her eyes and maintain eye contact.

By the time D was 21 weeks old, her parents reported that she was making much more eye contact and producing lots of facial expressions. They described her as more visual. For example, her eyes followed Dad when he left the room or walked past her, and she visually tracked a sign language conversation between Mom and Dad. D's parents also interpreted her gestures as if they were early signs. For example, on one videotape, Dad was feeding D her lunch. When he stopped to get another spoonful or to wipe her face, D waved her arms up and down, a gesture her parents interpreted to mean she wanted more. Mom pointed out that this body language was her first sign language. During one videotaped interaction, Mom was giving D a bath in the kitchen sink, and the infant was clearly enjoying the experience. Mom moved close to D, directly in front of her face, and signed FUN FUN BATH, YES FUN BATH RIGHT? YES. F-E-E-T IX:feet CLEAN F-E-E-T IX:feet NOW IX:me (This is fun! Taking a bath is fun, right?

Yes! Yes! Hey, these are your feet. I'll clean your feet now.). D smiled and laughed, maintaining eye contact, watching Mom's face and hands until the signing stopped. When Mom started washing D's feet, D stopped smiling and looked in the direction of the camera.

Linking ASL Signs and Fingerspelling

Like other researchers, we found that name signs, usually produced with a handshape representing the first letter of the name, were used early and often with the two children in our study. Our first video record of this practice occurred when Dad used D's name sign with her at 17 weeks 5 days of age. Interactional linguistic routines such as HI D and WHERE D LOOK-FOR++ appeared repeatedly on the videotapes in the early months of D's second year (1;0-1;6). When A was born and D was 20 months old, there was much discussion with D of her sister's name sign and her own. One and one half years later, when A was 1;6 and D was 3;1, our data showed a marked increase in the use of name signs for family and friends and the process whereby ASL signs and fingerspelled names are linked. At this time, Mom described how A was now really trying to communicate with them, comprehending simple requests and producing SIGN + POINT utterances. She then called the researcher's attention to A's finger movements, explaining that A was trying to fingerspell. Mom's response to A incorporated spelling WHERE YOUR F-E-E-T? WHERE YOUR F-E-E-T? YOUR YOUR F-E-E-T (Where are your feet? Where are your feet? These are your feet.).

Later in the same videotape, Dad was with both girls and urged D (3;1) to spell her name for the camera. She was reluctant so they began by spelling D-A-D together. Then, D successfully spelled her own 7-letter name independently, to her father's delight. Dad continued coaching D, and they spelled A's name and A-R-L-E-N-E, connecting the initialized name sign and the spelling of the name in each instance. They also spelled M-O-M, linking a sign that is not initialized (MOTHER) with the spelled translation. Dad then encouraged D to spell her name quickly, that is, to fingerspell it, which she does, producing a rapid sequence of three hand configurations, the first, second, and last letter of her name. A (1;6), observing this interaction, held her hand, palm out, away from her body while moving her fingers, and Dad told the researcher that she was fingerspelling. Maxwell (1988) described this exaggerated finger wiggling as scribble spelling and identified it in her data when Alice was between 2;11 and 4;5. According to Maxwell, it was used by the child only to indicate awareness of a fingerspelling sequence and never in place of a specific meaning.

Signs, Fingerspelling, and English in Print.   An interactional context that becomes increasingly central to parent–child dialogue involving fingerspelling is one characterized by the presence of written English.

Early examples of what Akamatsu and Andrews (1993) referred to as let-ter-calling, identified in their earliest videotapes at 2;0, appeared in video-tapes of D at 1;8 and 1;10, as reported in Blumenthal-Kelly (1995). In the first instance, D and her father were playing with a toy made of alphabet blocks that spin. He began the interaction by connecting the letter C printed on the block to the name sign of the researcher (C hand in neutral space, shaking back and forth). D then pointed to the letter D and fingerspelled the letter D. Dad then elicited the other two letters she had learned the names for, A and B, and the game ended. Two months later, D not only connected the fingerspelled letter to the printed letter, but through a finely tuned, scaffolded interaction with her parents she was able to connect the first letter of family members' names (D, A, Mom, Dad) with the signs for those names and the letters in print as they appear on the alphabet blocks. Two of the name signs were initialized (the chil-dren's names), and two were not (MOTHER and FATHER, made with the 5 hand configuration).

When D and A are each 2;9, we find qualitative and quantitative changes in fingerspelling during parent–child interactions. Fingerspelled words are still relatively rare during parent–child conversations and, al-though some of the words are more than seven letters in length, they oth-erwise continue to fit the description of fingerspelling during the first two and one half years of the child's life. However, interactions that link fingerspelling with printed text become much more prevalent near the end of the third year. Book sharing provides perhaps the most common environment for this kind of interaction involving English print. Maxwell (1984), reporting on her study of one Deaf child learning to read, described an activity wherein the child, at 2;8, identified letters of the alphabet in a book and associated them with familiar signs having that same hand con-figuration. In our videotape of A at 2;9, mother and daughter were looking at an alphabet book that presents each letter of the alphabet accompanied by a word beginning with that letter and a picture of the object represented by the word, for example, A, Apple, picture of apple. An example of a type of complex chaining structure that appears frequently in our data oc-curred when A noticed the letter C and the accompanying picture of cats. Mom pointed to the page, signed CAT, C, and pointed to the page again, signing MOTHER FATHER BIG CAT C-A-T, touching the page again and run-ning her finger along the printed word cat. She then retrieved a book on numbers that they had shared earlier, opening it to a page with a picture of kittens on it. Mom ran her finger along the printed word kittens and signed BABY CAT K-I-T-T-E-N, with her hand positioned so that she was spelling directly over the printed word. She then produced a C hand configuration over the printed word cat and a K hand configuration over the printed word kitten, signing DIFFERENT. A then continued the analysis by match-ing the c in the next word, duck, with the large printed C on the previous page, signing TWO C. During this brief interaction, signs, printed text, and fingerspelling were utilized to accomplish multiple communicative, linguistic, and cognitive objectives, all within the context of mutually enjoyable, reciprocal play.

Eventually, as A turned the pages of the book, she came to a letter she recognized as the first letter of her name. She pointed to the letter in the book, made the fingerspelled letter, and pointed to herself. Mom then confirmed and provided her name sign. This was the beginning of a sequence of interactions wherein A's attention shifted from the objects depicted in the pictures to a game connecting name signs of family and friends to letters of the alphabet represented in the book. She asked Mom where her (Mom's) letter was and Mom showed her the fingerspelled letter M, by-passing the sign MOTHER, asking M WHERE MINE M? A pointed to the letter M in the book. Next, they linked sign, fingerspelled letter, and printed letter for Daddy (FATHER, not an initialized sign) and D's name (initialized name sign). When they reached N in the book, A thought it was M for a second time. Mom told her no and traced the letter on the page for her. A recognized that it was an N not an M and demonstrated that she knew it was connected with her grandmother's name sign (not initialized), signing NANA (index touching side of chin twice) and then forming the fingerspelled letter N. She then asked about GRANDFATHER and her aunt, two more signs that were not initialized. Mom provided the first letter of the fingerspelled words translating those signs, G and M respectively, and A hunted for the corresponding pages in the book. What is notable about these interactions is that multiple connections were made between familiar initialized and noninitialized signs, the first fingerspelled letter of the names for those signs, and the printed letters of the English alphabet. That is, Mom was showing A, within an increasingly complex print-based interactional context, that the fingerspelled translations of signs do not always begin with the same handshape used for the sign, a process we can surmise began much earlier, as it had with her sister (around 20 months of age), when printed letters of the alphabet on a variety of toys were linked with family members' name signs and fingerspelled names. Padden (1991) claimed that children between the ages of 3 and 4 are beginning to understand the rules of English orthography. These interactions between A and her mother illustrate one of the strategies Deaf parents use to assist their children in learning the rules of English orthography and in mastering the rather complex set of relationships among ASL, fingerspelling, and written English.

CONCLUSION

First and foremost, the Deaf parents in this study were concerned about meaningful, comprehensible interactions with their children. They knew from their own experiences as Deaf people negotiating Deaf and Hearing worlds that learning to use vision efficiently and appropriately would enable their children to progress linguistically, cognitively, and socially in culturally appropriate ways. From the earliest weeks of their infants' lives, these bilingual Deaf parents engaged in finely tuned, mutually enjoyable interactional exchanges with their daughters through child-directed ASL that was modified in ways that served to capture their daughters' attention and maintain their interest. Fingerspelling occurred in this signed discourse when the children were only weeks old, but it did not play a prominent role in early communication. We began to see an increase in the prevalence and functional diversification of fingerspelling as the children moved into toddlerhood and demonstrated their developing interactional and linguistic competencies.

Our analysis focuses on the first three years, confirming and supplementing Blumenthal-Kelly's (1995) findings from her case study of the older child in this family and presenting new results from the analysis of her sister's development. Although our findings when the girls are 2;0 to 3;0 generally support the conclusions of earlier researchers, there are two notable exceptions. Scribble spellings and invented spellings reported in Maxwell (1988) at 2;11 and 4;5 respectively appear much earlier in our data. By 1;6 scribble spelling appeared in A's data, indicating the infant distinguished spelling as an activity that is distinct from signing. (We found the same result in our analysis of a Deaf infant in another Deaf family. She produced scribble spelling at 1;6 in a context similar to the one in this report, i.e., the infant had been watching her mother spell a name to her older sister.) Two months later, the parents in our study encouraged the naming of individual letters of the alphabet during play, and there was an increase in the children's use of name signs for family and friends. Early in the third year (2;0-2;6), both girls produced their first sign-like attempts to fingerspell whole words (eg., C-H-P for chip, A-L for Mal, F-L-E-A for waffle, L-I-S for Lisa, E-F for Jeff, C-E for rice, C-A-E for cake, O-Y for toy). In the second half of the third year, they attempted to spell and fingerspell their own names, and they invented fingerspelled names for their dolls at 2;6 and 2;9, more than 2 years earlier than Maxwell's child.

Although books were part of parent–child interaction from infancy, in the third year, they became increasingly prominent as contexts for interactions involving fingerspelling, with explicit attention to letters and words in print. Using a variety of strategies including letter calling, chaining structures, and play practice with name signs and their fingerspelled translations, Deaf parents mediate English print for their children. The picture that emerges is one of children acquiring representational systems (i.e., ASL, fingerspelling, and English literacy) simultaneously within developmentally appropriate contexts that resemble the everyday lives Deaf people live as they move between languages and worlds.

REFERENCES

Akamatsu, C. T. (1985). Fingerspelling formulae: A word is more or less than the sum of its letters. In W. Stokoe & V. Volterra (Eds.), *SLR '83: Proceedings of the third international symposium on sign language research* (pp. 126–132). Silver Spring, MD: Linstok Press.

Akamatsu, C. T., & Andrews, J. M. (1993). It takes two to be literate: Literacy interactions between parent and child. *Sign Language Studies, 81,* 333–360.

ASL in schools: Policies and curriculum. (1993). Washington, DC: College for Continuing Education, Gallaudet University.

Battison, R. (1978). *Lexical borrowing in American Sign Language.* Silver Spring, MD: Linstok Press.

Blumenthal-Kelly, A. (1995). Fingerspelling interaction: A set of deaf parents and their deaf daughter. In C. Lucas (Ed.), *Sociolinguistics in deaf communities* (pp. 62–73). Washington, DC: Gallaudet University.

Erting, C. J., Prezioso, C., & Hynes, M. (1994) The interactional context of deaf mother-infant communication. In C. J. Erting & V. Volterra (Eds.), *From gesture to language in hearing and deaf children* (pp. 97–106). Washington, DC: Gallaudet University.

Evans, C., Zimmer, K., & Murray, D. (1994). *Discovering with words and signs: A resource guide for developing a bilingual and bicultural preschool program for deaf and hearing children.* Winnipeg, Manitoba: Sign Talk Children's Centre.

Grosjean, F. (1992). The bilingual and the bicultural person in the hearing and in the deaf world. *Sign Language Studies, 77,* 307–320.

Haslett, B., & Samter, W. (1997) *Children communicating: The first five years.* Mahwah, NJ: Lawrence Erlbaum Associates.

Johnson, R. E. (1994). Possible influences on bilingualism in early ASL acquisition. *Teaching English to deaf and second- language students, 10*(2), 9–17.

Johnson, R. E., Liddell, S. K., & Erting, C. J. (1989). *Unlocking the curriculum: Principles for achieving access in deaf education* (Gallaudet Research Institute working paper 89-3). Washington, DC: Gallaudet University.

Kantor, R. (1982). Communicative interaction: Mother modification and child acquisition of American Sign Language. *Sign Language Studies, 36,* 233–282.

Launer, P. (1982). *Early signs of motherhood: Motherese in American Sign Language.* Paper presented at the Meeting of the American Speech-Language-Hearing Association, Toronto, Canada.

Maestas y Moores, J. (1980). Early linguistic environment: Interactions of deaf parents with their infants. *Sign Language Studies, 26,* 1–13.

Maxwell, M. (1980). *Language acquisition in a deaf child: The interaction of sign variations, speech, and print variations.* Unpublished doctoral dissertation, University of Arizona, Tuscon.

Maxwell, M. (1984). A deaf child's natural development of literacy. *Sign Language Studies, 44,* 191–224.

Maxwell, M. (1988). The alphabetic principle and fingerspelling. *Sign Language Studies, 61,* 377–404.

Mayberry, R., & Waters, G. (1991). Children's memory for sign and fingerspelling in relation to production rate and sign language input. In P. Siple & S. Fischer (Eds.), *Theoretical issues in sign language research* (Vol. 2, pp. 211–230). Chicago: University of Chicago.

Mayer, C., & Wells, G. (1996). Can the linguistic interdependence theory support a bilingual-bicultural model of literacy education for deaf students? *Journal of deaf studies and deaf education, 1*(2), 93–107.

Padden, C., & Humphries, T. (1988). *Deaf in America: Voices from a culture.* Cambridge, MA: Harvard University Press.

Padden, C., & Ramsey, C. (1998). Reading ability in signing deaf children. In P. Prinz (Ed.), *ASL proficiency and English literacy acquisition: New perspectives.* Frederick, MD: Topics in language disorders, 18 (4), 30–46.

Padden, C. A. (1991). The acquisition of fingerspelling by deaf children. In P. Siple & S. Fischer (Eds.), *Theoretical issues in sign language research* (Vol. 2, pp. 191–210). Chicago: University of Chicago.

Padden, C. A. (1996). Early bilingual lives of deaf children. In I. Parasnis (Ed.), *Cultural and language diversity and the deaf experience* (pp. 99–116). New York: Cambridge.

Padden, C. A., & LeMaster, B. (1985). An alphabet on hand: The acquisition of fingerspelling in deaf children. *Sign Language Studies, 47,* 161–172.

Ramsey, C. (1997). *Deaf children in public schools.* Washington, DC: Gallaudet University.

Strong, M. (1995). A review of bilingual/bicultural programs for deaf children in North America. *American Annals of the Deaf, 140*(2), 84–94.

Supalla, S., Wix, T., & McKee, C. (in press). Print as a primary source of English for deaf learners. In J. Nicol & T. Langendoen (Eds.), *Title forthcoming.* Malden, MA: Blackwell.

Tharp, R. & Gallimore, R. (1988). *Rousing minds to life: Teaching, learning, and schooling in social context.* New York: Cambridge University Press.

Intuitive Parenting, Communication, and Interaction With Deaf Infants

Lynne Sanford Koester
The University of Montana
Hanuš Papoušek
Max-Planck Institute for Research in Psychiatry
Sybil Smith-Gray
Gallaudet University

In this chapter, we summarize and offer theoretical and clinical interpretations of findings from various analyses of mother and infant behaviors during face-to-face interactions in the first year of life. These results are based on a longitudinal study of deaf and hearing mothers and infants carried out at Gallaudet University beginning in 1988 under the leadership of Dr. Kathryn Meadow-Orlans. Having worked and published in the field of childhood deafness for many years, Dr. Meadow-Orlans recognized the need for greater understanding of the needs and capabilities of deaf infants in order for early interventionists and caregivers to provide the most appropriate environments for these children. In addition, she was aware of the importance of including deaf parents in such investigations in order to gain insights about their natural strategies for interacting with deaf children to optimize visual attention and to maintain communication without relying primarily on vocalizations for this purpose. This resulted in funding for one of the largest studies to date comparing mother–infant dyads in all four hearing status combinations and included gathering observational and interview data over the first 18 months of the child's life (see MacTurk, Meadow-Orlans, Koester, & Spencer, 1993, for a complete description of design and methodology).

Several questions were of primary concern to the analyses reported here:

What maternal behaviors support and maintain successful interactive dialogue with a deaf infant?

What characterizes effective responsiveness with a deaf infant for whom access to parental vocalizations is compromised?

In what ways do parents, whether deaf or hearing, intuitively compensate for differences in perceptual abilities in deaf and hearing infants?

From a clinical perspective, are there qualitative differences in the early interactions between deaf and hearing infants and their parents that might be predictive of long-term consequences?

Face-to-face encounters between parents and infants are frequent and expected occurrences in the lives of most families in the Western world. These early interactions provide ample opportunity for researchers to observe the mutuality and reciprocity thought to be so important during parent–infant exchanges. Behaviors that are often used as indices of effective interactions, such as maintaining or breaking eye contact, motherese and infant cooing or babbling, touching and comforting (including self-regulation by the infant), and expressions of joy or displeasure, have all been documented as part of this study and will be summarized below (see also, Koester, 1995; Meadow-Orlans, 1997; Spencer & Lederberg, 1997; Spencer & Meadow-Orlans, 1996).

INTUITIVE PARENTING AND APPLICATIONS TO DEAF INFANTS

Papoušek and Papoušek (1987, 1990) developed the theory of intuitive parenting in which they describe the skillful yet often overlooked communication strategies used by parents when interacting with their babies—nonconscious behaviors that in fact are ideally suited to support the human infant's natural inclination to adapt to its social world. In addition to furthering our understanding of typical parent–child exchanges, this perspective also has the potential to illuminate our perceptions of parenting in exceptional populations. As a guiding model behind the current research,

Intuitive parenting has thus been applied to variations in parenting behaviors that may be related to deafness on either side of the dyad, parent or child, but can have important consequences regardless of the origin (Koester, 1992, 1994). Of course, interactive difficulties can result when disruptions occur in those subtle parenting behaviors that normally require very little thought and yet are necessary to sustain and enhance the parent–infant relationship. On the other hand, this theory also helps researchers become more observant and aware of the many nonconscious ways in which parents may be compensating quite appropriately for a child's hearing loss and may therefore lead to useful insights for early intervention personnel and educators of deaf children.

One example can be seen in the ways deaf parents modify their sign language when communicating with an infant. The patterns noticed by Erting, Prezioso, and Hynes (1990), for example, are strikingly parallel to those documented in vocal motherese: Signs are simplified and highly repetitive but also more influenced by the partner's gaze than sign communication among deaf adults. In other words, when the infant is looking at the mother, her signing is likely to occur near her face rather than within the larger space used among adult signing partners; when the infant looks away or at another object, the deaf adult is more likely to sign near the object or to reach into the infant's visual field for effective communication. This finding has been supported by similar observations in other cultures, such as reported by Masataka (1992, 1998) in regard to Japanese Sign Language directed to deaf infants. Spencer and Lederberg (1997) also provided evidence of syntactic simplification, visual displacement of signs, and use of shorter signed utterances to younger deaf children (12-month-olds).

DISRUPTIONS AND COMPENSATIONS WHEN AN INFANT IS DEAF

The developmental and educational delays experienced by some deaf children may be the result of difficulties hearing parents and teachers have in making the necessary adaptations or providing the scaffolding needed to help transmit knowledge and skills to the deaf child (Wood, 1991). This Vygotskian emphasis on the dialectical nature and social imbeddedness of the child's early interactive experiences also informs the research of Jamieson (1994). Observing hearing parents with deaf preschoolers, she found that even after effectively establishing eye contact prior to giving instructions, these parents often proceeded as if the child's auditory capacity was completely intact (Jamieson, 1988). As a result of using a simultaneous auditory–visual style of teaching, these parents essentially made very little adaptation to the deaf child's perceptual and learning needs. As Jamieson (1994) noted, "It appears that hearing adults, both parents and teachers, face a tremendous challenge in trying to unlearn habitual communication patterns and to replace them with patterns more appropriate to the visual mode" (p. 446).

These conclusions may also be relevant to interactions with the younger deaf subjects who have been the focus of our own investigations. However, an earlier study by Wedell-Monnig and Lumley (1980) stressed the early visual compensation observed between deaf infants and their hearing parents, noting that this may in fact contribute to delayed diagnosis if hearing parents misinterpret the infant's heightened visual sensitivity as response to environmental sounds or voices. That is, these parents may achieve a level of communication with their deaf baby through eye contact, facial expressions, and touch, especially in the early months. According to Wedell-Monnig and Lumley, however, a "common symbolic language" may still be missing in these dyads, with potentially deleterious long-term consequences (p. 766).

A number of researchers reported that hearing mothers tend to be highly directive with deaf children (Meadow, Greenberg, Erting, & Carmichael, 1981; Nienhuys & Tikotin, 1983) and as a result may not be sufficiently sensitive to the child's need to explore the surroundings visually (Spencer, Bodner-Johnson, & Gutfreund, 1992). As Spencer et al. observed, overly directive efforts to elicit and sustain a deaf infant's attention preclude the parent's sensitive responsiveness to the baby's cues. The same authors showed that deaf mothers with deaf infants are more likely to wait for the infant to look at them before signing or responding to the child's focus of attention. Such coordination of gaze patterns is of particular importance for the deaf child who must rely on vision for both receptive language input and for exploration of the external world (Waxman & Spencer, 1997).

Deaf parents with deaf children may provide important insights for hearing parents and early interventionists regarding optimal strategies for communicating with a deaf infant. Having grown up themselves without hearing (except in cases where they became deaf later in life), these deaf parents may in fact model intuitive parenting in ways that have to date been largely unexplored. Even deaf parents who do not use a formal system of sign communication appear to incorporate gestures extensively during spoken interactions with their deaf children; de Villiers, Bibeau, Helliwell, and Clare (1989) interpret this as an unconscious facilitation of the child's access to parental language input. Similarly, Spencer et al. (1992) report that dyads in which both mother and child are deaf often utilize strategies rarely observed among hearing partners, but that result in highly responsive and contingent interaction patterns.

Some of the more varied and multimodal forms of stimulation observed particularly by deaf parents in our own analyses include highly animated facial expressions, visual–gestural games (and of course sign communication), and frequent, vigorous tactile contact. Furthermore, many hearing mothers with deaf infants also become quickly adept at enhancing their usual visual and tactile stimulation. This represents an important adjustment by hearing mothers to the heightened visual needs of a deaf child, even though it may not occur immediately or automatically. (We note for example, that these adjustments appeared more frequently among the mothers of 9-month-old deaf infants in our study than when the infants were younger.) Many infants had only recently been diagnosed as deaf at the time of our 6-month observation, so their hearing mothers may have required some time to accept this news, understand its implications, and begin to modify their behaviors in ways that better met the deaf infant's perceptual and attentional needs. A variety of parental modifications in other modalities add to the list of intuitive behaviors observed in parents with deaf children or parents who themselves are deaf, as elaborated on next.

Maternal Vocalizations

It is difficult indeed for caregivers not to respond to the coos, babbles, and pleasant vocalizations of a human infant. These social signals typically elicit imitative and nurturing responses from caregivers and often lead to some of the infant's first lessons in turn taking with a social partner. Vocal exchanges thus play an important role in furthering and refining interactions between parents and their offspring, even before infants are themselves able to imitate the language to which they are exposed. A deaf child with hearing parents may, at least until the parents are able to make informed decisions about their preferred method of communication, be affected by the lack of experience with an accessible language system; the effect may extend to the socioemotional realm, with negative consequences in areas such as affect regulation, self-awareness, and self-esteem (Marschark, 1993).

Parental vocalizations clearly influence and shape the emerging language skills of infants, but their significance is even more far reaching. Early vocal exchanges also provide important affective information and cues to help the infant identify significant figures in the social world. As Fernald (1984) asserted, the characteristics of motherese, evident in so many languages and cultures, make speech particularly salient for human infants and contribute in important ways to the infant's development of meaning, particularly the understanding of affective messages. According to Kirkman and Cross (1986), "Deaf children, even more than hearing children, need to have their attempts at vocalization reinforced by incorporating them into the development of an affectional bond; such imitative babbling has both linguistic and emotional ramifications" (p. 61).

In an analysis of the acoustical patterns of both deaf and hearing mothers in the Gallaudet study (Traci & Koester, 1998), we were surprised by the extent to which Deaf mothers modified their own vocalizations depending on the hearing status of their infant. In other words, and lending further support to the application of intuitive parenting concepts to this population, it is apparent that deaf mothers use their voices more and incorporate more features of motherese when interacting with a hearing baby. On the other hand, it is the hearing mothers with deaf infants who appear to exaggerate their pitch excursions the most, as if to compensate for the infant's limited auditory perception. It is important to add, however, that concomitant facial expressions, head movements, and use of other sensory channels while vocalizing may also function to make these maternal utterances more salient even to a deaf child.

Another finding from this study (Koester, Brooks, & Karkowski, 1998), indicating that hearing mothers increase their use of vocal games when interacting with a deaf baby, is consistent with this view. Again, this demonstrates parental efforts to make vocal communication more salient and accessible to an infant with a hearing loss. *Vocal games,* as we define them, typically involve animated visual and often tactile cues and thus represent an important compensatory adaptation when interacting with a deaf baby. In these interactions, parental vocalizations are augmented by exaggerated play with sounds, perhaps accompanied by visual stimulation such as in peek-a-boo games, as well as animated facial expressions particularly when eye contact is achieved. Vocal games are by definition multimodal events and therefore more easily perceived (and obviously enjoyed) by the deaf infant. It is encouraging to see that hearing mothers are already using such strategies with their 9-month-old deaf infants.

Tactile Contact

Numerous researchers have demonstrated the importance of touch during interactive dialogues between caregiver and child (e.g., Brazelton, 1984; Field, 1993; Koester, 1995; Malphurs, Raag, Field, Pickens, & Pelaez-Nogueras, 1996; Stack & Muir, 1990, 1992). In addition to soothing or comforting a fussy baby, tactile contact contributes to the child's emerging awareness of boundaries between self and other, and to the development of reciprocity and communication skills in a variety of modalities. However, relatively little is known about the patterns of this early tactile contact that may contribute to its effectiveness, characteristics across different cultures, or the extent to which caregivers rely on touch in various contexts.

Gusella, Muir, and Tronick (1988) instructed mothers to use vocal and facial expressions but no touching while interacting with their 3-month-old infants. Results indicated a gradual decrease in the time infants spent smiling and gazing at their mothers. That is, when touch was removed from the interaction altogether, mothers were less able to maintain their infant's pleasure and participation. Stack and Muir (1992) also observed infant smiling and gaze behaviors while eliminating the mother's facial affect and vocalizations rather than touch; in this case, the role of tactile contact took on an even greater significance. That is, mothers resorted to more active patterns of touch in their efforts to maintain the infant's positive affect and eye contact.

As mentioned earlier, studies of spoken language directed to infants have increased researchers' awareness of the variety and complexity of parental behaviors—in the case of speech, the patterns of melodic contours, pitch ranges, rhythms, and repetitions all contribute to the infant's heightened responsiveness to motherese (Cooper & Aslin, 1990; Fernald, 1989; Papoušek & Papoušek, 1987; Papoušek, Papoušek, & Symmes, 1991). We examined parallels in the ways in which deaf and hearing parents touch their babies, focusing on durations of tactile contact during interactions and characteristics such as intensity and active or passive types of touch.

Dyads in which one or both partners are deaf offer a unique opportunity to observe the possible functions of touch in terms of optimizing or enhancing communication when the auditory modality is limited. In these dyads, touch may play an even more important function than usual as it is often necessary for eliciting visual attention, alerting the child that signed communication is forthcoming, or maintaining contact and providing reassurance even when the deaf child has looked away. Deaf mothers, having grown up with the need to rely on multiple sensory modalities for communication, provide interesting insights into the use of tactile contact during early interactions with either a deaf or hearing infant; in either case, the child needs to be attentive to various kinds of nonauditory communication occurring within the deaf family. Such naturally occurring adaptations provide impressive examples of parents' nonconscious compensatory behaviors that support the attentional needs and the emerging interactive skills of the young infant (Papoušek & Papoušek, 1987, 1990).

Mothers with deaf infants appear to use somewhat more active patterns of tactile contact with their infants, an adjustment that represents an important means of intuitively compensating for an infant's hearing loss. This use of a highly salient sensory channel for eliciting and maintaining visual attention is particularly necessary for a child learning to communicate in a visual–gestural modality. That is, touch may be even more important when a visual–gestural mode of communication is being used as it frequently serves to regain the infant's visual attention to a signing partner. Analyses reveal that deaf mothers with deaf infants in our sample emphasized short duration touches (less than 1 second) with infants at both 6 and 9 months of age. Brief episodes of tactile contact such as this appear to be examples of a tap-sign strategy used to alert the infant to forthcoming sign communication.

Clearly there are numerous subtle adjustments that parents make without any conscious awareness or planning but that in many cases may serve to support the perceptual, linguistic, and cognitive capabilities of a child without hearing. Of course the parent–child relationship is not a one-way street, and there may be equally subtle cues on the part of the infant that in turn help to instruct the relatively naive parent about strategies that are effective, pleasurable, and which the child would like to have repeated. In the process of learning how to communicate with each other, parents must also be sensitive to this feedback from the infant. We now turn our attention to some of the behavioral contrasts we observed between deaf and hearing infants, highlighting those that were somewhat unexpected or particularly important for parents who have not had previous experiences with deafness.

WHAT INFANTS CONTRIBUTE TO THESE INTERACTIONS

Repetitive Movements

We observed that infants who are deaf, as well as those whose parents are deaf, spend more time engaging in repetitive physical activity such as kicking, rhythmically extending and flexing the arms or hands, and so forth (Merritt, Terwilliger, & Koester, 1998; Oller & Eilers, 1998). One possible interpretation is consistent with the idea of attunement as described by Stern (1985) in which the similar activity levels reflect a sharing by deaf mothers and their infants of each others' level of physical engagement during these early interactions. Of course, the deaf mothers we observed were frequently signing to their infants, so their infants may have been responding by mirroring this repetitive activity—that is, by frequently moving their own hands and arms. This activity by the infant may then be interpreted (particularly by deaf parents) as a precursor to sign communication and responded to with praise and encouragement. In fact, this may occur regardless of the infants' hearing status: Those who are born into deaf families will most likely grow up using sign language at home, even if they themselves are able to hear.

Eye Gaze

Maintaining eye contact or visual attention to the social partner is of particular importance for a child who is deaf or for one who is interacting with a deaf caregiver (Koester, Karkowski, & Traci, 1998). As Robson (1967) pointed out, visual fixation and following are among the earliest volitional acts of the infant. The visual modality allows the infant to control sensory input by closing the eyes or looking away so as to eliminate external sensory input even within the first months of life.

In our studies, we found that 6-month-old infants with deaf, signing mothers alternate their gaze back and forth between mother and the surroundings more frequently but sustain their gaze to their social partner longer than do those with hearing mothers. By contrast, infants at this age whose mothers are hearing spend more time looking around the room (usually with mother vocally labeling and narrating in the background). By age 9 months, it is apparent that hearing infants with hearing mothers look away from the mother most frequently during interactions. It should be remembered, however, that for this group eye contact is least important to the success of an interaction as hearing infants can access spoken language input regardless of their focus of visual attention.

Self-Regulation

Infant self-regulatory behaviors offer important insights into the child's abiltiy to modulate responses to distress, overstimulation, or displeasure (Lipsitt, 1983) and may also reveal the degree to which an infant perceives a particular experience as distressful. Using the maternal still-face paradigm, we compared these regulatory mechanisms in both deaf and hearing infants, revealing some interesting differences. We noted, for example, that 6-month-old deaf infants display more self-regulatory behavior during actual face-to-face interactions with a hearing mother than do infants in the other groups; however, these same infants decrease this behavior during the still-face (nonresponsive mother) episode, which is when infants usually increase their self-regulation strategies. By 9 months of age, both groups of deaf babies (that is, with either hearing or deaf mothers) spend more time in self-regulatory activities in general than do their hearing peers. As would normally be expected, 9-month-old infants in all hearing status groups increase their use of these strategies during the still-face episode as compared to the interactive episodes (Terwilliger, Kamman, & Koester, 1997).

Another interesting finding is that infants with deaf mothers appear to be the most distressed during the still-face episode, as seen in greater displays of negative affect (struggle or protest). Deaf mothers themselves are often highly active and animated with their infants and may thus be more entertaining and engaging as partners; if so, then the still-face episode that disrupts this responsiveness may be a greater deviation for the infant, therefore eliciting a more negative reaction. Infants with hearing mothers, on the other hand, appeared to increase their protestations more gradually over the three episodes we observed.

Infant Vocalizations

Deaf as well as hearing infants produce vocal sounds such as cooing. In the Gallaudet study, for example, we found essentially no differences in the amount of affectively positive or negative vocalizations emitted by deaf or hearing 9-month-old infants. In the presence of caregivers, these sounds often initiate a dialogue, with parents responding as if the baby is already a conversational partner. With hearing parents, early dialogues require listening to the infant, imitating or prompting the infant to vocalize again, and pausing or waiting for the infant to take a turn (Mayer & Tronick, 1985). The hearing infant therefore experiences what Papoušek and Papoušek (1991) refer to as a modeling/imitative frame, receiving feedback and reinforcement for vocalizing and encouragement for the further development of conversational skills. There are innumerable opportunities for hearing infants to expand their vocal repertoire in response to spoken linguistic feedback. This process includes not just the imitation of language units but learning how to control relevant aspects of sound production such as tone of voice, melodic contours, volume, temporal patterns, and consonant-like sounds (Papoušek & Papoušek, 1991). Both infant and caregiver must be viewed as part of a variable and dynamic system, as proposed by von Bertalanffy (1968) in which every utterance as well as every pause has potential meaning.

For hearing parents, the diagnosis of deafness in a child can have a profound and unsettling effect on their confidence as parents, particularly in their ability to communicate effectively: "The diagnosis of deafness forces hearing parents abruptly to confront basic differences between themselves and their child, with the knowledge that there is a fundamental way in which they cannot share that child's experience" (Kirkman & Cross, 1986, p. 54). In a more recent study, Gregory (1995) observed that hearing parents sometimes refrained from speaking to their deaf child, assuming there was simply no point and finding that spoken communication was difficult. As we described previously however, many important and salient features of early communication with an infant (such as exaggerated facial expressions and the heightened use of tactile contact) co-occur with language input and may be of particular significance during interactions with a deaf child.

CLINICAL IMPLICATIONS

This section focuses on the clinical impact that the specific maternal and infant behaviors under investigation in our research can have on the quality of parent–infant interactions, particularly when deafness is a factor. Ultimately, the parent–infant relationship as a whole is affected when there is a perturbation or situation on either side that interrupts the normal sequence of development or the positive flow of social and emotional exchange between the two partners. Maternal behaviors that appear to compensate for sensory modality differences between themselves and their infants are particularly relevant for early intervention with clinically at risk parent–infant dyads.

The clinical observation of parent–infant interactions requires a skilled eye that is attuned to the dialectical give and take inherent in a family systems approach, as described earlier. It is difficult to conceive of other instances in behavioral science research in which the saying "the whole is greater than the sum of its parts" could be more true, regardless of an individual's perspective as observer, child participant, or parent participant. Even the brief observations used in our research reveal many examples of well adapted interactions and the multiple ways, both subtle and overt, in which each partner responds to and shapes the other's behavior. Gradually, behaviors coded as discrete acts of parents and infants merge to form impressions of signals and reactions that appear to be either smooth and well organized, or disconnected and frustrating on both sides. Researchers and clinicians alike may notice the distinct subjective experience of no longer observing individual actions and reactions but rather the fluid psychological motion of the dyadic unit as a whole.

Many clinicians hold the belief that disturbances in the early parent–child relationship significantly influence future development of the young child. The strength of this belief is reflected in the fact that relationship disorders is one of the five axes listed in the *Diagnostic Classification of Mental Health and Developmental Disorders of Infancy and Early Childhood* (1994). The *Diagnostic Classification: 0-3* manual indicates that formal clinical assessment of the parent–infant relationship should involve an evaluation of the behavioral quality of the interactions, the affective tone of the interactions, and the degree of psychological involvement. We stress that these features of parent–infant interactions are important regardless of whether deafness is a factor. However, our research findings primarily address each of these areas of parent–infant interactions within the context of a deaf partner in the dyad.

Behavioral Quality of the Relationship

The behavioral quality of the parent–infant relationship includes aspects of mutual responsiveness, sensitivity, and emotional regulation similar to some of the dynamics observed in our own research. The concept of intuitive parenting offers important insights regarding the optimal patterns that clinicians seek to observe, quantify, and describe in their attempts to rate the behavioral quality of any parent–infant relationship.

As previously discussed, this perspective addresses communication strategies that parents use intuitively to meet the adaptive needs of their infants. The particular features of a parent's communication style that may be expressed for this purpose are far ranging and complex. Nonetheless, it can be said that the nonconscious aim of the deployment of intuitive parenting strategies is to support and enhance the behavioral quality and the adaptive needs of the parent–infant relationship. The question then becomes in what ways do parents intuitively adjust their own behaviors so as to support their infant's early adaptive needs, particularly when either the parent or the infant is deaf.

It is difficult to measure and operationalize the rather abstract qualities such as sensitivity, reciprocity, and responsiveness that reportedly contribute to the behavioral quality of the parent–infant relationship. However, our research findings suggest that there may be a constellation of behaviors (such as maternal tactile contact, infant eye gaze, and infant self-regulatory behaviors) that have particular relevance for operationalizing these concepts for deaf infants. The results imply that these particular maternal and infant behaviors may contribute significantly to the fluid functioning and reciprocal exchanges with the dyad in these cases. When this occurs, state regulation, emotional predictability, and a generally positive affective tone should follow.

Nevertheless, it is to be expected that there will also be cases in which these compensatory behaviors do not appear, perhaps due to stress or depression or lack of support experienced by the parent. Our results lead us to conclude that the behavioral quality of the early relationship between a deaf infant and hearing parent may be enhanced by education awareness, information dissemination, and of course modeling techniques. For example, playback of carefully selected videotaped observations, drawing the mother's attention to specific moments when she did achieve mutual attention and shared positive interactions with her baby, may improve her sense of self-efficacy and effectiveness as a parent with a deaf child. On the other hand, showing hearing parents videotaped examples of deaf parents' intuitive modifications of their behaviors, such as signed motherese or tapping the baby before a signed communication (see Spencer & Lederberg, 1997, for further discussion of this phenomenon), may also be an effective intervention strategy. It is particularly important in this case, however, to do so with a great deal of care and awareness of differences between deaf and hearing cultures in regard to such matters as personal space and tactile contact during interactions.

Affective Tone.   *Affect* is a clinical term that refers to the communication of meaning beyond the physical display of a feeling state. The affective tone of the parent–infant relationship is of critical importance because it determines the overall mood of the dyadic exchanges. The clinical concern regarding the affective tone of the parent–infant relationship is one of intensity (in either direction) and the degree to which intense affect serves to dysregulate the quality of the interactions.

For example, a dyadic exchange between parent and infant may involve behaviors such as verbal teasing and tickling, initially leading to positive affect such as laughing or squealing. However, if these exchanges remain intense over time, the effect can be *dysregulation*: Very similar actions now take on a negative quality, better characterized as verbal and physical intrusiveness and resulting in negative affective exchanges—grimacing, scowling, or crying on the part of the baby. The result is the establishment of a negative or hostile mood. This is pertinent to some findings regarding hearing mothers with deaf children (for example, see Meadow-Orlans & Steinberg, 1993) indicating a tendency to be more directive and even intrusive when compared to mothers with hearing children. Although this may be a natural result of the parents' efforts to maintain attention and elicit responses from the deaf child, clearly the possible outcome of negative affect during these early interactions (if it becomes a predictable pattern) is neither desirable nor rewarding for either social partner.

The most relevant findings from our research regarding the area of affective tone involve maternal facial and affective expressiveness, infant affective responses, and maternal and infant vocalizations. Our findings suggest, for example, that parents modify their facial and affective expressiveness and their vocalizations in response to the hearing status of their children—in particular, appearing more animated and incorporating a greater variety of modalities during communication with deaf infants. Again, the intuitive parenting model and the clinical framework for examination of parent–infant relationships suggest that parental adjustments are made to meet the adaptive needs of the infant and thereby support and enhance the behavioral qualities of the relationship overall. In this case, animated behaviors that serve to make the mother's communication and play more salient to a deaf child appear to be highly appropriate modifications of the usual parental repertoire.

Psychological Involvement.   Psychological involvement as a concept applied to the assessment of parent–infant relationships focuses on the impact that "parental attitudes and perceptions of the child (i.e., the meaning of the child's behaviors to the parents)" can have on the relationship (Diagnostic Classification: 0-3, 1994, p. 48). The literature in infancy studies is replete with findings addressing the effects of parental attitudes and expectations on child development in various domains of functioning, including cognitive and motor abilities (Trad, 1992).

Although it is difficult to operationalize the construct of psychological involvement for the purpose of assessing the parent–infant relationship, we believe our research has in fact succeeded in providing a unique example of how this might be done.

Our findings involving repetitive movements by deaf babies, and the distinctly different meaning attributed to these movements by deaf mothers as compared to their hearing counterparts, have strong implications for the concept of psychological involvement. As previously discussed, we observed that deaf mothers tend to interpret their infants' repetitive hand and arm movements as a precursor to sign communication, regardless of the infant's hearing status. As a result, deaf mothers respond to this type of rhythmic activity with praise and encouragement, whereas hearing mothers do not (hearing mothers, in fact, reported a somewhat negative interpretation in which they perceived this physical activity as a sign of their infant's hyperactivity). This is a case in which the consequences of even a subtle behavior on the part of the infant can play a significant role in the subsequent emergence (or suppression) of these cues into more recognizable forms of communication.

The most direct explanation for these differential responses to repetitive movements is rooted in the varying life experiences of deaf and hearing mothers and in the way these experiences affect their perceptions and expectations of their infants' behaviors. Deaf mothers with deaf children do not typically experience the same struggles and conflicts reported by hearing mothers with deaf children in regard to methods of communication, schooling, or cultural identity. Even in the case of deaf mothers with hearing infants, there is likely to be encouragement of the use of gestures and manual forms of communication, assuming that in both families the primary language will be visual–gestural. The many opposing philosophies and opinions about education of children who are deaf present a confusing and often stressful picture to hearing parents. It is almost inevitable that this bewilderment will in some way be communicated to the young child, even if it is only in the parent's hesitancy to respond to the infant's early use of gestures to communicate needs, desires, and feelings. As Spencer and Lederberg (1997) noted, many of the hearing parents in this same study changed their minds about a preferred mode of communication with their deaf infant during the course of our observations (i.e., over the first 18 months of the child's life). It seems reasonable to assume that this ambivalence alone must have some impact in terms of potential disruption of the compensatory parental behaviors that seem so important to establishing effective communicative exchanges with a deaf infant.

CONCLUSION

From the 1960s to the 1990s, there has been a vast amount of research on parent–child interactions, with most investigations focusing on presumably normal mother and child dyads. Some questions and insights resulting from these efforts, such as the degree to which an infant is securely attached to the caregiver, have received much attention not only in the academic literature but also in the popular press. Society generally acknowledges the impact of the caregiver–child relationship on the developing child. Increasingly, the influence of fathers, siblings, and out of home caregivers is also being examined, so that gradually a more complete picture of the socioemotional world of the infant is emerging.

As part of this expanding knowledge, research must necessarily include those dyads and families in which one or more individuals experience some kind of disability or challenge to their normal functioning (see Calderon & Greenberg, chap. 10, this volume). Although many Western societies have made impressive strides in accommodating and including persons with disabilities in all areas of life—schools, the work place, athletic competition, and so forth—there is still relatively little comprehensive data regarding the early development of children who are deaf or who grow up in families with deaf parents. In this chapter, we take some initial steps to rectify this situation by providing an overview of some of the most interesting results of our observations comparing deaf and hearing infants in their first year of life as they interact with their hearing or deaf mothers.

REFERENCES

Brazelton, T. B. (1984). Discussion of "Philosophers on Touch". In C. C. Brown (Ed.), *The many facets of touch: The foundation of experience: Its importance through life, with initial emphasis for infants and young children* (pp. 10–12). Skillman, NJ: Johnson & Johnson Baby Products Co.

Cooper, R. P., & Aslin, R. N. (1990). Preference for infant-directed speech in the first month after birth. *Child Development, 61,* 1584–1595.

de Villiers, J., Bibeau, L., Helliwell, K., & Clare, A. (1989, April). *Speech and gestural communication between oral deaf children and oral deaf mothers.* Paper presented at the biennial meeting of the Society for Research in Child Development, Kansas City, MO.

Diagnostic classification of mental health and developmental disorders of infancy and early childhood. (1994). Washington, DC: National Center for Infants, Toddlers and Families.

Erting, C. J., Prezioso, C., & Hynes, M. O. (1990). The interactional context of deaf mother-infant communication. In V. Volterra & C. Erting (Eds.), *From gesture to language in hearing and deaf children.* Berlin, Germany: Springer.

Fernald, A. (1984). The perceptual and affective salience of mothers' speech to infants. In L. Feagans, C. Garvey, R. Golinkoff, M. T. Greenberg, C. Harding, & J. N. Bohannan (Eds.), *The origins and growth of communication* (pp. 5–29). Norwood, NJ: Ablex.

Fernald, A. (1989). Intonation and communicative intent in mothers' speech to infants: Is the melody the message? *Child Development, 60,* 1497–1510.

Field, T. (1993). Enhancing parent sensitivity. In N. J. Anastasiow & S. Harel (Eds.), *At-risk infants: Interventions, families and research* (pp. 81–89). Baltimore: P.H. Brookes.

Gregory, S. (1995). *Deaf children and their families.* Cambridge, England: Cambridge University Press.

Gusella, J., Muir, D. W., & Tronick, E. Z. (1988). The effect of manipulating maternal behavior during an interaction on three- and six-month-olds' affect and attention. *Child Development, 59,* 1111–1124.

Jamieson, J. R. (1988). *Deafness and mother–child interaction: Scaffolded instruction and the learning of problem-solving skills.* Unpublished doctoral dissertation, McGill University, Montreal, Canada.

Jamieson, J. R. (1994). Teaching as transaction: Vygotskian perspectives on deafness and mother-child interaction. *Exceptional Children, 60,* 434–449.

Kirkman, M., & Cross, T. (1986). Conversations between mothers and their deaf children. In T. Cross & L. Riach (Eds.), *Aspects of child development* (pp. 53–63). Melborne, Australia: AE Press.

Koester, L. S. (1992). Intuitive parenting as a model for understanding parent–infant interactions when one partner is deaf. *American Annals of the Deaf, 137*(4), 362–369.

Koester, L. S. (1994). Early interactions and the socioemotional development of deaf infants. *Early Development and Parenting, 3,* 51–60.

Koester, L. S. (1995). Face-to-face interactions between hearing mothers and their deaf infants. *Infant Behavior and Development, 18,* 145–153.

Koester, L. S., Brooks, L. R., & Karkowski, A. M. (1998). A comparison of the vocal patterns of deaf and hearing mother-infant dyads during face-to-face interaction. *Journal of Deaf Studies and Deaf Education, 3:4,* 290–301.

Koester, L. S., Karkowski, A. M., & Traci, M. A. (1998). How do Deaf and hearing mothers regain eye contact when their infants look away? *American Annals of the Deaf, 143,* 5–13.

Lipsitt, L. (1983). Stress in infancy: Toward understanding the origins of coping behavior. In N. Garmezy & M. Rutter (Eds.), *Stress, coping and development in children* (pp. 161–190). New York: McGraw-Hill.

MacTurk, R. H., Meadow-Orlans, K. P., Koester, L. S., & Spencer, P. E. (1993). Social support, motivation, language, and interaction: A longitudinal study of mothers and deaf infants. *American Annals of the Deaf, 138,* 19–25.

Malphurs, J. E., Raag, T., Field, T., Pickens, K., & Pelaez-Nogueras, M. (1996). Touch by intrusive and withdrawn mothers with depressive symptoms. *Early Development and Parenting, 5*(2), 111–115.

Marschark, M. (1993). Origins and interactions in social, cognitive, and language development of deaf children. In M. Marschark & M. D. Clark (Eds.), *Psychological perspecives on deafness* (pp. 7–26). Hillsdale, NJ: Lawrence Erlbaum Associates.

Masataka, N. (1992). Motherese in a signed language. *Infant Behavior and Development, 15,* 453–460.

Masataka, N. (1998). Perception of motherese in Japanese sign language by 6–month-old hearing infants. *Developmental Psychology, 34*(2), 241–246.

Mayer, N. K., & Tronick, E. Z. (1985). Mothers' turn-giving signals and infant turn-taking in mother-infant interaction. In T. M. Field & N. A. Fox (Eds.), *Social perception in infants* (pp. 196–216). Norwood, NJ: Ablex.

Meadow, K. P., Greenberg, M. T., Erting, C., & Carmichael, H. (1981). Interactions of deaf mothers and deaf preschool children: Comparisons with three other groups of deaf and hearing dyads. *American Annals of the Deaf, 126,* 454–468.

Meadow-Orlans, K. P. (1997). Effect of mother and infant hearing status on interactions at twelve and eighteen months. *Journal of Deaf Studies and Deaf Education, 2*(1), 26–36.

Meadow-Orlans, K. P., & Steinberg, A. G. (1993). Effects of infant hearing loss and maternal support on mother–infant interactions at eighteen months. *Journal of Applied Developmental Psychology, 14,* 407–426.

Merritt, D., Terwilliger, L., & Koester, L. S. (1998, April). *Deaf infants' rhythmic behaviors when face-to-face with a nonresponsive mother.* Poster session presented at the joint conference of the Rocky Mountain Psychological Association and the Western Psychological Association, Albuquerque, NM.

Nienhuys, T. G., & Tikotin, J. (1983). Pre-speech communication in hearing and hearing-impaired children. *Journal of the British Association of Teachers of the Deaf, 7*(6), 182–194.

Oller, K. D., & Eilers, R. E. (1998, July). Prospective evaluation of language learning in infants with delayed babbling. In N. Masataka & K. Oller (Co-Chairs), *Effects of environmental inputs on the development of babbling in hearing and deaf infants.* Symposium conducted at the biennial meeting of the International Society for the Study of Behavioural Development, Berne, Switzerland.

Papoušek, H., & Papoušek, M. (1987). Intuitive parenting: A dialectic counterpart to the infant's precocity in integrative capacities. In J. D. Osofsky (Ed.), *Handbook of infant development* (2nd ed., pp. 669–720). New York: Wiley.

Papoušek, H., & Papoušek, M. (1990). The art of motherhood. In N. Calder (Ed.), *Scientific Europe: Research and technology in 20 countries* (pp. 382–387). Maastricht, Holland: Scientific Publishers.

Papoušek, H., & Papoušek, M. (1991). Preverbal vocal communication from zero to one: Preparing the ground for language acquisition. In M.E. Lamb & H. Keller (Eds.), *Infant development: Perspectives from German-speaking countries* (pp. 299–328). Hillsdale, NJ: Lawrence Erlbaum Associates.

Papoušek, H., Papoušek, M., & Symmes, D. (1991). The meanings of melodies in motherese and tone and stress languages. *Infant Behavior and Development, 14,* 415–440.

Robson, K. S. (1967). The role of eye-to-eye contact in maternal–infant attachment. *Journal of Child Psychology and Psychiatry, 8,* 13–25.

Spencer, P. E., Bodner-Johnson, B. A., & Gutfreund, M. (1992). Interacting with infants with a hearing loss: What can we learn from mothers who are deaf? *Journal of Early Intervention, 16,* 64–78.

Spencer, P. E., & Lederberg, A. R. (1997). Different modes, different models: Communication and language of young deaf children and their mothers. In L. B. Adamson & M. A. Romski (Eds.), *Communication and language acquisition: Discoveries from atypical development* (pp. 203–230). Baltimore: Paul Brookes.

Spencer, P. E., & Meadow-Orlans, K. P. (1996). Play, language, and maternal responsiveness: A longitudinal study of deaf and hearing infants. *Child Development, 67,* 3176–3191.

Stack, D. M., & Muir, D. W. (1990). Tactile stimulation as a component of social interchange: New interpretations for the still-face effect. *British Journal of Developmental Psychology, 8,* 131–145.

Stack, D. M., & Muir, D. W. (1992). Adult tactile stimulation during face-to-face interactions modulates five-month-olds' affect and attention. *Child Development, 63,* 1509–1525.

Stern, D. N. (1985). *The interpersonal world of the infant: A view from psychoanalysis and developmental psychology.* New York: Basic Books.

Terwilliger, L., Kamman, T., & Koester, L. S. (1997, April). *Self-regulation by deaf and hearing infants at 9 months.* Poster session presented at the annual meeting of the Rocky Mountain Psychological Association, Reno, NV.

Traci, M. A., & Koester, L. S. (1998, July). *Fundamental frequency in speech directed to deaf or hearing infants by Deaf or hearing mothers.* Poster session presented at the biennial meeting of the International Society for the Study of Behavioural Development, Berne, Switzerland.

Trad, P. V. (1992). The role of parents in infant development. In P. V. Trad (Ed.), *Interventions with infants and parents: The theory and practice of previewing* (pp. 35–62). New York: Wiley.

von Bertalanffy, L. (1968). *General systems theory: Foundations, development, applications.* New York: Braziller.

Waxman, R. P., & Spencer, P. E. (1997). What mothers do to support infant visual attention: Sensitivities to age and hearing status. *Journal of Deaf Studies and Deaf Education, 2*(2), 104–114.

Wedell-Monnig, J., & Lumley, J. (1980). Child deafness and mother–child interaction. *Child Development, 51,* 766–774.

Wood, D. (1991). Communication and cognition: How the communication styles of hearing adults may hinder—rather than help—deaf learners. *American Annals of the Deaf, 136*(3), 247–251.

5

Impact of Child Deafness on Mother–Toddler Interaction: Strengths and Weaknesses

Amy R. Lederberg
Amy K. Prezbindowski
Georgia State University

The presence of a deaf child has considerable impact on a hearing family ... As early as infancy, there are reports of disruption in the development of reciprocal interactions between hearing mothers and their deaf infants. A few investigators have found these differences minimal (Greenberg & Marvin, 1979; Lederberg & Mobley, 1990; van Ijzendoorn, Goldberg, Kroonenberg, & Frenkel, 1992), but their findings are atypical (Musselman, MacKay, Trehub, & Eagle, 1996). (p. 556)

Most research investigating the impact of deafness on early mother–child interaction has compared hearing mothers and their deaf infants or toddlers to hearing children and hearing mothers. Those studies, almost without exception, found hearing/deaf (Hd) interactions problematic compared to those of hearing/hearing (Hh) dyads (Meadow-Orlans, 1997). (p. 26)

These quotes are representative of the prevailing view of the impact of child deafness on early hearing mother–deaf child interaction, but the picture they convey may be unduly ominous. Because of our training, behavioral scientists tend to focus on results that show significant differences between groups, perhaps because behavioral scientists know the null hypothesis cannot be proven. However, this may result in a more negative picture than exists in reality. The goal of this chapter is to review research on interactions between hearing mothers and deaf toddlers to identify positive, as well as negative, aspects of adaptations by hearing parents with deaf toddlers during the second year of life. Strengths, adaptive behavior, and signs of resiliency observed in hearing mother–deaf child interaction are noted, as well as aspects of early interaction that are problematic or detrimental to development.

This goal, to identify strengths and weaknesses in the relationship between deaf children and their hearing mothers, is a particularly appropriate topic for this volume because it follows in the tradition of the trail-blazing book *Sound and Sign* by Schlesinger and Meadow (1972). We are most concerned with deaf children born to hearing parents because they represent the vast majority of deaf children. From the late 1970s to the late 1990s, earlier identification of deaf children, particularly those of hearing parents, and stronger legal requirements for early intervention have resulted in their enrollment in early intervention programs at younger ages than ever before (Harrison & Roush, 1996). Before the age of 3 years, many early intervention services focus on supporting and facilitating the child's interactions with his or her parents (usually the mother; Pitt & Diaz, 1998). Professionals in these early intervention programs clearly are limited in the time they have with parents; they need to identify those aspects of the mother–child interaction requiring intervention and those developing along a typical pathway in order to provide the most useful parent education in a timely and cost-effective manner.

It is our contention that understanding the positive aspects of interactions between hearing mothers and their deaf children is as important as identifying areas in which deaf children and their hearing mothers experience problems. By depicting hearing mothers in the literature as deficient in their interactions with their deaf children, researchers bias professionals working with these mothers to focus on negative aspects of hearing mother–deaf child interaction. A balance of fostering hearing mothers' natural competencies to communicate with and meet the needs of their deaf children, along with identifying aspects of mother–child interaction that need modification, is most likely to prepare mothers to benefit from intervention programs.

Three methods have been used to identify strengths and weaknesses in mother–child interaction. First, the majority of research compares hearing mother–deaf child (Hd) dyads with hearing mother–hearing child (Hh) dyads. This comparison allows an individual to draw conclusions about the ways in which hearing mother–deaf child interaction is impacted by the child's hearing loss. Differences in dyadic functioning are seen as strengths or weaknesses depending on whether they are facilitative of development. Some of the differences may be positive adaptations to the child's needs (e.g., increase in visual communication), whereas others may be seen as areas of concern (e.g., increase in control).

Second, deaf child–deaf mother (Dd) dyads are included in some studies, providing an opportunity to tease apart the impact of hearing loss and the lack of a common communication system on the interaction between parent and child. Studies including Dd dyads are important to developmental theory because they also allow researchers to determine if communication modality (visual instead of auditory) has a significant impact on development. More importantly, from an interventionist's point of view, the observation of interaction patterns in Dd dyads provides a model of the kinds of positive adaptations possible when parents interact with their deaf children. As a result, these studies can be useful in interpreting the strengths and weaknesses in Hd dyadic interaction.

Third, characteristics of the Hd dyadic interaction can be related to outcome measures (e.g., language level) to determine which aspects are related to a positive developmental outcome. Cause and effect cannot be determined in correlational research, but these studies serve as a starting point from which important variables can be identified for later empirical research.

The review of research presented in this chapter relies heavily on two longitudinal studies that complement each other. The Infancy Research Group at Gallaudet (Meadow-Orlans, Spencer, Koester, and MacTurk) observed four groups of infants: Hd, Hh, Dd, and Dh dyads at 9, 12, and 18 months. Lederberg, Everhart, Mobley, and Prezbindowki observed Hd and Hh dyads at 22 months and 3 and 4 years of age. Thus, the studies have the potential for allowing us to capture the impact of child deafness on hearing mother–deaf child interaction from infancy through preschool. In this chapter, we primarily focus on the findings during the second year of life to gain a more complete description of the impact of child deafness at this young age (see Lederberg, 1993, for a broader review). For years, Meadow-Orlans and Lederberg have been puzzled about why their results conflict in a number of ways, with Meadow-Orlans' research showing more differences between Hd and Hh dyads than Lederberg's research. In this chapter, we present supplemental analyses conducted on these data to elucidate the factors that resulted in the different pattern of results.

Both studies described mother–child interaction in multiple ways, used similar coding schemes, and included samples of a reasonable size (i.e., at least 20 dyads per group). In order to achieve a large enough sample, they included children who varied in degree of hearing loss and communication method. They included only infants or toddlers already identified and enrolled in early intervention programs and excluded children with other disabilities. Therefore, children in these two samples are advantaged in comparison to the general deaf population, but they are representative of a large proportion of deaf children who are in early intervention programs.

There are some notable differences in the studies' samples. Families participating in the Infancy Research Group's study were more highly educated than the families in Lederberg's study: 70% of mothers in the Infancy Research Group's sample had a college degree and 35% had additional postgraduate education, in contrast, only 41% of mothers in Lederberg's sample had completed college and only 7% had postgraduate education. There was greater racial diversity in the Lederberg sample; 20% of the children were minorities (African American, Hispanic), but there were no minorities in the Hd dyads in the Infancy Research Group. The dyads in the Infancy Research Group represented greater geographic diversity. They came from five different metropolitan areas across the country, and the Lederberg sample came from only one.

We include other studies to complement the findings of these two studies where appropriate. However, we purposely excluded studies that have small samples (i.e., less than 10 deaf subjects). Although these studies are invaluable in identifying *potential* strengths and weaknesses, we believe it is misleading to use the characteristics of a few dyads to describe a whole group (e.g., Hd dyads) because of the wide variability of functioning.

These studies examined the impact of child deafness on mother–child relationships by comparing Hd and Hh dyads on attachment and three componants of mother–child interaction: the quality of interaction, maternal communicative control, and dyadic joint attention. In addition, individual differences within Hd dyads are examined to document relations between the quality of maternal behavior and outcome variables.

ATTACHMENT

Since the 1970s, assessment of the quality of the attachment bond has become a widely accepted way to describe the quality of the early mother–child relationship. The quality of attachment, as described by Bowlby (1969) and Ainsworth (1973), is usually assessed by the "strange situation" procedure, which consists of seven 3-minute episodes during which the infant is separated from his or her caregiver twice. Classification of the quality of mother–infant attachment is made based on the infant's behavior during these separation and reunion episodes and is conceptualized according to the infant's feeling of security in the presence of a caregiver.

Securely attached infants will use their caregivers as a secure base of exploration and venture out to examine an unfamiliar environment when their caregivers are present. When under stress (e.g., after being left alone or with an unfamiliar adult), securely attached infants will, on reunion, seek proximity to their caregivers and be comforted by their presence. Infants who do not seem to derive the same sense of security from their caregivers (i.e., insecurely attached infants) will show one of two patterns of behavior. Avoidant insecurely attached infants do not seek to be in contact with their caregivers when stressed. In fact, they frequently actively avoid contact with their caregivers on reunion by turning their backs or even crawling away. Ambivalent or resistant insecurely attached infants will usually seek proximity on reunion, but they will show their ambivalence about their caregivers by turning away from the caregivers or by angrily batting away offered toys. These infants also frequently will not get the comfort they seek by the presence of the mothers and continue to be upset throughout the reunion episode.

Research suggests that security of attachment is derived from the infant's experiences with his or her caregiver. Secure attachments are developed when caregiving is characterized by prompt responsiveness to crying, sensitivity to infants' signals during feeding and play, contingent and consistent interactions, and warmth and affectionate behavior. All of these maternal characteristics have been related to infants' security of attachment (see deWolff & van Ijzendoorn, 1997, for a meta-analysis).

In addition to the importance of attachment as a way of describing infant's relationships with his or her caregiver, quality of attachment seems to have broad impact on infants' socioemotional adjustment. Theorists posit that attachment contributes to the infant's development of a sense of self (e.g., Am I a valued member of this interaction?) and to the development of a working model of the infant's effectiveness in relationships (e.g., Am I able to elicit the care and attention I need from my caregiver?) that persists throughout childhood and adulthood. An infant's security of attachment, as assessed at 12 or 18 months, is associated with increased motivation and independence in problem-solving situations at age 2 and more positive peer and adult relations during early and middle childhood (Thompson, 1998).

There are several reasons why deaf children have been hypothesized to be at increased risk for developing insecure attachments: Increased stress and depression associated with the diagnosis of deafness may cause a hearing mother to neglect her deaf infant; Deaf infants may perceive their hearing mothers as insensitive because their mothers' natural way of comforting them is through the voice; Poor communication between infant and mother may lead to a sense of insecurity; Controlling, dominant types of interaction by hearing mothers of deaf children appear insensitive.

Contrary to our hypotheses, there is now evidence that child deafness does not interfere with the development of a secure attachment. Lederberg and Mobley (1990) found almost identical numbers of securely attached deaf and hearing toddlers (see Table 5.1). Koester and MacTurk (1991) from the Infancy Research Group also found no differences in security of attachment in their Hd and Hh dyads (see Table 5.1). Deaf and hear-

TABLE 5.1
Proportion of Securely Attached Toddlers
in Lederberg and Mobley (1990) and Koester and MacTurk (1991)

	Group	
Sample	Deaf Toddlers	Hearing Toddlers
Lederberg and Mobley		
Complete sample	56% (23/41)	61% (25/41)
Noncollege graduates	42% (11/26)	50% (12/24)
College graduates	80% (12/15)	76% (13/17)
Koester and MacTurk	75% (15/20)	90% (18/20)

Note. Numbers in parentheses represent the number of securely attached infants over the total number of dyads.

ing toddlers seem equally likely to perceive their mothers as providing sensitive, responsive emotional support.

Therefore, although parents may be depressed due to their children's recent diagnosis of hearing loss and communication may be less than optimal between hearing parents and their deaf children, these data suggest that parents are able to change their interaction patterns to meet the emotional needs of their deaf infants. Koester, Papoušek, and Smith-Gray (chap. 4, this volume) suggest that much of early interaction is based on intuitive parenting, which is a system mutually regulated by infant and parent. This includes both parents attending to cues signifying that their infant is alert and ready to interact as well as parents using appropriate visual and vocal strategies to gain and maintain their infant's attention. Hearing parents do appear to adapt to their deaf infants' needs as evidenced by an observed increase in the amount of visual communication and behavior hearing mothers use with their deaf children (at 9 months, Koester, 1995; at 12 and 18 months, Spencer, 1993; and at 22 months and 3 years, Lederberg & Everhart, 1998a).

It is possible that the similar rates of securely attached deaf and hearing toddlers in these studies may be a result of the Hd dyads being enrolled in intervention programs (Marschark, 1993). However, Lederberg and Mobley (1990) found that the length of time the deaf toddlers were in the intervention program (1–20 months) did not relate to security of attachment. In addition, the high rate of insecurity among the dyads in the Lederberg and Mobley study suggests that some intervention programs were not particularly successful.

Although deaf and hearing toddlers showed similar rates of secure attachments in each of these studies, the studies varied considerably in the percentage of children who were securely attached. Whereas Koester and MacTurk (1991) found less than 20% of their toddlers insecurely attached, almost 50% of the deaf and hearing toddlers were insecurely attached in Lederberg and Mobley's (1990) study. The high proportion of securely attached infants in the Gallaudet study is most likely due to their advantaged sample. Research with hearing infants shows that, in large samples, typical levels of secure attachment average 66%. Among children at high risk due to socioeconomic circumstances, secure attachment drops to closer to 50%, but advantaged samples can have more than 75% secure attachments (Thompson, 1998). In the Lederberg and Mobley sample, the proportion of infants who were securely attached to their college educated mothers was similar to the Gallaudet sample and significantly higher than the proportion of infants securely attached to their noncollege educated mothers, $X^2 (1, N = 82) = 8.30, p < .01$, (see Table 5.1). Thus, it seems it is the mother's characteristics rather than her child's deafness that is the cause of the insecurity. Sensitive parents seem to be able to adapt to a variety of special needs of their infants and toddlers in such a way as to make them feel secure in their care, with maternal characteristics impacting on whether they provide sensitive parenting. This finding is consistent with the conclusions reached by van Ijzendoorn et al. (1992) based on a meta-analysis of attachment studies: "In clinical samples, the mother appears to play a more important role than the child in shaping the quality of the infant–mother attachment relationship" (p. 840).

In sum, although child deafness does not put a child at risk for developing an insecure attachment, this research suggests that among infants and toddlers in any intervention program, just as with a group of typically developing hearing children, there will be infants who have an insecure attachment to parents who are not able to meet their needs.

MOTHER–CHILD INTERACTION DURING FREE PLAY

The impact of child deafness on mother–child relationships has traditionally been examined by noting defining features of maternal and child behavior during free play. Researchers have used a variety of different methods to capture the impact of child deafness on these interactions. We include three lenses in this chapter: global ratings of the quality of mother–child interaction, use of communication to control the child, and development of joint attention. Each will be described in turn.

Quality of Interaction

Comparisons of Interaction Between Hd and Hh Dyads

Schlesinger and Meadow (1972) pioneered the use of rating scales to capture the impact of child deafness in the way hearing mothers socialize and play with their deaf children. Observers rate the characteristics of mother–child interaction using 5-point Likert-like scales after watching a videotape. These rating scales are designed to describe individual differences in the quality of mother–child relationships.

In the Gallaudet research study, Meadow-Orlans and Steinberg (1993) rated mother–infant interaction for five maternal characteristics, four infant characteristics, and three dyadic characteristics. Child deafness influenced the quality of hearing mothers' behavior. Hearing mothers of deaf infants were less sensitive, less flexible, less warm, and showed less consistency in their interaction than mothers of hearing infants. Infant and dyadic ratings were not significantly different. In a follow-up study, Meadow-Orlans (1997) found that the quality of the behavior by *deaf* mothers of deaf infants did not differ from that of hearing mothers of hearing infants. Thus, it is not child deafness per se that impacted on maternal behavior but rather the mismatch between maternal and child hearing status.

Lederberg and Mobley (1990) rated mother–toddler interaction for 10 maternal characteristics, 9 child characteristics, and 3 dyadic characteristics. Ratings of Hd and Hh dyads differed significantly *only* on ratings of communicative competence. Contrary to Meadow-Orlans and Steinberg (1993), the quality of maternal behavior was not significantly different in the Hd and Hh dyads. The differences in the outcomes for these two studies may be attributed to differences in samples and statistical designs and differences in the definition of maternal sensitivity and responsiveness. An examination of each of these follows.

First, we approximated a replication of Meadow-Orlans and Steinberg's (1993) study by reanalyzing the data from Lederberg and Mobley using a statistical design closer to theirs. We conducted a multivariate analysis of variance (MANOVA) on the three maternal rating scales from our study (sensitivity, positive affect, stimulation) that most closely resemble three used by Meadow-Orlans and Steinberg (sensitivity/nonintrusiveness, overall affect, involvement), using only child hearing status as the between-subject variable. Because Meadow-Orlans and Steinberg's sample was primarily college educated, we also split the Lederberg and Mobley sample into college graduates ($n = 32$) and non-college graduates ($n = 50$). Table 5.2 displays the means and standard deviations of these scales for Meadow-Orlans and Steinberg's sample and Lederberg and Mobley's two subsamples.

Analyses of the subgroups in the Lederberg and Mobley (1990) study revealed a significant difference in maternal sensitivity between the Hd and Hh dyads for the college graduates but not for the noncollege graduates (see Table 5.2). College graduates with hearing toddlers were rated significantly more sensitive than college graduates with deaf toddlers. The one-point differential was very similar to that found by Meadow-Orlans and Steinberg. This effect seems to be due to the extremely high ratings that the college graduate mothers of hearing toddlers received (14 re-

TABLE 5.2

Mean Ratings of Maternal Behavior in Meadow-Orlans and Steinberg (1993) and Lederberg and Mobley (1990)

Meadow-Orlans and Steinberg				Lederberg and Mobley			
All Dyads				College Educated Dyads		Noncollege Educated Dyads	
Ratings	Hd	Hh	Ratings	Hd	Hh	Hd	Hh
Sensitivity	3.3	4.2	Sensitivity	3.9	4.8a	3.9	4.1
	(1.4)	(1.0)		(1.1)	(0.4)	(1.2)	(1.3)
Affect	3.2	4.0	Positive Affect	3.5	3.4	2.9	3.5
	(1.4)	(1.2)		(0.8)	(1.0)	(1.4)	(1.1)
Involvement	3.6	4.0	Stimulation	3.4	3.9	3.2	3.5
	(1.3)	(1.3)		(0.8)	(0.8)	(1.1)	(1.0)

Note. Data are mean ratings on 5-point scales for maternal behavior. Data in parentheses are standard deviations. Data for Meadow-Orlans and Steinberg are from their publication. Data for Lederberg and Mobley were calculated for this chapter.
[a]Difference between college educated Hd and Hh dyads, t (30) = 3.13, $p < .01$.

ceived a rating of 5, and 3 received a rating of 4 on the 5-point scale). The ratings of college graduates with deaf toddlers were much more variable (2–5) as were noncollege graduates of either deaf or hearing toddlers (1–5 and 2–5, respectively). These results suggest that highly educated mothers are almost universally able to be sensitive to their hearing toddlers' cues in this free play situation, although some highly educated mothers were much more likely to be out of tune with their deaf toddlers, as were some nonhighly educated mothers with either deaf or hearing toddlers.

The second major source of the discrepant results from these two studies was the definition of maternal sensitivity. Meadow-Orlans and Steinberg (1993) defined *highly sensitive mothers* as those who are responsive, do not interrupt their infants' activities, pace appropriately, and play instead of teaching their infants. In Lederberg and Mobley (1990), *overall sensitivity* (used in the analysis reported on Table 5.2) was defined more narrowly as the mother's ability to be in tune with her child by accurately perceiving her infant's signals or cues and responding appropriately to his or her interests, activities, or affective states. Lederberg and Mobley then rated mother–child interaction on three additional scales thought to contribute to maternal sensitivity: (a) *intrusiveness,* the frequency with which a mother's behavior interrupts or abruptly interferes with the child's ongoing activities; (b) *pacing,* the ability to appropriately time changes in activities; and (c) *developmental appropriateness,* mother's engagement in activities that are too hard or too easy for the child. Meadow-Orlans and Steinberg's study incorporated these three aspects of mother–child interaction into their definition of maternal sensitivity rather than analyzing them separately.

Although, like Meadow-Orlans and Steinberg, Lederberg and Mobley conceptualized maternal nonintrusiveness, pacing, and developmental appropriateness as components of overall sensitivity, the pattern of results suggests that this was only true to a limited degree. Correlations between sensitivity and the other scales ranged from moderate (intrusiveness, r (80) = .53, pacing, r = .59) to low (developmental appropriateness, r = .18, because mothers were almost always appropriate). Furthermore, some mothers were perceived as insensitive but nonintrusive by the raters. Although there was an impact of child deafness on the overall sensitivity of college educated mothers, there was none for intrusiveness, pacing, or developmental appropriateness. Thus, in the Lederberg and Mobley (1990) study, what seemed to distinguish the college educated mothers of deaf toddlers from those of hearing toddlers was not intrusiveness but rather how sensitive they were to their children's signals. This is consistent with Koester's (1995) suggestion that one of the major tasks of intervention programs is to help hearing mothers learn what their deaf toddlers' cues or signals mean.

Pressman, Pipp-Siegel, and Yoshinaga-Itano (1998) studied the quality of mother–toddler free play using another sample (n = 42) of deaf or hard of hearing (HOH) and hearing toddlers. These authors used two rating scales, sensitivity and structuring/intrusiveness, developed by Biringen and Robinson (1991) to measure "maternal emotional availability in mother–child interactions" (p. 258). *Maternal sensitivity* included responsiveness to child cues, positive affect, and affect regulation. *Maternal structuring/intrusiveness* was defined as the degree to which the mother provides optimal support of learning by following the child's lead and structuring the interaction appropriately and by not interrupting ongoing activity. These scales seem similar to (although with additional components) the sensitivity and intrusiveness scales used in Lederberg and Mobley (1990). Pressman et al. found that mothers of deaf and hearing toddlers did not differ in their sensitivity or intrusiveness during free play. These results suggest again that child hearing loss does not have a consistently negative impact on hearing mothers' sensitivity or intrusiveness. The impact of child deafness on maternal sensitivity may depend on the sample studied (e.g., education and social support, see Meadow-Orlans & Steinberg, 1993) and the definition of sensitivity used.

Relations Between Maternal Responsiveness and Outcome Variables

Although child deafness may not consistently influence maternal sensitivity, a different and perhaps more important question is what impact differences in the quality of maternal interaction have on the deaf or HOH child's development. To address this question, relations between the quality of maternal behavior and outcome variables (e.g., language growth) are examined. Even in studies where there were no differences between mothers of deaf and hearing toddlers (e.g., Lederberg & Mobley, 1990; Pressman et al., 1998), mothers within each group differed in how responsive, warm, and so forth they were with their toddlers. Research has studied relations between the quality of mother–child interaction and attachment, child's play, and language growth.

Attachment.   Lederberg and Mobley (1990) hypothesized that the quality of maternal behavior would be related to the toddlers' security of attachment. However, security of attachment was only minimally related to maternal behavior. Although mothers of securely attached toddlers reinforced their children more than did mothers of insecurely attached toddlers, they did not differ on measures of sensitivity or affect. In fact, surprisingly, mothers of insecurely attached and securely attached toddlers were rated the same on sensitivity (insecure, $M = 4.06, SD = 1.15$; secure, $M = 4.13, SD = 1.04$), intrusiveness (insecure, $M = 3.94, SD = 0.89$; secure, $M = 3.98, SD = 1.12$), pacing (insecure, $M = 3.91, SD = 0.89$; secure, $M = 4.08, SD = 0.96$), and developmental appropriateness (insecure, $M = 4.79$, $SD = 0.59$; secure, $M = 4.81, SD = 0.39$). Koester and MacTurk (1991) also found no relation between attachment security and Meadow-Orlans' maternal ratings. Thus, the sensitivity or responsiveness measured in both studies seems different from sensitivity that contributes to the development of a secure attachment. This may be because mothers were observed in a free play situation, and infants' feelings of security may be more related to maternal sensitivity during stressful situations (de Wolff & van Ijzendoorn, 1997).

Play.   Although the quality of maternal behavior in the free play situation did not relate to attachment, it does seem to be important for other aspects of development. Research with hearing children supports the hypothesis that mother's behavior influences the sophistication of her child's play. Spencer and Meadow-Orlans (1996) analyzed the relation between maternal responsiveness (a composite scale comprised of sensitivity, flexibility, and consistency) and the deaf and hearing infants' level of play (manipulative, relational, and pretend) at 12 and 18 months. Maternal responsiveness did not relate to infants' play at 12 months. However, maternal responsiveness was a significant contributor to differences in the amount of time spent in the highest subcategory of pretend play—preplanned pretend play—at 18 months. This type of play, which is based on symbolic representation, was the most cognitively advanced play observed at 18 months. This suggests that maternal responsiveness may encourage deaf and hearing toddlers to engage in a higher level of play, which could in turn facilitate their general cognitive development.

Language. The quality of maternal behavior may be related to deaf and HOH children's language development. Spencer (1998) found that maternal sensitivity (the composite of Meadow-Orlans five maternal behavior scales) at 12 months correlated with deaf or HOH 18-month-olds' language. Pressman et al. (1998) found that maternal emotional availability (a composite of maternal sensitivity and nonintrusiveness) at 2 years significantly contributed to the amount of language growth deaf or HOH children experienced over the next year (i.e., by the time they were 3). Interestingly, in this study, maternal sensitivity seemed to contribute to language growth for deaf but not hearing children. Lederberg did not find maternal sensitivity at 2 years to be related to deaf children's language level at 3 years. This may be because Lederberg's sample was much more language delayed than either Spencer's or Pressman et al.'s.

In summary, maternal sensitivity in free play does not seem to relate to the development of a secure attachment, but it does seem to have a significant impact on deaf toddlers' symbolic play and language development.

Maternal Communicative Control

Another dimension of maternal behavior that has been studied more than any other is maternal directiveness (Musselman & Churchill, 1993). Unlike the previous dimensions, directiveness has traditionally been studied by examining the characteristics of maternal communication and language rather than overall interactional style. These studies almost uniformly find that mothers of deaf children (as well as mothers of children with mental retardation) are more directive than mothers of hearing children (Musselman & Churchill, 1993). This increased directiveness has been cited as a contributing factor to deaf and HOH children's language delay and to child passivity. However, during the 1990s researchers have realized that maternal directiveness or control is not a unitary dimension and that some types of control may have a positive impact on development whereas others may have a negative impact.

Tannock (1988) proposed that there are three distinct ways mothers may control interactions with their children:

> *Response control* refers to a mother's tendency to use commands, questions, and other behavior to elicit a response from the child. *Topic control* refers to the mother's tendency to redirect the child's attention to mother–selected topics by using utterances or turns that are unrelated to the child's ongoing activity or topic. *Turn-taking control* addresses the extent to which mothers dominate the interaction by contributing long and frequent turns. (p. 154)

Each of these different types of control seems to be caused by different factors and have different effects on child development.

Response Control. Research consistently suggests that mothers of oral deaf or HOH children (2½–5 years) use more response controls (e.g., get the ball, look at me) than mothers of age-matched hearing children (see Gallaway & Woll, 1994, for a review). Lederberg and Everhart (1998b) also found mothers of deaf toddlers used more action and attention-getting directives than mothers of hearing toddlers. Although some have suggested that the use of response controls is a reaction to a sense of powerlessness (Schlesinger, 1985), research suggests that it is an intuitive adaptation to deaf children's linguistic delay; mothers of deaf children use the same amount of response controls as mothers of language-matched hearing children (Cross, Nienhuys, & Kirkman, 1985).

Research on the impact of response controls on language development is complex and contradictory; research with deaf children has shown both positive and negative relations between the amount of response controls mothers use and their deaf children's language (see Musselman & Churchill, 1993, for a review). The effect of response controls on language may depend on the child's level of language and mode of communication. However, results are so inconsistent that Musselman and Churchill concluded:

> The obtained patterns of relationships, however, are complex, suggesting that parent training programmes should be selective when attempting to decrease parents' overall levels of control. Taking into account the overall pattern of findings, ... directiveness should vary with children's language level and other characteristics. The findings for TC children are congruent with those from other studies that suggest that high control strategies are beneficial for children at the one-word stage. (p. 287)

In sum, hearing mothers of deaf children seem to make an intuitive adaptation to their children's level of linguistic competence by being more directive. However, it is not at all clear that this behavior should be interpreted as positive or negative.

Topic Control. Research with hearing children suggests that maternal language that is following or contingent on the young child's attention facilitates early language learning. Spencer (1991) found that communication and social behavior by mothers of deaf and hearing toddlers was highly contingent on their child's attention. At 12 and 18 months, approximately 80% of mothers' visually based social responses to deaf and hearing infants were contingent on the infants' attention. Although the spoken communication of mothers of hearing infants was significantly more contingent than that of mothers of deaf infants, they were both highly contingent (88% vs. 82%, respectively). In their sample, Lederberg and Everhart (1998b) found no effect of child deafness on mothers' topic control. Communication by mothers of deaf and hearing children was highly responsive to their children's attention (88% and 90% of utterances, respectively, were contingent). In addition, the majority of new topics started by mothers were in response to their children's attention or actions (deaf = 59%; hearing = 60%). This research is encouraging. It suggests that many hearing mothers are sensitive to their deaf infants or toddlers' interests and attention, and, therefore, maternal topic control, at least as defined in these studies, is not the source of most deaf toddlers' language delay.

Turn-Taking Control. Turn-taking control or dominance is usually measured by the proportion of communicative utterances contributed by mothers. Although research suggests that mothers of deaf preschoolers are more dominant than mothers of hearing preschoolers, this does not seem to be the case with younger deaf children. Neither Spencer (1991) nor Lederberg and Everhart (1998a) found differences between the Hd and Hh dyads in how much mothers contributed to the interaction. For both deaf and hearing infants and toddlers, mothers contribute the vast majority of communications at this young age (starting at 86% of dyadic communications at 12 months and decreasing to a mean of 78% at 22 months).

In sum, child deafness did not seem to impact on maternal topic or turn-taking control during infancy and toddlerhood. In addition, although mothers of deaf toddlers seem to use more response controls than mothers of hearing toddlers, this may not have a negative impact on deaf children's development.

Joint Attention

Research with typically developing toddlers suggests that another important way to characterize mother–child interaction is to examine the child's engagement/attention states. In the first year of life, infants primarily attend to only one aspect of their environment (either *object* or *person engagement*). However, during the second year they spend increasing amounts of time in joint attention, attending to both objects and people in the environment. Joint attention is considered an especially important engagement state because the infant integrates his or her attention to two or more aspects of the environment, enabling parental input to influence his or her perceptions of the environment.

There are three different ways that infants achieve joint attention. Initially, joint attention is scaffolded by caregivers' facilitation of infants' interactions with objects in the environment without the infants' acknowledgment of the mothers' participation, called *supported joint attention* (e.g., infant stacks rings while mother holds base). As infants mature (after 12 months), they become capable of engaging in more complex forms of joint attention. Specifically, infants begin to actively alternate their attention between interactive partners and objects in their environment, called *coordinated joint attention* (e.g., infant stacks rings while alternating gaze between rings and involved mother). Then, as language develops, children integrate language into episodes of joint attention. In other words, receptive and expressive language begin to mediate interaction between mothers and children, with language influencing the children's behaviors and thoughts, called *symbol-infused joint attention* (e.g., mother says, "No, not that one." Child puts ring down. "Put this one next.").

Spencer and Waxman (1995) examined joint attention in Hd, Hh, and Dd dyads at 12 and 18 months. All three types of dyads spent similar amounts of time in joint attention at each age, with an increase from 12 (38%, 35%, and 37%, respectively) to 18 (54%, 58%, and 61%, respectively) months. However, analyses of the different kinds of joint attention revealed some group differences. Dd dyads spent significantly more time than Hd dyads in coordinated joint attention, the engagement state in which children actively attend visually to both people and the environment. Coordinated joint attention is especially important for deaf children who access communication through the visual modality. Other researchers in this volume (Swisher, chap. 2; Mohay, chap. 9) have shown that deaf Mothers of deaf children are very good at scaffolding (or supporting) deaf infants' visual attention to themselves. Although this heightened visual vigilance was not present in Hd dyads, Hd dyads did not differ significantly from Hh dyads in the time spent in these prelinguistic joint attention engagement states. (Although not significant, Hd dyads spent less time compared to Hh dyads in coordinated joint attention by 18 months.)

Prezbindowski, Adamson, and Lederberg (1998) examined engagement states of Hd and Hh dyads at 22 months. Table 5.3, a composite of the results of Spencer and Waxman (1995) and Prezbindowski et al., displays the means and standard deviations of the proportion of time dyads spent in the different types of joint attention states at 12, 18, and 22 months. A comparison across these studies suggests that both Hh and Hd dyads increase the time they spend in joint attention from 18 to 22 months. However, by the age of 22 months, Hd dyads do not increase the time spent in joint attention as much as Hh dyads and, consequently, fall significantly behind Hh dyads in time spent in joint attention. This difference is due to the fact that by 22 months, Hh dyads spend about one third of their time in symbol-infused joint attention and the Hd dyads spent almost none. Thus, by the end of the second year of life, the use of language qualitatively changes the nature of mother–child interaction in Hh dyads but not in Hd dyads.

TABLE 5.3
Mean Percent Time Spent in Engagement States at 12, 18, and 22 Months

	Group							
	Hd			Hh			Dd	
Age in Months	12	18	22	12	18	22	12	18
Total joint attention	38	54	66	35	58	77	37	61
Supported joint attention	30 (20)	23 (18)	19 (14)	20 (12)	19 (14)	14 (11)	19 (9)	19 (13)
Coordinated joint attention	8 (9)	31 (23)	45 (20)	15 (14)	39 (23)	33 (19)	18 (17)	42 (19)
Symbol-infused joint attention			2 (3)			30 (29)		

Note. Data are mean percentage of time dyads spent engaged in an attentional state out of 10 minutes in a free play situation. Data in parentheses are standard deviations. Spencer and Waxman (1995) provided data at 12 and 18 months. Prezbindowski et al. (1998) provided data at 22 months.

Hd dyads compensate somewhat for their lack of symbol-infused joint attention by spending significantly more time in coordinated joint attention. In fact, at 22 months, Hd dyads spend almost 50% more time in coordinated joint attention than they do at 18 months. Thus, the extent to which deaf children actively include their mothers in their exploration of the world increases as they approach the end of their second year, but that increase is not as much as that which occurs with hearing toddlers.

These results suggest that language provides a unique means to attract and hold children in episodes of joint attention, which cannot be replaced by nonverbal communication. Because most of the language that these hearing mothers used was inaccessible to their deaf children, language did not serve as a means to attract and maintain the children's attention in joint attention states. This limitation prevented Hd dyads from engaging in a similar quantity (total time) and quality (complexity) of joint attention compared to Hh dyads. As a result, mothers of hearing children enculturate their children more (via parents' demonstration of problem-solving strategies and transmission of cultural information within this context) than hearing mothers of deaf children.

CONCLUSION

The comparison of Hd and Hh dyads informs us whether child deafness places an Hd dyad at increased risk for nonoptimal outcomes. Gallaway and Woll (1994) summed up the prevailing view in the field:

> Findings from these studies ... gave rise to the notion that deaf chil-
> dren might be suffering the secondary handicap of controlling, dis-
> couraging, and negative interactions with their mothers which
> would provide a less facilitative environment for language acquisi-
> tion and for social and cognitive development. (p. 199)

Similar to Gallaway and Woll, we caution people from accepting this conclusion. The research reviewed here suggests that child deafness does not
have general negative impact on mother–child *social* relationships in a
number of areas, including attachment, quality of maternal affective behavior, and maternal control. Thus, as Koester et al. (chap. 4, this volume)
argue, many mothers may be able to intuitively adapt to a variety of different affective needs during early development. Our review suggests that
negative interactions may be specific to certain samples and limited to
subsets of Hd dyads (e.g., as Meadow-Orlans & Steinberg, 1993, showed).
At this stage, however, any conclusions must be tentative. Although the
three studies reviewed here (the Gallaudet study, the Lederberg study,
and the Pressman et al. study) had relatively large sample sizes, there is
still not enough research to make firm conclusions.

Although Hd dyads may not be generally characterized by negative affect or nonreciprocal interactions, we do not mean that interaction in Hd
dyads is the same as interaction in Hh dyads. Research suggests that interactions in Hd dyads are more likely to be interrupted than those of Hh
dyads because of communication breakdowns (Lederberg & Mobley,
1990). Thus, although these communication breakdowns were not associated with increases in negative affect, they did result in a decrease in the
amount of interaction between mother and toddler (Lederberg & Mobley,
1990). Hearing mothers of deaf children seem to make some adaptations
to their child's communication needs by using more visual communicative devices and increasing the amount they touch their children (Spencer
& Lederberg, 1998). However, these accommodations are insufficient to
result in optimal communication. In addition, once language starts to mediate interaction between hearing toddlers and their mothers, the nature
of these interactions differs for the Hh and Hd dyads (Prezbindowki et al.,
1998). We are proposing that it is specifically the difficulty with communication, rather than the social relationship between hearing mothers and
their deaf toddlers, that disrupts development.

Optimal communication with deaf children is more intuitive for deaf
parents (Koester et al., chap. 4, this volume). Observations of deaf mothers communicating with their deaf children (e.g., Prendergast &
McCollum, 1996; Swisher, chap. 2, this volume) provide the foundation for
intervention programs such as the one developed by Mohay (chap. 9, this
volume). These programs provide intensive training for parents on
nonintuitive strategies that help hearing caregivers communicate more effectively with their deaf children. For example, parents are instructed on

ways to gain their deaf children's attention and taught strategies to make language visually accessible and salient.

The conclusion that child deafness does not have a major impact on several areas of the early social relationship does not mean that these areas are not important for the development of deaf children. On the contrary, individual differences *within Hd dyads* in the quality of the mother–toddler relationship affect developmental outcomes in multiple ways. For example, although child deafness per se did not put the child at risk for developing insecure attachments, some deaf children do develop insecure attachments, and an insecure attachment has an impact on the child's social development. In Lederberg and Mobley (1990), security of attachment had a stronger influence than hearing status on the toddler's social behavior. Although ratings of deaf and hearing toddlers did not differ, securely attached toddlers initiated more, responded more, showed more affective sharing, had a longer attention span, and were more likely to show pride after completing a task than insecurely attached toddlers. Thus, interventions that attempt to improve the quality of attachment may be appropriate for some Hd dyads. Research reviewed here suggests that maternal responsiveness during free play cannot be used to identify insecurely attached dyads. Instead, observations of maternal responsiveness to toddlers during times of stress may be more useful for identification of problem dyads.

Although differences in maternal responsiveness during free play did not relate to attachment, differences in maternal responding did relate to deaf toddlers' language, play, and joint attention (Pressman et al., 1998; Meadow-Orlans & Spencer, 1996; Spencer & Meadow-Orlans, 1996; Spencer, 1998). Although we feel that intervention programs for deaf toddlers need to make language learning their top priority, language learning needs to occur in a warm and responsive context for optimal development to occur. For individual dyads, increasing maternal responsiveness may be an important goal of intervention. Overall, however, dissemination of information to parents suggesting that intuitive parenting is sufficient to support typical growth in many areas of development may provide parents with a sense of competence in their ability to meet their children's needs in the months following the diagnosis of a hearing loss. This initial sense of mastery may help parents meet the challenges of learning nonintuitive ways of creating a language-rich environment for their deaf toddlers.

REFERENCES

Ainsworth, M. D. (1973). The development of infant–mother attachment. In B. M. Caldwell & H. N. Ricciuti (Eds.), *Review of child development research* (Vol. 31, pp. 1–95). Chicago: University of Chicago Press.

Biringen, Z., & Robinson, J. (1991). Emotional availability in mother–child interactions: A reconceptualization for research. *American Journal of Orthopsychiatry, 61*(2), 258–271.

Bowlby, J. (1969). *Attachment and loss: Vol. 1 Attachment.* New York: Basic Books.

Cross, T. G., Nienhuys, T. G., & Kirkman, M. (1985). Parent–child interaction with receptively disabled children: Some determinants of maternal speech style. In K. E. Nelson (Ed.), *Children's Language* (Vol. 5, pp. 247–290). Hillsdale, NJ: Lawrence Erlbaum Associates.

deWolff, M. S., & van Ijzendoorn, M. H. (1997). Sensitivity and attachment: A meta-analysis on parental antecedents of infant attachment. *Child Development, 68*(4), 571–591.

Gallaway, C., & Woll, B. (1994). Interaction and childhood deafness. In C. Gallaway & B. J. Richards (Eds.), *Input and interaction in language acquisition* (pp. 197–218). New York: Cambridge University Press.

Greenberg, M. T., & Marvin, R. S. (1979). Attachment patterns in profoundly deaf preschool children. *Merrill-Palmer Quarterly, 25,* 265–279.

Harrison, M., & Roush, J. (1996). Age of suspicion, identification, and intervention for infants and young children with hearing loss: A national study. *Ear and Hearing, 17,* 55–62.

Koester, L. S. (1995). Face-to-face interactions between hearing mothers and their deaf or hearing infants. *Infant Behavior and Development, 18,* 145–153.

Koester, L. S., & MacTurk, R. H. (1991). Attachment behaviors in deaf and hearing infants. In *Interaction and support: Mothers and deaf infants* (Final Report, Grant MCJ-110563). Rockville, MD: The Maternal and Child Health Research Program.

Lederberg, A. R. (1993). The impact of deafness on mother-child and peer relationships. In M. Marscharck & M. D. Clark (Eds.), *Psychological perspectives on deafness* (pp. 93–119). Hillsdale, NJ: Lawrence Erlbaum Associates.

Lederberg, A. R., & Everhart, V. S. (1998a). Communication between deaf children and their hearing mothers: The role of language, gesture, and vocalizations. *Journal of Speech, Language, and Hearing Research, 41,* 887–899.

Lederberg, A. R., & Everhart, V. S. (1998b). *Maternal control in deaf and hearing children.* Manuscript submitted for publication.

Lederberg, A. R., & Mobley, C. E. (1990). The effect of hearing impairment on the quality of attachment and mother–toddler interaction. *Child Development, 61,* 1596–1604.

Marschark, M. (1993). *Psychological development of deaf children.* New York: Oxford University Press.

Meadow-Orlans, K. P. (1997). Effects of mother and infant hearing status on interactions at twelve and eighteen months. *Journal of Deaf Studies and Deaf Education, 2*(1), 27–36.

Meadow-Orlans, K. P., & Spencer, P. E. (1996). Maternal sensitivity and the visual attentiveness of children who are deaf. *Early Development and Parenting, 5,* 213–223.

Meadow-Orlans, K. P., & Steinberg, A. G. (1993). Effects of infant hearing loss and maternal support on mother–infant interactions at 18 months. *Journal of Applied Developmental Psychology, 14,* 407–426.

Musselman, C., & Churchill, A. (1993). Maternal conversational control and the development of deaf children: A test of the stage hypothesis. *First Language, 13,* 271–290.

Musselman, C., MacKay, S., Trehub, S. E., & Eagle, R. S. (1996). Communicative competence and psychosocial development in deaf children and adolescents. In J. H. Beitchman, N. J. Cohen, M. M. Konstantareas, & R. Tannock

(Eds.), *Language, learning, and behavior disorders: Developmental, biological, and clinical perspectives* (pp. 555–570). New York: Cambridge University Press.

Pitt, L. H., & Diaz, J. (1998). Schools and programs in the U.S. *American Annals of the Deaf, 143,* 77–121.

Prendergast, S. G., & McCollum, S. G. (1996). Let's talk: The effect of maternal hearing status on interactions with toddlers who are deaf. *American Annals of the Deaf, 141,* 11–18.

Pressman, L. J., Pipp-Siegel, S., & Yoshinaga-Itano, C. (1998, April). *The relation of hearing status and emotional availability to child language gain.* Poster session presented at the International Conference for Infant Studies, Atlanta, GA.

Prezbindowski, A. K., Adamson, L. B., & Lederberg, A. R. (1998). Joint attention in deaf and hearing 22–month-old children and their hearing mothers. *Journal of Applied Developmental Psychology, 19* (3), 377–387.

Schlesinger, H. S. (1985). Deafness, mental health, and language. In F. Powell, T. Frinitzo-Hieber, S. Friel-Patti, & D. Henderson (Eds.), *Education and the hearing impaired child* (pp. 103–116). San Diego: College-Hill Press.

Schlesinger, H. S., & Meadow, K. P. (1972). *Sound and Sign.* Berkeley: University of California Press.

Spencer, P. E. (1991). Mother infant communication at twelve and eighteen months. In *Interaction and support: Mothers and deaf infants* (Final Report, Grant MCJ-110563). Rockville, MD: The Maternal and Child Health Research Program.

Spencer, P. E. (1993). Communication behaviors of infants with hearing loss and their hearing mothers. *Journal of Speech and Hearing Research, 36,* 311–321.

Spencer, P. E. (1998, July). *Communication, attention, and symbolic development: Mothers and infants as an interactive system.* Poster session presented at the biennial meeting of the International Society for Studies of Behavior Development, Bern, Switzerland.

Spencer, P. E., & Lederberg, A. R. (1998). Different modes, different models: Communication and language of young deaf children and their mothers. In L. B. Adamson & M. A. Romski (Eds.), *Communication and language acquisition: Discoveries from atypical development* (pp. 203–230). Baltimore: Brookes.

Spencer, P. E., & Meadow-Orlans, K. P. (1996). Play, language, and maternal responsiveness: A longitudinal study of deaf and hearing infants. *Child Development, 67,* 3176–3191.

Spencer, P., & Waxman, R. (1995). Joint attention and maternal attention strategies: 9, 12, and 18 months. In *Maternal responsiveness and child competency in deaf and hearing children* (Final Report, Grant HO23C10077). Washington, DC: U.S. Department of Education.

Tannock, R. (1988). Mothers' directiveness in their interactions with their children with and without Down Syndrome. *American Journal on Mental Retardation, 93,* 154–165.

Thompson, R. (1998). Early sociopersonality development. In W. Damon (Series Ed.) & N. Eisenberg (Vol. Ed.), *Handbook of child psychology: Vol. 3. Social, emotional, and personality development* (5th ed., pp. 25–104). New York: Wiley.

van Ijzendoorn, M. H., Goldberg, S., Kroonenberg, P. M., & Frenkel, O. J. (1992). The relative effects of maternal and child problems on the quality of attachment: A meta-analysis of attachment in clinical samples. *Child Development, 63,* 840–858.

Autobiographical Narrative on Growing Up Deaf

Annie Steinberg
University of Pennsylvania

I sometimes think that silence can kill you, like that terrible scene at the end of Kafka's The Trial when Joseph K. dies speechlessly, like a dog. In "The Metamorphosis," a story that is now lodged in everybody's unconscious, Gregor Samsa dies like an insect. To die is to be no longer human, to be dehumanized—and I think that language, speech, stories, or narratives are the most effective ways to keep our humanity alive. To remain silent is literally to close down the shop of one's humanity.

—Broyard (1992, p. 20)

Through the lens of experiences of children and adults who are deaf, this chapter examines the importance of discourse and narrative for the child who is deaf and the impact of deafness on shared narrative and the development of the child. Each person has a unique life history or personal narrative. Telling and retelling the stories of our lives helps us become aware of the significance of our experiences. Storytelling is meaningful and central to our lives not only because it allows us to explain our experiences and actions, but also because we are able to change the meaning of our experiences when we tell the story (Widdershoven, 1993).

Narrative identity has been defined as the "unity of a person's life as it is experienced and articulated in stories that express this experience" (Widdershoven, 1993, p. 7). Identity develops not only through the telling of the story, but also through the expression, elaboration, or containment of the experience. For the narrative to fulfill its promise, our cries for nurturing and comfort must be received by a receptive and knowing listener.

Whereas language is a code to represent ideas through a conventional system of signals, storytelling also involves the wish, perhaps even the need, to be recognized and understood. If a child whispers and receives no response, he will cry or speak louder or gesture more actively. If there is still no response, he may begin to act out with noise and a greater presence or eventually with silent withdrawal. Although parents and children may communicate many feelings and may understand one another in a deep and important nonverbal way from infancy through adulthood, beyond this language of affect (which is very often beyond words) there are many more complex stories, thoughts, and feeling states to share. Telling one's story or learning the story of another, whether as simple as the story of the day at school or as complex as pangs of existential angst, requires shared language. Without a common language, this sharing is reduced both quantitatively and qualitatively.

Meadow-Orlans and Schlesinger (Schlesinger & Meadow, 1972) observed mothers and toddlers engaging in dialog both with and without a shared language and followed these dyads over time. This pioneering work laid the foundation for Meadow-Orlans' research in child development, resulting in a heightened awareness of the need for creative modifications by hearing caregivers and deaf infants (as well as deaf caregivers and hearing infants) in order to dialog in a reciprocal fashion within a shared sensory modality. As paradigms emerged about optimal modifications, she addressed the impact of specific communication strategies and the challenges they present, the assimilation of overwhelming and conflicting professional advice, and the degree of parental support on the parent-child interaction (Meadow-Orlans, 1993). Meadow-Orlans' scholarship, creativity, and collegiality occurs in the context of a dialog and dialectical process; she lives, learns, works, and teaches by sharing and integrating her own experiences, knowledge, and interests with those of others. Because the development of the child who is deaf involves genetic and environmental variables, social and individual psychology, as well as the continuities and discontinuities of the developmental life cycle, this work has simultaneously drawn on and enhanced the strengths and scope of interest of her collaborators, and it has shaped the field as well. This chapter examines the importance of discourse, particularly narrative, in the life of the child who is deaf.

Both as a researcher and clinician in pediatrics and psychiatry, I have been privileged to learn about the experiences of many individuals who are deaf. This work has largely, but not exclusively, been conducted in the precious medium of language. Language is a tool used for communication, social interaction, learning, and creative outlets, acquired through a process involving biological maturation, cognitive preparedness, opportunities for interaction, and environmental exposure. While some may be positioned so as to best examine the trunk and others the legs of the elephant that is child development, no one can know any aspect of the elephant without first encountering its thick and wondrous skin. Skin is an often overlooked but essential organ—without this container, the body cannot survive. And so it is with language. And while language has often been described as essential to the process of individuation, Stern asserts that the opposite is equally true, that the acquisition of language is potent in the service of union and togetherness, uniting two mentalities in a common symbol system (Stern, 1985). For the child who is deaf and whose parent is hearing, creating a shared meaning and relatedness through language is a greater challenge. The absence of an available symbolic system in which to share personal knowledge or create a linguistic construct for an affective or emotional inner experience makes more likely the possibility of developmental arrest or delay.

Without words, without signs, without gesture or communicative silence, there is no ability to express inner experiences, thoughts, or feelings. Language is the major means we have of representing to ourselves and to others our understanding of the world or ourselves; and equally, it becomes the major means through which others will give back to us their view of us, which in turn will reshape and re-form us (Wright, 1991). If words, signs, and silence are containers, the container serves not only the individual, but also the dyad and the interchange. The container of language is designed to be shared. Without a shared language, the individual and dyad are trapped in an immutable abyss. Throughout the life cycle, the ability to contain an individual's experiences and communicate or share them with another is critical to the quality of life and the development and nourishment of the sense of self.

The quotes recorded in this chapter are excerpted from the stories of adults who are deaf as well as parents of children who are deaf. Many participated in studies examining experiences, including the lack of a shared language and the disrupted communication between members of the deaf community and the largely hearing workforce, health care provider community, or community at large. Although most interviews were conducted with adolescents or adults, a majority of the individuals referred frequently to their family of origin and experiences during early childhood or adolescence. Retrospectively, they shed light on how the child experiences the world and on what was transmitted by the parents who loved them and tried to make the right choices for them. Parents' accounts also reflect the child through the intersubjective narrative and in light of the dyadic nature of the child's development; as Winnicott once noted, "Without the mother, there is no baby" (Winnicott, 1958, p. 99). Specifically, the excerpts in this chapter are derived from the following research projects:

- A cross-sectional study of the experiences of parents of Hispanic origin after the identification of deafness in their children (Steinberg, Davila, Collazo, Fischgrund, & Loew, 1997).
- A prospective longitudinal investigation of the process of decision making and the manner in which it is influenced by values, expectations, beliefs, parental decision-making style, the recommendation of professionals, and external factors.
- Interviews with deaf adults about their knowledge, attitudes, beliefs, experiences, and community folklore related to general health, women's health, and mental health issues (Steinberg, Sullivan, & Loew, 1998).
- A study of the impact of loneliness, alienation, and perceived social supports on job satisfaction and job retention among young adults who are deaf (Steinberg, Sullivan, & Montoya, 1999).
- An investigation of the identity, family, education, work, social and community life, and the use of technology for adults who are deaf and were educated and raised with an emphasis on the development of speech and lip-reading skills.

Finally, clinical vignettes presented here are derived from work in an outpatient clinical setting, a school-based mental health program that partners the family with the school for both diagnostic and therapeutic interventions, a regional abuse prevention program, and an in-home family preservation program for families with deaf children and serious emotional or behavioral problems. Identifying information has been removed from this material to assure confidentiality for both clients and participants of the research projects.

SHARED LANGUAGE: THE FOUNDATION OF NARRATIVE

Most deaf children are born into families with hearing parents and are thus not immediately immersed in a fully accessible language. Regardless of the communication modality chosen by the parents, most children who are deaf lack access to shared family stories and such mundane conversations as plans for the day, the composition of a recipe, or the annoyance of a telephone sales pitch. Whereas hearing children acquire language without special efforts, children who are deaf (born to parents who are hearing) must be helped to gain exposure to language through the use of sign language, amplified auditory stimuli, or oral training in lipreading and speech. Primary, often unattained, goals are family adaptation to and acceptance of the child's special communication needs and the provision of a linguistically accessible home and school environment. Schools and programs serving children who are deaf also address these communication needs and help expose children to essential topics traditionally dependent on language for exploration, for example, the recognition and identification of internal emotional states and cognitive experiences, their containment in the vessel of language, and the use of cognitive skills to cope. These basic ingredients enhance the child's self-esteem and emerging sense of self. Without shared language, or at least full access to a language, mutual understanding, reciprocal dialogue, and the development of a healthy ego become more challenging tasks, as exemplified by Joe's story.

Joseph became deaf at 2 years of age as a result of meningitis. His great grandmother was suspicious of hospitals and doctors and removed him from the hospital in the middle of his course of antibiotics; deafness was not diagnosed until school entry 3 years later. In individual therapy exploring his destructive and rage-filled outbursts, he recalled how, after his illness, things began to happen without explanation. His great grandmother and primary caretaker disappeared when he was 4 years of age, but only much later did he learn that she had died. Shortly thereafter, his mother disappeared, but it was not until his therapy as a late adolescent that he learned that she had gone to jail on charges of possession of cocaine. Family violence erupted in the home without obvious antecedents or precipitants, and, to add insult to injury, Joseph was sodomized by a neighbor who gestured that he would be killed if he told anyone what happened.

Because Joseph's deafness was not recognized until he started school, he had no language in which to tell his story or explore what had transpired in his already eventful life. Even the basic building block, vocabulary, could not be assumed; when asked by several peers in group therapy to describe his childhood anger, Joe vehemently denied feelings of anger, frustration, exasperation, and so forth. The members of the group, who had come to learn of Joe's past, continued to challenge the veracity of what was expressed. Finally, in exasperation and earnestness, Joe elaborated,

I didn't have feelings. I didn't know feelings until I was age 9. "Age 9?" they queried. Yes, age 9. Age 9 I went to deaf camp. There, I learned signs, happy, sad, upset, angry, ugly. Age 9 I learned feelings.

One can only imagine the confusion and the lack of security and predictability in the world of this child. Without shared language or even basic labels for emotional states, self-regulation was not attained. This young man did not recognize these inner states of being as more generalized human experiences well known to others; he grew up withholding, angry, and isolated in his solitary existence.

The struggle for shared language is often enacted in play, drama, art, and psychotherapy. About 2 years after the initiation of therapy, Joe brought word finding puzzle books and challenged me to find the words contained within the blocks of what appeared to be random letters. He tested my ability to fingerspell words and demonstrated his own agility and speed. I observed this same desire to master words as well as to share the experience of a life of communicative challenge in the enactments of another child who wrote words on a piece of paper then folded and dramatically stored the paper in his pocket, impeding access to the word and demonstrating for me the frustration, impotence, and rage he had known.

Without access to information in the home, even cataclysmic family events are mysterious and inexplicable, and the resulting stress is multiplied exponentially by the absence of communication: This void is powerfully and poignantly recounted by adults who are deaf.

Mary was a 40-year-old woman who requested therapy to address her difficulty with intimate relationships. She grew up in a rural southern state and much of her home life and environmental experience was not accessible to her, as she was profoundly deaf and lived her childhood years without even occasional translation. She recalled what transpired around the time of her father's death when she was 8 years of age. She initially felt confused watching his skin become "yellow." She observed her family members closely for information, yet they did not express anything to her. In their denial of his impending death, she found herself alone. When her father disappeared from the house, she was given a one word explanation, which she did not understand: "coma."

Several weeks later, after returning to school from a holiday, she was called from the classroom by the headmaster, who appeared stern and solemn. She was frightened and tried to understand what she had done, but she was given a suitcase filled with her clothes and driven the two-hour journey home in silence. On arrival, her family appeared upset with her, and her mother cried and isolated herself in her room. Confused and bereft of landmarks or ways of responding, she placed her father's rowboat on the lake, sat on the boat near the dock, and described everything to the moon. She recalled that the moon comforted her and answered her questions. This dialog—with the moon reflecting in the lake—took place each night until her return to residential school.

It was almost 20 years before she came to understand the etiology of her father's disappearance, but by that time, the guilt and self-blame she had experienced and internalized in response to her family's grieving had become an important part of her personal narrative. This quiet dialog with the moon exemplifies the resilient child who invents a "God of listening" to quell the "yearning for witnessed significance" (Fleischman, 1989).

THE NEED FOR INFORMATION: IMPACT OF DEAFNESS ON NARRATIVE FLOW

Although vocal language is not necessarily the mediating symbol system of thought, the absence of shared language leaves many children without the opportunity to narrate or receive a story that will be understood. Reduced information transmission results in frequent misperceptions and misunderstandings for the child, as well as the transmission of oversimplified material and misinformation. In addition, when there is no shared language and little opportunity for dialog, false presumptions of cognitive deficits may result. Although Lisa recounted her story with a chuckle, this story typifies the unrealistic and developmentally inappropriate burden placed on a young child to access vital information:

I had been brought to the hospital to have my tonsils out. After my tonsils were taken out, I woke up from surgery, and the nurse was patting me on the shoulder. She was pointing to a cup of red liquid near a spitting dish. I was really thirsty and thought that it was for me to drink. The nurse was pointing to the cup and the spitting dish and nodding cheerfully. I nodded and smiled back at her, eager to drink it. The nurse didn't communicate well enough for me to understand that it was mouthwash for me to gargle, not to drink. The nurse was uncertain because I was deaf—she wasn't sure if I could understand or if I was retarded. I repeated what she was telling me, pointing to the cup and asking if it was for me. I didn't know—I couldn't read her mind. She said yes and left. I drank it—it was delicious! Anyway, when the nurse returned, she looked at the empty cup and asked me where it was. I copied her gesture and nodded yes. When I told her I had drunk it, she got very upset and called my extended family to come to the hospital for a conference.

Although legislation has mandated equal access to information in public facilities, implementation has been less than optimal in many hospitals and school settings. For the child who is deaf, when excluded from a conversation that all others share, the world is strange and surreal. Even when only portions of the dialog are missed, the discontinuities leave children confused and disoriented. Cognitive efforts are expended to piece together words, phrases, and situational context, rather than to respond to content, question, or learn.

When I was about 4 years old and entering a nursery school program, she left me there. My mother had told me about it in advance. I played with other kids, I was excited, said the final goodbye, she left. I sat down in a chair in a row with other kids. People were standing in front of us, and the kids were responding in unison. They were standing up or sitting down. Movements, and I was looking and what's doing. Why did everybody know what to do? What are the invisible strings that connect these children to the teacher? They all get up doing the same things. They might have been singing, I don't know. I kept questioning, what, what. We broke up, and the kids moved into different sections. Why don't I know? I had no idea in the world why I didn't know, so I went and hid under a table and stayed there until my mother came. I have a big memory of people telling me to come out from under the table. The teacher was coming, and I was curled up waiting for my mother to rescue me. The strange thing was that it wasn't until I was majoring in education and we went to visit a hearing class of children with an interpreter there interpreting the songs, things like that going on, and I said that's what was happening! Twenty years later, I found out. I finally found what was happening when I was 4. Little things like that which people take for granted. The world is a very strange place if you don't have support. It's like you being the only normal and a group of people communicating through ESP, and everybody communicating through ESP—you wonder what's going on.

Language is the medium in which the child learns and grows. Much of this learning occurs via a dialectical process (regardless of whether internal or external dialogue) in which contradictory theses or concepts are synthesized into a new and integrated judgement or perception. Children who are deaf often do not have this opportunity to dialog and struggle with information. Often missed also is the incidental learning that happens continually and without effort in stories conveyed at mealtimes, such as the news of the day, news of the family, the chores yet to be done and bills to be paid, visits to be made, and so forth. All have embedded critical information that fosters the development of social skills, interpersonal problem-solving skills, and life world knowledge. Oftentimes, living in the moment is simply unavailable to a child with a hearing loss whose family members complete conversations and then synthesize the contents of lengthy tales in a sentence or two or, more often, in an unfulfilled promise for an account later.

A typical holiday dinner where relatives came from all over and sat around a big table, and I sat there, too, every year it'd be the same thing, Thanksgiving or Christmas. And I would eat and look around and watch everyone talking, and then they would all laugh, and I would ask what it was about, and I always got the same answer. They'd say, I'll tell you later, but that I'll tell you later, meant, I'll tell you never. For example, I'd go to the movies with my brother or hearing friends, and the audience would all laugh, and I'd look around, and they'd say, oh, that's so funny, and I'll tell you about it when we get home, and that, too, meant never. (Eastman and Cassell, 1989)

The family meal can defy the most sensitive and inclusive parents; children and adolescents adapt expectations of meaningful conversation and information in such situations.

> We had 19 people coming for Thanksgiving last year, and no matter how we juggled the plates and chairs, my 14-year-old daughter, Bekah, and I were able to squeeze only 18 places at our rented table. Bekah, who is deaf and uses sign language to communicate, stood holding the extra plate. "You know," she told me, "I don't need to sit here. I'm not really going to understand what's happening anyway." Then she looked at my face, which must have shown my feelings, and signed, "No offense, Mom." I wasn't offended. I was, however, aching, because I knew just why she felt that way. When the kids were younger, they would all eat quickly and run off to play, and Bekah could be included in the games without much difficulty. But now they are all teenagers and young adults and they don't leave the table—the entertainment is talking. Even though there would be five of us at that Thanksgiving dinner who sign fluently when talking one-to-one with Bekah, in a larger group it doesn't work that way. The conversations get fast and funny and people interrupt, change topics, and crack jokes, and we all tend to drop our signs. Although I'm the best signer in the family, interpreting for 19 people while eating and attending to guests is impossible. Bekah misses alot, which is frustrating and hurtful. (Lichtman, 1998, p. W15).

In the most extreme of circumstances, the child who is deaf may be deprived entirely of opportunities to dialog with others in a shared language. Although many individuals become withdrawn or demonstrate regression, others (remarkably) remain resourceful and creative in their use of nonverbal communication. One teenager who had no formal sign language exposure recognized skepticism regarding her competence to describe her childhood experiences and forcefully told the gripping story of her life using solely gestural communication. Her narrative began with her toddler years and the illness that resulted in deafness and continued through childhood and early adolescence. She borrowed a pen to ignite an imaginary firecracker, pledged allegiance to represent classroom activities, covered her ears, and pointed to the sky to indicate the joy and exhilaration of a burst of fireworks.

When unable to tell the story or have it appreciated, a child or teenager might act out or demand that others take notice and help him or her achieve some degree of mastery. This story is told in behavior, physical presentation, and words and signs used provocatively to gain attention. Some children develop a sustaining internal dialog and others an imaginary friend, thus preserving the communicative self. Annette, a 5-year-old child who is deaf, imitated the behaviors of a dog throughout the day in school. Her teachers realized that this dog was hungry, always begging for food, eager to eat (she moved her plate to the floor and lapped up her food), and needed almost continuous attention. Annette dressed herself in shaggy clothes, scratched at the classroom door, panted, and left her hair unkempt. The prolonged nature of the enactment of this story persisted for almost one month, until the symptoms prompted the school staff to meet with Annette's mother, who revealed that her family was homeless and residing in an emergency shelter. (Although there was a limited allocation of food for her large family, a stray and roaming dog was usually greeted with squeals of delight as well as abundant table scraps.) The paradox of the well fed dog had not escaped Annette, who labored to make her situation known to others.

Role play is not uncommon for children who are deaf and who labor to share their story at home as well as in the classroom. Skillful parents and teachers help contain and organize the child's expressed social, emotional, and cognitive experience. Elaborate fantasies may carry children and adolescents to disquieting intensities of anger, frustration, aloneness, and pretend games such as playing house and the telling of family stories in role play activities give the child permission to share information about his or her experience without risking a more persistent role assumption of animals such as dogs, cats, cartoon characters, snakes, and so forth.

AFFECT CONTAINMENT IN THE NARRATIVE

From a mass of undifferentiated affect, individuals sort and categorize until they experience almost infinite varieties of emotional states about which they are conscious and can internally know and analyze. This affect is an important part of the text of the personal narrative. Does the young man who had no affective language as a child ("I didn't have feeling. I didn't know feeling until I was age nine.") have less of a capacity to know or experience emotions, or is the difference solely in the ability to contain in symbolic code and articulate the inner experience?

Words are used by the hearing child to internally modify behavioral responses. In an identification with the parent, words serve as transitional objects or links to the loved one, carried like a cherished security blanket and held tightly in times of stress. Actions become increasingly contained by language (I am so angry, mommy!). Words are meaningful with someone there to listen. The toddler shouts, stomps his feet, but no longer wails or tantrums without words as before. Later, individuals sort out the relationship between thoughts, feelings, and behaviors, and can often change their actions with this capacity for insight and working with the story internally as well as externally. Reflecting a child's feeling state, soothing when there is distress, giving language when there is none, are important to the developing knowledge of the child's affectivity and sense of self. The child who is not given an emotional mirror or the language container for emotions is left adrift.

Heather was an adolescent female who was severely neglected by her drug addicted parent and for several years was noncommunicative, with self-injurious behavioral outbursts. In sessions, she often sat in a fetal position and did not respond to questions beyond terse answers. Several years later and stabilized in a signing environment, Heather began writing and described a feeling of liberation from her depression; this letter represents a new expression of self for this young woman and an alternative to her internal preoccupations and acting out behaviors:

> Dear Dr. Annie, Hey do you know why I'm in foster care? I don't understand either. It is very weird to me. There is nothing good in my life. But only good foster family. But why do I have so many problems in my life? It only to be an embarrassment to me. I think I only person who don't have good life . I felt like this. It is truth. I feel like I have no special inside. I never said I am special that mean I'm not special. There is a list for you to read. Why I never to be susseful? I want to go whatever I wants without being stressing inside, fratrations, and idoit. I'm not idoit either. Here is for Dad qestions. Do you miss me? Do you like sign language? Do you love me? Do you know my name? Are you care about people who is deaf? Do you remember me? Do you know when is my birthday? Do you need somebody to help you?

With a newfound confidence in the use of written language and its potential for discourse, she began to live more in connection with others and, shortly thereafter, initiated a written imaginary dialog with her family of origin.

JoAnne was 13 when I began to see her after she was referred by her parents. She had no peer relations but had day long conversations with her dolls, who she dismembered when agitated. Emotionally labile, she alternated between inappropriate laughter and disinhibited tears and cried in her sleep. She was flooded with worries and when consumed by a worry could not continue a conversation without incessant interruptions. Choking, gagging, and coughing spasms occured when attempting to communicate (in sign language). She had difficulty containing her emotions, with spillover affecting peer relationships significantly, until she agreed to use a dialog journal:

> Why I feel alone because kid never talk to me never invite me sit with them, kids called me M.R. Kids always hate me pick on me and called me come short girl. I am very mad at kids that why. I feel alone a lot. Please help me.

Although the content of the dialog journal was gloomy for some time, the initiation of this conversation resulted in global improved performance in both work and interpersonal arenas. This opportunity for narrative discourse improved learning by providing increased motivation; diaries and journals not only offer practice in English writing and literacy but also offer students the opportunity to be heard. For this adolescent, the affectively charged drive to communicate may have contained the emotions in language and propelled her to interact with the reader, practicing engagement with others in a neutral and safe way.

ADAPTATION AND RESILIENCE: NARRATIVE AND MAKING SENSE OF ADVERSITY

The development of the narrative and the construction of personal life themes and meaning is critical for developmental tasks and life transitions (e.g., career changes, family and peer relationships, aging, bereavement; Luborsky, 1997). Competence involves the integration or coordination of emotions, communication, cognition, and behaviors to adapt successfully to life's challenges. As the child grows, inner visual or sensory images become stories that contain, describe, or give others a piece of their experience and make it less an inseparable part of their own. There is a powerful drive to have positive emotional experiences, to be competent, and to master what has been most difficult.

With early childhood traumas, whether normal developmental traumas such as daily brief separations from a parent or unimaginable tragedies, construction of narrative often creates as symbols of the past that frame, identify, or contain later experience. All of us develop symbols and metaphors in our inner thoughts, conscious and unconscious, and these symbolic threads are often woven through the fabric of our lives. Childhood deafness often results in sensory and communicative deprivation. When this is the case, it constitutes a trauma. Indefinite in its duration, it deprives the child of meaningful information, results in a sense of separation or interpersonal isolation, and yields repeatedly perceived memories, fears, altered attitudes about people, life, and the future. The cumulative trauma is the persistent void of shared communication with the parent and family members.

> There was never any goodnight kiss, tucking into bed, hugging, all through the school years. I hated going back to school passionately, begged Mom and Dad not to take me back, but they didn't understand what was happening. They took me back anyway. Mom still bemoans the fact that she sent me to that school but, also, she still can't accept the fact that I cannot talk and that people can't understand me.

Jackson (1992) described a healer as a person to whom a sufferer tells things, and, out of his or her listening, the healer develops the basis for therapeutic interventions. The psychological healer, in particular, is one who listens in order to learn and to understand, and, from the fruits of this listening, he or she develops the basis for reassuring, advising, consoling, comforting, interpreting, explaining, or otherwise intervening. Traditionally, the parent heals the child's wounds, but deafness often strips the parent of this role with a disorienting absence of shared language. The deaf child is often left to manage alone.

> While they were having conversations, I just sat down and watched them and ate my meal. I don't consider this that I am really lonely, this is normal lonely. When I feel lonely, like my heart's broken, this often happens during family gatherings. Relatives were invited; often times I felt left out and like my heart was broken.

Most of us long for connection with others, for intimate relationships, for our stories to be understood. Telling the human story involves not only cognitive reframing but also affective matching or empathic attunement. When someone listens to and understands a child who is deaf, the empathic attunement results in visible and palpable relief. From the child who insistently taps on his mother's leg or shouts "listen to me," to the ordinary day in a busy week, listening and responding can heal. For the child who signs, it can be seen in the delight expressed at discovering an individual can communicate in sign language. For the child who is deaf but relies on lip reading or residual hearing, there is a discernible relaxation with the recognition that the burden of communication will be shared.

Nisbet (1969) wrote that "metaphor is our means of effecting instantaneous fusion of two separate realms of experience into one illuminating, iconic, encapsulating image." Such "words which undergo a change or extension of meaning" can be transformative (Cox & Thielgaard, 1987, p. 99). They can serve as a container for feelings that are too overwhelming to be tolerated, describing the deepest experiences for which there may be no adequate vocabulary. Children and adolescents utilize metaphor in ASL, and this metaphor in space must be seen and responded to with empathic precision and never confused with a linguistic error. When resonating with another individual, shared metaphors in the narrative can be a useful vehicle for expressing and integrating affect and cognition in creating change. For the child who is deaf, shared language and narrative can heal the trauma of chronic communicative isolation and linguistic deprivation.

Listening to the narrative experiences of individuals who are deaf offers powerful testimony to human creativity and the drive to connect with others. Deafness serves as an exceptional model for the study of adaptation and resiliency, particularly in relation to the emergence of a sense of self. Deaf children and adults must overcome profound obstacles and endure adverse circumstances in order to share stories and live life in connection with hearing individuals. Assuming the burden of communication and the energy expended in approximating a shared language is a common narrative theme for adults and children alike.

> It was a constant struggle to understand hearing people around me because my hearing aid and my lipreading skill cannot pick up everything. I'm constantly doing a guessing game figuring out what hearing people are saying. So I have a list of matching words on one side, and the words are coming through my ear. I'm constantly matching them up, making sure that they make sense and that I'm on the same level of discussion with everyone. And so there have been times when a hearing person will go off the topic and which means I didn't get the cue of the transition to another topic, and my brain will still have imagined the key words. For example if we were talking about baseball, I would have a ready list of all the key words like strike, strikes out, or even of some famous players and stadiums or so forth, all the lingo related to baseball will be ready for matching. And then it goes off to another subject, talk about maybe to philosophy or addition, and then I'm starting hearing words that is all the sudden in terrible conflict; it doesn't match and uh, I'm trying to maintain my composure, my cool, to smooth over to the next transition without looking like a fool. I consider myself a survivalist in the hearing world; that's my definition myself, survivalist.

Whereas children yearn to be listened to, to be valued and understood, parents are driven to help their children grow optimally. They also need both to be listened to and to listen, to understand, and to resonate with their child. They are compelled to dialog and thus to share their language with their children. However, parents describe a diversity of perspectives on how they can best achieve healthy discourse with their child who is deaf. Values relevant to speech, hearing, and language are inextricably woven with perspectives on how to best achieve dialog with their child that will serve the child well later on in life. "Language is language is language," one parent proclaimed. She cared little about whether their discourse was in Swahili or Sign Language. For others "it was natural. I want my kid not to be like me but to be able to communicate on an oral basis." (The father added "And to verbally communicate. That's how the world is run.") "It hurt me a lot and still hurts me that I have never heard her tell me that she loves me." Speech is essential to their present and future stories. Some parents describe their powerful need for their child to speak in an emotionally connected way. "I would give anything to hear him say I love you." Another parent said, "and then, with this device, it's amazing. I'm just shocked. He called me Dad and Daddy, and gosh, it warmed my heart." To overcome the complexity that deafness added to their family's life, parents are prepared to expend energy, money, time, whatever is necessary to adapt to their unexpected obstacle to shared dialog. For each family, the solution is personally derived, utilizes their innate resilience and invulnerability, and may not match the perceptions or recommendations of professionals or advisors encountered.

Whereas parents struggle with finding the best communication vehicle for their family, the deaf child or adolescent must find a place within the family, community, and society. Their comfort in the context of both the family and community provides them with opportunities for the consolidation of identity.

> I was frustrated because my family was hearing, and they left me out. I felt different from them; sometimes I don't feel like I belong with them. Even though they are my family, there is love, but in other ways its different because I'm deaf, and they are hearing. I sit out from their activities. I get so upset just because I cannot communicate with them—I want to have fun with them. I wonder if its because I am deaf that I cannot be involved with them. My goal for this coming Thanksgiving or for a future Thanksgiving: I would like to host a Thanksgiving dinner party for any of my deaf friends who feel left out. They are welcome to come to a deaf Thanksgiving party. Someday..."

The development of a personal narrative has not only a profound impact on the individual child, adolescent, or adult, but also a communitywide influence on social perceptions, which, in turn, create a more hospitable culture and environment in which to grow. From the 1800s, when the deaf community held banquets in France and intellectuals flocked to witness wondrous deaf narrators, to the contemporary appreciation for folklore in the deaf community and the transmission of seminal stories to the community at large (e.g., Deaf President Now, etc.), narrative has empowered the entire community. Stories demand a community audience and compel societal acceptance and recognition of individuals who are deaf; they form the matrix of a powerful force that can advocate social change. This cultural and community identity consolidation also serves to preserve language, strengthens the self-esteem of children, adolescents, and adults, and assures children future role models.

Every child deserves to be "heard" and understood by a loving and empathetic adult. Regardless of modality, the adult(s) must both share a symbolic code or representational world with the child, reducing the solitary experience of an unexpressed existence, and help build a language system that can reflect, share, and modify inner cognitive and emotional experiences in the re-creation of the child's everchanging personal narrative.

REFERENCES

Broyard, A. (1992). *Intoxicated by my illness*. New York: Fawcett Columbine.
Cox, M., & Theilgaard, A. (1987). *Mutative metaphors in psychotherapy: The aeolian mode*. London: Tavistock Publications, Ltd.

Eastman, G. (Producer), & Cassell, J. (Director). (1989). *Deaf culture: Autobiographies* [Film]. (Available from Sign Language Videotapes, 1320 Edgewater St. NW, Suite B-10, Salem, OR, 97394).

Fleischman, P. R. (1989). *The healing zone: Religious issues in psychotherapy.* New York: Paragon House.

Jackson, S. W. (1992). The listening healer in the history of psychological healing. *American Journal of Psychiatry, 149*(12), 23–34.

Lichtman, W. (1998, November 22). A place at the table. *The Washington Post,* W15.

Luborsky, M. R. (1997). Creative challenges and the construction of life narratives. In C. Adams-Price (Ed.), *Creativity and later life: theoretical and empirical approaches.* New York: Springer.

Meadow-Orlans, K. P., & Steinberg, A. G. (1993). Effects of infant hearing loss and maternal support on mother–infant interactions at eighteen months. *Journal of Applied Developmental Psychology, 14,* 407–426.

Nisbet, R. A. (1969). *Social change and history: Aspects of the western theory of developments.* Oxford: Oxford University Press.

Schlesinger, H. S., & Meadow, K. P. (1972). *Sound and Sign: Childhood deafness and mental health.* Berkeley: University of California Press.

Steinberg, A., Davila, J. R., Collazo, J., Fischgrund, J., & Loew, R. C. (1997). A little sign and lot of love … attitudes, perceptions, and beliefs of Hispanic families with deaf children. *Qualitative Health Research, 7*(2), 202–222.

Steinberg, A., Sullivan, V. J., & Loew, R. C. (1998). Cultural and linguistic barriers to mental health service access: The deaf consumer's perspective. *American Journal of Psychiatry, 155*(7), 982–984.

Steinberg, A., Sullivan, V. J., & Montoya, L. A. (1999). Loneliness and social isolation in the workplace for deaf individuals during the transition years. *Journal of Applied Rehabilitation Counseling, 30*(1), 22–30.

Widdershoven, G. A. M. (1993). The story of life: Hermeneutic perspecitves on the relationship between narrative and life history. In R. Josselson & A. Lieblich (Eds.), *The narrative study of lives* (pp. 1–20). Newbury Park, CA: Sage.

Winnicott, D. W. (1958). *Collect papers: Through paediatrics to psycho-analysis.* London: Tavistock.

Wright, K. (1991). *Vision and separation: Between mother and baby.* Northvale, NJ: Jason Aronson, Inc.

The Deaf Child and Family
in Transition

Parents of deaf or hard of hearing children have to make a variety of decisions that parents of hearing children do not face. The confusing diversity of education and therapy programs, language methods, amplification technologies, and, more recently, the possibility of medical interventions available for deaf and hard of hearing children present parents with increasingly difficult choices. Parents often turn to doctors, educators, and early intervention specialists for information on which to base these decisions. Although professional assistance is often available to parents through early intervention programs, the quality of parents' experiences with early intervention and other professionals is quite varied. The four chapters in this section provide a look at the transition from issues related to the child within the family context to that of the family interacting with professionals who provide support services as parents negotiate the tangle of issues relating to raising and educating a deaf or hard of hearing child.

In the first chapter, Spencer reports on a case study of a deaf child in a hearing family that exemplifies the educational and medical issues, challenges, and decisions such families face. From the parents' first nagging doubts about the ability of their child to hear, to the hard decisions that all parents of deaf children have to make, Spencer provides a human perspective on our too often antiseptic, empirical view of development. This story of the ups and downs of hearing parents struggling to understand and provide support for their deaf child and their positive and negative experiences with professionals should serve as a caution for those who believe that a professional's role is to provide quick answers to complex questions.

Mertens, Sass-Lehrer, and Scott-Olson report parents' perceptions of experiences with their deaf and hard of hearing children and, especially, of the positive and negative aspects of their interactions with medical and other intervention professionals. Parents expressed a clear desire for unbiased information presented in a manner that shows respect for their knowledge and concern about their own child.

The next two chapters provide reports of intervention programs that are responsive to this request. Both emphasize the integral involvement of parents in educational programming efforts for deaf and hard of hearing children that are responsive to parents' needs as well as those of the children. Mohay synthesized empirical findings from her own and other studies to provide systematic guidance for hearing families as they accommodate their deaf and hard of hearing children's needs for visual communication. Mohay worked with deaf and hearing researchers to develop a curriculum in which hearing parents learn from and with deaf adults strategies that promote deaf and hard of hearing children's visual attention, communication, and early literacy skills. Initial studies found the curriculum to effectively provide hearing parents with communication tools that allow more comfortable, intuitive, and reciprocal interactions with their deaf and hard of hearing children. Thus, through the assistance of this curriculum, hearing parents can be empowered to provide their children with the kinds of interactive experiences known to support development.

Calderon and Greenberg describe the cooperative nature, as well as the challenges, of the venture between parents and appropriate professionals. Emphasizing the importance of socioemotional development for successful academic and personal growth, Calderon and Greenberg describe intervention programs that provide deaf and hard of hearing children and their families with support for the home to school transition. The PATHS program, in particular, was found to be an effective way to ensure that the "multiple, reciprocal interactions" in the deaf child's environment are drawn together in support of healthy development.

Every Opportunity:
A Case Study of Hearing Parents
and Their Deaf Child

Patricia Elizabeth Spencer
Gallaudet University

Every birth is a miracle. Except for the excitement that typically accompanies such a miracle, Maggie's birth was uneventful. After several days, she and her mother left the hospital to join her father and sister Sam (Samantha) in their colorful Victorian home in the older part of a midsized midwestern town of about 200,000 people in the United States. Maggie's extended family of aunts, uncles, and grandparents visited and admired this new addition to the family. Her parents, falling in love with Maggie almost immediately, adjusted for a second time to the demanding schedule of caring for a newborn. Sam, now 2 years old, became at the same time Maggie's protector and her competitor for the family's attention.

Maggie's mother and father were sensitive and experienced parents. By the time she was 4 weeks old, they noticed a difference between her behaviors and those of her older sister at the same age. Maggie seemed to be nonresponsive to sounds around the house like the buzzer on the oven timer and the telephone—and to their own calls to her when they were beyond her sight. They asked her pediatrician if perhaps Maggie's hearing should be tested. The doctor assured them that questions about a child's responsiveness to sound were common at this age and advised them to wait, to observe her carefully and to be patient. As time went on, Maggie's mother became more concerned about Maggie's ability to hear. Still, the parents were advised to wait for testing. Maggie's father, by his own report, tried to reassure her mother that nothing was wrong, but he also continued to keep a careful watch on Maggie's responsiveness.

By the time Maggie reached 6 months of age, her mother was convinced that she was not hearing. The pediatrician referred the family at last to a clinic in a nearby large city. Maggie's hearing loss—bilateral, sensorineural, profound—was diagnosed on the initial trip, and earmolds were poured for her hearing aids. That same day, her parents began their quest for information about ways to support Maggie's development. They felt confident about their parenting skills in general. After all, Sam was happy, healthy, and developing quickly. But this baby was deaf. What would they need to do for Maggie that was different from what they were doing for Sam? Where would they find the information and the resources they needed? What lay ahead for this tiny child and their family?

Maggie's father commented that when the hearing loss was finally diagnosed he was "sort of dazed there for a while." In contrast, he reported that Maggie's mother "hit the ground running—and it was pretty impressive to watch." According to him, Maggie's mother had been "worrying and worrying," but now she knew that Maggie was deaf. With the ambiguity resolved, Maggie's mother "didn't have to worry any more and set off to get things done." Almost immediately, Maggie's mother contacted the school to which they had been referred. School was just letting out for the summer, so the only person available was the program director. The director visited the family within days and continued to do so each week of the summer. With her, the family asked questions, talked about communication options, and began to learn to sign.

THE FAMILY[1] AND THE SETTING

Maggie's parents' approach to finding information, locating services, and making decisions about her experiences was a product of their own knowledge, experiences, and personalities. Both parents had graduated from college. Maggie's mother, a professional who worked for a local branch of a large corporation, went back to work after her maternity leave but continued to spearhead the family's information searches. Maggie's

[1] I am extremely grateful to Maggie's parents for allowing me to monitor her growth and for sharing their thoughts and feelings as they made important decisions. I also want to thank the teachers and therapists who spoke so openly with me and who demonstrated such dedication to the education of Maggie and other deaf children. Of course, I have altered some descriptive information about the family and professionals in an effort to keep their identity confidential.

father, who previously held an administrative position in a small company, found that he could conduct his business in a consultative manner from their home. After Maggie's diagnosis, he stayed home with both children and was usually responsible for getting them to doctor's visits and other appointments. He also had primary responsibility for getting Maggie to therapy visits and, as soon as she became old enough, to school.

In addition to support from a number of friends, many associated with their church, Maggie's parents had considerable support from their own families. One of Maggie's aunts previously taught deaf children and knew sign language. Although she lived in another part of the country, she provided information and support. An aunt and uncle in a nearby city began to study sign language. They became involved with the Deaf community, acquiring Deaf friends. Another aunt and uncle, living farther away, bought sign books to prepare for their next visit. Grandparents, also a great distance away, began to learn some signs and gave Maggie a series of sign language storybooks. In addition, a close family friend sat in on the sign language lessons during the summer.

The presence of so much family and community support provided an unusually positive environment for Maggie and her family. In addition, her parents' ability to obtain and evaluate information—as well as their confidence in their own general parenting skills—boded well. There was a satellite program for deaf children in town that was conducted by the state school for deaf students. The family's interaction with the program director immediately after Maggie's diagnosis was extremely helpful, and the parents appreciated this service. All in all, Maggie's family seemed to profit from an amazing constellation of positive support and resources. Even in this situation, however, their road was not an easy one. As Maggie grew, they had to revisit and revise decisions already made. They agonized, and sometimes disagreed, about the best course to take. They received negative as well as positive feedback from professionals with whom they worked, and despite an overall optimistic outlook, they continued to worry about whether they were doing the right things for Maggie.

DATA COLLECTION AND MY ROLE WITH THE FAMILY

I met Maggie's family when she was one year old while I was recruiting families to participate in a series of studies of the development of deaf infants that were conducted under the supervision of Kathryn P. Meadow-Orlans. Maggie and her family lived far from our research center, and I soon found that I could not replicate in the family's home the situations that we were using to collect data in our research lab. However, even at first contact, I was impressed with the way these parents obtained information and worked together to evaluate it as they made decisions about Maggie's therapies, the communication systems to use, and her educational services. I was impressed to find that both parents were signing consistently to Maggie and that her sister Sam was beginning to sign. I suspected that it would be fruitful to follow Maggie's early development in order to document successful language development by a deaf child with hearing parents. I was also intrigued to find that Maggie's family intended to use a bilingual approach to her language development: They intended to use both signs and Cued Speech. At my request, Maggie's parents agreed to let me return periodically to track her language development and to talk with them about the decisions they were making.

In addition to documenting Maggie's development, a major goal of this qualitative case study was to document the issues her parents faced and how those issues were resolved during her first 3 years of life. There has been much research in the past several decades emphasizing developmental challenges faced by deaf children whose parents are hearing and are, consequently, not native users of sign language (e.g., Moores & Meadow-Orlans, 1990). Many of these same reports noted the importance of hearing parents' acceptance of their child as a deaf person and their support for the child's development. In turn, work by Meadow-Orlans and her colleagues (Schlesinger & Meadow, 1972; Meadow-Orlans & Steinberg, 1993) pointed out the importance of support provided to parents to prepare them to maximize their parenting skills. Therefore, it was important to me to investigate Maggie's parents' attitudes about her deafness and sources of support they found to be effective.

I also wanted to find out from the parents how and where they found information about the variety of approaches to language development that were available. Although these data were collected in the late 1980s, issues prominent in the late 1990s in deaf education were already evident. "Simultaneous communication" or the use of English-based artificial sign systems, was under fire, criticized for its ineffectiveness in promoting literacy development. In its stead, use of ASL was recommended by many professionals and deaf adults (Johnson, Liddell, & Erting, 1989). Advocates of Cued Speech claimed that it provided more direct access to English literacy than other manual systems (Cornett & Daisey, 1992). Advocacy for oral education remained strong, and both tactile aids and more advanced traditional hearing aids were becoming available. Finally, multichannel cochlear implants were available for selected children (and were soon to be approved for general use with young children; Clark, Cowan, & Dowell, 1997). I thought that Maggie's parents, who had already demonstrated skills in finding information, might provide a model of the effectiveness with which available options could be sifted through and evaluated.

Collection of data from Maggie's parents depended primarily on interviews I conducted and audiotaped during visits to their home. As part of the infant research project, Meadow-Orlans revised a semistructured interview protocol first used in research conducted with Hilde Schlesinger (Schlesinger & Meadow, 1972). This protocol guides families in providing information about their children's initial diagnosis, subsequent stresses and supports they experienced, major events influencing the family and the deaf child postdiagnosis, child's developmental progress, and the parents' feelings about that progress as well as anticipated problems. I used this protocol in my first meeting with the family. In subsequent visits, interviews became more like conversations in which these highly articulate parents gave me news about Maggie's development and their own growth as they learned more about the world of deaf people. The parents also allowed me to videotape at home during mealtime and playtime. They and Maggie's teachers gave me permission to videotape Maggie at school, and I was able to talk with professionals who provided speech and communication therapy for her. This gave me multiple perspectives on Maggie's progress and family activities, providing a way to verify information obtained in the interviews. I visited Maggie's family a number of times over a 2-year period (approximately from her first to her third birthday), conducting interviews when Maggie was 12, 21, and 36 months old. Maggie was videotaped at school at 18 months and at home at 12, 24, and 36 months. I conducted a lengthy interview with the therapist providing Cued Speech training when Maggie was 21 months old and interviews with teachers when Maggie was 24 and 36 months old. I spent hours with the family in their home, once even staying overnight. Maggie and her family also visited me at my home.

It seems relevant to note here that my experience with young deaf children has been primarily with those in signing programs. I brought to this study an assumption that sign language was the most effective way to provide deaf children language and communication skills. I was aware of the disappointing results of the English-based artificial sign systems; however, I remained doubtful about the ability of hearing parents to accept or to learn ASL effectively. I had become interested in Cued Speech and had attended a weekend workshop to learn it, although I had never practiced its use. I was curious to find out whether it could be effective as a first language for deaf children, but I was doubtful. However, I did not discuss my own attitudes toward the language systems with Maggie's parents, and they did not ask. Because my university is associated quite strongly with use of sign language and is also the birthplace of Cued Speech, they may have assumed that I was open to both methods.

The analysis presented here was approached qualitatively and inductively. Audiotapes were transcribed and parents' comments were reviewed to identify themes or categories in their responses and their accounts of their thoughts and actions related to Maggie. The interview with the Cued Speech therapist was transcribed and coded, with the therapist's interpretation of family's decisions compared with information given me by the parents. Notes were taken from videotapes of Maggie at school and home; some of these videotapes were transcribed (notably one of extended interaction between Maggie and her deaf teacher, one of a family dinnertime conversation, and another of Maggie and her sister).

Videotape transcriptions provided observations of Maggie's cognitive, social, and language skills to supplement reports from family, school professionals, and brief direct testing.

MAGGIE AND HER FAMILY AT ONE YEAR

By the time Maggie was one year old, she was attending school. Services were provided on a satellite basis from the state school for the deaf five days a week for an hour each day. The school's official language policy mandated the use of Signed English in the classroom. In addition to school services, Maggie received speech therapy two days a week.

At this point, Maggie's parents had made their initial decisions about communication methods. At the time of diagnosis, her parents learned quickly about the classic conflicts between advocates of oral language and advocates of signing. Maggie's parents never considered a strictly oral approach. They accepted that Maggie needed to have language that she could perceive visually. However, they learned that deaf children are at high risk for academic difficulties and literacy problems, even when they learn sign language or an artificial sign system. Literacy was and continued to be a highly charged issue for this family. Reading and writing skills were of great importance to Maggie's parents. Having found reports proposing that Cued Speech provided a better method than English-based signing for providing deaf children visual access to English, they contacted the program that provided itinerant Cued Speech services in their area. Cued Speech—which provides manual information that represents speech sounds and supplements speechreading—immediately appealed to the parents. However, they knew most deaf adults prefer to sign, and a sign system was used at Maggie's school. Her parents were attracted to the elegance of signing during their early lessons. This attraction may have been enhanced because the person teaching signs began to visit them immediately after Maggie's diagnosis (see Calderon & Greenberg, chap. 10, this volume, for more about the importance of hearing parents' initial contacts with early interventionists).

Given the apparent merits of both signing and Cued Speech, the parents decided to use both with Maggie: a self-described "bilingual" approach. They planned to divide the day roughly in half. During one part of the day they would use Cued Speech with Maggie, and during the other part they would use English-based signing. They believed that the latter system would provide Maggie with an effective communication system, but they thought she would learn English through Cued Speech. They studied Cued Speech and were able to use it somewhat fluently. They set up weekly sessions for Maggie with the Cued Speech therapist in addition to other programs and therapies.

By one year of age, Maggie had been exposed to signs for 6 months. She already responded to and produced signs. She was observed by her parents to produce spontaneously signs for MOMMY, DADDY, BABY, and LIGHT. She also often imitated signs (one example was the sign BOAT). Maggie's mother noted that she often signed a sequence of POINT (to object) + EAT. According to her mother, this was an overgeneralization of the EAT sign—in her opinion, Maggie was using it to sign WANT. Her mother laughingly noted that Maggie was as likely to point to her teddy bear (when it was out of reach) and sign EAT as to point and sign this for a food item. She also pointed to objects frequently, looking up to her parents as though requesting that they provide the label for the object. They readily complied. Although they signed slowly and somewhat awkwardly, each had a reasonably large sign vocabulary. Sam also signed occasionally but was usually prompted to do so by her parents.

Maggie's parents indicated an ongoing interest in her ability to use speech. One of her grandfathers made a "light box" with red and green lights that flashed when someone vocalized into a microphone. Maggie's mother reported that the child learned this association and expressed puzzlement if she vocalized when the machine was unplugged and did not light up. Mother reported that the speech therapist said that Maggie "knows she has a voice and can use it," although Maggie "turned on her voice" only when prompted.

Themes that were already evident in the parents' comments at one year would continue to be expressed in later visits. They expressed pride in Maggie's accomplishments and appreciation of positive attitudes and support from educational professionals and family. When asked if they were receiving emotional support from school and other professionals, Maggie's mother replied, "(Yes) because we hear so much good stuff about how she is doing." Her father added, "Yeah. Also there is just generally a positive attitude. That is, all the professionals we meet have that same sort of attitude that (Maggie) is going to be great—we are going to have a good time—and we are going to see what we can provide for her and what we can get her to be able to do." Despite their pleasure in Maggie's growth to this point, her parents continued to search for information about educational and language options. They were thinking ahead and had serious concerns about literacy development.

Yet another theme emerged at the one year visit. In ways that were still subtle, Maggie's mother and father had somewhat different perspectives on her needs. This could be observed during each parent's videotaped interaction with Maggie. Her mother made careful attempts to produce English articles, be verbs, and verb inflections when signing, whereas her father had a more expressive but less English-like approach. In addition, Maggie's mother almost always combined signs with speech although her father sometimes signed without voice. Although both parents said that they did not equate English with speech, Maggie's mother held out a bit more hope than did her father that Maggie would learn to talk. Of the two parents, her mother expressed more concerns about literacy. In her father's words, "We have the same goals for Maggie, but perhaps we put different weights on them."

18 MONTHS

When Maggie was 18 months old, I videotaped in her classroom. One student was absent, leaving two children with two teachers: one deaf and one hearing. The hearing teacher used simultaneous voice + sign communication and focused her attention primarily on a hard of hearing child. The deaf teacher spent most of her time with Maggie and signed without voice.

As at home, Maggie produced single-sign and sign-plus-point expressions, although not signing often. She was able to engage in short conversations, to point to signed objects, and to label pictured objects. She preferred play with active toys (a pedalless cycle, climbing toys) and a set of small cars (which she moved around while making motor vocalizations) to more traditional classroom activities.

One positive aspect of the classroom was the supportive behaviors of the deaf teacher. As has been described for deaf mothers (Harris & Mohay, 1997; Spencer, Bodner-Johnson, & Gutfreund, 1992; Swisher, chap. 2, this volume; Waxman & Spencer, 1997) as well as deaf teachers (Mather, 1987), this teacher handled Maggie's still limited visual attention to communication masterfully. In fact, it appeared to be quite hard to direct or obtain Maggie's visual attention at this age. This was due at least in part to her interest in the objects around her and to her long and sustained attention episodes to those objects. Maggie played—mostly alone—and was fascinated by the properties of the objects with which she was playing.

Her deaf teacher, however, showed great patience and waited long periods of time for Maggie to look up at her. She signed every time Maggie glanced up at her. She also moved her hands down frequently to sign on or near objects with which Maggie was playing. The teacher's language was most often used to label or comment on the objects with which Maggie was engaged. Her comments were usually short—one to several signs—and occurred within Maggie's brief glances. The teacher sometimes tapped gently on Maggie to signal her to look up—with varying results. Thus, Maggie experienced daily conversations with a fluent signer who intuitively used signals for visual turn taking and patterns of language input like that provided by deaf parents for their toddlers.

The deaf teacher also provided Maggie's parents with opportunities to use sign language. Maggie's father and the teacher conversed daily. The teacher and her family also visited Maggie's home and were occasional dinner guests. The teacher's deaf daughter provided Maggie's parents with a model of what they considered to be a successful deaf adolescent. She was personable, self-confident, and secure in her identity as a deaf person. In addition, she had bilingual and bimodal communication skills.

Maggie's father told me about a parent meeting in which this young woman "was speaking and signing at the same time, and she was speaking in such a way that it would be intelligible to anybody you know … we were sitting there saying 'well, you know, if my kid never gets to speak any better than this, I think I can stand it.'"

In addition to the regular classroom, Maggie attended speech therapy sessions four or five times a week. One session was with the Cued Speech therapist, who also worked with Maggie's parents to reinforce their skills. Although I did not conduct formal interviews with Maggie's parents at this time, they each confided that they were beginning to reconsider their decision to use Cued Speech. They were having problems remembering to cue and were questioning the viability of their "half day for each" bilingual approach. They had only the therapist with whom to cue and gain fluency with the system. In contrast, they found that signing provided a functional communication method to use with Maggie and with other deaf persons they met.

21 AND 24 MONTHS

Parent interviews when Maggie was 21 months old were extensive. Maggie's parents were well into their fourth quarter of signing classes at the local community college and had once even found themselves on a list of potential interpreters for a meeting. They thought this was premature and laughed about it. However, they continued to find ways to practice and improve their signing. Their sign teacher told them that to learn to communicate in sign, they must have frequent meaningful interaction with persons who were fluent in sign. She set up pot luck dinners where hearing sign students could interact with deaf adults. Maggie's father described the deaf people at those events as "infinitely patient and willing to do anything for you."

Maggie's parents continued to express positive attitudes toward her as a deaf person. They also expressed comfort with Maggie's being deaf. Her mother commented,

> The thing, I guess, is after you sort of initially realize you have a deaf child—and then there are all sorts of things you need to do about that. But maybe it is just the process of doing those things, or maybe … in our case in particular, Maggie doesn't have any other learning problems and is learning so much so quickly … it is really rewarding to see that. In some ways, it is really nice to have a deaf child. I know it sounds kind of strange, but there's really no drawbacks to it.

Maggie's father commented that he and his wife discovered "being deaf can be a positive thing." He added that they noticed the strong sense of community among deaf people—a sense that he felt is often lacking among hearing people. Maggie's father believed that he had grown and had more opportunities because of her deafness: "Here, even with just the little bit of signing I know, there's a whole new bunch of folks—a whole different community—that I can get to know."

Data from videotapes made when Maggie was 24 months old support her parents' reports that she was developing well. During play sessions with each parent, Maggie showed precocious visual–spatial abilities and strong motivation to accomplish tasks. She was able to successfully put together puzzles containing more than five pieces, for example, to make a bear, and another that contained shapes including triangles, diamonds, and semicircles. Although her parents made suggestions, it was clear that she wanted to accomplish these tasks on her own. Maggie still did not give frequent eye contact to her parents while she worked on a puzzle or was otherwise engaged in object exploration. However, her parents were not upset by this and tended to wait for her to look up or to move their hands to sign near the objects. It is not clear whether the parents had seen these behaviors modeled or had adapted them spontaneously. They also tried to redirect Maggie's attention by tapping on her shoulder, but she rarely responded. The interactions were happy ones, though, because Maggie's parents did not try to actively compete with her interest in the toys and other objects. Maggie looked up at them spontaneously when wanting to share surprise, to obtain help, or to sign. In fact, her visual attention was most reliably directed toward her parents when she herself was signing. This happened more frequently than before because her sign vocabulary had increased noticeably. Her parents reported that she used "at least a hundred" different signs expressively and they recalled more than 40 of them easily. Her vocabulary included signs like ICE as distinct from COLD and from ICE CREAM. They also reported that Maggie combined pointing with more than one sign in utterances. For example, they remembered her pointing downstairs in the morning and then signing WANT DRINK. She reliably responded to yes or no questions and to requests for objects.

However, Maggie's parents began to express concerns about their own signing abilities and, therefore, their ability to provide Maggie with appropriate language input. Despite their pleasure at the social interactions with deaf adults provided in their sign class, Maggie's parents noted how avidly she attended to those fluent signers. She was more attentive where "fingers were flying," they said, than when they signed in their slower, less expressive way. During the past year they attended a summer camp for families with deaf children that also caused them concern. There, they were reminded of limitations in reading and writing frequently experienced by deaf students and were warned that the Signed English they were using was insufficient to provide Maggie with strong English competency. They had been admonished to sign at all times—even when they were not conversing with Maggie—and they had been impressed by the fact that deaf children of deaf parents almost always outperformed those with hearing parents who were new signers.

Maggie's parents appeared to reject the idea that she would have literacy problems. Maggie had started to sit and look at books alone and to label pictures in the books. Her mother was greatly encouraged by this. However, both parents worried about the other information they had been given. They expressed frustration with themselves and the fact that they knew "we need to be signing all the time" to give Maggie the opportunity to oversee conversations, but it clearly was not something they felt comfortable doing. For example, her father mentioned a situation in which he wanted to talk with his wife about handling a problem with the car and discuss how to respond to advice from the mechanic. He was sure that he could not do this fluently in sign and said that signing conversations like this would feel "unnatural" even when Maggie was in the same room and could easily oversee the conversation. Maggie's father, who was already by most standards a very competent hearing signer, also spoke poignantly about his recent distress on meeting a new deaf person and finding that he was unable to communicate with him. He reported thinking, "I am never going to learn this. My child is going to grow up and not understand me because I'm not going to be able to speak to her above a 3 year level." (He was told later that the deaf man with whom he was trying to communicate had developmental disabilities and that interpreters had problems communicating with him. However, this did not erase Maggie's father's memory of his distress.) Maggie's mother added, "Sometimes it is frightening to think maybe we aren't worried enough or not doing enough ... and I have heard people who have worked with deaf people saying the thing that bothers them the most is that they miss the background conversation. You need to be signing all the time or this person is not picking up everything. I know that this is true, and that makes me sad sometimes to think about it." However, the parents went on to chronicle their own attempts to build their sign skills, her mother commenting, "I find myself signing at my office, signing by myself, signing to animals ... (laughing)." Her father adds, "sitting around practicing fingerspelling without much thinking about it. ... We both try, but it's hard."

Thus, despite their confidence in Maggie's abilities, her parents appeared to worry about their own abilities. Maggie's mother reported with some anger that, at the family camp, she got the impression they were being told that they "could not raise a deaf child right. They just about said to us, 'You should just give her up to deaf people.'" It is not so surprising, then, that Maggie's mother asked me after I told her Maggie had performed well on a cognitive and language test, "But how does she compare to a child with deaf parents?"

At each visit, I asked Maggie's parents to evaluate her language development. They tended to begin by summarizing (even bragging about) her accomplishments in sign. Then, her mother would add information about

Maggie's progress in speech. At this visit, Maggie was reported to be able to differentiate and imitate long versus short sounds. (The Ling method was being used in speech therapy.) Both parents reported that Maggie vocalized more when she was wearing her hearing aids. However, neither had heard her produce any form of consonant–vowel combination.

Neither parent mentioned Cued Speech. When I asked about it specifically, they told me they were having serious second thoughts about using it. In fact, they had already decided to stop using it for routine communication, although they continued to think Maggie might use it later to support speech or literacy development: as "a tool for reading." Maggie's mother said she thought of it initially as the main method for communication, but "now I see it more as a tool to reaching speech and much less as a communication (method). Because I see that sign language can be so effective as the way you get across what you want to say. ... I see advantages to Signed English, which I think from an educational standpoint is really useful." Both parents now seemed to think of using Cued Speech rarely—"in addition to sign language and more of a tool rather than as the sole method of communication." They said that they might use it to introduce a word for which there is no sign or no sign that they know. (They indicated that they thought that fingerspelling, which might be used for this function by deaf adults, was too difficult for a toddler to understand.) The parents continued to think that Cued Speech could be used to teach speech during speech therapy sessions.

Why did Maggie's parents change their ideas about the usefulness of Cued Speech? In part, their attitudes changed as a result of their communicative experiences with Maggie, who was at this point still less than 2 years old. Her mother noted, "One of the things I had not realized until we tried it (Cued Speech) ... and found she might be able to understand some, but she can't give back any of it. She just does not have the (fine motor) skill." Her father added, "One of the good things about sign as opposed to cued speech is that it is easier to understand an approximation in sign. Of course, we react a lot more positively to an approximation of a sign than we do to an approximation of a cue. We can understand the sign but not the cue." Maggie's mother agreed, "You can't tell what she is trying to get across (in cueing), and since we are not understanding it, it's hard to be rewarding her for having tried it."

Maggie's parents also appeared to have had disagreements with the Cued Speech therapist. Although they had been pressed to cue entire sentences instead of single words, they found this to be difficult. Maggie's mother noted that cueing entire sentences was very slow because of their lack of skill. She preferred to use cues for single words "kind of as a label for things. Like when we started with sign, we would just sign whatever the object was in question. Then pretty soon we would start adding two words together and ... it seems we built up language more easily that way than starting out with a whole sentence. ... I think you need to start with building blocks and add on until you get to the sentence level comfortably." The Cued Speech therapist eventually approved this approach but only after considerable discussion. Maggie's mother reported having "talked to (the therapist) about Maggie not participating in the program (any longer) because we were getting such a guilt trip about her not performing." Maggie's father continued, "I think (the therapist) was under a lot of pressure to get results ... and I think she passed that (pressure) along (to us)." Her mother added that the pressure was "essentially to drop total communication ... and get serious about cueing."

At this visit, Maggie's parents told me about another deaf child in their town who was in the Cued Speech program. This child had had a single-channel cochlear implant. After meeting the child and her parents, Maggie's parents were unimpressed with her progress. Although the child was older than Maggie, she did not have Maggie's ability to communicate with her parents and other people in her environment.

That same week, the Cued Speech therapist spoke positively with me about Maggie's parents but expressed disappointment that the bilingual, Cued Speech and sign, experiment had been a failure. She continued to believe that it is possible for some families to implement the Cued Speech and sign combined approach, but she thought that Maggie's family was "not organized enough" to accomplish it. (She said that she herself would not have the organizational skills to do this either.) As we continued to talk, the therapist told me that her information about bilingualism was quite limited. She had read papers indicating that the two languages must be kept separate, "perhaps used in different places like one at home and one at school or by different people," but she had no previous direct experience. The teacher confirmed reports from Maggie's parents that they had found signing to be a more comfortable and useful means of communication. She also repeated their intent to use Cued Speech for introducing new words and perhaps for literacy purposes after Maggie was older. She noted how quickly Maggie's parents were learning to sign and commented that they seemed "naturally attracted" to signing. She agreed that signing was the best approach for Maggie's family even though she was going to continue to use Cued Speech with Maggie during speech sessions.

Thus, as Maggie approached her third year of life, she was developing well. Despite her progress, however, her parents had gotten more negative feedback from professionals this year than during her first year of life. The parents continued to evaluate Maggie's development positively and to maintain highly positive attitudes about deaf people in general, but they appeared to have entertained doubts about their own competence and ability to provide Maggie with the language environment she needed. They had also developed a bit of distrust of professionals. According to Maggie's father, "You get the feeling talking to Cued Speech fanatics or Total Communication fanatics that if you don't do this particular thing, your kid is going to be dumb as a rock for the rest of her life. Then you get out there and get to know more and more (deaf) people. ... You see people who came up in various systems and can communicate with a variety of people. Nothing (related to communication choice) seems to be so nearly earth shatteringly important as it did when we were first faced with this."

At this point in time, I expected Maggie would be raised in a signing environment and have frequent interaction with deaf adults and the deaf community. At other points in our extended conversation, it became apparent that her father was becoming increasingly interested in the use of ASL as opposed to the Signed English that was preferred by her mother. I suspected that this would be the next decision the parents would face. I was wrong.

THREE YEARS OLD

By 3 years, Maggie was a competent communicator. In a videotape I made of her and her sister Sam during outdoor play, Maggie was the picture of a happy, well-developing child. She twirled around in the yard, looking at and directing my attention to birds, flowers, and an airplane that flew so low and made such a loud noise that she could hear it. (As usual, she was wearing her hearing aids.) She chattered to me in sign, telling me to look at the birds as they flew by and announcing that her father was riding on the plane: "POINT(to plane) AIRPLANE. DADDY RIDE ON AIRPLANE." She went on to tell me (with a sly grin) that her father was actually flying the airplane. This conversation continued for several minutes. At dinner, she engaged in signed conversation (about the spaghetti and activities of the day) with her mother, father, and sister. At this point, her parents were unable to estimate the size of her rapidly growing sign vocabulary but confirmed that four-sign sentences were produced frequently.

During the interview at this time, there was little mention of Maggie's speech development. Maggie was still having speech therapy sessions several times a week. (The Cued Speech therapist was no longer in the picture, however, because her program had not been refunded by the district.) Maggie's father reported that she still enjoyed her speech therapy sessions. He stated that the sessions would stop if she ever gave any indication that she did not want to participate, but that had not yet happened. I observed a session at home and confirmed that Maggie participated happily. However, I noted no functional improvement in her speech skills over the past year. She was still not producing any true consonant–vowel combinations and produced nothing like canonical babbling. Her speech therapist, who signed in the sessions, was upbeat and provided engaging games. However, she agreed that Maggie was at a very early stage of speech development.

During the interview, Maggie's mother informed me that she and her husband were considering a cochlear implant for Maggie. Only once before, when they mentioned the other child in town who was deaf and had an implant, had this topic come up during interviews. I expressed surprise, but Maggie's mother insisted that they had mentioned it before and reminded me that they "were aware of it pretty much from the beginning just because another family in town (had done it)." She said that, despite their earlier negative evaluation of the benefits of the implant for the other child, she had heard recently that the child "was now trying to talk." She also noted that this child had only a single channel implant and that, if Maggie were implanted, it would be with the multichannel implant.

Although the decision to investigate a cochlear implant took me by surprise, in retrospect it can be seen as a continuation of themes that had been present in the interviews from the beginning. Her parents had been engaged continuously in searching for and evaluating options for Maggie's language development. They obtained information about cochlear implantation initially from an audiologist. Her mother said, "When she would have an audiogram, I would say, 'So, what do I need to do? Who do I need to talk to?'" The audiologist said, "Well, I think you need to consider a cochlear implant." Maggie's parents also asked a deaf professional about cochlear implants at the family camp they attended. Their question received an unambiguously negative response. However, they decided to interpret this negative response based on life experiences the deaf person shared with them—experiences that they reasoned made him especially sensitive to issues of surgery and attempts to change deaf people. It may have been easier to reach this conclusion because of their somewhat negative experiences at the camp.

Another theme that appeared to be involved in the cochlear implant decision was the parents' long-standing concern about literacy. Maggie's parents initially supported the use of Cued Speech as a way to provide her with competency in English and thus with an avenue into English literacy. Having found that the Cued Speech method was not initially beneficial in this regard, they dropped it. However, speech therapy continued five days a week, and Maggie's mother hoped that the use of simultaneous Signed English and speech would give Maggie a useful model of English. Now they were told at the camp that simultaneous English and sign tended not to promote high literacy skills. In addition, Maggie showed little progress in speech and auditory skills, and that avenue to English was doubtful. The parents believed that English literacy skills would depend on good knowledge, at least receptively, of the English language in a modality other than print. Thus, they continued to search for other options that might provide Maggie with more exposure to the structure of spoken English. Despite their pride in Maggie's accomplishments with signing, they had been led by professionals to expect that this was not enough to assure English literacy for Maggie.

The parents' consideration of a cochlear implant did not seem to be based on negative attitudes toward deafness or deaf persons. Although

Maggie's mother was concerned about "what deaf people have to put up with from the rest of society" and was concerned that Maggie's later employment opportunities might be limited, she was not willing to state that she wished Maggie were hearing. Her father said, "If I had the power to make all people hearing tomorrow, I wouldn't do it because my life is certainly a lot richer for Maggie being deaf. And if I had the power to make (her) hear tomorrow, I just don't know if I'd do it or not."

This attitude was also evident in their choice of a cochlear implant center. They initially contacted three centers for implantation. One center was too far away but supplied much readable information about the procedure. A second center was close to home. The parents attended a meeting in which the chief surgeon at that center "made the unfortunate statement that deaf people could not be as intelligent as hearing people. He said they would have problems with abstract thinking." Completely rejecting this concept, the parents decided they did not want to associate with that center. As they put it, "He (the doctor) just doesn't know about deaf people." They decided instead to associate with a center farther away with an implant team including several people knowledgeable about deafness who presented the implant as merely an additional "aid." These professionals informed the parents that although performance with the implant was variable across children, it would not "make Maggie into a hearing child." She would always be deaf.

As in earlier situations, Maggie's parents tended to be persuaded by positive rather than negative evaluations of Maggie and themselves. Their goal was to provide Maggie with every opportunity for learning and achieving, not to change her identity. Thus, they immediately rejected the surgeon who talked of negative effects of deafness. Similarly, they expressed open resentment of chastisement by the Cued Speech therapist and the warning that their failures to cue would limit Maggie's future abilities. It also appeared that the warnings they received at the family camp had effects opposite from those intended. Admonitions about the need to sign constantly (thus, the implication that they were not signing enough) and negative opinions about the form of signing they were using at home caused the parents to question their competence and, perhaps, to consider options in addition to signing for Maggie. In the long run, these parents (like most people) tended to be motivated by positive feedback and to resent or to ignore negative feedback.

Finally, the question of a cochlear implant for Maggie clarified further the difference in perspectives between the two parents that had been observed earlier. At the time of the 3-year interview, Maggie's mother was a strong proponent of the implant, but her father expressed ambivalence. Maggie's mother articulated a strong argument that, for Maggie to benefit from the implant, she needed to receive it early in life. Her mother admitted that outcomes from the implant were not yet predictable, however, she thought of the implant as a way to give Maggie more options later in her life. As the mother put it, "Our goal is to give both our children options ... to be sure they have the basic information, skills, to allow them to choose their own course later in life."

In contrast, Maggie's father commented disapprovingly that getting a cochlear implant was a bit like "trying to fix the deaf." He noted that they had always told Maggie that she was "fine as a deaf person, and I am ... hesitant to start carving on her to give her a little bit of speech." However, he also noted that Maggie herself could later make a decision about whether to use the implant device, saying that she could "always remove the processor" if she decided she did not want to use it.

This became a fulcrum around which consensus was established. After Maggie's father's statement, her mother reiterated that, based on her reading, speech is acquired best when it is acquired early. But, she stated that acquisition of speech was not necessary for the implant to be useful. "Maybe," she suggested, "the implant will let Maggie be a little more comfortable with hearing people and ... know what is going on around her in general." Her father added that if the implant merely allowed Maggie to hear that "one truck coming at her" it would be worth it. Her mother commented that Maggie could later rescind the decision, and that she might "choose to be a deaf person who doesn't hear anything and relies on her eyes and signing. Then that's fine." However, Maggie's mother concluded, it was now up to the parents to make a decision that could not wait until Maggie was older.

THE COCHLEAR IMPLANT

The cochlear implant team conducted extensive tests of Maggie's auditory abilities, cognition, and language skills. They emphasized the long hours of therapy required if Maggie was to benefit from the implant, and they talked to the parents about the increased efforts it would require from them. The implant team questioned whether the parents' consensus on the implant was strong enough and specifically questioned whether Maggie's father was willing to support her development of listening skills post–implant. These issues were eventually resolved, and Maggie had a cochlear implant by the time she was 4 years old. Because the implant team would document Maggie's development postimplantation, my own research involvement with the family ended.

However, I heard from the family again. Approximately 2 years later, I received a phone call at work. It was Maggie's father. We exchanged greetings; then he told me, "Hold on, there's someone else I want you to hear." I then listened as a child, a child who was obviously deaf but whose speech was almost entirely intelligible, read a lengthy passage from a child's book. It was Maggie.

Maggie's father took back the phone to tell me that her speech was not always that intelligible; "the print and reading help her pronunciation." He confirmed that she was improving her speech and her listening skills rapidly. "Of course," he assured me, "we still sign and probably always will. She is still deaf, but now she can talk."

DISCUSSION

It would be foolish to try to generalize from a single case study. However, a case study can provide an in-depth look at the complexities inherent in a situation. In some instances, a case study can provide an antidote to oversimplified and overhomogenized conclusions sometimes resulting from studies that emphasize the average or the commonalities among members of a group. Can this report of Maggie and her family enrich our understanding about influences on hearing families and their deaf children?

In the case of this family, there was little evidence of any prolonged period of grief in reaction to Maggie's being deaf. If her parents experienced this phenomenon, the feelings appeared to be well under control by the time she reached one year of age. This does not mean that they decided that Maggie's being deaf was a totally positive thing. However, they seemed to spend little time mourning any loss of the hearing child they were expecting to have and instead concentrated their efforts on assuring that Maggie would have every opportunity for a happy and productive life. The support that these parents valued most was that which provided them with information they could use to promote Maggie's development. Instead of wanting to talk about feelings of grief and loss, they appreciated opportunities to learn specifics about the potential of various communication systems. They were most appreciative of opportunities to meet and interact with older deaf children and adults. Thus, their story is a reminder that instead of making assumptions about the feelings and needs of hearing parents with deaf children, interventionists might spend time ascertaining the feelings and needs of individual families. Individualization of approaches to parent support may be as important as is individualization of programming and educational approaches for the child. (See Calderon & Greenberg, chap. 10, this volume, for amplification of this view.)

The degree to which Maggie's parents responded to feedback that was positive about her and about their own efforts but rejected negative feedback was striking. This general principle about effects of positive reinforcement is sometimes forgotten in professional–parent interactions. It was disconcerting to find that these parents, whose daughter was progressing so well socially and linguistically, felt reprimanded instead of rewarded by some of their contacts with professionals in deaf education. It is hard to see how causing parents to question their ability to provide an adequate environment for their child's development can have positive outcomes. I must admit that some of my own research and publications support the premise that hearing parents face inordinate difficulties in adapting to their children's deafness. However, there is information available showing that some hearing families (most of the research has focused on mothers) make positive adaptations in their interactions with deaf children (e.g., Lederberg & Prezbindowski, chap. 5, this volume; Prendergast & McCollum, 1996; Spencer, 1993). When providing services to families, it seems important to work from a strengths perspective (Saleebey, 1996), that is, to identify and reinforce their strengths instead of giving what may be an exaggerated impression of the difficulties they face.

In Maggie's case, her environment provided much positive support for development. Maggie and her family possessed strengths that were specific to their own innate abilities and individual life experiences. For example, Maggie had no cognitive, physical–motor, or medical disabilities to complicate her progress. She gave no evidence of attention problems, despite her relatively infrequent switches of attention between objects and parents during her first 2 years. Finally, although she was quite spirited and occasionally headstrong, she willingly participated in classroom and one-on-one therapy sessions. Similarly, Maggie's parents possessed some helpful attributes that are not universally characteristic of parents of deaf children. Although they were not wealthy, both were bright and well educated, able to understand and make use of available information. Being a two-parent family allowed a division of efforts, gave more time for attention to their hearing as well as their deaf child, and provided the luxury of having one parent home with the children. Large portions of the population of hearing parents of deaf children around the world do not have these advantages.

However, Maggie's family had benefits that could and should be provided to other hearing families. For example, the immediate attention they received from an educator after Maggie's diagnosis was a great help. Signing lessons provided in their own home—and the invitation to friends and other family members to participate in them—was reported to be especially helpful. This gave Maggie's parents other adults with whom they could sign, and sign lessons became a social occasion instead of evidence of their difference and isolation. They had the added practical advantage of having no need to find babysitters and transportation to the lessons. Being in their own home, they were able to remember readily objects they used frequently and daily routines for which they needed to learn signs.

Maggie's parents also benefited from opportunities to meet and interact with older deaf children and adults. This happened in large part due to the presence of a deaf teacher in Maggie's school program. In addition, the (hearing) teacher of the sign classes they attended provided opportunities for hearing persons to meet with deaf signers. These were not occasions for study or for being "taught." Instead, they were social occasions during which they were able to see and appreciate deaf persons as individuals—not as a monolithic and somehow foreign group. (Of course, this was possible only because deaf adults in the area were willing to give of their time to allow hearing parents these experiences.) Other hearing parents could also benefit from the presence of deaf teachers in early intervention programs, provision of services in the homes of families with infants and toddlers, and signing classes that emphasize functional use of the language and take a social instead of a traditional classroom approach to instruction.

An important lesson that may be derived from the story of this family is that positive acceptance of a deaf child may not imply that parents cease trying to provide the child with skills to allow access to hearing as well as deaf cultures. In fact, one thing that Maggie's parents learned from their experiences with deaf persons was that some deaf people can use speech functionally and still be part of the deaf community. They saw great advantages to this, and, although both parents appeared to be willing to accept that Maggie might not be able to use speech well, they felt that it was important to give her opportunities to try.

Finally, this family reminds interventionists not to assume that parents reach agreement on ways to support their deaf child's development without some amount of conflict. Although it is undeniably positive to have two parents involved with a deaf child's education and development, this can in some ways complicate the task of providing services to the family. In Maggie's case, her mother and father put different emphases on English and, to some degree, on speech and even literacy. They were able to handle these differences in the beginning: Maggie's mother signed her way, and her father signed his way; her mother used voice, and her father often did not. However, when the issue became one of a cochlear implant, no easy compromise was possible. There was serious disagreement that required energy from both parents for its resolution, with their eventual compromise that Maggie herself could decide whether to actually use the implant device when she became older. Given the strength of the parents' disagreement on this issue, it was particularly beneficial that they located a cochlear implant team that did not take sides in the discussion. Maggie's parents were treated with respect, given all the information available, and encouraged to make their own decision without pressure. This may have been an unusual team, but the model it provides should be as valuable for education and other service providers as for medical teams.

It is important to emphasize that Maggie's experiences with Cued Speech and with the cochlear implant should not be used to predict the experience of other children. Data on the development of a first language by infants and toddlers exposed to Cued Speech are rare (LaSasso & Metzger, 1998), and it is too soon to draw conclusions about its potential in that context. (In addition, practice in the late 1990s would not support the plan attempted by Maggie's parents and the Cued Speech therapist in which she was exposed to two languages at once, albeit during different periods of the day.) Available data about the course of development of young congenially deaf children who receive early cochlear implantation are also still relatively rare. Reports show great variability in outcome, and much of this variability is unpredictable based on current knowledge (Fryauf-Bertschy, Tyler, Kelsay, Gantz, & Woodworth, 1997; Osberger, Robbins, Todd, & Riley, 1994). In short, Maggie's amazing progress in spoken language skills after implantation cannot be called typical. Her progress calls into question, however, suggestions in the cochlear implant literature that use of signing postimplant will interfere with development of auditory and speech skills (e.g., Clark, Cowan, & Dowell, 1997; Geers & Moog, 1994).

CONCLUSION

This case study provides a picture of a deaf child whose rate of social, cognitive, and linguistic development during the first several years of life is consistent with general expectations for hearing children and deaf children whose parents are deaf. The fact that her parents are hearing and had never signed before she was diagnosed as deaf is a reminder that it is quite possible for hearing parents to competently support the development of young deaf children. The experiences of Maggie's parents demonstrate that families bring many strengths to the raising of their children (deaf or hearing). Interventionists can best support families by identifying and reinforcing those strengths while providing information that they can use when they make decisions for their child.

REFERENCES

Clark, G., Cowan, R, & Dowell, R. (Eds.). (1997). *Cochlear implantation for infants and children—Advances.* San Diego, CA: Singular Publishing.

Cornett, O., & Daisey, M. (1992). *The Cued Speech resource book for parents of deaf children.* Raleigh, NC: National Cued Speech Corporation.

Fryauf-Bertschy, H., Tyler, R., Kelsay, D., Gantz, B., & Woodworth, G. (1997). Cochlear implant use by prelingually deafened children: The influences of age at implant and length of device use. *Journal of Speech, Language, and Hearing Research, 40,* 183–199.

Geers, A., & Moog, J. (1994). Spoken language results: Vocabulary, syntax, and communication. *Volta Review, 96,* 131–148.

Harris, M., & Mohay, H. (1997). Learning to look in the right place: A comparison of attentional behavior in deaf children with deaf and hearing mothers. *Journal of Deaf Studies and Deaf Education, 2,* 95–103.

Johnson, R., Liddell, S., & Erting, C. (1989). *Unlocking the curriculum: Principles for achieving access in deaf education.* Washington, DC: Gallaudet University.

LaSasso, C., & Metzger, M. (1998). An alternate route for preparing deaf children for bibi programs: The home language as L1 and cued speech for conveying traditionally-spoken languages. *Journal of Deaf Studies and Deaf Education, 3*(4), 265–289.

Mather, S. (1987). Eye gaze and communication in a Deaf classroom. *Sign Language Studies, 54,* 11–30.

Meadow-Orlans, K., & Steinberg, A. (1993). Effects of infant hearing loss and maternal support on mother–infant interactions at 18 months. *Journal of Applied Developmental Psychology, 14,* 407–426.

Moores, D., & Meadow-Orlans, K. (1990). *Educational and developmental aspects of deafness.* Washington, DC: Gallaudet University Press.

Osberger, M., Robbins, A., Todd, S., & Riley, A. (1994). Speech intelligibility of children with cochlear implants. *Volta Review, 96,* 169–180.

Prendergast, S., & McCollum, J. (1996). Let's talk: The effect of maternal hearing status on interactions with toddlers who are deaf. *American Annals of the Deaf, 141,* 11–18.

Saleebey, D. (1996). The strengths perspective in social work practice: Extensions and cautions. *Social Work, 4*(3), 296–305.

Schlesinger, H., & Meadow, K. (1972). *Sound and sign: Deafness and mental health.* Berkeley: University of California Press.

Spencer, P. (1993). The expressive communication of hearing mothers and deaf infants. *American Annals of the Deaf, 138,* 275–283.

Spencer, P., Bodner-Johnson, B., & Gutfreund, M. (1992). Interacting with infants with a hearing loss: What can we learn from mothers who are deaf? *Journal of Early Intervention, 16*(1), 64–78.

Waxman, R., & Spencer, P. (1997). What mothers do to support infant visual attention: Sensitivities to age and hearing status. *Journal of Deaf Studies and Deaf Education, 2*(2), 104–114.

Sensitivity in the Family–Professional Relationship: Parental Experiences in Families With Young Deaf and Hard of Hearing Children

Donna M. Mertens
Marilyn Sass-Lehrer
Kim Scott-Olson
Gallaudet University

Families with deaf and hard of hearing (D/HH) children face many challenges that often begin before the confirmation of a hearing loss. The purpose of this chapter is to explore the experiences of families during the D/HH child's early years of life, that is, before the age of 7. Specifically, data are reported concerning the parents' experiences around the time of suspicion and diagnosis of hearing loss, the concerns parents had during those early years, and the implications for the professionals who provide medical, audiological, social, and educational services for these families.

SUSPICION AND DIAGNOSIS OF HEARING LOSS

Parents frequently experience a lag of approximately 6 months or more from the time they suspect a hearing loss to when the hearing loss is confirmed by a professional (Elssman, Matkin & Sabo, 1987; Harrison & Roush, 1996; Meadow-Orlans, Mertens, Sass-Lehrer, & Scott-Olson, 1997). The waiting time from initial suspicion of hearing loss to diagnosis and beginning early intervention services increases as severity of hearing loss decreases (Elssman, et al., 1987; Harrison & Roush, 1996; Mace, Wallace, Whan, & Stelmachowicz, 1991). Findings such as these raise questions concerning the nature of the relationship between parents and professionals around the time of the diagnosis of a hearing loss.

SOCIOEMOTIONAL DEVELOPMENT

For most parents, the behaviors associated with a hearing loss are unknown and are sometimes interpreted as childhood stubbornness, lack of attentiveness, or slow development. This is especially true for infants and toddlers who are hard of hearing (Meadow-Orlans, Sass-Lehrer, Scott-Olson, & Mertens, 1998). Hearing parents of young children who are deaf frequently describe their children as aggressive, disobedient, and easily frustrated (Marschark, 1993). Research over the past several years has shown that the root of social and behavioral disturbances is not the hearing loss per se but is more likely explained by a complex array of child, family, and environmental variables and interactions (Calderon & Greenberg, 1997). For example, research indicates that children with sensory impairments often use inappropriate behaviors to serve pragmatic functions such as getting attention, obtaining a desired object, or avoiding an unpleasant situation (Orelove & Sobsey, 1991). Marschark (1993) pointed out that behaviors of children who are D/HH are remarkably similar to descriptions of hearing children who experience insecure attachment to their mothers. In fact, the birth of a deaf child in a hearing family temporarily disrupts the parent–child relationship, family roles, and parental expectations in some families (Calderon & Greenberg, 1997) resulting in decreased responsiveness to the child. Parents who experience a prolonged period of uncertainty regarding the diagnosis are often confused by their child's inconsistent or seemingly unresponsive behaviors and may misinterpret these behaviors as rejection or deliberate disobedience. Unable to sustain a mutually satisfying relationship, parents may lose confidence in their ability to parent and reduce the quantity and quality of positive interactions with their child.

LANGUAGE AND COMMUNICATION

These youngsters' hearing losses may not be discovered until the child demonstrates a speech or language delay (Meadow-Orlans et al., 1997). The indications of hearing loss are often ambiguous and only detected by careful observations of a child's development. For the child with little usable hearing, language must be accessible visibly either through speechreading, sign language, or cues. Young children who are deaf in hearing families are at risk for delays if there are no adult language models consistently available to them (Marschark, 1993). Without skills for effective communication, families are also unable to transmit an understanding of the family's culture and values essential to the development of positive self-identity and self-esteem (Henderson & Henderschott, 1992). The acquisition of language, whether signed or spoken, depends on the degree to which family members are responsive to their children's communication needs and to the extent that children are able to access and process the language visually or auditorily (Sass-Lehrer, 1999).

FAMILY–PROFESSIONAL RELATIONSHIPS

Professionals may unwittingly contribute to a delay in diagnosis by convincing parents that they are just overly worried or anxious parents. Nonetheless, parental frustration over the lack of a definitive explanation for their child's delay in language development or in seemingly inappropriate behavior creates anxiety and raises concerns that something is wrong. Level of stress appears to be related to the timeliness of identification of hearing loss (Meadow-Orlans, 1994; Quittner, 1991; Quittner, Glueckauf, & Jackson, 1990). Parents of children who are D/HH frequently wait months before a hearing evaluation is complete and the exact nature of the hearing loss is determined, thus leaving parents baffled by unanswered questions about their child's development and expectations for the future. Professionals are an important source of support for families during this time (Greenberg, 1983; Roush, 1994).

Early intervention designed to work with families and assist them in promoting the growth and development of their D/HH child has been the goal of family advocates and policymakers for many years. This approach, referred to by many different names including family-centered, family-focused, and family-directed services, calls for the development of partnerships with families in the planning and implementation of early intervention services. Although professionals agree that this approach is ideal, a survey by Roush, Harrison, and Palsha (1991) revealed that many fall short in their practice of providing family-centered services. A lack of sensitivity and knowledge on the part of the professional may present barriers to establishing effective relationships with families and providing appropriate information and services (Sass-Lehrer, Gerner de Garcia, & Rovins, 1997).

Families with children who are D/HH are extremely heterogeneous in their culture, language, economic resources, and family structure, as well as the individual differences in their children (Meadow-Orlans & Sass-Lehrer, 1995). Sensitivity and understanding of each family's unique perspective and the issues and concerns that are most important to them are essential for professionals providing effective and appropriate early intervention services. Researchers and practitioners recognize that the single best method for identifying family perspectives about what works and how best to address individual needs is to ask the families themselves (Mertens, 1998; Rossetti, 1996).

Areas of interest for the study arose from a review of previous research on parental experiences of parents of D/HH children and a quantitative national survey of such parents (Meadow-Orlans et al., 1997). The research questions themselves emerged from the inductive analysis of the qualitative data collected in this study and were refined through an iterative process as the qualitative data analysis proceeded. The emphasis found in all four questions on the family–professional relationship is influenced by an assumption associated with the emancipatory paradigm—that those with less power (generally parents) have an opportunity to speak to those with more power (generally professionals; Mertens, 1998). The four questions that frame the organization of the data reported here are

1. What characterized the nature of the relationship between parents and professionals at the time of early suspicion and diagnosis of hearing loss?
2. How do parents describe their concerns about their child's socioemotional development in terms of behavior problems and their interactions with professionals related to this area?
3. How do parents describe their concerns about their child's linguistic and communicative development and their interactions with professionals related to this area?
4. What advice do parents have for increasing professionals' sensitivity (including those who provide medical, audiological, educational, and other related services) in their interactions with each other?

METHODOLOGY

Meadow-Orlans et al. (1997) conducted a national survey of families with D/HH children about early intervention services and parental satisfaction with those services. Data were collected through questionnaires completed by 404 parents of children born in 1989 or 1990. The data reported in this chapter are based on the responses of 40 hearing parents who were selected from the 404 respondents in the national survey. There are two other components of the study that are still in process, and, therefore, are not reported here. Focus groups were conducted in four metropolitan areas with high concentrations of D/HH people. Additional interviews are being conducted with specific subgroups of parents who were not adequately represented in the first 40 phone interviews (such as deaf parents).

Participants

Forty hearing parents were selected at random from the parents who participated in the national survey, excluding only those residing in a city in which a focus group was conducted. Characteristics of the children whose parents participated in this study are summarized in Table 8.1. Of the 40 parents, 37 were mothers and 3 were fathers.

TABLE 8.1

**Characteristics of Deaf or Hard of Hearing Children
for Parents in Phone Interviews**

Child's Gender	
Girl	18 (45%)
Boy	22 (55%)
Age Diagnosis Confirmed (in months)	
Deaf	$M = 11.1$ (SD = 7.2)
Hard of hearing	$M = 26.6$ (SD = 20.9)
Overall	$M = 18.3$ (SD = 16.6)
Child's Hearing Status	
Deaf	22 (55%)
Hard of hearing	17 (43%)
D/HH	1 (2%)
Presence of Behavior Problems IEP	
No	34 (85%)
Yes	4 (10%)
No answer	2 (5%)
Presence of Additional Disabilities	
No	22 (55%)
Yes	16 (40%)
No answer	2 (5%)
Race/Ethnicity of Child	
White	31 (77%)
Black	3 (7%)
Hispanic	3 (7%)
Mixed race	3 (7%)

Instruments and Procedures

Telephone interviews were conducted using a semistructured questionnaire. The interviewer had the survey for each respondent and a list of issues to address, for example, diagnosis, concerns, services provided, and
so forth. The issues that stimulated the development of the research questions for this paper emerged through the interviewer's reference to the respondent's survey responses for each of the major issues in that study. For
example, the issue of the circumstances surrounding diagnosis of the
hearing loss surfaced by the following type of question

Interviewer:	I see here on the survey that you filled out that a parent suspected the loss initially?
Parent:	Right.
Interviewer:	And was that you?
Parent:	It was me and my ex-wife yeah. I adopted her, see I'm not her biological father. Yeah it was my wife and I, we knew something was wrong but we couldn't quite put a finger on it.
Interviewer:	uh hmm … and how did you know something was wrong? (Survey 85)

The parent then shared his concerns about the child's possible hearing
loss and told the story of how the diagnosis of deafness was delayed by 6
months from the time of their first suspicions.

The expression of concerns specifically related to developmental areas
of behavior and language also arose spontaneously from the parents in response to questions about general concerns after the hearing loss diagnosis was confirmed.

Each interview took about 30 to 60 minutes. The phone interviews were
tape recorded with the permission of the respondent. The tapes were transcribed and entered into a computerized data base using Ethnograph, a
qualitative data analysis software program. The analysis of the data proceeded by coding or categorizing parent responses based on themes that
emerged from the data. The coding of the interviews was a team process.
One team member coded the first interview and shared her coded transcript with another team member. After extensive discussion and revision
of the codes, a code book was developed for use in coding the second interview. Three members of the team reviewed the second coded transcript and made additional revisions to the coding of that transcript and the
code book. Team members then each took two interviews and coded
them independently. These were compared, and the process was repeated until agreement was reached as to identification and definition of
the important codes. After three iterations, the only differences in coding

were in the number of lines that were included for each coded segment (some team members were a bit more inclusive in the segments coded to provide more context; others tended to be less inclusive with an eye to brevity when reading the coded segments after analysis). The remainder of the transcripts were coded independently by team members and reviewed by one other team member after the codes were entered.

Analysis was accomplished by searching for terms related to the themes that emerged during the coding process using Ethnograph, which can find segments of text using one or more code words. Much more data were generated in this process than can be presented in this chapter, thus the results that are presented are illustrative rather than comprehensive. The decision about what to include was based on the notion of providing information that could enhance understanding of the conditions surrounding diagnosis, social, or language development.

RESULTS

The results are organized as answers to the research questions that are repeated here.

What characterized the nature of the relationship between parents and professionals at the time of early suspicion and diagnosis of hearing loss?

Parent comments revealed that one explanation for delay of diagnosis resulted from the dismissal by professionals of expressed concerns as emanating from overly worried parents. The following comment illustrates one parent's perceptions of her interactions with professionals when she first suspected a hearing loss:

> But I still felt a sense that he should have been responding to his name, and he wouldn't turn his head when somebody would call him. So I took him to the pediatrician, and he said, "No, there's nothing wrong with him, you're just a worried mom. This is your first child, and you know you're paranoid." So, I mean, it took 6 months to finally make the doctors do a test on him which I was not pleased that it took that long you know … to have them tell me it was just all in my head basically. (Survey 251)

The age of diagnosis for hard of hearing children is significantly later than for deaf children. The experiences of the child and the parents during that extended time can have severe consequences for both parties, as illustrated in the following comment:

And everybody said he could hear. And he really could because it was only a high frequency loss, you know. And apparently he got very good at lip reading in those developmental years because he responded and because I guess they said he could hear uh, he only could not hear 25% of the sounds. So I guess that's why it eluded us for years. But the damage was that he had uhm damaged his self-esteem so much because ... the kids would say, "How come he talks funny? How come he talks like a baby?" And he had that all the time, I guess. And so what happened is, he stopped talking. And there would be days at preschool where he would go through the whole day without saying a word to a single person. And uh, in preschool they were having problems with him, you know it was a combination, he didn't want to talk and his self-esteem was low. Uh, he was easily intimidated. And there was like, oh a long period of time where he would wet his pants every single day because he didn't want to ask the teacher when he wanted to go to the bathroom. So you know we had a lot of these problems along the way. And we never knew it was hearing related. (Survey 186)

Another parent of a late-diagnosed, hard of hearing child added a different dimension to our understanding of how diagnosis can be delayed because most parents do not want their child to have a hearing loss. She said

I just really wish that the doctors, you know, were more familiar, you know, even otolaryngologists in our area are the very people who looked me in the face and said, "It is not a hearing problem. Look I can look right at her and talk, ask her a question, and it's obvious she can hear me." I mean it's things like that, that it took me so long to figure out what it was, and of course, as a parent you know, you, I and my husband would much prefer, if that weren't it. You know. So it's easy to accept, to stay in denial, if you have the support of a doctor. (Survey 344)

This parent expressed the pain some parents feel when they learn that their child has a hearing loss and the inclination to deny this situation. Parents can take comfort in denial, especially when it is combined with the support of the authority figure represented in the doctor.

How do parents describe their concerns about their child's socioemotional development in terms of behavior problems and their interactions with professionals related to this area?

In some instances, parents realized that the behavior problems they observed were exacerbated by the late diagnosis of the hearing loss. For example

It's a preschool program for kids with disabilities and behavioral problems. And when my wife and I first got married, her ex had custody. And when we got her, there were some behavioral problems when we took custody of her and that's why we put her in there, and then after she'd been in that program for about 6 months is when we found the hearing loss. We think that probably had something to do with the behavior problems. (Survey 85)

One parent felt guilty for punishing her daughter for misbehaving before she found out that she had a hearing loss. She reported that her interactions with professionals assisted her in dealing with the behavior problems:

(deep breath) I just wanted to know how to deal with it really. Uhm, my biggest thing was I felt guilty because I had been I guess, punishing her for not listening or not responding, but she really didn't hear me so … (laughter), but that's what I didn't know then. Once we found out what was wrong, they kinda helped me deal with it rather than, uhm, I guess you know going through this disciplining her all the time, where you know punishing. And I can just remember punishing her for you know misbehaving; we found different ways of uhm of dealing with her behaviors, because we understood why she was doing it. So like I said not punishing her, but working with her. (Survey 111)

Additional disabilities, such as an attention deficit or autism, created additional tensions for some families. For example

We were more concerned with him being a person … he needed constant supervision. They lost him twice at the child development center because he just walked off, you know he just wandered off even though there was an aide out there watching. He was supposed to be transitioning into the regular classroom but the teacher couldn't deal with him, and she finally just gave up and said she couldn't deal with him, that he was too disruptive to the class, and that he would just get up and walk out of the classroom and stuff, and she couldn't keep an eye on him. (Survey 115)

Provision of services a long distance from home also added to challenges in the behavioral area. Another family added to this dimension as follows:

And it's hard because uhm, sometimes you know if my son gets in trouble or something they want me to drive 150 miles, 300 miles to come to get him. And that's so hard on you. And uhm here it is I'm barely making it, and I'm a struggling mother, and they want me to, I mean I know this is my kid and this is coming out wrong, but you gotta understand the background behind it. If you're poor and they want you to come get your kid you don't have the gas, your car barely runs, and I don't think that they see that. But there's nothing I can do because there's nothing up here for him so I can put him close to me. (Survey 53)

This illustrates the compounding of problems that result when services are offered a far distance from home and the family is poor. The family's ability to have an active role in controlling behavior problems is impeded further by limited access to services because of distance and economics. The next section addresses parental concerns about language and communication. For many children, the lack of a satisfactory means of communication goes hand in hand with poor social adjustment.

How do parents describe their concerns about their child's linguistic and communicative development and their interactions with professionals related to this area?

For the hearing parents in this study, concerns about communicating with their child were intense. One parent commented

Ahh boy. Well my first ... my first ... primary concern was how I was going to talk to him. How was I going to teach him and uh relate to him as I did with my hearing daughter. That was my biggest concern. He obviously could not hear what I had been saying for the last year, so that didn't work. So I ... I uhm, I was like ... what do I do? (Survey 37)

Barriers to communication resulted in some behavior problems that parents described as very frustrating for themselves and for their children. The barriers came in the form of a lack of knowledge of appropriate communication systems and inadequate access to services in order to learn to communicate effectively. For example, one parent comment illustrates the complex relationship between knowledge of and access to sign language classes and behavior problems:

Well, the sign language, I mean it was very little sign language and uh the lady who was to teach him sign language he was getting very little time with her at all. You know 20 minutes at the max every week, and that just wasn't enough. He had to have this every day, and he wasn't getting that. And you know we saw him regressing a lot. And his behavior wasn't getting any better you know, and we talked at length with them about it you know, and they just kinda shrugged it off, like it's normal, it's natural. Well it wasn't. Because we were having a harder time with him at home than anybody realized. It was just getting to the point where we couldn't handle it. Just a lot of frustration. (Survey 231)

Other parents reinforced the relationship between frustrations associated with inadequate communication skills and behavior problems. One family found a viable solution in the advice a psychologist gave them when their 4-year-old daughter lost all the rest of her hearing.

And then over one weekend, when she was almost 4, she lost all the rest of her hearing. I did take her … to some psychologist who works just with deaf families … because we were having so many behavior problems with her. And he said basically, "You have to just find a way for her to communicate. That's the big problem. Either we have to start signing with her or she has to, we've taken away everything, so we have to give her something back and that's why she's so frustrated." And uh so that was something we kind of pursued on our own, uhm during that sort of crisis period. (Survey 80)

Parents struggled with the decision as to which communication system was appropriate for their child and how they could facilitate their child's development in this area. One mother who is hard of hearing had this concern, "Finding out if he could wear hearing aids or how much of a loss he had … or if it was something that was going to affect the speech the rest of his life … just general things" (Survey 115).

Another mother's comments illustrate the difficulty surrounding the discussion of appropriate communication choices.

If you just stuck with sign, uhm my thinking was, he's locked in this deaf world. Uhm he has to fit in with both, try to fit in with both sides of the family. My brother has three young children that are his age. Hm I wanted him to be able to socialize and be able to communicate with these boys, cuz my family, my siblings and I were always close growin up … with our cousins. Uhm and on my husband's side, you know he has cousins and they didn't need to be made to sit there and look at him like he's stupid. And that was my feeling one time and I thought no. Uh I'm not going to send him away like some people always used to say years ago. And I had him, God trusted me, God didn't trust somebody who runs some school. Uhm … that means God thinks I know what I should do. I'll figure it out as we go. And I decided he would have to fit into both worlds. And I told him when he was real little once he had a hearing aid on. And he said, you know he would nod at me when he heard me when I would get him up and hold him close and be talking to him … I'd say, "We're gonna try to learn some sign language to come into your world and you're gonna cross over and you're gonna fit into our world because I'm not gonna let go," you know? "God gave you to me, uh, I'm hanging on tight. You're stuck, you're not getting away." And he just kinda ... you know ... when he was old enough to understand that at about a year and a half and two, he'd smile. And you know, you could tell in his eyes he understood. And I'd say, "You're gonna have to actually work to say words and talk to us, and we're gonna have to work to do some of the basic sign language." (Survey 37)

Parents who want to do what is best for their children need information from professionals who can both understand the family's needs as well as explain clearly the options and possible consequences of various choices.

What advice do parents have for increasing professionals sensitivity in their interactions with each other?

Parents who participated in the telephone interviews, like those who participated in the national survey (Meadow-Orlans et al., 1997), generally were quite satisfied with the services provided to them by professionals, especially teachers. The themes that emerged from the parents with regard to giving advice to professionals included the opportunity to make informed choices with adequate provision of information on which to base those choices, being treated with respect, and being meaningfully involved in the decision-making process.

The following exchange between the interviewer and one parent illustrates these themes:

Interviewer: Uhm, what kind of advice, if any, would you give to professionals on how to make parents feel more involved or more comfortable with what's going on with their child?

Parent: Hmmmm. Nobody ever asked me that before. I can tell you what I didn't like and then maybe you can extrapolate from there. I didn't like being petted on the head and given sort of pat, rote answers to problems and issues that I was dealing with. And I especially didn't like it—and nobody really did this to my face—but you got the impression that social workers and people in the business sort of refer to parents as in the third person as though I was sort of childlike like my child was. And if I had just been given credit for being a reasonably intelligent person who was interested in being involved and aggressive in helping my child, I would've appreciated that. I also would've appreciated as much facts, as many facts, as were available. Because a lot of times, when you have a child that is very ill or has an uncertain future, the medical profession is hesitant to just tell you what they're thinking. And so you end up worrying about things you don't even have to worry about because no one will say "I think this is happening, or I think that's happening." So those are the two things that probably made me most uncomfortable over the process. (Survey 121)

Other parents continued this theme in terms of the time of first suspicion and diagnosis of their child's hearing loss, for example:

I think ... when their child is first diagnosed, you feel like all the control has been ripped out of your hands. Everything is now in someone else's hands, and the most important thing seems to be to give some element of control or choice, maybe choice is a better word, some element of choice back to the parent and also to the children, so the parents feel like no one's treating them like a child. I would much rather have been given, just inundated with all this information of different methodologies, different, uh resources so that we could experiment and try different things so we could see how the children track. I mean one might do better with one method and one might do better with another, and allowing the families to have more information I think would make the families then more flexible, but everybody's educated in their field to such an extent that they feel like their methodology is the best. And it's kinda what we ran into ... is we were spoken to in a real condescending manner when we would suggest something different than what they were offering. It was like they didn't want to adapt anything or change any of their services or their methods to accommodate something a little different. (Survey 348)

Parents also deepened this notion of a need for feeling respect for their child as a person with feelings and for their feelings related to dealing emotionally with the new knowledge that their child is deaf or hard of hearing. One parent recommended the following:

First and foremost, they must remember ... these people are scared, these people don't know what's going on, don't know what to expect, talk to them like ordinary people, no matter what their income, religion, background, anything. Just sit down face to face and you let them, uhm, know everything. Quit just, you know, putting people off. That is very important. I mean because parents will try harder if things are explained to them. A lot of parents you know would, uh, they can accept it after awhile. (Survey 38)

Another parent provided advice related to the subject of honesty and appropriate recognition of limitations, so as not to give false hope. She said

> As far as the oto-ologist goes, you know when we first found out about his deafness, with the hearing aides you know they were forcin' us to have him to wear 'em. Forcin 'em on him which he hated 'em you know right off the bat, you know cuz they were new and something all new to him and frightening. And they were saying "well if he wears these, he's gonna be pickin' up speech left and right," and well with his type of hearing loss at that time, we didn't know was that you know it was impossible. So we were thinkin', well if he puts these on his speech is gonna be, he's just gonna be pickin' up words left and right, and as we found out that wasn't the case. And I think you know, we were really aggravated because they got our hopes up about that. You know be more honest about it. And let the parents know, that they may or they may not let you know, and as time goes on, but in (name of child)'s case you know it hasn't been that way. You know we got our hopes up that as soon as he put on his hearing aides that his words his speech you know he was just gonna be talkin'. And uh they kinda lead us to believe that at first you know. That uh you know he wears these, no problem, he's gonna be able to talk normal just like everybody else you know, and we found out that wasn't the case. And that was pretty disturbing, you know? (Survey 231)

Some of the parents' comments were directly related to interactions with school personnel and indicated a desire for a high level of meaningful parent involvement. For example

> Uhm, I guess probably provide more of a time to either observe or even to meet some of the teachers involved. We have her, uhm, like her oral interpreter we've met and we talk on a regular basis. But it wasn't until last week we had her IEP, and that was the first time we'd met her speech teacher at all. And so, you know, I guess, I mean maybe that's just uh some teachers are gonna be more willing to get the parents involved than others. But uhm, I enjoy the day, the reports and updates on how she's doing you know in school and how she's doing as compared to the hearing children in there. (Survey 101)

Other parents reinforced the need for meaningful parental involvement in the planning of their child's educational programs. Still others described conflicts between themselves and school personnel concerning the appropriate amount of speech therapy.

CONCLUSIONS AND IMPLICATIONS

The discovery of hearing loss often takes parents on a circuitous journey from suspicion to diagnosis. Although parents tend to be the first to suspect the condition, many do not obtain a firm diagnosis for several months (Harrison & Roush, 1996; Thompson & Thompson, 1991). Complicating the diagnosis of hearing loss are lack of information and misunderstandings within the professional community regarding the age at which hearing loss can be determined and services initiated to support the development of the child and work with the family. The results of this study reveal problems associated with delayed diagnosis and thus underscore the necessity for early identification of hearing loss through newborn hearing screening programs. Although a number of states are adopting legislation to implement systems of newborn hearing screening, the diagnosis of hearing loss is still too often delayed by professionals who dismiss parents' concerns resulting in severe consequences for both child and family members. Parents are often consciously or unconsciously a party to a delay in diagnosis because of their own hopes that the problem will just go away.

Support for families, especially during the time when hearing tests are conducted and diagnosis is confirmed, is also critical to the family's adjustment and their efforts to accommodate the needs of the child with a hearing loss (Calderon & Greenberg, 1997). Parents in this study indicate that support from professionals is especially important and appreciated but not always available. Medical and other early intervention professionals have a particularly powerful role to play, especially in view of the tendency by many hearing parents to want to deny the presence of a hearing loss in their child. Training of medical and other health care personnel to recognize the signs of hearing loss and the importance of immediate referral for evaluation and services is still warranted (Calderon & Greenberg, 1997).

Parents' descriptions of their children's behavior illustrated the many ways that hearing loss can be manifest in behavior problems. Especially if the diagnosis is late, parents reported punishing their child for not listening and not responding. The effects of hearing loss on the manifestation of behavior problems is exacerbated in children who have additional disabilities such as an attention deficit or autism. Frustration in communication is a major contributor to the problems parents report. Professionals should pay attention to disruptive behaviors as a possible indication of hearing loss and recognize the power of communication for reducing problems related to behavior (Orelove & Sobsey, 1991). Some children with additional disabilities need simplified signs, adapted signs, or augmentative communication and skilled professionals who can work with these children and coach their families to use effective tools for communication and strategies for promoting positive behaviors.

Families also need accurate information and access to resources to support their ability to make informed decisions about important issues such as which communication and language approach fits the needs of their child best and what educational programs and service options are available to them. Families whose children are D/HH report, however, that professionals sometimes cite the best interests of the family to excuse their own biases or provide only selective information about important issues. Professionals need to explore their own biases and beliefs that may interfere with their efforts to provide effective services to families (McAdoo, 1993).

The parents in this study welcomed the opportunity to provide advice to the professionals that serve families with D/HH children. Their advice included listen to parents, do not patronize, provide information regarding the full range of choices, involve parents in the decision making, and recognize that conflicts will arise in the parents' and the professionals' views. One parent's comments at the end of her phone interview summarizes the importance of this study as follows: "I hope that it helps somebody else. I really hope it helps some other parent some day—that would make me feel good. Yeah."

Additional research is needed to explore parents' experiences beyond that reported here. This study was based solely on data from self-report on a questionnaire and phone interview. A richer picture could be developed by adding additional dimensions derived from observation of family dynamics. In addition, families with different characteristics could be explored, such as identifying differential experiences for families in which the parents are deaf or members of racial or ethnic minority groups, or families in which the child has an additional disability or whose diagnosis occurred later than average. Another population of interest is families who have chosen to use cochlear implants for their communication enhancement. Such research could provide professionals with more complete information on the needs of diverse families of D/HH children.

ACKNOWLEDGMENTS

The authors wish to acknowledge Kathryn P. Meadow-Orlans for her work on this research and the Gallaudet University Research Institute for funding. We are grateful to the parents who by sharing their time, memories, and advice with us made this work possible.

REFERENCES

Calderon, R., & Greenberg, M. (1997). The effectiveness of early intervention for deaf children and children with hearing loss. In M. Guralnick (Ed.), *The effectiveness of early intervention* (pp. 455–482). Baltimore: Brookes.

Elssman, S., Matkin, N., & Sabo, M. (1987). Early identification of congenital sensorineural hearing impairment. *The Hearing Journal, 9,* 13–17.

Greenberg, M. T. (1983). Family stress and child competence. *American Annals of the Deaf, 128,* 407–417.

Harrison, M., & Roush, J. (1996). Age of suspicion, identification, and intervention for infants and young children with hearing loss: National study. *Ear and Hearing, 17*(1), 55–62.

Henderson, D., & Henderschott, A. (1992). ASL and the family system. *American Annals of the Deaf, 136,* 325–329.

McAdoo, H. P. (Ed.). (1993). Family ethnicity: A challenge for the future. In H. P. McAdoo (Ed.), *Family Ethnicity: Strength in Diversity* (pp. 332–334). Newbury Park, CA: Sage.

Mace, A. L., Wallace, K. L., Whan, M. Q., & Stelmachowicz, P. G. (1991). Relevant factors in the identification of hearing loss. *Ear and Hearing, 12,* 287–293.

Marschark, M. (1993). *Psychological development of deaf children.* New York: Oxford University Press.

Meadow-Orlans, K. P. (1994). Stress, support and deafness: Perceptions of infants' mothers and fathers. *Journal of Early Intervention, 18,* 91–102.

Meadow-Orlans, K. P., Mertens, D. M., Sass-Lehrer, M., & Scott-Olson, K. (1997). Support services for parents and their children who are deaf or hard of hearing: A national survey. *American Annals of the Deaf, 142*(4), 278–293.

Meadow-Orlans, K. P., & Sass-Lehrer, M. (1995). Support services for families who are deaf: Challenges for professionals. *Topics in Early Childhood Special Education, 15,* 314–334.

Meadow-Orlans, K. P., Sass-Lehrer, M., Scott-Olson, K., & Mertens, D. M. (1998). Children who are hard of hearing: Are they forgotten? *Perspectives in Education and Deafness, 16*(3), 6–8, 24.

Mertens, D. M. (1998). *Research methods in education and psychology: Integrating diversity with quantitative and qualitative approaches.* Thousand Oaks, CA: Sage.

Orelove, F., & Sobsey, D. (1991). Communication skills. In *Educating children with multiple disabilities: A transdisciplinary approach* (2nd ed., pp. 297–334). Baltimore: Brookes.

Quittner, A. L. (1991). Coping with a hearing-impaired child: A model of adjustment to chronic stress. In J. H. Johnson & S. B. Johnson (Eds.), *Advances in child health psychology* (pp. 206–223). Gainesville: University of Florida Press.

Quittner, A. L., Glueckauf, R. L., & Jackson, D. N. (1990). Chronic parenting stress: Moderating versus mediating effects of social support. *Journal of Personality and Social Psychology, 59,* 1266–1278.

Rossetti, L. (1996). *Communication Intervention: Birth to Three.* San Diego: Singular Publishing Group, Inc.

Roush, J. (1994). Strengthening family–professional relations. In J. Roush & N. Matkin (Eds.), *Infants and toddlers with hearing loss.* Baltimore: York Press, Inc.

Roush, J., Harrison, M., & Palsha, S. (1991). Family-centered early intervention: The perceptions of professionals. *American Annals of the Deaf, 136,* 360–366.

Sass-Lehrer, M. (1999). Techniques for infants and toddlers who are deaf or hard of hearing. In S. Raver (Ed.), *Strategies for infants and toddlers with special needs: A team approach* (2nd ed., pp. 259–297). New York: Prentice Hall.

Sass-Lehrer, M., Gerner de Garcia, B., & Rovins, M. (1997). *Creating a multicultural school climate for deaf children and their families.* Washington, DC: Gallaudet University.
Thompson, M., & Thompson, G. (1991). Early identification of hearing loss: Listen to parents. *Clinical Pediatrics, 30,* 77–80.

Language in Sight: Mothers' Strategies for Making Language Visually Accessible to Deaf Children

Heather Mohay
Queensland University of Technology

Despite changes in educational practices, advances in hearing aid technology, and even the development of cochlear implants, the majority of deaf children continue to experience delayed language acquisition, educational underachievement, and difficulties in parent–child communication. These characteristics cannot be attributed to an inherent lack of intelligence or lower academic potential on the part of deaf children, as was so frequently assumed in the past (see Paul, 1998), nor is it reasonable to ascribe them to a lack of commitment to the children's development on the part of parents or teachers (Ramsey, 1997). Explanations of these disappointing outcomes have also been frequently sought in psycholinguistic theories of language acquisition, however, these are spurious as they are based on evidence from the spoken language acquisition of hearing children. Comparisons of the interactions of hearing mother–hearing child dyads with those of hearing mother–deaf child dyads have invariably found anomalies in the interactions of hearing parents with their deaf children, and these were held responsible for the children's delayed language development and consequent impoverished educational achievements. This deficits model led to a belief that parents simply needed to boost their language input to deaf children to compensate for their impaired hearing (see Gregory, 1985). Unfortunately, this advice failed to substantially improve the children's language development.

Deafness per se cannot be held responsible for the children's suboptimal development as deaf children of deaf parents demonstrate few of the communication problems and developmental delays observed in deaf children of hearing parents (Ackerman & Woll, 1990; Bellugi & Klima, 1985; Bonvillian, Orlansky, & Novak, 1983; Volterra, 1983). It therefore seems logical to compare the experiences of deaf children of deaf parents to deaf children of hearing parents in order to identify factors that may prevent the adverse developmental outcomes that have plagued the lives of so many deaf children.

Unlike deaf parents, most hearing parents have had no experience with deafness when their child's hearing loss is identified. Hearing parents are therefore likely to experience more stress at the time of diagnosis followed by higher levels of anxiety associated with mastering new and complex information about their child, navigating an often less than supportive bureaucratic system (Deslandes, 1994; Freeman, Carbin, & Boese, 1981), and making decisions about educational placements that are likely to have long-term ramifications for their child. Subsequent requirements to comply with educational programs and keep appointments with a myriad of specialists maintain the pressure on parents. Meadow-Orlans and Steinberg (1993) suggested that these stressors are likely to have an adverse effect on the quality of parent–child communication and hence on language acquisition. Support and counseling programs have been shown to beneficially affect parent–child interaction (MacTurk, Meadow-Orlans, Koester, & Spencer, 1993; Meadow-Orlans & Steinberg, 1993) but have not fully remedied the children's lag in language development.

Another explanation suggests that the early exposure to sign language experienced by deaf children of deaf parents greatly enhances their language development and permits relaxed and easy parent–child communication (Harris & Mohay, 1997; Schlesinger & Meadow, 1972). This firm foundation in language then supports the acquisition of literacy during the school years. Such arguments led many educators to believe that the introduction of manual communication would resolve the language learning problems of their deaf pupils. Undoubtedly, it has led to improvements in parent–child and teacher–child communication (Greenberg, 1980; Greenberg, Calderon, & Kusche, 1984; Meadow, Greenberg, Erting, & Carmichael, 1981). Nevertheless, language acquisition continues to be problematic and the language development of most deaf children remains significantly delayed (Johnson, Liddell, & Erting, 1989). Spencer (1993a, 1993b) argued that this delay may be attributed to three factors: (a) the late identification of hearing impairment and consequent delay in the introduction of sign language, (b) hearing parents need to learn to communicate manually, and (c) the consequent lack of hearing parents' proficiency in sign during children's early years when language acquisition should be at its height.

A report by Meadow-Orlans (1997) put yet another perspective on the communication difficulties experienced by hearing parents and their deaf children. Her finding that not only these dyads but also deaf parents with hearing children experience less than optimal communication suggests that the mismatch in hearing status of communicative partners has a profound effect on the quality of their interactions. It might be expected that deaf parents would have no difficulty communicating with their hearing children as these children are able to use the visual channel to receive communication in the same way that deaf children do. It does, however, appear that when there is a mismatch in the primary communication channel used by the participants in an interaction, there is increased risk of breakdown in the flow of communication and in the enjoyment of the interaction.

Until the 1990s, the effect of the channel of communication used for language acquisition was largely ignored, although this has major implications for the establishment and maintenance of communication. Hearing children rely on audition for language input and are therefore free to observe objects and events in their environment while listening to what their parents are saying about these objects. Thus, language can overlay activities, and the link between the two is readily made. For deaf children the situation is different. Even when they have some residual hearing, they must rely heavily on vision to make sense of their environment and the communication that takes place within it. Hence, for deaf children to acquire language, it must be visible to them on the lips, hands, or both, of their communicative partners. As vision is a directional sense, deaf children must regularly shift attention between their activities and their interlocutor in order to obtain both linguistic information and the information from the environment that gives the language its meaning. Consequently, input from the two sources is received sequentially rather than simultaneously, making the link between language and meaning less obvious than it is for hearing children who can listen to language and at the same time visually attend to their environment (Wood, 1982). Accordingly, deaf children must not only be able to see language, but the links between language and meaning must be made explicit. The mere introduction of manual communication is insufficient to meet the language learning need of deaf children if other aspects of the linguistic environment are not also modified to address their reliance on visual information.

Harris and her colleagues (Harris, 1992; Harris, Clibbins, Chasin, & Tibbitts, 1989) drew an important distinction between language input and language uptake and pointed out that although deaf parents typically communicate with their children less frequently than hearing parents, most of their language is both visually accessible and meaningful to their children. Several recent studies identified the strategies used intuitively by deaf parents (but rarely by hearing parents) to ensure that their communication meets the language learning needs of their deaf children. A number of comprehensive reviews of these modifications have been presented (Koester, 1994: Mohay, 1992b, 1993; Swisher, 1992; Waxman & Spencer, 1997). Although some of the adaptations can be seen to parallel "motherese" in spoken language, many are specifically geared to ensure the visibility and intelligibility of communication to deaf children. In marked contrast, even when they elect to use manual communication, hearing parents continue to operate primarily in an auditory-verbal language environment and either fail to adjust their language to make it visible to their deaf child or attempt to achieve this in clumsy and intrusive ways, such as turning the child's face toward them. Data presented by both Jamieson (1994) and Waxman and Spencer (1997) suggest that hearing mothers have a very limited repertoire of visually oriented attention strategies that they can call on when communicating with their deaf child and tend to rely on object related strategies that have only limited success.

It seems logical that hearing parents of deaf children should be encouraged to use the communication strategies used so successfully by deaf parents. My colleagues and I therefore set ourselves the dual tasks of documenting these strategies and constructing an intervention package that could be used to teach hearing parents to integrate the strategies into everyday interactions with their deaf children. (It should be emphasized that the package we aimed to develop was not intended to stand alone but rather to complement existing early intervention programs. Furthermore, it was not intended to teach the use of sign language, and for the most part the techniques included were to be equally applicable whether oral or manual forms of communication were used.)

IDENTIFYING COMMUNICATION STRATEGIES

From both the literature and our own observations, we identified a number of behaviors frequently used by deaf parents to enhance communication with their children. These strategies fell into in six broad categories.

Nonverbal Communication

Facial expression, body language, and gesture are important components of communication that are used more frequently by deaf parents than by hearing parents. De Villiers, Bibeau, Ramos, and Gatty (1993), for example, reported that deaf mothers used more gestures than hearing mothers, and Meadow-Orlans, MacTurk, Prezioso, Erting, and Day (1987) as well as Swisher (1992) found deaf mothers made greater use of facial expression to convey feelings and more frequently smiled to provide positive feedback to their children. Nonverbal feedback can therefore provide incentives for children to look at their parents thus encouraging the development of looking patterns that support communication in the visual modality.

Gaining and Directing Attention

This area includes strategies for gaining the child's attention (i.e., directing the child's attention to the speaker or signer) as well as strategies for maintaining language input while directing the child's attention to interesting objects and events in the environment (i.e., directing attention away from the speaker or signer).

Breaking the Child's Line of Gaze and Gaining Attention Using Movements of the Hands and Body.   Deaf children must learn to look at their communicative partner in order to obtain information. To establish this pattern of behavior, it is essential to create situations where looking at parents can be reinforced. One way that deaf parents achieve this is by attracting the child's attention, by waving a hand or an object in front of the child or moving their head from side to side in the child's visual field, and providing rewarding feedback (e.g., smiling, clapping, or signing) when the child looks at them (Kyle, Woll, & Ackerman, 1989). These tactics are used most often with very young children and appear to have the function of training the children's attention.

Using Touch to Gain the Child's Attention.   Touch is another strategy used by deaf parents to gain (and train) their children's attention (Mohay, 1988). Typically deaf parents are much more persistent in, and insistent on, gaining their child's attention by this means than hearing parents (Harris & Mohay, 1997). Deaf parents also use touch to provide positive feedback to their children and to reassure them of their presence when they are outside the child's visual field (Meadow-Orlans & Steinberg, 1993).

Using Pointing to Direct Attention While Still Permitting Language Input.   Hearing parents characteristically direct a child's attention to an object or event by pointing to it and then talking about it (Swisher & Christie, 1989). Although this works well with hearing children, it is not effective with deaf children as both the object of interest and the speaker (signer) can seldom be seen at the same time, hence the message is lost. Kyle, Ackerman, and Woll (1987) reported that deaf parents frequently use the tactic of gaining the child's attention, telling them what they are going to see, then directing their attention to the relevant object or event. Alternatively, they may direct the child's attention to the object, then displace their signs to a location between the child and the object so that both sign(s) and object can be seen at the same time. As pointing is such a commonly used means of directing children's attention to objects of interest, it is essential that parents learn to use it in a manner that does not detract from their deaf children's language learning opportunities.

Making Language Salient

Language must stand out from all the other environmental stimuli that impinge on children so that they come to recognize that it carries information that is relevant to them and should be attended to.

Reducing the Frequency of Communication so That it Is Recognized as Worthy of Attention. To perceive language, deaf children must divide their attention between their activities and the person with whom they are communicating. This constant switching of attention can be extremely disruptive and interfere with what they are doing. It is therefore important to ensure that communication is meaningful, relevant, and worth looking for, or the child will not voluntarily direct visual attention to the communicative partner (an all too common feature of the interaction of deaf children with their hearing parents). Several studies have shown that deaf parents typically communicate with their children less often than do hearing parents and frequently wait for the child to look at them before communicating (Gregory & Barlow, 1989; Mills & Coerts, 1990; Mohay, Luttrell, & Milton, 1992; Spencer, Bodner-Johnson, & Gutfreund, 1992; Woll & Kyle, 1989). As a result, their communication is visually accessible, occurs when the child is likely to be receptive, and only minimally disrupts the child's activities. Children accordingly come to recognize the importance of communication and to accept parental demands for attention.

Reducing the Need for Divided Attention

The necessity to switch attention regularly between activities and interlocutor not only disrupts activities but also places added cognitive demands on deaf children as they attempt to make sense of the language input (Wood, Wood, Griffith, & Howarth, 1986). Unlike hearing children who can simultaneously listen to language and observe the relevant referent, deaf children must retain information in memory as they shift visual attention from one source of information to the other.

Using Short Utterances. Deaf parents typically use short utterances when communicating with their children, thus minimizing both disruptions to the children's activities and the demands on their memory (Harris, 1992; Spencer et al., 1992; Woll & Kyle, 1989).

Positioning Self and Objects in the Child's Visual Field.   If speakers or signers place themselves so that both they and the objects of interest to the child are within the child's visual field, the necessity for the child to make significant shifts of attention in order to see both language and referent is markedly reduced. Hearing parents often attempt to achieve this by sitting opposite the child, thus creating a rather artificial and stilted interactional arrangement. Deaf parents tend to sit to the side or even behind the child and curve their body around so that the child can both see them and feel them thus achieving the same results in a more subtle way and at the same time providing the child with reassurance about their presence even when no communication is taking place (Jamieson, 1994; Mohay, Milton, & Hindmarsh, 1996).

Moving Hands or Face, or Both, Into the Child's Visual Field.   The previous strategies referred to the fairly passive positioning of interactants during an activity. Another group of strategies used by deaf parents involves actively shifting position or displacing signs during the course of an interaction. A number of researchers (e.g., Kyle et al., 1987; Maestas y Moores, 1980; Schlesinger & Meadow, 1972) reported that deaf parents frequently displace signs from their own signing space into the child's or make signs onto the child's body. Both strategies ensure that the signs are salient and are perceived with minimal need for the child to redirect attention from other objects of interest.

Linking Language and Meaning

Because deaf children receive language input and information from the environment sequentially, the links between language and referent are less obvious than they are for hearing children who can receive information from the two sources simultaneously. Deaf parents employ a number of mechanisms to clarify the meaning of their language.

Bracketing.   Kyle and his colleagues (Ackerman, Kyle, Woll, & Ezra, 1990; Kyle, 1990; Kyle et al., 1989; Woll & Kyle, 1989) appear to have been the first to use this term to describe a convention that deaf parents use to clarify the meaning of their language when communicating with young children. It refers to the practice in which a sign or a phrase is placed at both the beginning and end of an utterance. This phenomenon is frequently observed, for example, when parents name an object, then point to the object, and then present the sign for the object again and also when they ask a question by presenting a question sign followed by pointing and a repetition of the question sign.

Modifying Signs.   Three related strategies that also help explicate the meaning of utterances are (a) displacing signs so that they are made on or close to an object thus highlighting the link between the two (Spencer & Lederberg, 1997), (b) repeating signs, and (c) enlarging and prolonging signs. These strategies all increase the probability of the child attending to the sign and promote understanding by giving the child longer to assimilate the messages (Erting, Prezioso, & Hynes, 1990).

Extending Language and Stimulating Imagination

Storytelling and book reading facilitate language development and expand children's imagination (Marschark, 1997; Ninio & Bruner, 1978). Regrettably, they are activities that hearing parents have great difficulty engaging in with their deaf children (Lartz, 1993; Mogford, Gregory, & Keay, 1979; Mohay, Schlesinger, & Kelly, 1984). Deaf parents, on the other hand, readily tell stories or read to their children. In the process, they incorporate many of the strategies outlined earlier into these more complex forms of language usage. Although few new communication strategies are involved, the ways in which they are used and combined led us to believe that these two specific language learning situations merited particular attention.

Having identified the methods used by deaf parents to support communication with their children, a number of issues still had to be addressed. The first related to identifying the most effective way of teaching these techniques to hearing parents of deaf children. The second concerned the ability of hearing parents, who were so attuned to auditory language input, to learn these communication strategies and to integrate them successfully into their day to day interactions. Finally, it was necessary to ask whether teaching parents these skills had any beneficial effects on the children's language development. I address each of these issues in turn.

TEACHING THE COMMUNICATION STRATEGIES TO HEARING PARENTS

The involvement of deaf people in the project was essential for several reasons. Most importantly, they were the ones who used the communication techniques that we wished to convey to hearing parents spontaneously and most effectively in their daily interactions. They also represented positive role models for the deaf children involved in the program. Finally, their presence gave the hearing parents the opportunity to interact with deaf adults, which we hoped this would allay their fears about deafness and provide an entree into the deaf community if they chose to use it.

We conducted three studies to develop and evaluate techniques for teaching the communication strategies. A review of the literature revealed several reports of short-term intervention programs designed to improve interactions between mothers and their young children who had various types of disabilities (Clark & Seifer, 1983; Field, 1979; Kogan, 1980). All the studies claimed significant success in modifying maternal behavior and improving mother–infant interactions. Although none of the studies had included deaf children, our first attempt at teaching the communication strategies was based on the methods they used. This involved a 6 week intervention in which mothers were prompted to use the communication strategies used by deaf mothers while they engaged in a half hour play session with their deaf child. The sessions were videotaped and the prompts were given by an observer who watched the interactions through a one-way mirror and gave directions to the mother via a "bug in the ear." Following each session, the mother was given video feedback on her performance, and she heard the soundtrack of the videotape played back through Helos equipment, which simulated what the child would have heard during the play session.

The parents reported that they found the program helpful and believed that they had learned some new communication strategies. The videotape evidence, however, suggested that although they were able to use a range of strategies when prompted, these were not incorporated into their spontaneous communication. Observations made 6 weeks after the final session showed that the parents used few of the techniques and that there was little improvement in the quality of communication with their deaf children in terms of accessibility, success rate, or responsiveness to the child (Mohay, Turner, & Milton, 1992). On reflection, we realized that we were not asking for the minor modifications to communication that the other studies required of the mothers; rather, we were asking for a total revision of their communication style. Our prompting program was overloading the mothers with information and giving them insufficient time to practice any of the new communication strategies. In addition, they were given no written information to refer to or to share with other members of the family after the training sessions (Mohay, 1992a; Mohay, Milton, & Hindmarsh, 1997).

As a result of this experience, we developed a set of instructional materials built around the grouping of communication strategies outlined earlier in this chapter. The set comprises 10 modules, each dealing with specific methods for making language accessible and meaningful to deaf children, along with a module on storytelling and one on book reading that require the combination of many of the strategies. Included in each module is an information sheet, a set of video clips showing deaf parents using the targeted communication strategies, and some suggested activities for practicing their use. The modules are all self-contained and can be used independently. However, they are sequenced so that later ones tend to build on and reinforce skills that have already been learned. Parents are encouraged to practice each technique until they feel comfortable using it before progressing to the next module.

In our second study, we used a modeling program in which a deaf assistant visited the home of a hearing family who had a deaf child for approximately one hour a week, taking with her the materials for a particular module and demonstrating the communication techniques included (Mohay, Milton, & Hindmarsh, 1996; Mohay, Milton, Hindmarsh, & Ganley, 1998). This program took, on average, 8 to 12 months to complete.

In the last study, we pilot tested a combination of the previous two methods, using prompting to reinforce strategies demonstrated in the modeling program. We had hoped to run the two programs in parallel, with the modeling program operating in the children's homes and the prompting program in the early intervention center that the children attended. However, constraints on the mothers' time due to their work commitments and funding cuts to the early intervention program made this impossible. The two teaching methods were therefore implemented in the family homes on alternate weeks (Mohay, Milton, & Hindmarsh, 1997). This program took approximately 12 months to complete and was more cumbersome to administer than the modeling program alone.

EVALUATION OF PARENTAL RESPONSE

In all three studies, parents reported that they learned new communication techniques. However, as stated earlier, when the intensive prompting program was used these techniques were not incorporated into the mothers' spontaneous communication, and little improvement was seen in their interactions with their deaf children.

The parents were enthusiastic about the modeling program. They all reported initially feeling apprehensive about having to communicate with a deaf adult but unanimously agreed that this experience had been extremely beneficial. Analysis of videotapes made during the program showed that the hearing mothers effectively incorporated many of the strategies used by deaf parents into their spontaneous communication. As a result, a higher proportion of their communication became visually accessible to the children, and their interactions were more successful and less frustrating (Mohay et al., 1998).

Similar results were found for the combined modeling and prompting program, with little improvement in outcome from the addition of the prompting component. This may have been because the circumstances for the implementation of the program were not ideal. The program became somewhat disjointed with a deaf person visiting the family home one week for the modeling program and a hearing person the next to provide the prompting program. Had it been possible to geographically separate the two programs, so that they were seen to reinforce each other, the combination may have been more successful.

CHILDREN'S LANGUAGE DEVELOPMENT

Because Australia has a very small and widely dispersed population (approximately 18 million people spread across an area roughly the same as that of the United States), and because childhood deafness occurs relatively infrequently (about once in every thousand births), it was difficult to recruit sufficiently large numbers of children to participate in the studies. Study populations were therefore small and heterogeneous and control groups poorly matched or nonexistent. (The first study had four study children and four comparison children, the second had four study children, and the third had six study children.) Consequently, it is difficult to ascertain with any accuracy the impact of the programs on the children's language development. In all three studies, there was some evidence that the children's language acquisition accelerated during the families' participation in the program, however, a much larger long-term study is required to confirm these impressions.

CONCLUSIONS

For the reasons outlined previously, it was not possible to conduct a rigorous evaluation of the intervention materials and teaching methods or to assess their impact when used in conjunction with different early intervention programs. Much larger scale and better controlled studies are required to provide this information. However, we believe that our program is based on sound scientific research and theory and that the results of our pilot studies show promising results. We anticipate that the program will have benefits for hearing parents and their deaf children irrespective of the mode of communication they choose to use as it incorporates a wide range of strategies that can be expected to enhance parent–child communication.

We focused our efforts specifically on improving the management of joint attention, which has been recognized as crucial for language learning (Bruner, 1983; Tomasello & Farrar, 1986) but fraught with problems for deaf children of hearing parents (Wood, 1982). To achieve this, we aimed to supplement the meager range of visually oriented attention strategies utilized by most hearing parents of deaf children (Jamieson, 1994; Waxman & Spencer, 1997) by introducing an array of strategies used successfully by deaf parents to ensure that language is both visually accessible and intelligible. In this way, more of the language used by hearing parents should become accessible to their deaf children, increasing opportunities for language acquisition. Furthermore, as parents become increasingly sensitive to their child's need for visually accessible language input and able to employ a wider range of strategies for making language accessible, it is expected that communication with their children will become more successful, responsive and rewarding.

In view of Meadow-Orlans and Steinberg's (1993) suggestion that increased parental stress adversely affects parent–child interaction and interferes with language learning opportunities, our program also contains elements that we anticipate will reduce anxiety and thus enhance parent child interactions. These center around the role of the deaf assistants who are indeed the linchpin of the program. Not only do they demonstrate the use of the interactional strategies, they also provide a positive image of deaf people and give hearing parents the opportunity to become acquainted with a deaf adult (something that most of them have not previously experienced) thus reducing their fears and ignorance about deafness. The associated stress reduction is expected to enable the parents to interact in a more relaxed and appropriate fashion with their deaf children. The deaf assistants also act as positive role models for the deaf children, supporting the development of positive self-esteem and providing additional opportunities for language input that further aids language development.

Our pilot studies suggest that the modeling program is likely to be the most cost effective of the three tested. Prompting is likely to have some benefits when used to reinforce communication strategies but probably would be better incorporated into a center based early intervention program or used sparingly within the home when parents are having difficulty using a particular communication strategy. Whatever teaching techniques are used, it is vitally important that the strategies included in the program are reinforced by *all* advisers working with the child and family if maximum benefits are to accrue.

ACKNOWLEDGMENTS

Numerous people contributed to this research and the research that led up to it. Leonie Milton, who is profoundly deaf, has been the mainstay of the research over many years. She visited the families, coordinated the deaf assistants, coded videotapes, and did many of the administrative jobs that enabled the project to run smoothly. Bronwen Dean, Donna Smith, Allana Dwyer, and Alison Shanley were the deaf assistants who worked with the families, and Robyn Luttrell, Karen Turner, Gabrielle Hindmarsh, Kay Ganley, Colleen Buckley, and Felicity Long acted as hearing assistants at various stages of the project. The families who participated in the studies need to be particularly thanked for their generosity in inviting us into their homes and being willing to give up their time to enable us to develop and refine a program that had no proven benefit for their children but that we hope will benefit deaf children in the future.

The research presented in this paper was supported by grants from the Australian Research Council, the Queensland State Education Department, the Charles and Sylvia Viertel Foundation, and the Victorian School for Deaf Children Research Foundation.

REFERENCES

Ackerman, J., Kyle, J., Woll, B., & Ezra, M. (1990). Lexical acquisition in sign and speech: Evidence from a longitudinal study of infants in deaf families. In C. Lucas (Ed.), *Sign language research: Theoretical issues* (pp. 337–345). Washington, DC: Gallaudet University Press.

Ackerman, J., & Woll, B. (1990). Deaf and hearing children learning to sign and speak: from birth to three years. In J. Kyle (Ed.), *Deafness and sign language into the 1990s* (pp. 54–61). Bristol, England: Deaf Studies Trust.

Bellugi, U., & Klima, E. (1985). The acquisition of three morphological systems in American Sign Language. In F. Powell, T. Finitzo-Hieber, S. Friel-Patti & D. Henderson (Eds.), *Education of the hearing impaired child.* San Diego: College Hill.

Bonvillian, J. D., Orlansky, M. D., & Novak, L. L. (1983). Developmental milestones: Sign Language acquisition and motor development. *Child Development, 54,* 1435–1445.

Bruner, J. (1983). *Child's talk: Learning to use language.* Oxford, England: Oxford University Press.

Clark G. N., & Seifer R. (1983). Facilitating mother–infant communication: A treatment model for high-risk and developmentally delayed infants. *Infant Mental Health Journal, 4,* 67–82.

Deslandes, S. (1994). *Factors which influence early management decisions of hearing parents of hearing impaired children.* Unpublished master's thesis, Flinders University, Adelaide, South Australia.

De Villiers, J., Bibeau, L., Ramos, E., & Gatty, J. (1993). Gestural communication in oral deaf mother–child pairs: Language with a helping hand. *Applied Psycholinguistics, 14,* 319–347.

Erting, C., Prezioso, C., & Hynes, M. (1990). The interactional context of deaf mother infant interaction. In V. Volterra & C. Erting (Eds.), *From gesture to language in hearing and deaf children* (pp. 97–106). Heidelberg, Germany: Springer-Verlag.

Field, T. M. (1979). Interaction patterns of pre-term and term infants. In T. M. Field, A. M. Sostek, S. Goldberg, & H. H. Shuman (Eds.), *Infants born at risk: behaviour and development* (pp. 333–356). New York: SP Medical and Scientific Books.

Freeman, R. D., Carbin, C. F., & Boese, R. J. (1981). *Can't your child hear?* Baltimore: University Park Press.

Gregory, S., & Barlow, S. (1989). Interactions between deaf babies and their deaf and hearing mothers. In B. Woll (Ed.), *Language development and sign language* (pp. 23–35). Bristol, England: International Sign Linguistics Association.

Greenberg, M. T. (1980). Social interaction between deaf preschoolers and their mothers: The effects of communication method and communicative competence. *Developmental Psychology, 16,* 465–474.

Greenberg, M. T., Calderon, R., & Kusche, C. (1984). Early intervention using simultaneous communication with deaf infants: The effect on communication development. *Child Development, 55,* 607–616.

Gregory, S. (1985). Advising families of young deaf children: Implications and assumptions. In J. Harris (Ed.), *Clinical psychology in action: Linking research and practice* (pp. 50–70). London: Croom Helm.

Harris, M. (1992). *Language experience and early language development: From input to uptake.* Hillsdale, NJ: Lawrence Erlbaum Associates.

Harris, M., Clibbens, J., Chasin, J., & Tibbitts, R. (1989). The social context of early sign language development. *First Language, 9,* 81–97.

Harris, M., & Mohay, H. (1997). Learning how to see signs: A comparison of attentional behaviour in eighteen month old deaf children with deaf and hearing mothers. *Journal of Deaf Studies and Deaf Education, 2,* 95–103.

Jamieson, J. (1994). Teaching as transaction: Vygotskian perspectives on deafness and mother–child interaction. *Exceptional Children, 60,* 434–449.

Johnson, R., Liddell, S., & Erting, C. (1989). *Unlocking the curriculum: Principles for achieving access in deaf education* (Working paper 89–3). Washington, DC: Gallaudet University.

Koester, L. S. (1994). Early interactions and the socioemotional development of deaf infants. *Early Development and Parenting, 3,* 51–60.

Kogan, K. (1980). Interaction systems between preschool handicapped or developmentally delayed children and their parents. In T. Field, S. Goldberg, D. Stern, & A. M. Sostek (Eds.), *High risk infants and children: Adult and peer interactions* (pp. 227–246). New York: Academic Press.

Kyle, J. (1990). *BSL development.* Final report. Centre for Deaf Studies. Bristol University.

Kyle, J., Ackerman , J., & Woll B. (1987). Early mother–infant interactions: Language and pre-language in deaf families. In P. Griffiths, A. Mills, & J. Local (Eds.), *Proceedings of the Child Language Seminar,* University of York, England.

Kyle, J., Woll, B., & Ackerman, J. (1989). *Gesture to sign and speech: Final report to ESRC.* Bristol, England: Bristol University, Centre for Deaf Studies.

Lartz, M. N. (1993). A description of mothers' questions to their young deaf children during story book reading. *American Annals of the Deaf, 138,* 322–330.

MacTurk, R. H., Meadow-Orlans, K. P., Koester, L. S., & Spencer, P. E. (1993). Social support, motivation, language and interaction: A longitudinal study of mothers and deaf infants. *American Annals of the Deaf, 138,* 19–25.

Maestas y Moores, J. (1980). Early linguistic environment: Interactions of deaf parents with their infants. *Sign Language Studies, 26,* 1–13.

Marschark, M. (1997). *Raising and educating a deaf child.* New York: Oxford University Press.

Meadow, K. P., Greenberg, M. T., Erting, C., & Carmichael, H. (1981). Interactions of deaf mothers and deaf preschool children: Comparisons with three groups of deaf and hearing dyads. *American Annals of the Deaf, 126,* 454–468.

Meadow-Orlans, K. P. (1997). Effects of mother and infant hearing status on interactions at twelve and eighteen months. *Journal of Deaf Studies and Deaf Education, 2,* 26–36.

Meadow-Orlans, K. P., MacTurk, R. H., Prezioso, C. T., Erting, C. J., & Day, P. S. (1987). *Interactions of deaf and hearing mothers with three and six month old infants.* Paper presented at the biennial meeting of the Society for Research in Child Development, Baltimore, MD.

Meadow-Orlans, K. P., & Steinberg, A. G. (1993). Effects of infant hearing loss and maternal support on mother infant interactions at 18 months. *Journal of Applied Developmental Psychology, 14,* 407–426.

Mills, A., & Coerts, J. (1990). Functions and forms of bilingual input: Children learning sign language as one of their first languages. In S. Prillewitz & T. Vollhaber (Eds.), *Current trends in European Sign Language research* (pp. 151–162). Hamburg, Germany: Signum Press.

Mogford, K., Gregory, S., Keay, S. (1979). Picture book reading with mother: A comparison between hearing impaired and hearing children at 18 and 20 months. *Journal of the British Association of Teachers of the Deaf, 2,* 43–45.

Mohay, H. (1988, August). *The effects of hearing status on the methods of attention getting used by mothers and infants.* Paper presented at the 24th International Congress of Psychology, Sydney, Australia.

Mohay, H. (1992a). Incorporating our knowledge of deaf mother/child interaction into early intervention programs for deaf children of hearing parents. In *Early diagnosis and options for deaf/hearing impaired students* (pp. 7–17). Proceedings of the conference of the Australian Educators of Deaf Students.

Mohay, H. (1992b). What do deaf mothers do that's different? In *Early diagnosis and options for deaf/hearing impaired students* (pp. 1–6). Proceedings of the conference of the Australian Educators of Deaf Students.

Mohay, H. (1993). Joint attention between deaf mothers and deaf children. In R. E. Asher (Ed.), *The Encyclopedia of Language and Linguistics* (pp. 3914–3915). Oxford, England: Pergamon.

Mohay, H., Luttrell, R., & Milton, L. (1992). How much, how often and in what form should linguistic input be given to deaf infants. In G. Lawrence (Ed.), *Pathways for the future* (pp. 121–131). Proceedings of the Australian and New Zealand Conference for Educators of the Deaf, Brisbane, Australia: The Australian Association of Teachers of the Deaf.

Mohay, H., Milton, L., & Hindmarsh, G. (1996, August). *A word in your eye: Making language accessible to deaf children.* Paper presented at the 26th International Congress of Psychology, Montreal, Canada.

Mohay, H., Milton, L., & Hindmarsh, G. (1997). *Learning from deaf parents how to make language visible to young deaf children* (pp. 227–232). Proceedings of the Twentieth Conference of the Australian and New Zealand Association of Educators of the Deaf, Adelaide, South Australia.

Mohay, H., Milton, L., Hindmarsh, G., & Ganley, K. (1998). Deaf mothers as language models for hearing families with deaf children. In A. Weisel (Ed.), *Issues unresolved: New perspectives on language and deafness* (pp. 76–87). Washington, DC: Gallaudet University Press.

Mohay, H., Schlesinger, H., & Kelly, P. (1984, August). *Looking at picture books with hearing and hearing impaired children.* Paper presented at the Australian Child Development Conference, Perth, Australia.

Mohay, H., Turner, K., & Milton, L. (1992, July). *An intervention program for hearing mothers of deaf children.* Paper presented at the National Human Development Conference, Brisbane, Australia.

Ninio, A., & Bruner, J. (1978). The achievement and antecedents of labeling. *Journal of Child Language, 5,* 1–15.

Paul, P. V. (1998). *Literacy and deafness.* Needham Heights, MA: Allyn & Bacon.

Ramsey, C. L. (1997). *Deaf children in public schools.* Washington, DC: Gallaudet University Press.

Schlesinger, H., & Meadow, K. (1972). *Sound and sign: Childhood deafness and mental health.* Berkeley: University of California Press.

Spencer, P. E. (1993a). Communication behaviours of infants with hearing loss and their hearing mothers. *Journal of Speech and Hearing Research, 36,* 311–321.

Spencer, P. E. (1993b). The expressive communication of hearing mothers and deaf infants. *American Annals of the Deaf, 138,* 275–283.

Spencer, P. E., Bodner-Johnson, B. A., & Gutfreund, M. K. (1992). Interacting with infants with a hearing loss: What can we learn from mothers who are deaf? *Journal of Early Intervention, 16,* 64–78.

Spencer, P. E., & Lederberg, A. R. (1997). Different modes, different models: Communication and language of young deaf children and their mothers. In L. B. Adamson & M. A. Romski (Eds.), *Research on communication and language disorders: Contributions to theories of language development* (pp. 203–230). Baltimore: Brookes.

Swisher, M. V. (1992). The role of parents in developing visual turn taking in their young deaf children. *American Annals of the Deaf, 137,* 92–100.

Swisher, M. V., & Christie, K. (1989). Communication using a sign code for English: Interaction between deaf children and their mothers. In B. Woll (Ed.), *Language development and sign language* (pp. 36–44). (Occasional monograph No. 1) International Sign Linguistics Association. Bristol, England: Centre for Deaf Studies.

Tomasello, M., & Farrar, M. J. (1986). Joint attention and early language. *Child Development, 57,* 1454–1463.

Volterra, V. (1983). Gestures, signs and words at 2 years. In J. Kyle & B. Woll (Eds.), *Language in sign: An international perspective on sign language* (pp. 109–115). London: Croom Helm.

Waxman, R., & Spencer, P. (1997). What mothers do to support infant visual attention: Sensitivities to age and hearing status. *Journal of Deaf Studies and Deaf Education, 2,* 104–114.

Woll, B., & Kyle, J. (1989). Communication and language development in children of deaf parents. In S. von Tetzchner, L. S. Siegel, & L. Smith (Eds.), *The social and cognitive aspects of normal and atypical language development* (pp. 129–144). Heidelberg, Germany: Springer-Verlag.

Wood, D. (1982). The linguistic experiences of the prelingually hearing impaired child. *Journal of the British Association of Teachers of the Deaf, 4,* 86–93.

Wood, D., Wood, H., Griffith, A., & Howarth, I. (1986). *Teaching and talking with deaf children.* Chichester, England: Wiley.

Challenges to Parents and Professionals in Promoting Socioemotional Development in Deaf Children

Rosemary Calderon
University of Washington
Mark T. Greenberg
Pennsylvania State University

There is no doubt that the diagnosis of a profound hearing loss in the child of hearing parents elicits within the parents a complex array of emotions including sorrow, confusion, guilt, anger, and a strong desire to do the right thing to help their child (Meadow, 1980; Roush, 1994). The diagnosis of hearing loss brings the initiation of ongoing contact with professionals who will play a significant role with the child and family over the next several years. These professional contacts will likely include medical doctors, audiologists, early interventionists, special education teachers, speech therapists, counselors, interpreters, and so forth. Additional contacts with other parents of children with hearing loss and paraprofessionals are also likely to occur either in person or via the internet, which is becoming an increasingly used resource of which parents are availing themselves. The child's need for specialized educational and professional resources will likely be a lifelong process for the child and family (Marschark, 1997).

Given the emotional upheaval and information overload parents often experience, it is no wonder that many parents feel confused about the numerous complex issues surrounding hearing loss (Meadow-Orlans & Sass-Lehrer, 1995). Parents question their ability to evaluate and to determine the best plan of action to help their child develop necessary life skills and realize their academic potential. For many parents, the support, guidance, and advice of a professional can subdue much of their initial anxiety. For both parents and professionals, actualizing the potential in deaf children is challenging and complex. For deaf children with hearing parents, the most profound effect that hearing loss has is on communication development and the subsequent effect on the child's academic and socioemotional development. This impact cannot be overstated (Marschark, 1993a, 1993b; Meadow, 1980). This chapter explores the challenges to parents and professionals and discusses the strategies parents and professionals can utilize with deaf children to promote positive socioemotional development across childhood. For the purposes of this chapter, we focus on hearing parents of children with severe to profound hearing loss as it is this group of families that has the greatest challenge in raising their child and interfaces most frequently with professionals. There are two main factors that we believe greatly impact the development of socioemotional competence in deaf children. First is the important influence that family and community ecologies have on children (e.g., educational settings, day care, church, neighborhoods, and other professional and community resources). Second is the importance of parents' and professionals' own understanding of critical socioemotional skills that they can model and directly teach to the deaf children in their care.

The need to address these challenges as a cooperative venture between parents and professionals has grown dramatically since the 1970s as most deaf children are likely to reside with their hearing families (Meadow-Orlans & Sass-Lehrer, 1995; Moores, Cerney, & Garcia, 1990). Previously, the majority of deaf children were sent to centralized residential state schools where they essentially lived apart from their families for the majority of their school years. Raising deaf children was left to the professionals with little input or contact from the child's family. The deaf school often became the child's family and professionals became the decision makers for the deaf child's well-being.

The education of deaf children has changed dramatically since the 1960s with better and earlier intervention for parents and families and more options for nonresidential school programs (Moores, Cerney, & Garcia, 1990; Roush & Matkin, 1994). Thus, the process of parents and professionals working together is a relatively new concept and practice. Although it may seem logical to think that family characteristics and needs would be considered as critical factors in the development of children with hearing loss, surprisingly, family resources and needs are seldom considered in the planning and provision of services. The absence of a central role for families exists despite a number of studies that indicate parent attitudes, social support, expectations, and problem solving skills are related to the academic and social development of deaf children in early and middle childhood (Bodner-Johnson, 1986; Calderon & Greenberg, 1993; Calderon, Greenberg, & Kusche, 1991; Watson, Henggeler, & Whelan, 1990).

This gap between the identified need to build greater family–school involvement and current practice is demonstrated by the following three indicators: First, there are few family or parent service programs relevant to school-age deaf children; Second, historically, schools have been remiss in involving families in the education process during the middle childhood years (ages 6 to 14) and rarely continue necessary services that were provided for families during early intervention (e.g., advanced sign language classes, exposure to deaf adults, preventive parenting classes); Third, it is rare for families to receive a systematic assessment of their qualities or characteristics in order to determine the appropriate services for each individual family (Greenberg & Calderon, 1984). Thus, neither a developmental perspective nor a school–family inclusion model typically are involved in the provision of intervention services to the deaf child and his or her family across childhood and adolescence.

In summary, increasing numbers of children are now educated in neighborhood schools and remain at home rather than reside in state residential schools. These changes in educational policy dramatically altered the ways in which hearing families want, can, and need to involve themselves with their deaf children, their schooling, and professionals. Given the rapid shift in responsibility for raising and educating deaf children, feelings of isolation, uncertainty, frustration, and disappointment (in parents, professionals, and children) may result if there is a lack of preparation, knowledge, and cooperation in assuming these roles.

As Brofenbrenner (1979) and others (Weissberg, Caplan, & Sivo, 1989) suggested, person-centered models of development must be integrated with ecological models that examine how development is affected by systems-level factors. These variables include the nature of each ecological setting in which the child interacts (e.g., family, school, neighborhood, church, peer group), the linkages among those systems (e.g., school–family communication), the indirect influences of others on the family and school, and cultural values.

WHY FOCUS ON SOCIOEMOTIONAL DEVELOPMENT?

Establishing healthy socioemotional development is a critical foundation for life success. Furthermore, competencies that are generally accepted as defining healthy socioemotional development are also applicable to helping individuals realize their academic and vocational potential (Feuerstein, 1980; Goleman, 1995). In short, we believe that regarding the whole child involves viewing personal growth and understanding as critical educational goals.

Greenberg and Kusche (1993) include the following characteristics as central to socioemotional competence:

1. Good receptive and expressive communication skills.
2. The capacity to think independently.
3. The capacity for self-direction and self-control.
4. Understanding the feelings, motivations, and needs of self and others.
5. Flexibly adapting to the needs of a particular situation.
6. The ability to tolerate frustration.
7. The capacity to tolerate the frequent ambivalence in feelings, cognitions, and internal structures and thus acknowledge inner conflicts, needs, and desires.
8. The ability to rely on and be relied on by others.
9. Understanding and appreciating an individual's own culture and values and those of others (especially subcultures within a multicultural society such as the United States).
10. Using skilled behaviors to maintain healthy relations with others and to achieve socially approved goals.

Although this is not an exhaustive list of skills to delineate socioemotional competence, it does profile several necessary characteristics for successful development. These skills are achieved over time and each possesses its own developmental trajectory dependent on an individual's growth from infancy to adulthood (Weissberg & Greenberg, 1998). In other words, mastery of these skills for any person is a lifelong process, and each person develops these skills to a greater or lesser degree depending on their own temperament and personality, family values, educational background, peer relationships, societal and cultural norms, and so forth.

Unfortunately, as a group, deaf children and adolescents demonstrate reduced mastery in many of these areas of competence and thus are at risk for a number of adverse outcomes (Emerton, Hurwitz, & Bishop, 1979; Meadow, Greenberg, Erting, & Carmichael, 1981). These include low academic achievement, underemployment, as well as higher rates of social maladaptions (violence, drug and alcohol problems) and psychological distress and disorder (Greenberg & Kusche, 1989; Marschark, 1993b). However, not all deaf children develop adjustment problems, and the impact of deafness is influenced by several factors, including the quality of the family environment, parental adaptation to deafness, family coping, the nature of school and community resources, as well as the child's own characteristics and transactions with his or her ecology.

It is the joint responsibility of parents and professionals (i.e., teachers and counselors) to assist deaf children to successfully master these socioemotional competencies. Parents and professionals are put in the position of being role models and advocates for deaf children. This is not an easy task and requires much caring, thoughtfulness, training, and concerted effort and collaboration between parents and professionals across the child's development. There are two critical issues that heighten the challenge to parents and professionals in promoting socioemotional competence in deaf children, these being developing effective and positive communication with the child and building social networks for the child.

Developing Effective and Positive Communication

Meaningful, elaborated, engaged, and smooth communication is critical for the transmission and education of socioemotional competence (see Marschark, chap. 16, this volume). Children from families with poor communication are likely to show one or more of the following patterns when under stress: an absence of communication about important issues or feelings, withdrawal behaviors, or aggressive or impulsive actions that are often modeled after frequent physical punishment by their parents (Greenberg, Kusche, & Speltz, 1991). Poor communication in the family and ecology contributes to the development of fewer and less flexible coping resources, an impoverished sense of self-worth, less trust in the ability to control an individual's life, deficits in the ability to understand the social world, and serious behavioral problems.

Deaf children's access to and development of meaningful, elaborated, engaged, and smooth communication often is severely limited (Marschark, 1997). For many (if not most) adults living and working with deaf children, sign language is a second language acquired later in life and is never as natural as their native spoken language. Therefore, in addition to the deaf child's communication difficulties, many hearing individuals (parents, teachers, therapists, vocational counselors, etc.) have a great fear of being misunderstood or not understood at all. This (often unconscious) fear, as well as less than optimal communication skills, often leads individuals to talk down to or reduce the linguistic and cognitive complexity of communications to deaf children. For example, a word/sign such as *good* might be substituted for *proud* although the latter would teach a new and critical concept. In addition, some important concepts and feeling words that are commonly used with hearing children do not have signs in the existing contrived sign systems, and often the hearing adults (teachers, parents) do not know the ASL equivalent of the concept. Because of this, certain concepts are either not introduced, must be fingerspelled, or are imprecisely represented by another sign that does not adequately express the concept.

This combination of fear of misunderstanding or being misunderstood and communication deficiencies in adult role models results in an insidious form of linguistic overprotection. Moreover, there is an obvious circularity in this process; a lack of linguistic exposure results in deaf children having more limited vocabularies. Due to their more limited comprehension, speakers or signers offer them less complex and less mature communications. As a result, deaf children often appear immature because they are typically exposed to simplified as well as limited communications. For this as well as many other reasons, it is critical that deaf children be exposed to fluent communicators during their early development. To do so requires extensive and extended training for teachers in use of alternative communication modes in addition to spoken language. Further, it is critical that parents as well as children receive regular exposure to deaf adults along with ongoing family support and education programs (Calderon & Greenberg, 1997).

Building Social Networks for Children

Healthy socialization with both adults and peers results in children becoming increasingly capable of demonstrating more mature forms of self-control and of using higher-order cognitive processes. Intimate attachment to parents and peers as well as a feeling of belonging to a social network are important in healthy identity development. A social network might include a variety of individuals such as relatively close friends, members of the extended family, coworkers or classmates, neighbors, casual acquaintances, and members of organizations or groups in which an individual actively participates. This less intimate social support can be a powerful influence on mental health and coping ability. Both intimate attachments and an individual's social group can be invaluable resources for coping with stress by providing a variety of functions including emotional support, information, advice, feelings of solidarity, and actual physical or financial assistance. Although the capacity for forming intimate attachments and social networks outside the immediate family is incipient during the preschool years, it is continually undergoing reorganization (differentiation and integration) throughout childhood and adolescence.

As a whole, deaf children in hearing families tend to experience a significant degree of isolation within both their immediate and extended families and their communities. Previously, deaf children and adolescent's networks developed through attendance at a residential school, as well as through special summer camp experiences and participation in athletic, activity-based, and fraternal networks involving other deaf peers and adults. As enrollment at residential schools dramatically declines, deaf children are at greater risk (especially in rural areas) as they may not have access to social networks where they feel they belong and that can help to normalize the experience of being "an outsider in a hearing world" (Higgins, 1980, p. 22).

As more deaf children are educated in mainstream settings and thus have fewer early and adolescent experiences with deaf adults, the nature and function of the deaf child's social network may be of particular importance for the following reasons. First, a social network provides a sense of connection or feeling of belonging to some type of community. For a deaf person, it could be either the deaf world or the hearing world or both. However, given that most deaf children grow up as a minority with few or no role models to help them establish their identity, the feeling of belonging is both quite important and in some cases difficult for the individual to establish (Reagan, 1990). Second, a social network opens up new channels of information for the individual and thus provides the individual with more coping options, for example, different alternative solutions to problems. Individuals who are isolated or have deficient social networks are likely to be less able to deal adequately with stress for the variety of reasons mentioned previously.

LAYING THE FOUNDATION IN EARLY INTERVENTION: PARENT–PROFESSIONAL COLLABORATION

Perhaps the most challenging time for hearing parents and involved professionals is the diagnostic and early intervention period, which is characterized by parents as the most emotionally stressful time (Calderon & Greenberg, 1997; Meadow-Orlans, 1987; Roush, 1994). The emotional loss felt by parents of not having a "normal" child is complicated by the urgent demand by professionals of parents to make a decision about early intervention options. Given parents' lack of knowledge about hearing loss, they often feel inadequate to make such decisions. These decisions are often presented as imposing a life-long, intractable impact on their child. Parents search for information from other parents, professionals, and via advanced technology (e.g., the internet). This often leads to information overload, opposing positions, strong emotions, and feelings of mass confusion and being overwhelmed rather than the assurance and clarity that parents are hoping to find.

Professionals, on the other hand, feel pressed to begin intervention as soon as possible knowing that much precious time has already been lost, and the longer the child goes without intervention, the more pronounced the deficits will be in language, communication, and preacademic skills. Additionally, and unfortunately, professionals in the field of deafness continue to lack consensus on how best to intervene early with deaf children (Roush, 1994), especially in the areas of communication and education approaches. It is also of concern that amplification technology (e.g., digital hearing aids, cochlear implants, FM systems) is increasingly available to younger and younger deaf children (e.g., cochlear implant approval for 18-month-olds in the United States [Nucleus 24, 1998] and as young as 8 months in Germany [S. Norton, personal communication, July, 1998] and is developing faster than outcome research investigating the benefits is accomplished. This imbalance of rapid technological advances and lagging outcome research may create high levels of false hopes and become a major distraction from helping families deal more directly with the adjustment of having a deaf child.

Thus, from the beginning, professionals and parents may have different priorities and approaches in understanding and working with the child's hearing loss. These differing priorities between parents and professionals, lack of professional consensus, and advanced but unproven technology only underscore the challenge in bringing parents and professionals together to work as a team and staying focused on the overall development of the child. If parents are to feel competent in raising their deaf child and understand the big picture, significant importance must be given by early interventionists and other professionals to facilitating and supporting the parents' ability to step back, reflect on their feelings, and make a strategic plan with specific short and long-term goals and objectives for their child and themselves as a family. From our years of work with deaf children and their families, it is clear that each child and family is unique, and no one approach or intervention program is appropriate for every family. Families need a setting where professionals can (a) be empathic to their emotional response, (b) provide unbias information, (c) initiate implementation of varying options available for intervention with their deaf child, and most importantly, (d) support parents in developing and using the necessary skills to evaluate and determine whether the strategies they are now using are of benefit to reaching their defined goals and objectives.

The main goals of professional support should be to validate the parents' feelings and, if necessary, help to sort and identify those feelings, empower the parents in their decision making and evaluative roles, elevate their feelings of competency, forge a true partnership between parents and professionals, and begin the process of early intervention. In this way, whatever options a family chooses are continuously monitored, evaluated, determined as effective or ineffective by both parents and professionals, and alternate approaches can be implemented. Within this framework, professionals can model, encourage, and promote effective problem solving skills and reflective thinking in parents. This allows parents to come to their own conclusion on what works for their child with a better understanding of what else may need to be added or changed to further their child's attainment of the identified goals over time.

One such program that promotes parents' partnership with professionals and a continuous evaluative process in a family oriented intervention plan is the Diagnostic Early Intervention Program (DEIP; Moeller & Condon, 1994; Moeller, Coufal, & Hixson, 1990). This program was developed at the Boys Town National Research Hospital. Families are enrolled in DEIP immediately following the identification of hearing loss. DEIP is designed to support families in their understanding and exploration of intervention needs and options over several months. This allows parents to have some breathing room and support following the diagnosis while still providing a broad array of interventions to the child within a multidisciplinary team.

Specific objectives of the DEIP are as follows:

1. To support the parent and family in understanding and coping with a child's hearing impairment.
2. To guide the family in the stimulation of their child's language, auditory, and speech development while helping them understand and cope with the impact of hearing impairment.
3. To assist the family in developing an objective information base to support decision-making and goal selection processes.
4. To gain a comprehensive understanding of the family's and child's needs through diagnostic teaching and discovery and transdisciplinary evaluation.
5. To provide a mechanism within the school district for longitudinal monitoring of the decision-making process and its efficacy. (Moeller & Condon, 1994, p. 165)

The main objectives of the DEIP program are to avoid the various pitfalls incumbent in more traditional early intervention methods that tend to stress deficit-focused models, make predictions about the long-term outcome of the child, move too quickly into a task-related problem solving mode, and give the impression that experts have the answers and parents know little of how to help their child. DEIP recognizes what each family brings to the situation and builds on the parents' and child's strengths.

At the end of their participation in DEIP, families settle on the approach that best works for them and their child. Families are then transitioned as smoothly as possible into an intervention program that can continue to build on the foundation laid by DEIP with the hope they will continue to expect, accept, and encourage parents to be full partners in the intervention process. Outcome results of the DEIP program indicate that parent satisfaction and comfort level with follow-up program choice and communication modality increased dramatically following participation in DEIP. Prior to the use of DEIP, 50% of families studied reported making changes in program choice or communication modality in the early elementary grades, whereas only 4.5% made such changes after participating in DEIP (Moeller & Condon, 1994). Unfortunately, programs like DEIP are not the norm, but should universal screening of hearing loss in newborns become a reality (National Institutes of Health, 1993) and diagnosis made within the first weeks of life, programs like DEIP will hopefully become the standard practice following early diagnosis.

The DEIP approach is not to discount the significant role more traditional early intervention programs play in the lives of deaf children and their families. It is clear that the majority of families report strong positive regard for their interventionist (Roush & Matkin, 1994). The main point that distinguishes DEIP from more traditional early intervention programs is the emphasis on parents developing feelings of competence, good decision making, and developing equal partnership with professionals in understanding what is best for their child.

All early intervention programs, to some degree, take on the enormous challenge of helping the deaf child catch up in the area of language and communication development, appreciating the implications such development has for later academic and socioemotional success. Despite acknowledging this association, traditional early intervention programs generally overlook encouraging parents to learn and use affective vocabulary with their young deaf children. As a result, deaf children have been shown to demonstrate significant delays and deficits in recognizing and correctly labeling affective internal states in themselves and others (Kusche 1984; Kusche, Garfield, & Greenberg, 1983; Odom, Blanton, & Laukhuf, 1973).

At graduation from a typical 0 to 3 early intervention program, which children usually enter at around 20 months of age (Calderon, Bargones, & Sidman, 1998b; Strong, Clark, Johnson, Watkins, Barringer, & Walden, 1994), it is rare that deaf children have caught up to their age appropriate language and communication skills. Does this mean that early intervention has failed? Likely not if the intervention program also focused on the parents' understanding of hearing loss, devised a clear plan of action with the family for continued progress with the child after early intervention is discontinued, and empowered the parents to know that they are and will be the main learning models for their deaf children. A study by Calderon, Bargones, and Sidman (1998a) demonstrates the impact of parent involvement during early intervention on their deaf children's later preschool and early elementary school communication skills, academic development, and socioemotional adjustment. Their results showed that higher levels of maternal involvement in early intervention predict better prereading scores, fewer behavior problems, and continued maternal involvement in the child's later school programs. These findings demonstrate that getting and keeping parents involved, motivated, and aware of meeting their child's needs can have a positive and lasting impact on the child's academic and socioemotional development.

Transitioning through the diagnostic and early intervention phase is an important milestone for most families. The completion of this phase sets the tone and foundation with parents with regard to future choices they will make for their deaf child (Calderon, Bargones, & Sidman, 1998b).

However, parents will continue to experience emotional upheaval and be faced with making more significant decisions for their child but with increasingly less support and guidance from professionals. Appreciating this transitional leap, it is important to promote independent, evaluative thinking, and parent–professional partnerships.

Transitioning to Formal Schooling

The shift from receiving family-centered, home-based services to enrolling the child in school can be quite unsettling for many families and children (Harris, 1982). This transition is often difficult because of the child's young age, limited options for educational programs, and the discontinuation of a family specific advocate. Although most early interventionists facilitate the enrollment of the child into a school placement, they do not tend to stay involved beyond enrollment. Families often experience the loss of their family support person as quite significant (Thompson, 1994). Educational institutions rarely have the financial or personnel resources to provide parents with a similar support person as their early interventionist and, in general, do not offer services or resources for families except for the occasional sign language class (Greenberg & Calderon, 1987).

In addition to losing the support offered by early intervention programs, parents are often faced with few options for educational programs within their own immediate community. This is especially true for families living in rural communities but not uncommon for urban families. Deaf children often need to commute 2 to 4 hours a day to attend their school program. The distance makes it very difficult for the parent to engage in the child's program. By parents' report, more often than not, school officials are not very encouraging and do not expect parents to be involved in their children's educational process. This is unfortunate because preliminary research suggests that parent involvement can have important, long lasting benefits for the child. Similar to hearing children, deaf children with parents who are involved in the child's early formal education program show higher levels of academic success and socioemotional functioning as measured by early reading assessments and teacher and parent ratings of externalizing (acting out) symptomotology (Calderon, Bargones, & Sidman, 1998a).

Thus, during the school years, while parents continue to play crucial roles in their children's lives, teachers and other adult role models begin to exert an important influence on children's development. Teachers provide children with alternative role models and demonstrate ways of using cognitive and affective processes for handling frustration, emotional turmoil, and interpersonal conflict. Teachers can have a major influence on children's emotional development and social competence. As children make their way from family-based to school-based services, they gain new opportunities for communication and language development, peer interactions, and structured support to help them develop more effective communication and social networks. At this juncture, parents routinely need to find resources on their own to increase their communication skills and arrange for appropriate supplementary services for their child (e.g., speech and language therapy, audiology services, recreational activities, etc.). Parents should be encouraged to be assertive and persistent in advocating for services from the various systems with which their child is involved.

THE CHALLENGE TO SCHOOL PERSONNEL: ADMINISTRATORS, EDUCATORS, AND COUNSELORS

Although the general intent of education is to prepare young people to reach their highest potential and to transmit the norms and values of society, we believe that current outcomes necessitate a reexamination of current practices in deaf education. Within the traditional focus of most educational efforts with deaf children there appears to be a lack of clarity concerning both the goals of education and the procedures needed to achieve them in the classroom.

Most instructional time in the classroom (as well as preparatory teacher-training experiences) is spent on academic subjects, speech, and communication skills. Yet rehabilitation counselors and mental health professionals recount that many of the vocational difficulties of deaf adults that lead to unemployment, underemployment, and lack of advancement are social and interactional, stemming from poor self-concept, lack of appropriate assertiveness, and poor social comprehension. Teacher-training programs in deaf education often do not require sufficient coursework in cognitive and personality and social development; as a result, most graduates do not have state-of-the-art information or knowledge of specific instructional techniques to teach socioemotional competency skills. Moreover, inservice training in school programs is frequently inadequate for teaching new skills. We found that the implementation of Public Law No. 94-142 (United States Code, 1975) resulted in the development of many smaller, geographically dispersed programs. These programs have few teachers and often no administrator, curriculum specialist, or even psychologist who works solely with students with hearing loss and possesses the necessary skill and knowledge to provide appropriate training (Committee on the Education of the Deaf, 1988).

In summary, systemic problems exist in the field of deaf education, including limited parent education after the preschool years and poor teacher training in the areas of emotional development and social cognition. Many teachers and schools are not well equipped to prevent or remediate socioemotional difficulties and their consequences. There is a clear need to develop preventive and remedial school-based interventions to ensure the healthy development of deaf children.

The PATHS Curriculum: A Developmental, School-Based Model for Teaching Socioemotional Competency Skills

Recognizing the systemic problems in current approaches to educating deaf children, Greenberg and his colleagues developed and evaluated the implementation of a school-based curriculum, Promoting Alternative Thinking Strategies (PATHS), designed to improve the social competence and reduce the behavioral difficulties of deaf children (Kusche & Greenberg, 1993). The PATHS curriculum is a comprehensive approach for teaching self- and interpersonal understanding. The goals of the PATHS curriculum are to teach children how to develop and maintain self-control, increase their awareness of and ability to communicate about feelings, and to assist them in conflict resolution through improving their problem-solving skills. Another focus of the curriculum is teaching concepts and words useful in logical reasoning and problem solving (e.g., if then, why because, and or, accident on purpose, before after, etc.). Because deaf school-age children make up a heterogeneous population, PATHS was designed for use with a variety of developmental levels (late preschool to grade 6).

Lessons are taught by teachers (after extensive training on use of the curriculum) on a regular basis throughout the elementary years, and there are extensive methods of generalization to help build and solidify these skills outside the classroom context. The PATHS curriculum model encourages the transformation of the classroom from a didactic model to one of dialogue and social interchange. PATHS was conceptualized as both a specific set of lesson procedures and a global model for structured education. Although PATHS focuses on the development of social-thinking skills, the problem-solving paradigm and other component processes can be effectively harnessed for academic subjects (e.g., reading, mathematics, and social studies). For example, the children can apply the problem-solving process when feeling frustrated or confused in mathematics, or to issues regarding story conceptualization in reading, and so forth.

Results from the initial investigations of the PATHS curriculum with deaf children indicate significant improvements in social problem-solving skills, affective awareness, emotional adjustment, frustration tolerance, and the children's behavior (Greenberg & Kusche, 1993). Since its inception, the PATHS curriculum has undergone a number of revisions and expansions of the curriculum and is now being used with deaf and hearing children in the United States, the Netherlands, Belgium, Canada, Australia, and Great Britain. A study conducted in Great Britain comparing groups of deaf children who received the PATHS intervention for one year and those who did not showed significant differences between the two groups. Those children who participated in the PATHS intervention demonstrated higher scores on emotional understanding (ability to recognize and label emotions) and on measures of self-image and emotional adjustment by teacher report (Hindley, Reed, Jeffs, & McSweeney, 1988).

Although we have thus far focused on elementary school-age children, the processes of social understanding in PATHS can also be applied to the problems of early and middle adolescence. Following an initial mastery of the basic PATHS concepts, there are various areas of instruction that can be incorporated into the PATHS paradigm, such as alcohol and drug abuse prevention, sex education, and AIDS awareness. Continued use of a PATHS-like curriculum in middle school and high school takes on new meaning at these ages as teenagers can utilize more abstract thinking and engage in more sophisticated problem solving and emotion regulation. Greenberg, Kusche, and colleagues (Greenberg & Kusche, 1993; Kusche, Greenberg, Calderon, & Gustafson, 1987) found that teachers successfully applied skills learned during the PATHS lessons to such issues as peer pressure, substance abuse, contraceptive decision making and sexuality, and parent–adolescent communication. There is a great need for the development of similar curriculum models for deaf adolescents and young adults who are going through the transition to college, vocational training, or the world of work.

In summary, the PATHS curriculum provides teachers with a systematic and developmental procedure for reducing adverse factors that can negatively affect a child's adaptive behavior and educational experiences. PATHS is designed to help children develop specific strategies that promote reflective responses and mature thinking skills, become self-motivated and enthusiastic about learning, obtain information necessary for social understanding and prosocial behavior, generate creative alternative solutions to problems, and learn to anticipate and evaluate situations, behaviors, and consequences. These skills increase the child's access to positive social interactions, thereby providing opportunities for a greater variety of learning experiences, which, in turn, reduce isolation. Increasing self-control and reflective thinking skills also ameliorates underachievement and promotes skills that help prevent the genesis of other types of problematic behaviors (e.g., alcohol and drug abuse). In addition, as PATHS activities become a regular part of the school day, less instructional time and teacher energy are needed for correcting behavioral problems; as a result, classroom climate is improved and teacher frustration and burnout are reduced. Because parents find the goals of PATHS to be central to the goals they have for their child, Greenberg & Kusche (1993) have begun to develop various avenues for greater parent participation. These include an extensive parent handbook, a structure for regular parent meetings, and homework activities that the child and parent complete together. These topics are discussed in detail in *The PATHS Curriculum Instructional Manual* (Kusche & Greenberg, 1993).

CURRENT AND FUTURE NEEDS TO FACILITATE
HEALTHY ADAPTATION IN DEAF CHILDREN

Given our extensive clinical and research experience in schools, intervention programs, and clinical settings for deaf children and their families, we believe that the further development of programs and services is necessary to fill current program gaps in the following three areas.

Programs and Services for Parents and Families

Programs should offer services to mothers and fathers that will teach, encourage, and expand parents' affective awareness and use of problem-solving skills. Such a framework could be utilized as a model for parental discussion and support groups. An increase in parental success at solving problems is likely to increase feelings of mastery and control. This in turn, provides deaf children with influential, competent, and resourceful parental role models.

Program services should facilitate the development of strong support networks for parents, especially as children enter school and fewer resources are readily available for the parents and family.

Parent support and guidance should continue throughout childhood. This should include advanced sign language classes, family weekend retreats, exposure to deaf adults, and problem-solving groups to address deaf adolescent issues.

A developmental approach should be emphasized in providing services to families. Recognition of parents' different needs at different emotional and life stages and children's age-related needs is critical for developing appropriate services.

School-Based Programs and Services

Given the interrelatedness of familial effects and children's school performance, educators, counselors, school administrators, and other related professionals should be encouraged to develop ways to involve families in the educational process of their children (e.g., designating the role of a Parent Educator to facilitate parent–school and parent–child involvement).

There should be training on and use of comprehensive curriculums to teach and promote socioemotional competency skills.

Curricular materials on Deaf culture, Deaf history, and ASL should be developed for use in school programs for children across educational settings (see Stone, chap. 13, this volume).

Broader Community Programs and Services

Development of program coordination between vocational rehabilitation counselors and school personnel will help to facilitate the transition between the worlds of school and work.

CONCLUSIONS

Emotional and social competence are critical aspects of development for all children, and the development of these skills is a lifelong process. However, our experience from the late 1970s reinforced our beliefs that there is a need to directly and explicitly focus on teaching socioemotional skills to deaf children and to emphasize, beginning in early intervention, the powerful role parents and professionals can play in promoting social competence. With deaf children in particular, parents and professionals need not only directly address the needs of the child, but must consciously interweave the systems of the school, family, and community to work together to meet the child's needs. The child's developmental integration occurs from a relational standpoint—in relation to the ecology of the school (teacher–student, teacher–principal, teacher–parent, and peer–peer interactions) and the home (family interactions). No single main effect (the ecology alone, personal characteristics of the participants, or the nature of the intervention itself) will determine the outcomes. Instead, there is a need to conceptualize the multiple, reciprocal interactions among persons and environment that determine healthy, competent behavior (Brofenbrenner, 1979; Weissberg, Caplan, & Sivo, 1989).

Beginning with the earliest phase of diagnosis and continuing through young adulthood, we cannot stress enough the importance of parents and professionals working together as equal partners in setting goals and objectives and monitoring the child's progress. There is a continual need to evaluate and revise what is best for the child, eventually making the child a partner in that process as well. As with any child, the parent of a deaf child can take great pride in watching him or her develop into a confident and successful adult. There is no reason a deaf child cannot master to the same degree or better than a hearing child the list of socioemotional competence skills listed at the beginning of this chapter. With consistent use of validated, effective intervention programs, the wellknown deficits in deaf children's socioemotional development can be ameliorated or prevented. As we tried to elucidate, from the perspective of professionals, parents, and the child, an individual does not learn to be aware of his or her inner feelings nor develop competence and confidence in his or her decision making and independent thinking by being told what to do or being dependent on other people to do things for him or her. In the same fashion, deaf children can only become socially and emotionally competent if given the same opportunity to develop self-awareness, independent thinking, and good problem-solving skills over the course of their development.

ACKNOWLEDGMENTS

We are deeply indebted to Kathryn Meadow-Orlans for her mentorship to both of us over the past 20 years. It was her keen insights, depth of understanding, and empathy with deaf children and their parents that has so greatly affected our own thinking and service to deaf children.

REFERENCES

Bodner-Johnson, B. (1986). The family environment and achievement of deaf students: A discriminant analysis. *Exceptional Children, 52,* 443–449.

Bronfenbrenner, U. (1979). *The ecology of human development.* Cambridge, MA: Harvard University Press.

Calderon, R., Bargones, J. Y., & Sidman, S. (1998a, April). *Outcomes of early intervention for children with moderately- severe to profound hearing loss: Family, child, and program factors.* Poster session presented at the biennial International Conference on Infant Studies, Atlanta, GA.

Calderon, R., Bargones, J. Y., & Sidman, S. (1998b). Characteristics of hearing families and their young deaf and hard-of-hearing children: Early intervention follow-up. *American Annals of the Deaf, 143,* 347–362.

Calderon, R., & Greenberg, M. T. (1998). Considerations in the adaptation of families with school-aged deaf children. In M. Marschark & M. D. Clark (Eds.), *Psychological perspectives on deafness* (pp. 27–47). Mahwah, NJ: Lawrence Erlbaum Associates.

Calderon, R., & Greenberg, M. T. (1997). The effectiveness of early intervention for children with hearing impairments. In M. J. Guralnick, (Ed.), *The effectiveness of early intervention: Second generation research* (pp. 455–482). Baltimore: Brookes.

Calderon, R., Greenberg, M. T., & Kusche, C. A. (1991). The influence of family coping on the cognitive and social skills of deaf children. In D. S. Martin (Ed.), *Advances in cognition, education, and deafness* (pp. 195–200). Washington, DC: Gallaudet University Press.

Committee on the Education of the Deaf. (1988). *Toward equality: Education of the deaf.* Washington, DC: U.S. Government Printing Office.

The Education for All Handicapped Children Act of 1975, Public Law No. 94-142, 20 United States Code § 1401 et. seq.

Emerton, G., Hurwitz, T. A., & Bishop, M. E. (1979). Development of social maturity in deaf adolescents and adults. In L. J. Bradford & W. G. Hardy (Eds.), *Hearing and hearing impairment* (pp. 451–460). New York: Grune & Stratton.

Feuerstein, R. (1980). *Instrumental enrichment.* Baltimore: University Park Press.

Goleman, D. (1995). *Emotional intelligence.* New York: Bantam.

Greenberg, M. T., & Calderon, R. (1984). Early intervention for deaf children and their families: An analysis of outcomes and issues. *Topics in early childhood special education* (Vol. 3:4, 1–9).

Greenberg, M. T., & Calderon, R. (1987). Parent education. In J. Van Cleve (Ed.), *Gallaudet encyclopedia on deaf people and deafness* (Vol. 2, pp. 264–268). New York: MacMillan.

Greenberg, M. T., & Kusche, C. A. (1989). Cognitive, personal, and social development of deaf children and adolescents. In M. C. Wang, H. J. Walberg, & M. C. Reynolds (Eds.), *The handbook of special education: Vol. 3. Research and practice* (pp. 95–129). Oxford, England: Pergamon.

Greenberg, M. T., & Kusche, C. A. (1993). *Promoting social and emotional development in deaf children: The PATHS project.* Seattle: University of Washington Press.

Greenberg, M. T., Kusche, C. A., & Speltz, M. (1991). Emotional regulation, self-control, and psychopathology: The role of relationships in earl childhood. In D. Cicchetti & S. L. Toth (Eds.), *Rochester symposium on developmental psychopathology: Vol. 2. Internalizing and externalizing expressions of dysfunction* (pp. 21–56). Hillsdale, NJ: Lawrence Erlbaum Associates.

Harris, R. I. (1982). Early childhood deafness as a stress-producing family experience: A theoretical perspective. In C. Erting & R. W. Meisegeier (Eds.), *Social aspects of deafness: Vol. 1. Deaf children and the socialization process* (pp. 155–232). Washington, DC: Gallaudet College.

Higgins, P. C. (1980). *Outsiders in a hearing world: A sociology of deafness.* Beverly Hills, CA: Sage.

Hindley, P., Reed, R., Jeffs, J., & McSweeney, M. (1988). *An evaluation of a social and emotional intervention for deaf children.* Unpublished manuscript, St. Georges Hospital, London.

Kusche, C. A. (1984). *The understanding of emotion concepts by deaf children: An assessment of an affective education curriculum.* Unpublished doctoral dissertation, University of Washington, Seattle.

Kusche, C. A., Garfield, T. S., & Greenberg, M. T. (1983). The understanding of emotional and social attributions in deaf adolescents. *Journal of Clinical Child Psychology, 12,* 153–160.

Kusche, C. A., & Greenberg, M. T. (1993). *The PATHS curriculum.* Seattle, WA: Developmental Research and Programs.

Kusche, C. A., Greenberg, M. T., Calderon, R., & Gustafson, R. N. (1987). Generalization strategies from the PATHS project for the prevention of substance use disorders. In G. Anderson & D. Watson (Eds.), *Habilitation and rehabilitation of deaf adolescents: 1986 conference proceedings* (pp. 263–304). Sulphur, OK: Steven Ray.

Marschark, M. (1993a). Origins and interactions in social, cognitive, and language development of deaf children. In M. Marschark & M. D. Clark (Eds.), *Psychological perspectives on deafness* (pp. 7–26). Hillsdale, NJ: Lawrence Erlbaum Associates.

Marschark, M. (1993b). *Psychological development of deaf children.* New York: Oxford University Press.

Marschark, M. (1997). *Raising and educating a deaf child: A comprehensive guide to the choices, controversies, and decisions faced by parents and educators.* New York: Oxford University Press.

Meadow, K. P. (1980). *Deafness and child development.* Berkeley: University of California Press.

Meadow, K. P., Greenberg, M. T., Erting, C., & Carmichael, H. S. (1981). Interactions of deaf mothers and deaf preschool children: Comparisons with three other groups of deaf and hearing dyads. *American Annals of the Deaf, 126,* 454–468.

Meadow-Orlans, K. P. (1987). An analysis of the effectiveness of early intervention programs for hearing-impaired children. In M. J. Guralnick & F. C. Bennett

(Eds.), *The effectiveness of early intervention for at-risk and handicapped children* (pp. 325–362). New York: Academic Press.

Meadow-Orlans, K. P., & Sass-Lehrer, M. (1995). Support services for families with children who are deaf: Challenges for professionals. *Topics in Early Childhood Special Education, 15*(3), 314–334.

Moeller, M. P., & Condon, M. (1994). D.E.I.P.: A Collaborative Problem-Solving Approach to Early Intervention. In J. Roush & N. D. Matkin (Eds.), *Infants and toddlers with hearing loss: Family centered assessment and intervention* (pp. 163–192). Baltimore: York Press.

Moeller, M. P., Coufal, K., & Hixson, P. (1990). The efficacy of speech-language intervention: Hearing impaired children. *Seminars in Speech and Language, 11*(4), 227–241.

Moores, D. F., Cerney, B., & Garcia, M. (1990). School placement and least restrictive environment. In D. F. Moores & K. P. Meadow-Orlans (Eds.), *Educational and developmental aspects of deafness* (pp. 115–136). Washington, DC: Gallaudet University Press.

National Institutes of Health. (1993). *Consensus development conference statement: Early identification of hearing impairment in infants and young children.* Bethesda, MD: Author.

Nucleus 24 Innovative System. (1998, July). BLOEDEL News Update.

Odom, P. B., Blanton, R. L., & Laukhuf, C. (1973). Facial expressions and interpretation of emotion-arousing situations in deaf and hearing children. *Journal of Abnormal Child Psychology, 1,* 139–151.

Reagan, T. (1990). Cultural consideration in the education of deaf children. In D. F. Moores and K. P. Meadow-Orlans (Eds.), *Educational and developmental aspects of deafness* (pp. 73–84). Washington, DC: Gallaudet University Press.

Roush, J. (1994). Strengthening family-professional relations: Advice from parents. In J. Roush & N. D. Matkin (Eds.), *Infants and toddlers with hearing loss: Family centered assessment and intervention* (pp. 337–350). Baltimore: York Press.

Roush, J., & Matkin, N. D. (Eds.). (1994). *Infants and toddlers with hearing loss: Family centered assessment and intervention.* Baltimore: York Press.

Strong, C. J., Clark, T. C., Johnson, D., Watkins, S., Barringer, D. G., & Walden, B. E. (1994). SKI*HI home-based programming for children who are deaf or hard of hearing: Recent research finding. *Infant-Toddler Intervention: The Transdisciplinary Journal, 4,* 25–36.

Thompson, M. (1994). ECHI: The University of Washington. In J. Roush & N. D. Matkin (Eds.), *Infants and toddlers with hearing loss: Family centered assessment and intervention* (pp. 253–275). Baltimore: York Press.

Watson, S. M., Henggeler, S. W., & Whelan, J. P. (1990). Family functioning and social adaptation of hearing impaired youths. *Journal of Abnormal Child Psychology, 18,* 143–163.

Weissberg, R. P., Caplan, M. Z., & Sivo, P. J. (1989). A new conceptual framework for establishing school-based social competence promotion programs. In L. A. Bond, B. E. Compas, & C. Swift (Eds.), *Primary prevention and promotion in the schools* (pp. 255–296). Newbury Park, CA: Sage.

Weissberg, R. P., & Greenberg, M. T. (1998). Community and school prevention. In I. Siegel & A. Renniner (Eds.), *Handbook of child psychology: Vol. 4. Child psychology in practice* (5th ed., pp. 877–954). New York: Wiley.

The Deaf Child at School

The educational system and the policies and practices of teachers and administrators who represent it impact children's social development and acculturation as well as their acquisition of traditional academic skills. For most children, school also provides ongoing contact with peers and thus is another important source of socialization, influencing their personal as well as academic images of themselves. In the curricula presented and the kinds of social opportunities they present, schools simultaneously influence and reflect the attitudes and expectations of the culture in general.

For many deaf and hard of hearing children, school can have even more impact than for hearing children. When lack of a shared language system interferes with communication between a child and other family members, interactions with peers and teachers at school provide an especially potent context for social and personal development. Because most deaf children are born into families of hearing persons, school is frequently a primary avenue for acquiring information about being deaf, for making contact with other deaf people, and increasingly for the development of deaf children's understanding of themselves as a part of a vibrant and identifiable cultural group.

The chapters in this section address three elements of the school environment: placement in separate or mainstreamed schools, the curriculum or the content taught in the schools, and the characteristics of deaf students as learners. The first two chapters in this section discuss effects of various school placements from rather different perspectives. Experiences in special or separate schools are compared with those in local, mainstreamed classrooms where there is much opportunity for interaction between deaf and hearing students. Stinson and Foster provide descriptions of models of educational service delivery predominant in education of deaf children in the United States. They conclude that mainstream placements are associated with higher academic achievement, but special schools better support personal socioemotional development. The authors also note that the two kinds of placements have taken on additional meaning for many students who have accepted the idea that the inclusive placements are for the best students. The inability to be successful in such a placement is seen as a personal failure.

Nash discusses intended and unintended effects of policies in the United States that promote mainstream educational placements for deaf students. These policies and their effects, he argues, can only be fully understood as they relate to basic American attitudes about individualism and individual control over one's fate. Inability to succeed in the mainstreamed educational environment can lead to increased isolation and may be blamed on a student's having a negative self-concept or other "character-related" disability. Thus, stigma that might have resulted previously from the presence of a physical disability (such as being deaf or hard of hearing) may be reinterpreted and perceived to be due to personal weakness.

In the third chapter, Stone posits that deaf children's self-esteem and concepts of self can be enhanced by educational experiences with curricula based on Deaf culture and emphasizing the history, the accomplishments, and the character of the Deaf community. Increased feelings of self-worth can provide deaf and hard of hearing children with personal resources to challenge the barriers they encounter and to promote the development of their inherent strengths and abilities.

Dyssegaard's chapter provides a view of opportunities and challenges faced by deaf and hard of hearing students in two developing nations: Mongolia and Nepal. Dyssegaard has been an on-site observer of and advisor for changes in educational services in these two countries. Her observations suggest that increased quality of educational practice, wider access to signed communication, higher expectations for students' achievement, and provision of opportunities to identify with other deaf and hard of hearing children have strongly positive effects on academic and personal outcomes.

The next two chapters focus on the diverse needs and characteristics of deaf and hard of hearing children as learners. Akamatsu and Musselman report analyses from a longitudinal Canadian study of deaf children whose development was assessed from early childhood through adolescence. The children's cognitive development was analyzed across groups based on etiology of hearing loss (genetic versus non-genetic) and experience with sign language. The authors document complex interactive effects of heredity and language experience, illuminating sources of heterogeneity of learning styles in the population.

Marschark also emphasizes the significant variability within the population of deaf students. Both that variability and the variability between deaf and hearing students, as well as the continuing lack of consistent academic progress observed among deaf students, call for a closer look at the sources and effects of individual differences. The author argues that an educational model appropriate for hearing students often is inappropriately applied to curricula and educational approaches for deaf students. In other cases, theoretical bases for educational approaches developed specifically for deaf students are incomplete, inflexible, and may lack full recognition of the diversity of experiences and characteristics of the population. Marschark challenges researchers, educators, other intervention specialists, and parents to work together to develop a more complete and sensitive model of deaf children as learners so that their optimal development may be more successfully promoted.

In her afterword, Meadow-Orlans applies the wisdom of her years of study of deaf and hard of hearing children and adults to provide an integrated overview of the major ideas presented in the chapters in this book. She reminds us of progress already made but guides us toward contemplation and future study about the many needs to be met before deaf and hard of hearing children have access to social and academic opportunities that maximize the development of their potential.

Socialization of Deaf Children and Youths in School

Michael S. Stinson
Susan Foster
Rochester Institute of Technology

Socialization is concerned with the influences of the diverse social agents, ranging from the family to the culture, on children's psychological and social development. Socialization is necessary for developing children who are integrated into society as respected participants (Damon, 1984). If the family unit is the first and major vehicle for socialization of children, schools run a close second (Shaffer, 1985). Generally, parents see the beginning of school as an opportunity for their children to meet new peers and adults and to interact in social settings beyond those of home and neighborhood. Getting on the school bus the first day of kindergarten is exciting and stressful precisely because it is recognized as a rite of passage from a closely knit social environment into a larger setting.

Schools affect students' social and emotional development, as well as their academic development. Schools help students become aware of the rules, norms, and expectations of society and help students move toward eventual economic self-sufficiency. In understanding school socialization processes, it is also important to know the physical, instructional, and social contexts of the educational experience because these contexts affect development (Shaffer, 1985).

The transition from family to school, and the role of schools as a socialization mechanism, is a defining experience for all children. But what about children who are deaf or hard of hearing? What is this experience like for them? How is it the same as or different from the experience of hearing children? What kinds of adaptations must these children, their teachers, and hearing peers make in order to ensure that their developmental experience holds the same opportunities as for hearing children? What kinds of educational conditions enhance socialization of deaf children, and how can these conditions be developed in school settings? These are the central questions that we will attempt to address through this chapter.

The chapter is divided into three sections. In "Elements of Socialization," we describe those key processes that are essential to the social development of deaf and hard of hearing youths[1] in school settings, including access to (a) formal as well as informal communications, (b) peer interactions, and (c) the unwritten curriculum. These processes enhance students' acquisition of social information and eventual acculturization through incidental learning experiences (unplanned events), social engagement with others, and the development of a positive individual as well as group identity. In "Educational Practice and Socialization," we describe those educational practices that either promote or inhibit the development of optimal conditions for socialization in schools, including predominant models for education of deaf and hard of hearing students and placement trends since the mid-1970s, the impact of these models on socialization, and new and innovative educational models and practices that may enhance socialization of deaf and hard of hearing students in a variety of educational settings. The chapter concludes with recommendations for future research and innovative practice regarding the personal and social development of deaf and hard of hearing persons in school settings.

PROCESSES OF SOCIALIZATION

Participation in several fundamental kinds of processes is essential for the effective socialization of all students, including those who are deaf or hard of hearing. In this section, we describe each of these processes, as well as their outcomes for personal and social development.

Formal and Informal Communications

Most communication is a form of social engagement. It can be formal or informal, planned or spontaneous, structured or unstructured, or some-

---

[1]As used here, students who are deaf or hard of hearing are those with sufficient hearing loss to participate in special education services designed specifically for this group.

thing in between. Communication in school settings can be formal, informal, or a combination. One example of formal, planned, structured communication is when a teacher stands before the class and lectures on a specific topic; another is when the student reads from a textbook and responds to questions listed at the end of the chapter. Examples of informal communications include hallway banter between teachers or students, passing notes in class, or conversations on the bus.

Often the distinction has been made that formal communication is used in schools for academics, whereas informal communications are reserved for social interactions. Although this may be true in a very broad sense, there is also a great deal of overlap between the two. Teachers may assign students to work in groups. In a discussion format, communication may be focused on an academic topic, but it is informal in the sense that it is often unstructured, and the form of engagement may be spontaneous. Similarly, students may find themselves using a more formal communication style at a debate club meeting, during a chess match, or while being briefed by the basketball coach for an upcoming game. All students, including deaf and hard of hearing students, need access to both formal and informal communication in school settings.

Peer Interactions

Communication, especially informal communication, is the foundation for interactions and the development of peer relationships. Peer interaction can range from formal, such as a structured cooperative work group in class, to informal, such as chatter in the lunch room. True friendships and group affiliation may be more likely to occur when there are many opportunities for informal interaction that occur regularly over a sustained period of time. Students develop friendships and social groups based on common interests, values, and behaviors, all of which are shared through casual conversations. Grapevines, whispers in class, and yelling in the hallway are all examples of the kinds of conversations that characterize peer interactions.

Extracurricular Activities and Unwritten Curriculum

The *unwritten curriculum,* to use Garretson's (1977) phrase, is a bridge between formal interactions in the classroom and informal or spontaneous interactions such as those described previously. Extracurricular activities such as school sports, clubs, class field trips, and student government are all important components of the unwritten curriculum. Just as in less formal peer relationships, participation in extracurricular activities provides students with opportunities for leadership, contribution to a group goal, understanding and negotiating diverse perspectives within the group, as well as dealing with issues of acceptance or rejection (Holland & Andre,

1987). These activities may be more accessible to students with a wider range of social skills because they are generally moderated or facilitated by an adult.

Why is access to the unwritten curriculum, including informal communications, peer relationships, and extracurricular activities, so important to the effective socialization of students? In her study of deaf children in a mainstream and in a separate class setting, Ramsey (1997) explored the "situated nature of learning and development" (p. 1). Her descriptions of schooling contexts "focus on children as social beings, schools as sites where group life dominates and takes on great importance, and on interaction with others as the driving force in learning and development" (pp. 1–2). Following this train of thought, we propose that students gain various social skills and knowledge through individual relationships as well as participation in social groups at school. Study teams or lab partnerships may enhance a student's ability to master course material, but they may also develop into friendships beyond the class. Often, groups of students will stake out their lunch table and meet there regularly to plan out of school activities or discuss fashion, friendships, and life in general. Through these relationships, they learn how to listen as well as express personal feelings, how to become a leader or supporter, how to participate without dominating the relationship or group, and how to handle confrontation or rejection as well as acceptance.

In short, much (some would argue most) of the learning that occurs in school takes place outside the classroom. Students share information about which teachers are easy or hard, who is dating whom, why Sally was suspended for three days, which courses to avoid, and why it is or is not cool to smoke. Students overhear the conversations of teachers, peers, and school administrators, integrating this information into their understanding of how the school functions. Through informal conversations, they learn how to interpret their feelings, get along with others, lead or follow, set goals, and how to think about themselves.

Social engagement within school settings helps to develop self-esteem in students. Students who have friends and are able to actively participate in one or more extracurricular activities are more likely to feel good about themselves and to feel connected to their environment (Asher, Parkhurst, Hymel, & Williams, 1990; Holland & Andre, 1987). Conversely, those who are always outsiders to the group, who are never included in casual conversations, or who describe themselves as lonely and without friends are likely to have much lower levels of social self-confidence and self-esteem.

Lastly, social connection to peers either individually, within informal cliques, or through membership in formal extracurricular clubs and activities is essential to the development of the student's individual as well as cultural and social identity. Sports engender an understanding of healthy competition and teamwork. By joining school clubs, students become engaged with their school communities and develop a sense of civic responsibility. These are the same skills that will enable them to become a department manager or member of a development team in work situations. Positive peer experiences help to develop self-esteem and a feeling of connection to a larger social group. Through less formal social interactions, they learn how to work with a difficult person or network with others. By working out difficult relationships, they learn how to advocate for themselves in later life, discover the line between assertiveness and aggressiveness, and develop collaborative work skills.

EDUCATIONAL PRACTICE AND SOCIALIZATION

In the previous section, we propose that in order for socialization in schools to occur, deaf and hard of hearing students need access to informal as well as formal communications, peer relationships, the unwritten curriculum, and extracurricular activities. We now turn to an examination of the impact of major forms of educational practice on the socialization of deaf and hard of hearing students. This section begins with a brief description of predominant educational models serving deaf and hard of hearing students, as well as placement trends since the mid-1970s. The focus then shifts to a discussion of the impact of predominant educational models on the socialization of deaf and hard of hearing students. The section concludes with a discussion of new and innovative educational models and practices that may enhance socialization of deaf and hard of hearing students in a variety of educational settings.

Predominant Educational Models, Public Policy, and School Placement Trends

Historically, there have been two predominant educational models for deaf and hard of hearing students—separate (residential/day) schools and mainstream programs in local schools. Each has a number of distinguishing features. Although there is much diversity in separate schools for deaf children, the typical school has 150 to 200 students. High school students tend to reside at the school, and among these students there may be a number who transferred from a mainstream program (Moores, 1996). In recent years, simultaneous communication has been the predominant method for communication at both elementary and high school levels. There is generally an excellent range of special services, such as audiologists, counselors, and psychologists. There is an extensive array of academic and vocational courses and a wide range of athletic and social programs.

Students who are mainstreamed attend classes in regular schools that enroll predominantly hearing students. There are two major types of mainstream programs. The first is a regional program, which includes resource rooms that are part of a local public school for hearing students. Deaf and hard of hearing students receive special instruction in self-contained classes or resource rooms and typically attend selected classes that are primarily for hearing students. The size of these programs varies considerably from more than 100 students to just a few (Moores, 1996). The second type of mainstream program is one where students are enrolled in their local neighborhood school. The students generally are placed in classes with hearing students, although they are visited by an itinerant teacher who provides special instruction. There is much variation in the extent to which students receive such instruction.

Educational philosophy, as reflected in public policies, had a great impact on the patterns of school placement in this country. The development of separate residential schools occurred at a period in the United States when all students with special educational needs were seen as best educated separately from their "normal" peers. However, since the mid-1970s, the trend has turned sharply away from separate programs for all students with disabilities in support of placing these students in classes with nondisabled peers. Public Law No. 94-142, also known as The Education for All Handicapped Children Act, supports placement in "the least restrictive environment (LRE)" for all students with disabilities. Although there is debate over whether the LRE is a requirement (Kellogg, 1997), it is at least recommended that

> special classes, separate schooling or other removal of handicapped children from the regular educational environment occurs only when the nature or severity of the handicap is such that education in regular classes with the use of supplementary aids and services cannot be achieved satisfactorily. (The Education for All Handicapped Children Act of 1975, Part B, Section 612, No. 5B)

Generally, inclusion is seen as the least restrictive school placement, with residential schools being the most restrictive. Thus, the law has often been interpreted as supporting the notion that disabled students must fail in the mainstream before being placed in separate day or residential programs.

The Individuals With Disabilities Education Act (IDEA) of 1997 incorporated a greater sensitivity to the communication needs of deaf and hard of hearing students, including the recognition that these students have a right to "opportunities for direct communications with peers and professional personnel in the child's language and communication mode, academic level, and full range of needs, including opportunities for direct instruction in the child's language and communication mode" (Council for Exceptional Children, 1998, p. 20). Although it is not clear yet whether this will herald a return to separate programs for deaf students, it may open the door for deaf professionals in public schools, as well as the development of innovative educational programs for deaf and hard of hearing students that incorporate communication ease within a mainstream setting.

These changes dramatically altered the numbers of students in separate residential and mainstream schools, and the students in these different settings have different communication characteristics and academic skills. Data from the annual survey of deaf and hard of hearing children and youth show that approximately 70% of the students are educated in local schools (i.e., mainstreamed), approximately 22% are educated in residential schools, and 8% are educated in local, separate day schools. There has been a steady trend toward educating more students in local schools since the late 1970s (Schildroth & Hotto, 1994, 1996). Students in mainstream settings tend to have less severe hearing losses than do those in separate schools (Schildroth & Hotto, 1994). In addition, students in mainstream settings are more likely to be younger and less likely to have an additional disability (Allen & Karchmer, 1990).

Impact of Predominant Models on the Major Processes and Outcomes of Socialization

As noted previously, there have been two major types of educational programs for deaf and hard of hearing students: separate residential and public mainstream. In this section we examine the impact of each of these models on the processes of socialization for deaf students.

Formal and Informal Communication. Students' communication experiences are different for those in mainstream settings and in special classes, and there also may be differences between communication in special classes in public schools and residential ones. In residential schools, there is greater emphasis on sign communication than in mainstream programs. The sign communication occurs in forms with and without speech used simultaneously. Because teachers tend to be fluent signers, and because communication with peers is generally in sign, the residential setting offers the best access to communication for many students who are profoundly deaf and who rely on a visual form of communication (Lane, Hoffmeister, & Behan, 1996). Allen and Karchmer (1990) found that teachers in residential schools were more likely to be deaf (though still a minority of the teaching staff), to have greater experience teaching deaf students, and to more often supplement their learning of sign from interactions with deaf students and deaf coworkers. All of these factors are likely to contribute to these teachers' proficiency in sign.

Although the predominant language in residential schools continues to be simultaneous communication in which the teacher speaks and signs the words in English word order, there has recently been considerable experimentation with using ASL in instruction, and some schools have bilingual programs in which the philosophy is to develop competence in ASL

first and then use this competence as the base on which to build competence in English (Strong, 1995).

For students who are educated in mainstream classes with hearing students, the most common form of communication is spoken English. To follow the classroom discourse, these students rely on lipreading, aided by
residual hearing. Many students use frequency modulated (FM) systems
in which the teacher wears a wireless microphone that sends a direct signal to the child's hearing aid (Johnson, 1998).

Support services in mainstream classes, such as interpreters,
notetakers, and speech-to-print systems increase access to formal communication. Interpreters sign and mouth the words as they are spoken by
the teacher and other students so that they are more understandable.
Speech-to-print systems are growing in use but are used considerably less
often than interpreters (Bervinchak & Bolesky, 1998; Stinson & Stuckless,
1998). With this system, the student sees a real-time display of the classroom dialogue in printed English. The text is generally produced by an
in-class captionist. The student also benefits from being able to review the
text after class by reading the text file on a computer screen or by reviewing a paper printout.

Even when support services are good, students may still have difficulties communicating, participating, and learning in the mainstream classroom (Stinson & Antia, in press). The lag time of 2 to 6 seconds between
the speaker's voicing of information and the corresponding signing of that
information contributes to difficulty in class participation; by the time the
student receives the interpreted question or comment, hearing students
may have already responded (Stewart & Kluwin, 1996). Interviews with
students and observations in classrooms indicate that barriers to classroom participation include the rapid rate of discussion, rapid turn taking,
rapid change of topics, the high number of speakers involved in the discussion, and more than one student talking at a time (Saur, Layne, Hurley, &
Opton, 1986; Stinson, Liu, Saur, & Long, 1996). Additionally, even teachers
who have been trained in the use of interpreters may still forget that deaf
students are attending to them when they focus on the interpreter or that
they must not turn their back to the class while speaking (Ramsey, 1997).

An additional problem is that support services such as interpreting are
generally limited to facilitating formal communications within the classroom (Ramsey, 1997). This is particularly true in secondary school settings, where interpreters are assigned to a class rather than to a student.
Once students are in the hallway, lunchroom, or the bus, they are usually
on their own regarding communication with peers. As a result, they often
report limited or superficial conversations with peers, and many say they
feel left out of the casual discussions that characterize most out of class
communications between students (Foster, 1989; Mertens, 1989). Hearing
students must be prepared to repeat or write notes, and deaf students
must be comfortable asking students to do this when necessary. Commu-

nication among hearing and deaf students outside school (for example, to check homework tasks, share ideas, or ask for a date) requires knowledge and comfort on the part of both hearing and deaf students. If a telephone conversation is required, hearing students must be comfortable with the relay, and deaf students must have ready access to a telecommunications device for the deaf (TDD).

Peer Relationships. School placement decisions, in combination with the experience of success or failure to access information through formal or informal communications, greatly impact opportunities for interactions of deaf and hard of hearing students with peers. In residential schools, there is a critical mass of peers and adults with whom the students can interact easily and where they benefit from a variety of positive social experiences (Foster & Emerton, 1991; Moores, 1996). Individuals who attended residential schools have commented on how one of their special benefits is the development of close, long-lasting friendships (Foster & Emerton, 1991). In all these ways, residential schools are the traditional places for socializing deaf children into the deaf community. Perhaps most important, students have access to informal communications in these settings and are therefore able to acquire information through incidental learning techniques such as observing the conversations among adults in public settings or learning about which teachers are the most demanding through casual conversations with peers at the lunch table.

In regard to peer interactions of deaf students in mainstream programs, concern has been expressed that primarily because of communication difficulties, a frequent consequence of mainstreaming is social isolation, rather than integration, and this kind of social experience is not conducive to the deaf child's social development. Students may experience feelings of loneliness because they cannot easily participate in social activities with peers due to communication difficulties (Foster, 1989). They are also the conversations that are most difficult for deaf students to access and the most resistent to intervention by professionals and support service personnel. An interpreter might be acceptable during a biology lab but would not be welcome when students gather at the back of the school to sneak a cigarette and share weekend plans. Research on students educated in public schools suggests that students with a range of hearing loss experience an absence of close friendships (Antia, Kreimeyer, & Eldredge, 1994; Stinson & Antia, in press; Stinson, Whitmire, & Kluwin, 1996; Tvingstedt, 1993). Research has also shown that deaf adolescents consistently felt more emotionally secure and more accepted in relationships with deaf peers than in those with hearing peers. This is generally true regardless of whether the student is in a residential (or separate day) school or in a public school program either large or small (Foster, 1989; Stinson & Whitmire, 1991; Stinson, Whitmire, & Kluwin, 1996).

Extracurricular Activities.   In addition to a large group of peers and adults who use sign communication in separate day or residential programs, there is also a wide range of athletic and social programs in which all the participants are deaf. These programs offer links to social organizations for deaf people, sponsor special cultural activities, and support ASL. These activities provide more leadership opportunities than are available in the mainstream setting. They also provide more opportunities for deaf students to rise to positions of leadership in the club or organization.

Extracurricular activities in mainstream settings may be easier for deaf students to access than informal peer interactions because they include elements of both formal and informal communications. Interpreters are often available for these activities, and there are generally adults involved to monitor or lead the activities of the group. However, deaf students may still experience difficulty with peripheral conversations among students, spontaneous or unplanned activities, or achieving roles of prominence or leadership in the group (Holcomb, 1990; Stewart & Stinson, 1992).

Self-Esteem.   How might school placement decisions affect deaf and hard of hearing students' self-esteem? On the one hand, social isolation resulting from spoiled communications with hearing peers will almost certainly lower self-confidence and self-esteem as it relates to social engagement. Being a full and equal participant in student organizations, clubs, sports, activities, and so forth, which is much more common in separate schools, may enhance the student's sense of social and individual competence.

On the other hand, deaf students often express regret or disappointment when they are removed from mainstream settings. Just as called for in Public Law No. 94-142, these students interpret their educational placements in terms of personal accomplishment or failure. The following quotations, from interviews with deaf college students about their past school experiences, capture this sentiment:

> Student #1: I was [at the school for the deaf] for 3 months, and they realized I was too advanced, so they moved me to a small program for deaf students at a hearing school.
>
> Student #2: Started at 2 in a deaf program in a public nursery school. Then in kindergarten I was half time mainstreamed and half time in the deaf program. But I didn't make it through the hearing program, so I stayed in the deaf program full time, first and part of second grade.

In a similar vein, deaf students often speak with pride of their graduation from mainstream schools, stressing their belief that they received a better education and learned how to interact with hearing people. In the words of one college student,

> I benefitted from going to a mainstreamed school ... since we're in a hearing world, you kind of have to adapt to the environment around you. ... I'm learning how to get along with hearing peers, how to get along with hearing people around me, learning how to keep up. It's helped me a lot. (Foster, 1989, p. 72)

Quantitative studies with questionnaires or rating scales designed to tap self-esteem indicate that self-esteem is not related to educational placement. Five studies reported since 1984 do not show significant differences in the self-esteem of students who are mainstreamed or who are in special classes or schools (Cohen, 1991; Gans, 1995; Jacobs, 1989; Larsen, 1984; Shaffer-Meyer, 1991). Three older studies provided mixed results regarding the relationship between placement and self-esteem (Craig, 1965; Farrugia & Austin, 1980; Schlesinger & Meadow, 1972). One qualification to this proposition may be that self-esteem is associated with an interaction of the students' language-communication proficiency and the specific school setting. In one study, mainstreamed students with better English language skills had more positive self-images than mainstreamed students with weaker language skills, but there was not this difference in self-esteem in residential students with different levels of language skills (Shaffer-Meyer, 1991).

Three studies found that higher self esteem is associated with greater academic achievement (Desselle, 1994; Joiner, Erickson, Crittenden, & Stevenson, 1966; Koelle & Convey, 1982). One also found that children who had higher self-esteem were more likely to have parents who included signing in communication with them, and those with lower self-esteem were more likely to have parents who did not sign (Desselle, 1994). This study was conducted with children who attended a southern residential school, and one question is whether this relationship would also hold for children with varying degrees of hearing loss and with those in different types of educational programs.

Cultural and Self-Identity

A related question, which is closely tied to socialization through schooling, is whether it is preferable for schools to socialize students for the deaf community or the predominant society. Is the goal to prepare the student to function competently in a society in which hearing people are predominant, or is the goal to promote integration of the child into the deaf community and comfort with deaf culture? The previously considered issues of school placement and communication clearly impact on cultural and identity issues. Traditionally, residential schools effectively socialized students to become comfortable with deaf culture. Deaf adults serve as role models and may help children to identify positively with deaf people. Although public schools provide for extensive practice in interacting with hearing individuals, much of the experience may be frustrating. Assimilation into the predominant hearing society may be limited, and when these individuals turn toward the deaf community, they may proceed awkwardly (Glickman, 1996).

The concept that there is a culture within the deaf community has emerged more strongly as deaf individuals recognize that they share special common abilities and ways of relating to others who are deaf (Padden & Humphries, 1988). These common abilities have to do with language (ASL) or ways of communicating, values that may not be the same as those commonly held by hearing persons (Leigh & Stinson, 1991). The residential school is the setting where the deaf child has been traditionally socialized to acquire these values and to identify with the deaf community. Students come into contact with many deaf role models, including deaf staff, older deaf students, and deaf alumni. Allen and Karchmer (1990) reported that whereas 20% of the teachers in residential schools was deaf, only 1% of the teachers in mainstream programs was deaf, and the proportion of deaf teachers may have increased since that report. These contacts with deaf individuals, especially for deaf children of hearing parents, may contribute significantly to acquisition of deaf culture and a positive view of deafness. For students who have been exposed to both deaf and hearing schools, the experiences over a lifetime of isolation among hearing people and a sense of belonging among deaf people results in a shift from hearing to deaf culture (Foster, 1996).

Glickman (1996) suggested that for individuals to develop comfort with deaf culture and a healthy integration of deafness into their identity, they must at some point have an immersion experience with deaf culture, which means being surrounded by deaf peers and adults. Such immersion is clearly more likely to occur in a residential program. This proposition is consistent with a cultural deaf perspective on the impact of school placement on identity development. A cultural deaf perspective contrasts the supportive environment of the residential school with a view of mainstreaming as isolating the deaf students from each other and from integration with deaf culture (Glickman, 1996).

Given current trends in education, it is increasingly likely, at least for that 90% of deaf children who has hearing parents, that an immersion type of experience will not occur until adolescence, because younger students are more likely to be educated in local schools. Allen and Karchmer (1990) found that although 45% of the residential school students is in high school, approximately half that percentage of students in mainstream programs is in high school. Only 5% of the students in local programs that were not integrated was in high schools. These differences in percentages provide evidence for such a shift of older students from local to residential programs.

Along with the benefit of contact with many deaf peers and adults at residential schools, students have commented on feelings of being fundamentally separated—culturally, academically, socially, and physically—from hearing society. Students at residential schools noted a lack of experience with hearing people, not knowing what to expect in dealing with them and how to interact as effectively as possible. Students also noted missing the experiences of coming home every day from school, going out to play with neighborhood children, and being with parents and siblings every day, even though they were aware that such interactions often involved frustration and communication breakdown (Foster, 1989).

It may be argued that mainstream schools provide the same exposure to the culture at large as hearing students and, thus, provide the best opportunity to develop the skills and personal resources to function effectively in the larger (hearing) society. At the same time, the environment of the neighborhood public school is unlikely to support an interest in deaf culture and may complicate development of the students' self-identity (Glickman, 1996). Writing about his counseling experiences with deaf children and youth, Glickman suggests that the establishment of identity with deaf and hearing social groups is often a complex task for deaf adolescents, especially for those who have been mainstreamed. On the one hand, contact in the family, neighborhood, and school is predominantly with hearing individuals. On the other, it is generally easier for deaf individuals to communicate and establish friendships with each other. Orally trained students from mainstream programs with little experience with deaf culture may undergo internal conflict as they discover sign language and the deaf community. They may struggle in their efforts to clarify their affiliation with deaf and hearing cultures (Glickman, 1996). This struggle includes difficulty in developing a conception of themselves as a deaf person, in defining the nature of the relationships they have with other deaf persons, and also in the relationships with hearing individuals. For individuals to be comfortable with themselves in their relationships, these separate perspectives on relationships with hearing and with deaf individuals also probably need to be integrated in some way. The following quotation from Charlson, Strong, and Gold (1992) illustrates some of the difficulty an adolescent can have in establishing an identity as either a deaf or a hearing person:

I don't like the fact that I have trouble talking to people. It seems like people look at me as a hearing person, but in reality I'm really not. But I think I act like a hearing person, but I think I can call myself hard of hearing in some ways because I think I'm in between deaf and hearing, I'm in between them. (p. 264)

EDUCATIONAL PHILOSOPHIES AND INNOVATIONS

The trend toward mainstreaming deaf and hard of hearing students, soft-
ened by the recognition of these students' special needs for communication and social interaction with peers and direct communication with
professionals, has resulted in a variety of program efforts and innovations
since the late 1980s.

Mainstreaming Versus Inclusion

A controversial issue in the education of students in local public schools is
the extent that an inclusive approach should be used as opposed to a
mainstream approach. Inclusion and mainstreaming are educational
practices as opposed to integration (academic and social), which is an
outcome of these practices. When examining these practices from the
perspective of placement, the key issue is the physical setting in which
children receive their education. From this perspective, inclusion implies
that children who are deaf or hard of hearing receive most, or all, of their
education in the regular classroom. Mainstreaming implies that these students receive their education in the regular public school but not necessarily within the regular classroom. Thus, children can be mainstreamed
for math or art or recess but may attend a resource room or a
self-contained classroom for the remaining school day. The term *mainstream* can refer to more extensive placement in classes with hearing
peers. The term refers to a broader range of placement options than does
inclusion (Stinson & Antia, in press).

   Philosophically, the difference between mainstreaming and inclusion
is that mainstreaming implies that the child will adapt to the regular classroom, whereas inclusion implies that the regular classroom will adapt to
the child. To successfully mainstream a child it is necessary to evaluate the
child's readiness to function within the classroom. In a mainstream setting, the classroom teacher is the gate keeper, turning away children who
are unable to function within the existing classroom structure and curriculum. In contrast, in an inclusive setting, the classroom practices are expected to change to accommodate individual children. Another
philosophical division between the two concepts is classroom membership. Mainstreaming implies that the deaf and hard of hearing students are
visitors in the regular classroom, whereas inclusion implies that these children are members of the regular classroom. The following continuum represents the range of school placement options, from residential programs
to those public school settings that practice full inclusion.

Regional Programs

It seems helpful for students in mainstream settings if they have opportunities for contact with deaf adults and deaf peers. All adolescents struggle to

find appropriate social roles and identities, and it is helpful if they have choices in social relationships and opportunities to explore these options and experiences (Damon, 1984). For deaf students, exploration of these options probably requires regular contact with a sufficiently large group of deaf peers of similar age. Mainstream programs that include a separate program for deaf students, such as a regional program, may offer the best possibility for such exploration because they have many deaf students and because they are also likely to provide opportunities for students to learn about the cultural aspects of deafness (Foster, 1989).

Regional or centralized mainstream programs attended by a number of deaf students also provide opportunities for social interaction with deaf peers. Many educators supported this practice over placement in local public schools because it is likely to result in more positive social experiences. Deaf students themselves have commented on how they benefitted from this type of program. There, students gained experience in relating to hearing students, but at the same time there are usually closer, more comfortable relations with deaf peers. When relationships with hearing peers got difficult, there were always deaf friends to provide support (Charlson, Strong, & Gold, 1992; Foster & Emerton, 1991; Reich, Hambleton, & Houldin, 1977).

In the late 1990s, there has been educational and political movement to increase the number of regional programs. For example, many organizations in California banded into the California Deaf Education Coalition, which recently created a plan for development of regions for providing and administering programs for deaf and hard of hearing students and for coordination between these programs and the state special schools that serve deaf students (California Deaf Education Coalition, 1996).

Coenrollment Programs

In coenrollment programs, deaf and hard of hearing and hearing students learn together in a classroom that is cotaught by a regular education teacher and a teacher of the deaf. The coenrollment model provides deaf and hard of hearing students with opportunities for academic and social integration that may not occur in self-contained or resource classrooms. The deaf and hard of hearing students have many opportunities to become true social members of the class because they are involved in all classroom activities with a stable group of peers. Because coenrollment classrooms include multiple deaf and hard of hearing students, the opportunities for interaction with other deaf and hard of hearing peers are a central part of the model (Kreimeyer, Crooke, Drye, Egbert, & Klein, 1998).

IMPLICATIONS FOR PRACTICE

Interviews with deaf persons about their experiences in various kinds of school settings suggest that often they feel they must choose between opportunities for social development and academic growth (Foster, 1989). They believe that they will have more choices and more demanding courses in mainstream school programs, and research (e.g., Allen, 1986) suggests they may be correct. On the other hand, research also suggests that mainstreamed deaf and hard of hearing students may be severely limited in terms of friendships, participation in extracurricular activities, and in learning from all the incidental exchanges that occur in school settings. Students should not have to choose between one kind of experience and the other; both are important. What can or should educators do to maximize the chance that deaf and hard of hearing students will experience the full range of their development needs during their school years? We have several suggestions that should be taken as examples, not an exhaustive list.

First, counselors and educators who work with deaf students and their parents need to consider the impact of different educational settings on the academic, communication, and social development of deaf children and youth. Careful attention must be given to individual differences in placement and monitoring of student progress. In some cases, flexibility will be critical to student success. For example, a student may need different placements at different times during his or her development. In other cases, students may need the option of moving between two placements on a regular basis, that is attending a separate program for most of the day but joining a mainstream class for certain courses. In every case, decisions should revolve around the needs of the student rather than the convenience of the schools.

Second, programs with inclusive approaches need to make special efforts to make the full range of formal and informal school activities accessible to deaf students. Relatedly, special attention must be paid to assessment of communication access in the classroom and school context, including the impact of communication barriers on the development of social and academic networks among students. Group work, informal learning situations, and extracurricular activities may require additional accommodations or creative strategies to facilitate full inclusion of deaf students. These efforts may require that schools move beyond traditional methods of inclusion, for example, to establish experimental classrooms where new techniques are tested or coenrollment is practiced.

Third, both separate and mainstream programs must recognize and compensate for limitations inherent in their settings. In regard to academic development, deaf students need access to a full range of educational options, including college preparation and advanced placement courses and vocational or technical training. Deaf students also need opportunities to learn about both deaf and hearing cultures and to interact with deaf and hearing peers. Mainstream schools may consider offering both deaf and hearing students courses in sign language and deaf culture. Mainstream and residential schools may wish to develop liaisons for extracurricular activities or experiment with a coenrollment program.

Lastly, there is a need for continuing research on effective practice regarding education of deaf and hard of hearing students. Ramsey's (1997) observational study of a mainstream and separate class for deaf students details the social and linguistic communities that develop in school contexts and the impact of these contexts on deaf students. Prolonged and close study of how support services are implemented in a dynamic and complex setting such as a schoolroom is critical to understanding the limits as well as the potential of these services. Much of what has been completed to date focuses on the challenges to academic and social development that deaf students face in various kinds of school settings. However, we know very little about how to improve these experiences and how to resolve the problems. This is the task that researchers must now address.

REFERENCES

Allen, T. E. (1986). Patterns of academic achievement among hearing impaired students: 1974 and 1983. In A. N. Schildroth & M. A. Karchmer (Eds.), *Deaf children in America* (pp. 161–206). San Diego, CA: College Hill Press.

Allen, T., & Karchmer, M. (1990). Communication in classrooms for deaf students: Student, teacher, and program characteristics. In H. Bornstein (Ed.), *Manual communication: Implications for education* (pp. 45–66). Washington, DC: Gallaudet University Press.

Antia, S. D., Kreimeyer, K. H., & Eldredge, N. (1994). Promoting social interaction between young children with hearing impairments and their peers. *Exceptional Children, 60,* 262–275.

Asher, S., Parkhurst, J., Hymel, S., & Williams, G. (1990). Peer rejection and loneliness in childhood. In S. Asher & J. Coie (Eds.), *Peer rejection in childhood* (pp. 253–273). New York: Cambridge University Press.

Bervinchak, D., & Bolesky, C. (1998). *Real-time captioning: Equal access for deaf students.* Unpublished manuscript.

California Deaf Education Coalition. (1996). *An innovative approach for critical change: Proposal for a California office of education for deaf and hard of hearing.* Sacramento, CA: Author.

Charlson, E., Strong, M., & Gold, R. (1992). How successful deaf teenagers experience and cope with isolation. *American Annals of the Deaf, 137,* 261–270.

Cohen, B. S. (1991). *A comparison of self-concept scores in secondary-aged hearing-impaired students enrolled in mainstreamed and self-contained classes.* Unpublished doctoral dissertation, Pace University, New York.

Council for Exceptional Children. (1998). *IDEA 1997: Let's make it work.* Reston, VA: Author.

Craig, H. B. (1965). A sociometric investigation of self-concept of the deaf school child. *American Annals of the Deaf, 115,* 79–85.

Damon, W. (1984). *Social and personality development.* New York: Norton.

Desselle, D. D. (1994). Self-esteem, family climate, and communication patterns in relation to deafness. *American Annals of the Deaf, 139,* 322–328.

Farrugia, D., & Austin, G. (1980). A study of the socio-emotional adjustment patterns of hearing-impaired students in different educational settings. *American Annals of the Deaf, 120,* 391–405.

Foster, S. (1996). Communication experience of deaf people; an ethnographic account. In I. Parasnis (Ed.), *Cultural and language diversity: Reflections on the deaf experience* (pp. 117–135). New York: Cambridge University Press.

Foster, S. (1989). Educational programmes for deaf students: An insider perspective on policy and practice. In L. Barton (Ed.), *Integration: Myth or reality?* (pp 57–82). London: The Falmer Press.

Foster, S., & Emerton, G. (1991). Mainstreaming the deaf student: A blessing or a curse? *The Journal of Disability Policy Studies, 2,* 61–76.

Gans, J. (1995, July). *The relation of self-image to academic placement and achievement in hearing impaired students.* Paper presented at the 18th International Congress on Education of the Deaf, Tel Aviv, Israel.

Garretson, M. (1977). The residential school. *The Deaf American, 29,* 19–22.

Glickman, N. S. (1996). The development of culturally deaf identities. In N. S. Glickman & M. A. Harvey (Eds.), *Culturally affirmative psychotherapy with Deaf persons* (pp. 115–153). Mahwah, NJ: Lawrence Erlbaum Associates.

Holcomb, T. K. (1990). *Deaf students in the mainstream: A study in social assimilation.* Unpublished doctoral dissertation, University of Rochester, Rochester, NY.

Holland, A., & Andre, T. (1987). Participation in extracurricular activities in secondary school: What is known, what needs to be known? *Review of Educational Research, 57,* 437–466.

Jacobs, J. L. (1989). *A comparison of deaf pupils in residential and mainstream settings on self-concept.* Unpublished doctoral dissertation, Spalding University, Louisville, KY.

Johnson, C. (1998). *Amplification in inclusive classrooms.* Unpublished manuscript.

Joiner, L. M., Erickson, E. L., Crittenden, J. B., & Stevenson, V. M. (1966). Predicting the academic achievement of the acoustically impaired using intelligence and self-concept of academic ability. *Journal of Special Education, 3,* 425–431.

Kellogg, R. C. (1997). Inclusion and deaf students: Some critical considerations. *The Nebraska Journal, 127*(1), 3–5.

Koelle, W. H., & Convey, J. J. (1982). The prediction of achievement of deaf adolescents from self-concept and locus of control measures. *American Annals of the Deaf, 127,* 769–779.

Kreimeyer, K., Crooke, P., Drye, C., Egbert, V., & Klein, B. (1998). *The development of a co-enrollment model of inclusive education for deaf and hard of hearing children.* Unpublished manuscript.

Lane, H., Hoffmeister, R., & Behan, B. (1996). *Journey into the DEAF-WORLD.* San Diego, CA: Dawn Sign Press.

Larsen, D. S. (1984). *An investigation of the relationship between self-concept of hearing-impaired students and other selected variables.* Unpublished doctoral dissertation, Brigham Young University, Provo, UT.

Leigh, I. W., & Stinson, M. S. (1991). Social environment, self-perceptions, and identity of hearing-impaired adolescents. *Volta Review, 93,* 7–22.

Mertens, D. (1989). Social experiences of hearing-impaired high school youth. *American Annals of the Deaf, 134,* 15–19.

Moores, D. F. (1996). *Educating the deaf* (4th ed.). Boston: Houghton Mifflin.

Padden, C., & Humphries, T. (1988). Deaf in America: Voices from a culture. Cambridge, MA: Harvard University Press.

Public Law 94142. (1975). *U.S. Code Congressional and Administrative News,* 94th Congress, 1st session, 89 STAT. 781.

Ramsey, C. L. (1997). *Deaf children in public schools: Placement, context, and consequences.* Washington, DC: Gallaudet University Press.

Reich, C., Hambleton, D., & Houldin, B. K. (1977). The integration of hearing impaired children in regular classrooms. *American Annals of the Deaf, 122,* 534–543.

Saur, R. E., Layne, C. A., Hurley, E. A., & Opton, K. (1986). Dimensions of mainstreaming. *American Annals of the Deaf, 131,* 325–330.

Schildroth, A. N., & Hotto, S. A. (1994). Deaf students and full inclusion: Who wants to be excluded? In R. Johnson & O. Cohen (Eds.), *Implications and complications for deaf students of the full inclusion movement* (pp. 7–30). Washington, DC: Gallaudet University.

Schildroth, A. N., & Hotto, S. A. (1996). Changes in student and program characteristics. 1984–85 and 1994–95. *American Annals of the Deaf, 141,* 68–71.

Schlesinger, H. S., & Meadow, K. P. (1972). *Sign and sound: Childhood deafness and mental health.* Berkeley: University of California Press.

Shaffer, D. R. (1985). *Developmental psychology: Theory, research and applications.* Monterey, CA: Brooks/Cole.

Shaffer-Meyer, D. (1991). *The self-concept of mainstreamed hearing-impaired students.* Unpublished doctoral dissertation, University of Northern Colorado, Colorado Springs, CO.

Stewart, D., & Kluwin, T. N. (1996). The gap between guidelines, practices, and knowledge in interpreting services for deaf students. *Journal of Deaf Studies and Deaf Education, 1,* 29–39.

Stewart, D., & Stinson, M. S. (1992). The role of sport and extracurricular activities in shaping socialization patterns. In T. N. Kluwin, D. F. Moores, & M. G. Gaustad (Eds.), *Toward Effective Public School Programs for Deaf Students* (pp. 129–148). New York: Teacher's College Press.

Stinson, M., & Antia, S. (in press). Issues in educating deaf and hard of hearing students in inclusive settings. *Journal of Deaf Studies and Deaf Education.*

Stinson, M., Liu, Y., Saur, R., & Long, G. (1996). Deaf college students' perceptions of communication in mainstreamed classes. *Journal of Deaf Studies and Deaf Education, 1,* 140–151.

Stinson, M., & Stuckless, E. R. (in press). Recent developments in speech-to-print transcription systems for deaf students. In A. Weisel (Ed.), *Deaf education in the 1990s: International perspectives.* Washington, DC: Gallaudet University Press.

Stinson, M., & Whitmire, K. (1991). Self-perceptions of social relationships among hearing-impaired adolescents in England. *Journal of the British Association of Teachers of the Deaf, 15,* 104–114.

Stinson, M., Whitmire, K., & Kluwin, T. (1996). Self-perceptions of social relationships in hearing-impaired adolescents. *Journal of Educational Psychology, 88,* 132–143.

Strong, M. (1995). A review of bilingual/bicultural programs for deaf children in North America. *American Annals of the Deaf, 140,* 84–94.

Tvingstedt, A. (1993). *Social conditions of hearing-impaired pupils in regular classrooms* (Monograph No. 773). Malmo, Sweden: University of Lund, Department of Education and Psychological research.

Shifting Stigma From Body to Self: Paradoxical Consequences of Mainstreaming

Jeffrey E. Nash
Southwest Missouri State University

People with disabilities enjoy unprecedented participation in today's society. Yet, exclusion from full employment still exists; as do other forms of discrimination, and, across the country, disabled children may be managed within special classrooms and programs in ways that preclude them from participation with others and from achieving to their full potential (Mehan, Mercer, & Rueda, 1996). In this chapter, I suggest that both inclusion and exclusion depict the experiences of disabled people in general and the children of special education in particular. The dark side of the monumental gains of the last several decades, I show, is the result of the very way that people in the United States think about themselves and others. I argue that through an examination of the shifting meaning of stigma within the context of American individualism, how this paradox forms and persists can be understood.

The concept of *stigma* refers to processes of social interaction that discredit an individual's character or, as Goffman (1963) put it, "spoils identity." The ways that character may be discredited are complex and sometimes subtle, especially in modern society, and in order to understand how stigma operates for the disabled, the cultural beliefs that underpin the process must be explored. After exploring the paradoxical nature of American individualism as a belief system, I show that policies intended to include the disabled in society and remove the stigma of disability may actually result in exclusion in the form of transformed meanings of stigma.

STIGMA AND SOCIAL INTERACTION

According to Goffman's classic 1963 essay, "Stigma: Notes on the Management of Spoiled Identity," a marked, or stigmatized, relationship is one in which judgments have been made by one person about another with the effect of discrediting and marking that individual as somehow deviant and vulnerable to further discrediting (Jones et al., 1984). Goffman, one of the most influential sociological thinkers of the 20th century, stressed that stigma is primarily about the management of information regarding the self. Some stigma are of the body, but, in modern society, they are increasingly about character and who a person is (identity) and dependent on control of what one person knows about another (identity management). The judgments that people make to discredit one another are based in knowledge that is widely distributed throughout society—what some social scientists refer to as common sense knowledge (Mehan & Wood, 1974) or cultural knowledge (Spradley, 1972). This knowledge of everyday life consists of assumptions and judgments about others (what everybody knows about people who cannot hear, for example), or in other words, the basic beliefs and values that made up the way people think.

Although these ways of knowing may be factually incorrect and even stereotypical, they nevertheless are widely distributed among members of a given society. How a person or group of people become stigmatized is dependent on the social context in which it occurs.

In some societies, stigma is relatively fixed. These societies are typically nonmodern, and the examples Goffman (1963) used, Greek and early Christian times, are drawn from such societies. However, categories of experience become fluid and negotiable in modern society, and because rituals of interaction undergo transformations that make them appear to be under the control of individuals rather than structures of society (Goffman, 1974; Higgins, 1992), the experience of stigma likewise becomes a matter of competent interaction.

For this reason, Goffman (1963) stressed the importance of managing information about stigma and of the individual's control over his or her biography. Paradoxically, although modern society provides its members with the interpretive means to avoid stigma (it legislates against the fateful interpretation of social identity), it rearranges the context of interaction in such a way that all members of society become vulnerable to stigma. Discrepancies between how people wish others to see them and how others actually see them, once matters of fate, now become matters of interactional strategy.[1] In the context of modern society, therefore, stigma undergoes a transformation from collective to individual or self-meanings, and, in the process, the liberating tendencies of equalization become opportunities to stigmatize.

A further extension of Goffman's thinking suggests that although stigma may discredit character in a fateful social context, in the contemporary setting it does so increasingly. Goffman's account of stigma can be seen as an elaboration on a sociological insight (Weber, 1958) that when social order is rationalized (made formal through codification) individuals are liberated from fatefulness while new conditions of discrimination aimed at the individual social self are created. In other words, although discrimination and prejudice on the basis of some condition legally or rationally defined can be forbidden, discrimination and prejudice may shift to aspects of the self that are considered matters of character. The law may be followed but not necessarily obeyed. Put differently, the requirements of meeting a rule do not always suggest the accomplishment of the purpose of the rule.

Social policies, such as mainstreaming and the Americans With Disabilities Act (ADA) mandated legislation, are designed to increase participation in society and remove the stigma of disability. However, what might be happening is the creation of new conditions of stigma, that is, stigma may shift from the fatefulness of race, caste, and biology to the autonomous social self. With such a shift, individuals once relatively safe from the threat of stigma become vulnerable to it, and those once subject to stigma discover opportunities to escape it.

Goffman (1963) used cases of hard of hearing and deaf individuals as examples of stigmatic tendencies in interaction. What he did not entertain was the obverse implication of his theory—namely, how the very structures of society designed to obviate stigma by collective management of information (policy and law) may free individuals from one kind of stigma and subject them to another. It is the thesis of this chapter that, at least with regard to deafness, there is a tension between liberation from stigma of the body and vulnerability to individual experiences of it. Hence, in the United States today, deaf people in general and school-age children in particular experience less stigma of the fateful (structural) variety and more of the consequential (interactive) type. Although this shift is difficult to document, a broad outline of consequences of mainstreaming seems to support the thesis.

---

[1]Goffman (1963, pp. 2–3) referred to this as a distinction between virtual and actual identity. It is when there is a discrepancy between virtual and actual identity that stigma occurs. In fateful stigma, virtual and actual identities are the same, that is, both are discredited. In modern stigma, the discrepancy is a matter of who knows what about the other (that is, virtual identity is normal while actual identity may be discreditable).

SPECIAL EDUCATION AS THE EQUALIZATION OF FATE

The history of special education in the United States provides a chronicle of the meanings of being disabled and of how the stigma of disability has been managed and interpreted. Although there have been many shifts in policy and practice over the years (Higgins, 1990; Lane, 1984), and these relate to stigma as fateful or consequential, today mainstreaming is the law of the nation. Its significance and impact on disabled children and the disabled population of society is not immediately apparent, because, as Goffman demonstrated, the experience of stigma is transformed in the context of society. The policy of mainstreaming reflects trends and shifts in cultural knowledge of the meanings of disability. Only through a form of cultural analysis can the transformation of the experience of stigma be identified and understood.

The idea of mainstreaming emerged from a variety of social forces centered in strong cultural values of individualism and egalitarianism. These values are central to U.S. culture and are part of the complicated and multi-faceted ways people make sense of participation in society. Individualism may be described as a kind of cognitive map or a set of guide posts for thought and action. Because the organization of U.S. life has become increasingly choice driven, individualism often manifests itself in decision making and in the ways people account for their lives and the lives of others. The organization of these accounts, the ideas people have about who they are, and their relationships with others make up the social self (Nash & Calonico, 1996). By examining the social self in broad perspective, that map people seem to be following in their participation in society can be depicted.

Any action, therefore, can be seen in relationship to the basic elements of culture called precepts (Spradley, 1972). Mainstreaming is the result of a coming together of two major forces that are changing the specialized, residential education of yesterday into integrated, auxiliary, and support programs that are today's norm. The first force is the belief Americans have about equality of opportunity, especially within the context of educational institutions. The second is the changing set of beliefs about what a "normal" person is, which, of course, is bound up in the social self. In a different yet interrelated way, each has contributed to what I here call the American experiment in special education.

CULTURAL INDIVIDUALISM

Individualism has been defined in a variety of ways, but there are common themes in these definitions. Americans, for example, see themselves as linked to one another in a way that ensures equality among all citizens. This aspect of American individualism has attracted the attention of observers and critics since the United States first became a player in world politics and economics. Well known attempts include, from the French, Alexis de Tocqueville's *Democracy in America,* from the Germans, Max Weber's *The Protestant Ethic and the Spirit of Capitalism,* and American social scientists such as Robert and Helen Lynd's *Middletown USA,* Robert Bellah, Richard Madsen, William M. Sullivan, Ann Swidler, and Steven M. Tipton's *Habits of the Heart,* and Herbert Gan's *Middle American Individualism.* Although none of these studies concerns special education directly, each offers an insight into the U.S. belief in equality of opportunity, a belief that may be seen as a cultural precept (Spradley, 1972). As a precept, this belief functions as a rule or formula for decisions people make about their action in society. However, precepts, especially in a society undergoing rapid changes, may be organized paradoxically (Carbaugh, 1988), and they may even function as ideologies in a society that Swidler (1986) refers to as having an "unsettled culture."

Mainstreaming has had an unsettling effect on educational organizations (Bushman & Bushman, 1998; Sigmon, 1987). At the very least, it represents an extension of cultural precepts to a population heretofore excluded from dominant interpretations of the meanings of social action—members of society who are disabled. The paradoxical and unsettling nature of the meanings of being disabled in U.S. society can be better appreciated by a depiction of the relationships between cultural and individual social action for various aspects of the precept of American individualism. Following classic attempts to depict this core cultural value, I sketch the meanings of attempts to mainstream disabled children and, more generally, the meanings of being disabled in U.S. culture. These meanings and their paradoxical relationships fuel the shift of stigma from fate to consequence.

The Tyranny of the Majority

In his classic work, de Tocqueville (1864) noted a tendency for Americans to conform to what they imagined as a majority. This conformity to an average view, he observed, was particularly strong in small towns and rural areas of the 18th century United States. Although Americans express strong beliefs in religious, political, and personal liberty, in their attitudes toward the religions of others, in their tolerance of political opinions, and even their conceptions of representative government, they exert great pressure on one another to conform to a middle position. Hence, a majority opinion, even if it is a simple or perhaps even an imagined majority, may become the dominant position among a group of Americans. This tendency of the majority to act as if they represent consensus is the tyranny of the majority.

The tyranny of the majority embodies a paradox because group pressures mitigate against the exercise of individual liberties. Two beliefs support the paradox: All people should act independently according to their natural potentials, and all members of society do, indeed, have potential. Paradox is embodied in social action for disabled people, however, because a specific action or range of actions they may engage in may be seen as restricted by their disability and, therefore, not grounded in natural potential. A stigma may develop as a result of paradoxical injunctions between beliefs that all members of society have potential and knowledge that some are disabled. Finally, because a majority defines the needs of society, a ranking of potentials results, and things that disabled people can do are restricted by these definitions.

In Goffman's theory, stigma forms when actual and virtual identities do not coincide. People with disabilities are vulnerable to stigma of the self, as well as the body. Whereas what potential a person has is seen as more or less endowed, the value of the potential is structured by majority group pressures. As with any paradoxical belief, an individual asserts various interpretations of his or her predicament by stressing different sides of the paradox. A blind person may have musical potential, a deaf person grace of movement, and so on according to stereotypical understandings of the potentials of disabled individuals. Although the stereotypes do not describe what people actually do, they may represent the resolution of paradox in the mind of the majority (a form of tyranny).

Legitimate Social Control

Ideas of legitimate control, in the sense of who holds ultimate authority, are remarkably individualistic in U.S. culture. Max Weber (1958), a seminal German sociological theorist of the early 20th century, noted that Americans tend to evaluate one another in terms of beliefs about an individual's self-control. Hence, according to individualism, a person is the center of society, rather than a derivation of his or her social location. Likewise, a person is the center of control. A person achieves by virtue of hard work and diligence even if the results of such efforts are new and contrary to established practices.

As Weber (1958) suggested, precepts of cultural belief reflect images of society and individual. In turn, these images function as tool kits for action and interpretations of action. In the relief of American individualism, society becomes autonomous individuals dealing with one another according to available resources. As the classic observers pointed out and current public opinion polls corroborate,[2] these individuals stand united in distrust of large organizations and of any remote or abstract collective force.

---

[2]General Service Society (GSS) is an almost annual, "omnibus," personal interview survey of U.S. households conducted by the National Opinion Research Center. GSS data since 1972 show that Americans have been and remain suspicious of large organizations and government and have changed very little over this period in their highly individualistic views of themselves and others (Davis & Smith, 1996).

The Distribution of Inequality

As Lynd and Lynd (1929) demonstrated in their landmark study of Muncie, Indiana, during the 1920s and 1930s, Americans' lives are qualitatively different depending on their access to money and social advantages, yet they think of themselves as similar—equal in some fundamental sense. Individualism as a means of understanding social life is paradoxical. Although all have the right to speak their mind, some may speak in ways that deny the rights of others. Although all are individually responsible for their station in society, not all start in the same place. Although all strive to be at the top of their respective communities, not all can be at the top. Although all opinions and choices must be respected, some choose to express opinions of disrespect for others. Indeed, the paradoxical nature of individualism seems self-evident, but it still anchors the world views of Americans (cf. Carbaugh, 1988) and comes into play in making sense of disability, especially when coupled with other precepts. For example, the cultural value on individualism encourages deaf people to develop strong senses of their equality along with confidence that they can accomplish virtually any goal they can imagine. Yet, they often dramatically experience stress between aspirations and accomplishment, especially when opportunities for accomplishment are limited. In other words, like all Americans, for deaf people equality and individualism merge into a paradox between being like and unlike others at the same time.

Therapeutic Self Meanings

In their account of the community of Americans, Bellah, Madsen, Sullivan, Swidler, and Tipton (1985) point out that the heterogeneous nature of U.S. society and the mixing of cultural backgrounds of immigrants as well as the class system of consumption has resulted in conflicting and confusing pressures that cancel one another leaving a void in which a therapeutic or psychologized self emerges.

Bellah's critique suggests that Americans think increasingly in terms of self-development and less in terms of sacrifice and loyalty, more in terms of the self as the location of significance and less in terms of collective urgency. Although Americans remain a spiritual people in terms of their ideas of their place in the universe, they seem fragmented in their accounts of the nature of that universe. They may agree about the importance of spirituality, but they value individualism so much that their definitions of spirituality, when taken as a whole, may seem highly variable and even paradoxical. One individual's spiritual experiences become evidence to another that spirituality is on the wan; for example, weekend retreats for spiritual renewal can be seen as selfish indulgences.

Self as Denial of Fate

In the U.S. belief system, an individual possesses a self that is the controlling force in social life. This belief is reflected in law and, most importantly, in how Americans account for their places as well as the places of others in society. Although the role of forces impinging on the individual is acknowledged in accounts of why people are as they are, in the final accounting, it is the individual who must accept responsibility for his or her fate. It is an individual decision, made in the context of other individual decisions, that anchors social action. This U.S. concept of selfhood is woven into policy and institutional action.

Because the concept of self embodies paradox, it is inevitable that policy or institutional action will likewise be paradoxical. With regard to the great American experiment in mainstreaming disabled individuals into society, the paradox manifests itself in policies that express the ideology of individualism yet lack the collective force to be implemented. Although Americans can agree that being disabled is not the responsibility of the disabled individual, they nevertheless often expect from the disabled individual actions that are interpretable from the point of individualism. Hence, the articulation of policy and law that embodies basic cultural precepts of individualism is important to making sense out of the fate of disabled individuals in society. The articulation of such policy and law becomes an opportunity for understanding disabled individuals as responsible and autonomous.

A BRIEF REVIEW OF POLICY AND PHILOSOPHY

U.S. society, like most others world wide, has a history of disabled people that is shameful by contemporary standards yet reflects resolutions of the paradox between autonomy and fate. As Hewett (1974) wrote, individuals different in any physically observable way were routinely mistreated, shunned, isolated from social contact, and stigmatized. It was not until the early 19th century that institutional care was provided for the physically disabled. These facilities were total institutions in the sense that residents were forced to live in relative isolation from society. The complete scope of their social existence was defined by the boundaries of the asylums in which they lived.

However, with the advent of compulsory education, disabled children were forced to attend school. Still, those with special health needs could not be cared for in the public education classroom, and slowly over a 150 year period legislation was passed that established special classrooms and schools. In his critique of special education in the United States, Sigmon (1987) offered a chronology of milestones in U.S. special education. Beginning in 1817 with the founding of the American Asylum for the Education and Instruction of the Deaf and Dumb in Hartford, Connecticut, institutions and special schools were built for a variety of children with special needs. By the early 20th century, these facilities could be found in most major cities and states, and by the 1950s laws were passed that granted children with disabilities access to the same educational opportunities as able-bodied children.

American individualism as a cultural interpretation of self was being extended to all children, at least in principle. The process of individualizing disabled children reached an apex with the passage of national legislation known as Public Law No. 94-142, "The Education for All Handicapped Act of 1975." Under this act, all children were assured, by law, education within the least restrictive environment. In the ensuing years since passage of this act, various interpretations have been offered for the meaning of the phrase "least restricted environment." By 1987 Congress had mandated in all states, and made available funds for programs for children regardless of their disability, racial or social class background. (See Table 12.1 for further detail.)

Today the precepts of American individualism as they pertain to education have been extended to disabled children. While the full impact of this application is not complete, because implementation of the various acts and amendments varies, the idea of access to educational opportunities for disabled children has been affirmed repeatedly, and the overwhelming interpretation of access favors a mainstreaming approach. With notable exceptions, such as success of bilingual (ASL/English) Schools for the Deaf, the total institutional approaches that characterized education of deaf children until the 1960s seem to be waning in the face of both economic advantages of mainstreaming and the ideological fit between mainstreaming and individualism.

The parallels between reform of special education and civil rights legislation are so striking that Sigmon (1987) refers to the period since the 1960s and the passage of Public Law No. 94-142 as the "desegregation phase of special education" (p. 27). Because the parallel is obvious and because the impact of the educational desegregation of the races that comprises the U.S. population of school-age children has been subject to much debate and controversy (Wilson, 1987), it might be expected that the desegregation of school-age children by physical, emotional, and mental disability will likewise stimulate debate and controversy (Higgins, 1990, 1992). Moreover, it can be expected that some of the trends and consequences attributed to racial desegregation may well apply to understanding the great American experiment in mainstreaming.

PARADOXICAL CONSEQUENCES OF MAINSTREAMING

Because my focus is on the paradoxical nature of individualism, I propose to show how the consequences of mainstreaming reflect the paradoxical nature of individualism, much in the same way that the consequences of racial desegregation reflect the paradoxical nature of individualism. With regard to racial desegregation, the debate centers on two issues. First, the

TABLE 12.1

Selected Federal Legislation Related to Education of Handicapped Children

Year	Act or Amendment
1867	An act of Congress provided free entrance to the National Deaf–Mute College for limited numbers of poor deaf students from any U.S. state or territory.
1879	Federal Act of 1879. To Promote the Education of the Blind. Since its enactment has provided annual appropriations to the American Printing House for the Blind for the manufacture of educational texts and aids, free of charge, for use by legally blind students of less than college level throughout the U.S. and its possessions.
1956	PL 85-531. Cooperative Research Act. Congress earmarked $667,000 for special education for the mentally retarded. First major and contemporary piece written for special education at the national level.
1959	Federal funding for professional preparation in institutions of higher learning (college professors) for training future teachers of the handicapped.
1965	PL 89-10. Elementary and Secondary Education Act. This act provided direct educational aid to states for compensatory education to socioeconomically deprived youngsters. Legally, they are not considered handicapped.
1965	PL 89-36. Funds were provided for the first ever directly funded federal educational facility: The National Technical Institute for the Deaf, at Rochester Institute of Technology, for advanced vocational training.
1966	PL 89-694. The Model Secondary School for the Deaf, directly funded by U.S. government at Gallaudet College, Washington, DC.
1966	PL 89-750. Title VI. Included granting of direct aid to programs for handicapped children. It established the Bureau of Education for the Handicapped in Washington, DC.
1970	PL 91-230. Education of the Handicapped Act. Combined into one act a number of previously isolated legislative enactments related to handicapped children. Established some new programs: Regional Resource Centers, Services for Deaf–Blind Children, programs for learning disabled.
1975	PL 94-142. The Education for All Handicapped Act of 1975. Most comprehensive and significant piece of legislation regarding the education of handicapped, applies to all children ages 3 to 21, and denotes specific categories of impairment.
1976-1983	Several acts and amendments building on PL 94-142, expanding funds available and categories of children eligible.

Table 12.1 continued on next page

1986	PL 99-457. Education of the Handicapped Act Amendments of 1986. This reauthorization of PL 94-142 provided increased funding, mandated in all state programs for the "preschool handicapped" (ages 3 to 5), gave money for early intervention programs (birth to 3 years of age), and encouraged exploration of alternative approaches to special education.
1990	ADA. Provides a national mandate for the elimination of discrimination against individuals with disabilities. Provides consistent, enforceable standards addressing discrimination against individuals with disabilities; ensures that the Federal Government plays a central role in enforcing the standards established by this act on behalf of individuals with disabilities. Invokes congressional authority in order to address the major areas of discrimination faced day-to-day by people with disabilities.

Note.   From *Radical Analysis of Special Education: Focus on Historical Development and Learning Disabilities* (pp. 23–24), by S. B. Sigmon (1987), New York: The Falmer Press. Adapted with permission.

role of social class or economic well-being in relation to the cultural integrity of minority groups, and, second, the consequences of adaptations to integration, which have assumed the form of curriculum tracking.

Wilson (1987) advanced an interpretation of racial inequality within the context of American individualism that suggests that social class overrides inequality to a degree. Hence, as African Americans become better off in terms of economic and social advantages, they conform more and more in their interpretation of participation in society to the precepts of individualism. Those individuals who remain outside the experiences of middle-class lifestyles, however, become more unlike the general population, developing adaptive and distinctive meanings of selfhood and social participation. Wilson suggested that integration works only to the degree that the values and cultural interpretation of minority and majority populations come together under a general cultural framework, and, to the degree that this does not happen, the consequence of attempted integration is the polarization of a minority population.

Although Wilson's hypothesis is somewhat controversial (see Herring, 1989; Thomas & Hughes, 1986), he did offer a theoretical expectation that, when coupled with an appreciation of the strength and distribution of an individualistic worldview, can guide assessments of the impact of attempts to achieve equality in educational opportunities.

Wilson's theory implies two trends: Those children who more closely align in behavior and attitude with the fundamentals of individualism will profit from mainstreaming, whereas those who do not will be isolated and stigmatized according to new meanings of being different. This means that the effects of mainstreaming are to polarize the disabled population into two camps—a small number who are doing much better under the new expanded opportunities and a larger group who remain disadvantaged both socially and educationally. For example, special education programs housed within regular public schools often feed a few of the best students into hearing classes, while the majority of hearing impaired students remain within the self-contained classrooms. Although there is considerable debate about which group receives education under the least restrictive environment, there can be little doubt about the results—the better students profit in terms of expanded opportunities, at least in the sense of conventional expectations, such as opportunities to attend higher education, participate in extracurricular activities, and establish good reputations.

Several authors (Mehan, Mercer, & Rueda, 1996; Sigmon, 1987) suggested how such a polarization might take place. Sigmon wrote that the tendency in U.S. special education is to expand the concept of special education largely through the label of *learning disability*. School administrators want to show that they are accommodating the needs of students with disabilities, and they may seek monetary awards with which to accomplish this yet do not wish to fundamentally alter the missions of their institutions. A struggle ensues. Sigmon (1987) wrote, "This struggle has led to the inadvertent co-optation of special education by including millions of so called mildly handicapped children instead of concentrating on the best possible education for the moderately and severely impaired" (p. 97).

Sigmon and more recently Mehan, Mercer, and Rueda (1996) identified the polarization effects of individualism. Current numbers of children in various special education programs seem to bear out his conclusion. When looking at changes in numbers of children in selected programs (see Table 12.2), it can be seen that significant increase has occurred in the category of learning disabled. What lies behind this trend is the paradox of American individualism itself.

TABLE 12.2

Numbers of Children in Special Education, Percentage Distribution by all Disabilities and Percent Change Since 1979

Selected Categories	Number in 1995	Percent of All	Percent Change Since 1979
Learning disabled	2,487,900	51.2%	22%
Emotional disturbed	427,600	8.8%	−1.8%
Mentally retarded	553,920	11.4%	−11.6%
Hearing impaired	63,200	1.3%	−1.0%
Visual impaired	24,000	0.5%	0.04%

Note. For school year ending as shown. Age range varies somewhat from census year to year. *Statistical Abstract of the United States, 1998: The Natural Data Book.* U.S. Department of Commerce, Bureau of the Census. Table no. 287, p. 182.

That paradox plays itself out through each of the aspects of U.S. egalitarianism. First, the tyranny of the majority operates in seeking a way of making sense of differences in behavior and attitudes among children by selecting those children who can be worked with and who profit from educational intervention. Hence, disabled children who pose the greatest difficulty, although they often start in a regular classroom, are tracked into special classrooms and programs as a means of managing them. This has the effect of limiting opportunities for these children. Because budgetary considerations favor mainstreaming (programs that mainstream are generally less expensive than residential or specialized, self-contained programs), educators are less likely to seek funds for approaches that seem to be a retreat to institutional perspectives.

Proposals for constructing centralized schools for deaf children are often paired with proposals for incorporating special classes in existing facilities. With regard to deaf children, this resulted in a complete reversal of numbers of children in different educational facilities. In 1961, for example, nearly 70% of all deaf children were enrolled in residential schools. By 1996, according to the annual survey conducted by the *American Annals of the Deaf,* 71% of all children with severe to profound hearing loss "attend[ed] regular education school with hearing students" (Holden-Pitt, 1997). Although it is difficult to document, these pressures toward mainstreaming most likely result in advantages for those children whose behavior and attitudes parallel those of the hearing students in these schools, and these social skills, which may be interpreted as acting hearing (Johnson & Erting, 1989), may override excellent academic skills, that is, poor social skills take precedence over academic skills in placement decisions.

The tendency to reisolate profoundly hearing impaired children within regular schools is a part of the transformation of stigma. In other words, although deaf children are present in the regular school, they actually have a much different set of experiences from regular students and, at least socially, are in their own school. As a report from the Gallaudet Research Institute puts it, "In fact the overwhelmingly modal group comprising the Annual Survey data base are students with profound hearing loss who receive no academic integration with hearing students" (Allen, 1992, p. 382).

Deaf children with inappropriate social selves are tracked into special classes and deprived of the very expanded educational opportunities that mainstreaming philosophy seeks to provide. This tendency seems akin to de Tocqueville's tyranny of the majority—that tendency of Americans to press toward a middle ground of behavior and attitude thereby muting diversity.

Because the only truly legitimate social control, according to individualism, is that coming from the self, those incapable of controlling themselves are candidates for external controls. If a person acts in ways that do not make cultural sense, then someone else must assume responsibility on behalf of the person. Of course, in the history of education in the United States, the rationale for public compulsory education has been to instill a core set of cultural values and beliefs in the citizenry. In other words, core values rest on assumptions not only that all members of society will share them, but that they will learn about them in the same way.[3] Because values are embodied in language, it is impossible to separate questions of language and language acquisition from values. Just as children of immigrants were expected to learn U.S. core values in English, hearing impaired children face similar tacit assumptions that denigrate their learning and language.

A deaf child has special language development needs, for example, and these needs call into question assumptions about how language develops naturally (Meadow-Orlans, 1996). Children showing development most closely aligned with normal development will be advantaged in a setting operating under the assumptions of normalcy of language development. The frustration that teachers and parents may experience with the lack of normal development may well occasion special classrooms and programs that, once again, disadvantage the child outside the normative expectations of teachers and administrators. Hence, a deaf child whose speech is incomprehensible to his or her teachers and fellow students will be tracked in programs that isolate him or her from the mainstream (Higgins, 1990). Paradoxically, being in a hearing school becomes restrictive.

As inequality becomes a part of the mainstreamed or desegregated school environment, it justifies further restriction. This justification functions as the rationale for external social control. Little wonder, therefore, that disabled children, at least deaf ones, are more likely than the general school population to be seen as possessing behavior problems, and likely to be overrepresented in those special programs for categories of children whose behavior is seen as incorrigible and requiring isolation from the general population of students.

Once the presence of a disabled child in the mainstream environment is seen as problematic, therapeutic meanings of self can be applied so that the child's self-concept becomes the source of the problem, not his or her physical disability. Hence, the child is targeted for therapy designed to change his or her self-concept. Literature sights lack of self-esteem as a central problem for the disabled child (Meadows-Orlans, 1987). Once this shift in the locus of the problem has been made from physical disability to character disability, efforts are directed at remedial self-development, and these distance the disabled child from the general student population. Again, the paradox derives from individualism itself because opportunities are defined in terms of cultural expectations about the nature of the self in society. High self-esteem, a sense of individual empowerment, and

---

[3]This often took the form of Americanization with a strong emphasis on English which fostered a shift from ethnic mother tongues such as German and Italian to English, and from loyalty to "old world" ways to new values of individualism (Veltman, 1983).

self-motivation are normal; low self-esteem, poor motivation, and withdrawal are disabling. A child without the requisite self-concept mainstreamed into a school environment, therefore, is disadvantaged to the extent that he or she recognizes his or her departure from the norms of vital individualistic self-interpretation.

Finally, because it is in the arena of self and self-mastery that fate is denied, great value is placed on overcoming odds. Hence, those few students who meet cultural expectations of self-development are seen as heroic. The child who succeeds in the mainstreamed environment is, therefore, doubly exceptional—exceptional in the sense of being physically disabled and in the sense of conforming to culturally defined self-development.

CONCLUSION

In this chapter, I outline a theoretical sketch for assessing the great American experiment in mainstreaming. The experiment itself can only be fully appreciated in the relief of American individualism as a cultural system for understanding participation in U.S. society. The changes in the cultural system itself, its paradoxical nature with regard to issues of social control, the experiences of self, and inequality are reflected in the very policy of mainstreaming.

Improving the education of physically disabled children requires acknowledging the social processes that define participation in society. Although the extension of opportunities to disabled children is consistent with the philosophy of the integrity of the individual, the actual opportunities the policy affords children are double edged or paradoxical. Sigmon (1987) put it well when he wrote

> Mainstreaming is a dual edged concept as it allows some handicapped pupils to be in a more normalized program; but it also can be used to deprive truly handicapped youngsters of needed services to save local school districts money if these services are not fully funded by state governments via federal reimbursement. It is best to meet all of an exceptional child's needs, but this must be done with as little stigmatization, labeling and segregation as possible. (p. 84)

What I attempted to show is that the consequence of mainstreaming in general and in particular for deaf children is not simply one of economics and pedagogy; it is also rooted in the paradoxical nature of being an individual American. The U.S. way of understanding the self shifts the locus of disability from the body to the self.

REFERENCES

Allen, T. (1992). Subgroup differences in educational placement for deaf and hard of hearing students. *American Annals of the Deaf, 137*(5), 381-388.

Bellah, R., Madsen, R., Sullivan, W. M., Swidler, A., & Tipton, S. M. (1985). *Habits of the heart: Individualism and commitment in American life.* Berkeley: University of California Press.

Bushman, B. A., & Bushman, T. E. (1998). The Americans with Disabilities Act (1990): Its Impact on Higher Education, *SMSU Journal of Public Affairs, 2,* 21-38.

Carbaugh, D. (1988). *Talking American: Cultural discourses on Donahue.* Norwood, NJ: Ablex.

Davis, J. A., & Smith, T. W. (1992). *The NORC General Social Survey: A user's guide.* Newbury Park, CA: Sage.

de Tocqueville, A. (1864). *Democracy in America.* Cambridge, MA: Sever & Francis.

Gans, H. J. (1988). *Middle American individualism: The future of liberal democracy.* New York: The Free Press.

Goffman, E. (1963). *Stigma: Notes on the management of spoiled identity.* Englewood Cliffs, NJ: Prentice-Hall.

Goffman, E. (1974). *Frame analysis: An essay on the organization of experience.* Cambridge, MA: Harvard University Press.

Herring, C. (1989). Convergence, polarization, or what? Racially-based changes in attitudes and outlooks, 1964-1984. *Sociological Quarterly, 30,* 267-282.

Hewett, F. M. (1974). *Education of exceptional learners.* Boston: Allyn & Bacon.

Higgins, P. C. (1990). *The challenge of educating together deaf and hearing youth: Making mainstreaming work.* Springfield, IL: Thomas.

Higgins, P. C. (1992). *Making disability: Exploring the social transformation of human variation.* Springfield, IL: Thomas.

Holden-Pitt, L. (1997). Annual Survey. *American Annals of the Deaf, 142*(2), 108.

Johnson, R., & Erting, C. (1989). Ethnicity and socialization in a classroom for deaf children. In C. Lucas (Ed.), *Sociolinguistics of the deaf community* (pp. 41–84). San Diego, CA: Academic Press.

Jones, E., Amerigo, F., Hastorf, A. H., Markus, H., Miller, D., & Scott, R. A. (1984). *Social stigma: The psychology of marked relationships.* New York: Freeman.

Lane, H. L. (1984). *When the mind hears: A history of the deaf.* New York: Random House.

Lynd, R., & Lynd, H. (1929). *Middletown: A study of modern american culture.* New York: Harcourt Brace.

Meadow-Orlans, K. P. (1987). Understanding deafness: Socialization of children. In P. C. Higgins & J. E. Nash (Eds.), *Understanding deafness socially* (pp. 29–58). Springfield, IL: Thomas.

Meadow-Orlans, K. P. (1996). Socialization of deaf children and youth. In P. C. Higgins & J. E. Nash (Eds.), *Understanding deafness socially; Continuities in research and theory* (pp. 71–95). Springfield, IL: Thomas.

Mehan, H., Mercer, J. R., & Rueda, R. (1996). Special education. In *The encyclopedia of education and sociology.* New York: Garland Publishing Company.

Mehan, H., & Wood, H. (1974). *The reality of ethnomethodology.* New York: Wiley.

Nash, J. E., & Calonico, J. M. (1996). *The meanings of social interaction: An introduction to social psychology.* Dix Hills, NY: General Hall.

Sigmon, S. B. (1987). *Radical analysis of special education: Focus on historical development and learning disabilities.* New York: The Falmer Press.

Spradley, J. P. (Ed.). (1972). *Culture and cognition: Rules, maps and plans.* San Francisco, CA: Chandler Publishing Company.

Swidler, A. (1986). Culture in action. *American Sociological Review, 51,* 273-286.

Thomas, M., & Hughes, M. (1986). Race in America. *American Sociological Review, 51,* 830-841.

Veltman, C. (1983). *Language shift in the United States.* Berlin, Germany: Mouton.

Weber, M. (1958). *Protestant ethic and the spirit of capitalism.* New York: Scribner.

Wilson, W. J. (1987). *The truly disadvantaged: The inner city, the underclass and public policy.* Chicago: University of Chicago Press.

13

A Bold Step: Changing the Curriculum for Culturally Deaf and Hard of Hearing Students

Rachel E. Stone
Western Maryland College

I found out that I was not alone in my dream. My dream was that culturally deaf and hard of hearing people would go to a school with the curriculum supporting their experiences. I believe I had that dream when I was very young while attending a residential school with deaf students. Most of my learning experience was hearing-oriented, and the books we used were Eurocentric in nature. We read and studied everything about hearing people. The Wright brothers, wars, Presidents of the United States, inventions, etc. Everything was about people who were hearing. Nothing about deaf people. During the elementary years, I never had a teacher who was a role model. In my secondary years, I had a few instructors whom I considered my role models, and they were deaf just like me. Each time my classmates and I came into the classroom with deaf instructors, we would try to convince them to tell us their stories and avoid at all costs to study the subject we were supposed to learn unless the story was relevant to the course being taught. The classroom turned into a dream for us.

During those times, we rarely thought of ourselves as just a minority within a majority of hearing people. It was like stepping out of the hearing world and entering a world of our own. When the class was over, reality raised its head forcing us to suspend our dream temporarily until the next class. I always looked forward to watching deaf adults telling stories about their experiences, ranging from successful to agonizing. I never pinpointed why I enjoyed those particular experiences until I discovered that I belonged to a unique culture called deaf culture. It was not until I was 30 that I took a course discussing deaf culture and American Sign Language. At that time, I learned about Laurent Clerc and that he was deaf and helped establish the first school for deaf students in America in 1817! I wondered why it was necessary to learn about famous hearing people rather than to learn about deaf people like Clerc. Am I like other deaf people, not important enough too, to be part of the society? All those years were lost in the hearing world. I often wonder what I would be like if I had been brought up and taught from the deaf culture point of view. I believe without struggles and achievements we may not be where we are today. However, if we had studied and learned about Deaf people's lives while in school, we would be further ahead of where we are now.

—A personal conversation with a deaf adult

By the 1980s, the demand for wider representation of diverse cultural perspectives in school curricula was evident, and the argument was being made that students should be encouraged to view U.S. society through various cultural lenses (Nelson, Carlson, & Palonsky, 1996). Traditionally, it has been argued, the objective of public education in the United States has been to educate students for democratic participation, to encourage individual achievement through academic competition, and to promote and teach the values and traditions of U.S. cultural heritage.

According to Sizemore (1989), the curriculum is not only the content but how it is taught and how it is administered. Further, curricula result from political settlements and compromises over what is important to know (Goodson, Meyer, & Apple, 1991; Nelson, Carlson, & Palonsky, 1996). Curriculum writers choose certain heroes, events, and values to emphasize and praise and shift other people, other events, and other values to the margins of academic consideration or ignore them altogether. Students are more likely to learn about the fictionalized childhood experiences of George Washington and Abraham Lincoln than about the real lives of people like themselves. In other words, content, methods, and administration are all influenced by cultural values and belief systems about what students should learn in school.

One of the earliest efforts to infuse multicultural perspectives into a curriculum occurred in 1971 when the New Concept School in Chicago adopted an Afrocentric curriculum ("Alternate Schools," 1995). African American parents were disillusioned with traditional approaches and were seeking schools that would instill pride in their racial heritage. Supporters believed that such schools would provide African American children with a good education while helping them regain a sense of identity and community that was lost through integration. African history and culture were integral parts of this curriculum, which also included English, math, science, geography, social studies, and physical education. According to one teacher at the school, students were taught to look at the world through African eyes.

During a journey to Africa, Asante (1992), a supporter of empowerment and culturally centered education for African American children, noticed that children in Africa seemed more motivated than African American children. He concluded that in order to empower students, it is necessary to present information in such a way that students leave the classroom feeling that they are an integral part of the information. The academic content, then, becomes a center within the cultural context of the students' own experiences. Delpit (1988) added to this perspective, arguing that African American and poor students often suffer because educators do not provide them with knowledge of the rules needed to function in the culture of power. Her point was that those with power are frequently least aware of its existence, and those without power are often most aware of its existence.

African Americans are not alone in their interest in developing ethnic-centered curricula. Native American and Alaska Native educators also argue that it is by recovering the past and regaining a strong sense of identity using culturally appropriate curricula and instruction that Native American and Alaska Native children will achieve educational success. In the 1960s, tribal colleges in Arizona and New Mexico "nativized" their education by adopting tribe-specific curricula, and, in 1972, as a result of Native American activism, the Indian Education Act was passed, establishing that Native American people themselves, not the U.S. government, should decide what is best for Native Americans (Reyhner, 1994). More recently, in Native American Education in the Santa Fe schools, there has been a curricular shift from traditional education to one including the culture and language of Native Americans.

TEACHERS AS CULTURAL FACILITATORS

Although those opposed to the spread of multiculturalism in the curriculum are concerned that an emphasis on diversity will divide the United States culturally (Chavez, 1996; Schlesinger, 1996), even among supporters there is concern about teachers' readiness to be effective in implementing a multicultural curriculum. Teachers themselves have usually been educated in a Eurocentric curriculum and are most comfortable teaching what is familiar to them. An approach to teaching that incorporates multicultural perspectives is likely to present a challenge to teachers educated traditionally. There is a great need, then, for a multicultural curriculum for teacher education to enhance teachers' knowledge of different cultural traditions as well as to prepare them to adopt teaching approaches that will meet the needs of a diverse student population.

Two examples serve to illustrate the kinds of challenges facing teacher educators and school systems attempting to implement multicultural curricula. A 1995 article in the Indianapolis Star ("Living and Learning," 1995) described student teachers doing their practicum at a Navajo reservation school where Native American history and literature were incorporated into the curriculum. A former student teacher, now a principal, emphasized that Anglo educators who teach Navajos must be prepared to be treated as outsiders. The Navajos do not need to be saved. They have their own religion, culture, and customs, and educators who continue to assume that the majority culture is superior are considered arrogant and disrespectful.

Teachers' lack of familiarity with African American culture is illustrated by Hilliard (1989) in his article, "Teachers and Cultural Styles in a Pluralistic Society." He pointed out that teachers from a European cultural background have a linear storytelling style, whereas many African American children exhibit a spiraling storytelling style, with many departures from an initial point but with a return to the main storyline. Rather than understanding the children's storytelling as reflective of a cultural style, the teachers believe that the children's stories lack order and that the children are not skilled storytellers.

Regardless of cultural affiliation, advocates of a multicultural curriculum emphasize the importance of building a culturally centered curriculum in a positive educational setting. This type of curricula provides a connectedness with the students' life experiences and the experiences of their mentors and teachers. People from minority cultures seem to feel the need to create a critical link between their experience and that of the majority culture with the instructors' support.

DEAF EDUCATION: PAST AND PRESENT

For the past 200 years, deaf education has had one goal: to educate deaf and hard of hearing individuals for full participation in U.S. society by promoting, encouraging, and teaching the values and traditions of people living in the United States—who happen to be hearing. During the past two centuries, numerous philosophies and approaches for educating deaf and hard of hearing students have come and gone, but from the beginning, deaf education programs followed a curricula that excludes the deaf experience. The approach has been hearing centered instruction in which deaf students feel little connection with the curriculum. Students study the literature, history, and politics of hearing people without any mention of deaf people's accomplishments. The books they read are likely to have been written by hearing authors, and they are tested only for their knowledge of hearing culture and history. They are likely to learn more about the experiences and activities of nondeaf individuals than about the real lives of deaf people like themselves.

Most educators do not think about teaching hearing culture to hearing students, and it is simply assumed that the language of instruction is a spoken language. Nevertheless, whether educators are aware of it, information conveyed is hearing centered. Hearing students see successful hearing people when they study history. They are able to visualize themselves in similar roles, and they have numerous role models to admire. They are more likely to feel connected with the information presented in the traditional curriculum throughout their years in school. Furthermore, they have the opportunity to experiment with ideas, with leadership, and with relations with peers and adults in a culturally compatible milieu—all day, 180 days a year, every year from the age of 6 to 18.

Do deaf students have the opportunity to study and learn about people similar to themselves? Is there an existing curriculum that incorporates the culture, history, and language of deaf people? Ramsey (1997) found in her study of deaf students educated with hearing students in a public school setting that the deaf students turned to each other to address their cultural and communication needs. When deaf students are educated in a hearing-centered educational environment, do they feel connected even though they have not had the opportunity to learn about other people who share their experience? Where do students who are deaf and hard of hearing see themselves in history? Do they perceive their place in society as full participants? Do they have the opportunity to experiment with ideas related to themselves?

By continuing to teach from the perspective of a hearing-centered curriculum, teachers create limitations for deaf and hard of hearing students. Unlike their hearing counterparts, they do not have the opportunity to explore ideas, leadership roles, and relationships with others like themselves. What is the effect on the self-concept of deaf students when their identity as deaf people is unrecognized and undervalued in this way? Is this exclusively hearing centered approach not a form of cultural imperialism?

Deaf Studies in the 1990s

In the 1990s, schools for deaf and hard of hearing students played an important role in dispensing the history and culture of deaf Americans, and deaf people themselves argued for a more culturally sensitive curriculum. Corson (1992), a school superintendent who is deaf, suggested that the world of deaf individuals is shaped by what they have learned through the deaf experience—how they see themselves and view the world, what they have learned and have been taught. He noted that research in the areas of deaf language, culture, history, and arts has changed what individuals who are deaf know about themselves. Similarly, Moore (1996) pointed out that studying the lives of deaf achievers can inform people who are deaf about how these individuals communicated, raised families, made livings, and functioned with other deaf people as well as in the hearing community where they achieved and overcame obstacles. He stated that by learning about these successful deaf individuals, others can learn much about their past, identities, and dreams.

Deaf professionals stress that students should be taught about themselves and others like them before learning about those who are different (Bangs, 1993; Bienvenu, 1992). They believe that by educating students about their culture, their self-esteem and self-image will improve, and they will develop a sense of self-worth and pride. In order to be successful in the majority culture, students need to acquire a strong cultural foundation of their own. These writers argued that a culturally relevant curriculum will also result in increased participation in and access to society.

Bienvenu (1992) emphasized that the study of deaf people should not focus on deaf people's deficiencies and should not encourage a pathological zeal for curing deafness or helping deaf people become hearing. Instead, she suggested that the curriculum should adopt a cultural view focusing on deaf people's lives, their accomplishments, their language, and culture. It is also imperative that researchers study how deaf people have been perceived and treated historically so that we can better understand how they overcame attitudinal barriers and achieved empowerment as deaf individuals despite the obstacles.

Mather (1994) studied the storytelling activity of a hearing instructor and a deaf teacher with deaf and hard of hearing children. She found that the students were more responsive to the deaf teacher than the hearing teacher and were able to discuss the story in depth. Mather's interpretation is that the teacher with the same culture and language as the children was able to establish the rapport necessary to facilitate interaction and learning.

Since the late 1970s, in a limited number of deaf education programs, students have been allowed to learn about their cultural heritage and the role of their language in the academic setting. Deaf culture studies and ASL classes in these programs have been added as a one-week or one-month feature celebrating the lives of deaf people. Furthermore, Miller-Nomeland's (1992) survey of 120 programs for deaf students found that 68% teach deaf studies and 77% of these is at the high school level. Another study indicated that 71 (59.2%) kindergarten through high school programs offered short courses, workshops, and activities related to deaf studies (Bangs, 1993). Miller-Nomeland (1992) and Bangs (1993) identified the most frequent topics included in deaf studies curricula, and the lack of uniformity is clear. Miller-Nomeland's survey revealed that deaf culture, history, self-knowledge, communicative strategies, ASL, and assistive communication devices are the most common topics covered in elementary and secondary programs. Bangs found these topics most prevalent: deaf people in theater, TV, and film; sports and recreation; and written literature about and by deaf people. Bienvenu (1992) advocated more cultural representation in the curriculum, but, to date, no program has been identified that provides a comprehensive deaf studies curriculum from kindergarten to high school. Rarely are students provided with such courses on a daily basis. Apparently Jankowski (1997) was correct when she stated that educational professionals believe that world knowledge and competency in the society of the majority are far more important than minority linguistic and cultural considerations.

A NEW DIRECTION: A DEAF-CENTERED CURRICULUM

Bienvenu (1992) argued that hearing-centered education sends a message to deaf students that important people and people with power are hearing. Other writers pointed out that identity and self-concept among deaf students are often not clear due to lack of knowledge and awareness of themselves as members of a culturally unique group (Carty, 1994; Kannapell, 1994; Stone & Stirling, 1994). Grosjean (1992) advocated that deaf children be given the opportunity to learn about deaf culture and then hearing culture so that they will be able to interact with members of both. How can educators ensure that deaf students will become adults who are content with themselves and their lives? How can they gain a sense of pride and identity as deaf and hard of hearing individuals? Do students feel detached from their own culture because they have no cultural center as a result of the hearing-centered curriculum? As a departure from the traditional curriculum, Bangs (1993) proposed a new approach to education called Deafcentric education, teaching deaf students about deaf culture first.

Early and continuing instruction in a Deafcentric curriculum is necessary to help students become grounded in their culture, identity, and history. A strong sense of self will serve them well in interacting in both the deaf and hearing worlds. The question is how can educators balance the teaching of deaf culture with the teaching of other academic subjects such as mathematics, science, social studies, and English? In traditional deaf education, there is no place for deaf cultural studies because professionals believe they must prepare deaf and hard of hearing students for a predominantly hearing world, and they do not see Deaf cultural studies as supporting that goal. It is time for this narrow focus to change. Now educators must strive for an approach in which deaf cultural content is embedded throughout the curriculum.

CONCLUSION

Deaf education has not been entirely successful in educating students for full participation in the mainstream U.S. society. However, it is not the students who must change, it is the schools. Curriculum reform aimed at moving from a hearing-centered curriculum to a Deafcentric approach is proposed as a means of enabling deaf students to reach their full potential. The goal is for deaf students to participate fully in their own culture, perceiving, thinking, feeling, and carrying out discourse in the deaf world and to apply the knowledge they gain to their interaction within the world of the hearing majority. Some educators may find this proposal and the underlying critique of the status quo in deaf education unsettling. Others who want to see change and improvement in deaf education will welcome these ideas. The challenge here is for professionals to adopt a new vision and chart a new direction for the future. Furthermore, deaf people should be at the forefront of the planning for this change because deaf and hard of hearing people are the experts on their own lives, as they live them within both the deaf and the hearing worlds. The proposal advanced is that deaf students formally study the culture of deaf people and use the knowledge they gain to study the hearing world in which they live. If deaf education continues to teach students through a hearing-centered approach, the lack of connection between students and the curriculum will continue. A deaf-centered curriculum will enhance students' curiosity and energy and provide them with knowledge they can utilize in facing life's challenges and reaching their human potential.

REFERENCES

Alternate schools put emphasis on Africa. (1995, April 13). *The Indianapolis Star*, B6.

Asante, M. (1991/1992). Afrocentric curriculum. *Educational Leadership, 49,* 28–39.

Bangs, D. (1993). Deaf studies: Building bridges, building pride. In *Deaf studies III: Bridging cultures in the 21st century* (pp. 25–31). Washington, DC: Gallaudet University.

Bienvenu, M. (1992). Deaf studies in the nineties: Meeting the critical needs. In *Deaf studies for educators* (pp. 17–34). Washington, DC: Gallaudet University.

Carty, B. (1994). The development of deaf identity. In C. J. Erting, R. C. Johnson, D. Smith, & B. Snider (Eds.), *The deaf way: Perspectives from the international conference on deaf culture* (pp. 40–43). Washington, DC: Gallaudet University.

Chavez, L. (1995). Should multicultralism permeate the curriculum? In J. Noll (Ed.), *Taking sides: Clashing views on controversial educational issues* (8th ed., pp. 94–98). Guilford, CT: The Dushkin Publishing Group, Inc.

Corson, H. (1992). Deaf studies: A framework for learning and teaching. In *Deaf studies for educators* (pp. 7–16). Washington, DC: Gallaudet University.

Delpit, L. (1988). The silenced dialogue: Power and pedagogy in educating other people's children. *Harvard Educational Review, 58*(3), 483–502.

Goodson, I., Meyer, J., & Apple, M. (1991). Introduction: special issue on sociology of the curriculum. *Sociology of education, 64*(1), iii.

Grosjean, F. (1992). The bilingual and the bicultural person in the hearing and in the deaf world. In W. Stokoe (Ed.), *Sign language studies, 77* (pp. 307–320). Burtonsville, MD: Linstok Press.

Hilliard, A. (1989). Teachers and cultural styles in a pluralistic society. *National Education Association Today, 7*(6), 65–69.

Jankowski, K. (1997). *Deaf empowerment: Emergence, struggle and rhetoric.* Washington, DC: Gallaudet University.

Kannapell, B. (1994). Deaf identity: An American perspective. In C. J. Erting, R. C. Johnson, D. Smith, & B. Snider (Eds.), *The deaf way: Perspectives from the international conference on deaf culture* (pp. 44–48). Washington, DC: Gallaudet University.

Living and Learning. (1995, November 12). *The Indianapolis Star,* A1, D4.

Mather, S. (1994). Classroom turn-taking mechanism: Effective strategies for using eye gaze as a regulator. In C. J. Erting, R. C. Johnson, D. Smith, & B. Snider (Eds.), *The deaf way: Perspectives from the international conference on deaf culture* (pp. 627–632). Washington, DC: Gallaudet University.

Miller-Nomeland, M. (1992). Developing a deaf studies curriculum guide for preschool-eighth grade. In *Deaf studies for educators* (pp. 42–45). Washington, DC: Gallaudet University.

Moore, M. (1996). The great treasure hunt: What we can learn from researching "deaf history." In M. Garretson (Ed.), *Deafness: Historical perspectives: A deaf American monograph* (pp. 107–111). Silver Spring, MD: National Association of the Deaf.

Nelson, J., Carlson, K., & Palonsky, S. (1996). *Critical issues in education: A dialectic approach* (3rd ed.). New York: McGraw- Hill.

Ramsey, C. (1997). *Deaf children in public schools: Placement, context, and consequences.* Washington, DC: Gallaudet University Press.

Reyhner, J. (1994, April). *American Indian/Alaska Native education.* Bloomington, IN: *The Phi Delta Kappa Foundation.*

Schlesinger, A. (1995). Do black students need an afrocentric curriculum? In J. Noll (Ed.), *Taking sides: Clashing views on controversial educational issues* (8th ed., pp. 227–236). Guilford, CT: The Dushkin Publishing Group, Inc.

Sizemore, B. (1989). Curriculum, race, and effective schools. In H. Holtz, I. Marcus, J. Dougherty, S. Michaels, & R. Peduzzi (Eds.), *Education and the American dream* (pp. 88–95). New York: Bergin & Garvey.

Stone, R., & Stirling, L. (1994). Developing and defining an identity: Deaf children of deaf and hearing parents. In C. J. Erting, R. C. Johnson, D. Smith, & B. Snider (Eds.), *The deaf way: Perspectives from the international conference on deaf culture* (pp. 49–54). Washington, DC: Gallaudet University.

Emerging Educational Programs for Deaf Students in Mongolia and Nepal: A Special Report

Birgit Dyssegaard
Danish International Development Assistance

Children and adults with disabilities are among the poorest, most vulnerable, and most neglected groups in many developing countries (Swedish International Development Authority, 1995). Individuals with hearing loss are no exception. This chapter provides a firsthand account of observations made while providing assistance to educational programs for deaf students in Mongolia and Nepal, countries with limited economic resources and little history of effective education for students with disabilities. Although educational changes are emerging in these countries, there is not yet adequate data-based research to analyze and interpret the results of those changes. A primary goal of this chapter is to encourage such research identifying potential questions that research might fruitfully address. Systematic analysis of the effects of educational change in developing countries like Mongolia and Nepal can provide unique information about possibilities for deaf children's development in contexts very different from those that informed most previous experience. Therefore, in addition to providing a necessary data base for evaluation of program results in those countries, such research potentially broadens and enriches understanding of developmental processes, in general, for deaf children.

This chapter begins with a brief review of some pertinent international agreements and statements in support of increased efforts for education of persons with disabilities. Then, the stories of two deaf students in Mongolia are recounted. One student is a young child from a relatively affluent family in a major town; the other is a young herdsman from the countryside. Issues and needs for deaf education in that country are discussed and observations from the second country, Nepal, are then addressed. Finally, general issues related to changing educational practices and delivery of services in developing nations are discussed and suggestions for research efforts are outlined.

INTERNATIONAL SUPPORT FOR INCREASED EDUCATIONAL OPPORTUNITIES

In recognition of the difficulties faced by persons with disabilities, especially in developing countries, the international community issued a number of declarations and agreements confirming a commitment to the rights of all people to be included in society on equal terms. Although these declarations address a variety of issues related to the rights of persons with disabilities, the focus of this discussion is on portions of the declarations that address educational issues. For example, the United Nations Convention on the Rights of the Child states that, "a child with disabilities has the right to special care, education, and training to help him or her enjoy a full and decent life in dignity and achieve the greatest degree of self-reliance and social integration possible" (United Nations, 1989, Article 23).

In 1994, the United Nations General Assembly adopted the Standard Rules on the Equalization of Opportunities for Persons With Disabilities. Rule 6, Education, emphasizes that countries should ensure that education for persons with disabilities forms an integral part of national educational planning, curriculum development, and school organization. Although education in mainstreamed (or inclusive) contexts is recommended in this rule, it also states that

> education for deaf and deaf/blind persons may be more suitably provided in schools for such persons or special classes and units in mainstream schools. In the initial stage [of development of services], in particular, special attention needs to be focused on culturally sensitive instruction that will result in effective communication skills and maximum independence for people who are deaf or deaf/blind. (United Nations, 1994, Rule 6.9)

Other declarations, "World Declaration on Education for All" (United Nations Children's Fund, 1990) and "The Salamanca Statement and

Framework for Action on Special Needs Education" (United Nations Educational, Scientific and Cultural Organization, 1994), reiterated the international commitment to providing access to education for all persons with disabilities:

> The guiding principle that informs this framework is that schools should accommodate all children regardless of their physical, intellectual, social, emotional, linguistic, or other conditions. This should include disabled and gifted children, street and working children, children from remote or nomadic populations, children from linguistic, ethnic or cultural minorities and children from disadvantaged or marginalized groups. These conditions create a range of different challenges to school systems. In the context of this Framework, the term "special educational needs" refers to all those children and youth whose needs arise from disabilities or learning difficulties. Many children experience learning difficulties and thus have special educational needs at some time during their schooling. Schools have to find ways of successfully educating all children, including those who have serious disadvantages and disabilities. (UNESCO, 1994, paragraph 3)

This declaration, which addressed needs of all persons with disabilities, goes further and proposes that they preferably should be educated in an inclusive or mainstreamed context. It calls for the development of a pedagogy that is responsive to needs of all students and concludes, "A change in social perspective is imperative. For far too long, the problems of people with disabilities have been compounded by a disabling society that has focused upon their impairments rather than their potential." Soon thereafter, the United Nations Social Summit (1995) in Copenhagen adopted a declaration stressing that all persons, poor as well as wealthy, disabled as well as nondisabled, should have equal access to basic social services, especially education and health care services.

Thus, although the specifics of various declarations differ and the strength of a preference for inclusive versus separate educational settings for students with disabilities varies, there has been a strong international mandate to provide education for all persons in all countries. Of course, even the best and most progressive principles and statements do not ensure easy and fast implementation. Most often, the distance between the decision makers and the millions of people with disabilities who are supposed to benefit from these principles is very, very far. At best, many steps are involved in the process of changing the reality of life for individuals.

The Role of Denmark

The country of Denmark has taken an especially active role in providing direct assistance to developing countries throughout the world. These efforts are aimed primarily at the alleviation of poverty and its effects. Attention also has been directed toward enhancing the role of women, protecting the environment, and promoting good government and human rights (Danish International Development Assistance, 1994, 1997). These goals have been interpreted as providing a mandate for supporting efforts in education in the countries served and improvement of basic and primary education is one of the priority areas of Danish assistance to developing countries. Support for the education of children with special needs is increasingly seen as an integral part of this effort.

The Danish International Development Assistance program (DANIDA) began its first major special needs education program in Kenya in 1984. Experience in that country has been brought to current efforts in Uganda, Zambia, Mongolia, and Nepal. In accordance with most recent international declarations, education of children with disabilities in regular classrooms and in special classes located in local schools has been promoted.

My Role With DANIDA.   For more than 10 years, I have worked as an external consultant to DANIDA and assisted in the development of educational programs for children with special needs in developing countries. During the years of 1980 to 1983, I also had the opportunity to collaborate with Kathryn Meadow-Orlans and her colleagues at the Center for Studies in Education and Human Development at Gallaudet University. That work led me to a deeper understanding of the importance of communication on all aspects of human life and on child development. I now see development of interaction and communication skills in the widest sense as the most important issue for early intervention programs and special needs education. My previous work in Denmark as director of the special needs education department of the county of Copenhagen being responsible among others for development and implementation of programs for children and adults who were unable to use oral communication (deaf children as well as children and adults with autism), as well as my work within a neonatal intensive care unit, had shown me how desperately individuals at any age will struggle to interact and communicate with others. However, none of these experiences fully prepared me for the impact of working with deaf children served by new educational programs in developing countries. When I first encountered these children, they had been expected to develop oral communication without even the support of hearing aids. In reality, these children and their teachers could not communicate at any useful level, and most of the children communicated with each other through home signs only. These were thought to be the most fortunate deaf children in those countries, however, because most deaf children had no access to formal education of any kind.

Since my initial contact with these deaf students, I have seen the progress that can be made in relatively short periods of time when educational programs begin to teach and use signed language, when parents are empowered to take an active role in educational decisions, and when expectations for deaf children's accomplishments are raised.

Two stories from Mongolia demonstrate the pervasive benefits possible from educational change. These stories reflect the complications inherent in supporting educational change that is economically feasible and responsive to cultural sensitivities in a nonwestern country where families are reluctant to send their children away from home to attend school.

Mongolia is a vast country with enormous stretches of beautiful steppes, mountains, and desert areas. Now, as in centuries past, traditional herdsmen on horseback attend to herds of sheep, goats, cattle, camels, and horses. One quarter of the country's 2.2 million people live in the capital city of Ulaanbaatar, while another quarter live in the towns or centers of the 18 aimags (districts), and the rest live in smaller communities and family units. A large part of the population is nomadic, moving several times a year to find the best grazing for their herds. This lifestyle, well suited to harsh living conditions, depends on participation of all family members, even the youngest ones, to ensure survival.

Mongolia was heavily influenced and supported by the former Soviet Union since 1921. The dramatic political changes introduced by *Glasnost* and *Perestroika* in the Soviet Union were reflected in Mongolia and resulted in the initiation of a comprehensive program of economic, social, and political reforms in 1990. In 1991, the government of Mongolia undertook comprehensive national school reform and requested technical assistance from DANIDA in these reforms. A DANIDA supported program began in 1992 and was implemented by the Royal Danish School of Educational Studies (RDSES) in collaboration with Mongolian teacher training and educational institutions.

Prior to DANIDA/RDSES supported educational reforms, most Mongolian children with special needs either attended one of a few special (boarding) schools or stayed at home with no access to schooling. Teachers in the special schools had been trained in the Soviet Union as *defectologists*. Their training was based on a medical model, emphasizing the deficiencies of persons with disabilities and providing little support for rehabilitation or special education methods. Thus, expectations for achievement by the students were very low. The Danish effort focused on developing programs in local "regular" schools to serve children with disabilities, including those who were deaf. Regular primary school teachers were selected to participate in a pilot project and were provided information and training to work with deaf students. Two stories from that pilot project follow.

TULGA'S STORY: EDUCATIONAL OPPORTUNITIES IN A MONGOLIAN TOWN

Tulga was a 9-year-old deaf boy whose family's educational and economic status allowed them to be effective advocates for his education. The youngest of three children, he was the only son of a professional family. His mother was a teacher and his father was a lawyer from a prominent family in a small town that was the most important center of the aimag. Tulga's extended family was very close. He and his sisters got much attention from grandparents and other extended family members. Tulga was especially close to his grandfather.

Tulga was born hearing. He became very ill at 9 months of age and was admitted to the intensive care unit in a local hospital. Soon after his recovery, his parents discovered that he had lost all hearing in his right ear and could detect only very loud sounds made directly to his left ear. They immediately obtained a hearing aid for him, but aids and earmolds available in Mongolia were sized for adults. Tulga was never able to use the aid for more than a short period at a time. Because of the discomfort caused by the aid and his parents' doubts that it increased his hearing, Tulga soon stopped using the aid.

Tulga began preschool at age 3, as do most other children in Mongolian towns. His parents felt very lucky that the director of the preschool accepted him. This did not come easily. They had to plead for their son's admittance because of the traditional Mongolian attitude that children with disabilities should not be educated in the regular schools. In the preschool, Tulga tried to imitate the behaviors of the other children. In school photographs, he appears quite happy. However, no attempts were made to help him develop any form of communication beyond pointing. No one at school or at home knew of any method to use.

When Tulga finished preschool at age 7, he was allowed to begin the first grade in the local school where his mother was a highly esteemed teacher. A photograph from his first school day shows a serious-looking young boy dressed in a dark blue three-piece suit with a tie, carrying a brand new schoolbag that looks more like a businessman's briefcase than a child's bag. Tulga had good reason to look worried and serious. He started school with no way to communicate except for some gestures, pointing, and a few sounds. His new teacher was not able to communicate with him at all, and it soon became obvious that he was not learning but was merely copying classmates' work.

At this time (1995), the only other possibility for education of deaf children was admittance to the special school in Ulaanbaatar, which was a great distance from Tulga's home. His parents did not want to send their young son so far away. As his mother said,

> I do not understand how a young child can be expected to learn far away from the support and love of his parents and family, especially

when we have no way of explaining the situation to him or to be in contact with him.

Therefore, Tulga's father went directly to the president of Mongolia with a plea for support to establish a class for deaf children in his home town. The president referred him to the Ministry of Education, which referred him back to the governor of the aimag. The governor told Tulga's father that it was not possible to start a class for deaf children in their aimag because no one knew how many deaf children lived in the town or whether there were enough children to make a special class feasible. Tulga's father used resources at his disposal to conduct a survey of the town and identified about 90 deaf children and young people. However, when he presented the names of these persons to the aimag government, officials replied that there was no money to pay for training a teacher for deaf children. Resources were stretched, they stated, to provide sufficient teachers and classrooms for the growing number of normal children. To prove this point, the officials recounted how a special boarding school for children with mental disabilities in the aimag had been closed recently in order to provide room for regular classrooms.

Having exhausted their efforts to find a way for Tulga to receive an appropriate education at his current school, Tulga's parents approached another local school that was participating in the Danish-assisted pilot project. There, one teacher had been selected to include three children with disabilities in her first grade classroom and was being trained to assist with the children's integration into a regular classroom. Learning that this school was being visited by the Mongolian-Danish professional support team, Tulga's parents dressed him in his three-piece suit and brought him to the team. A member of the team and fresh from my stay at Gallaudet University, I immediately recognized the need for providing Tulga with access to an appropriate education that recognized his communication needs while not having to live apart from his supportive extended family.

The visiting team met with Tulga's parents and the director of the education center. It was agreed that the director would provide two teachers and a classroom for a special class for deaf children. DANITA/RDSES would fund transportation for the teachers to attend the special school in Ulaanbaatar for a one-month training course. Two teachers from each of the other three aimags involved in the special-needs pilot project were also invited for the training. The main objective of the training was to give the teachers basic skills in sign language. Even though the special school used signing only after students reached eighth grade, there were teachers available to provide sign language training. With such brief training, the pilot project teachers learned only basic sign language. They found that they had to rely frequently on fingerspelling to supplement their signs.

After this training, the two teachers from Tulga's aimag returned home. A group of 13 young deaf children were admitted to a first grade class that started at the beginning of the next school year with instruction provided in sign language. The teachers also organized a sign language course for students' family members and began teaching them basic signs and the sign alphabet. When the children first started school, they knew no formal sign language. They were unable to express even their names and ages. The teacher used the first 4 months of school to teach the children simple signs and the fingerspelling system she had learned in Ulaanbaatar. This allowed the children to communicate with each other and the teacher. Only Tulga had attended preschool; many of the other children needed to learn simple social skills and appropriate school behaviors before the teacher could focus on academic skills.

Tulga and his classmates completed the second grade. Tulga went to school happily every morning and changed from the sulky, serious boy who started school into a smiling, eager, outgoing child who often took responsibility for other children in his class, but he could also be mischievous and play around like any other school child. His parents reported that Tulga's friends were in and out of their house every afternoon after school, having a good time like other children their age. Because of the family sign classes, members of Tulga's family began to sign with him. His younger sister was particularly skilled, and his parents learned basic signs. Although communication was easier than before, they still found it difficult to discuss abstract topics. His father was pleased that Tulga could write and that they could use written communication. However, Tulga's father was still concerned about the ultimate level of academic skills that Tulga may obtain.

All the children in Tulga's class continued in third grade the next year. The children as a group seemed happy and eager to learn. The teacher reported that they covered the standard curriculum at the same pace as the classes of hearing children. After their first year of school, the deaf students won second place in a math competition among all first grade classes in the aimag, and half of them were given recognition for good penmanship. On an examination at the end of the second grade, half of the class scored *good* or higher, and all were passed on the exam.

Like other children in Mongolian schools, the deaf children were involved in dancing, drama, and poetry recitals. Children from the older classes often visited the class of deaf children, and some of the older girls taught the younger children the complicated steps of traditional Mongolian dances. Tulga was one of the best boy dancers in his class and performed with gusto and enthusiasm.

The school administration, as well as teachers, parents, and students, was proud of the special class. After some early incidents of hearing children teasing and making fun of the deaf children, the principal summoned all students to a meeting and explained that such behavior was not acceptable and that all children at the school should feel welcome. The deaf children are accepted both in the school and the community. When other students meet their deaf schoolmates outside school, they are friendly.

Tulga's story illustrates the difficulty faced by children with disabilities in Mongolia, even if they come from middle class, educated families. However, his parents' determination, combined with the willingness of local school officials to use outside assistance to train teachers and establish a special class, resulted in significant improvement of educational opportunities, not only for Tulga but for other deaf children in his district. The introduction of sign language at an earlier age than in the traditional boarding school as well as higher expectations for the deaf children's performance undoubtedly contributed to their success. However, Tulga's father's fears for his son's later education were not unfounded. Much effort will be required to assure appropriate educational opportunities for Tulga and other deaf children living in the towns of the aimag.

JARGALSAIHAN'S STORY: EDUCATIONAL ACCESS FOR A YOUNG HERDSMAN

Jargalsaihan's story illustrates the barriers faced by deaf children from the nomadic herdsman culture of Mongolia, who live in the countryside beyond the towns. Jargalsaihan was 23 years old when one of the teachers trained in the special needs project made a radio announcement and visited small villages in the aimag to inform families about the new program for deaf children. Jargalsaihan's family and several others with deaf adolescents and young adults responded to the announcement.

In answer to the family's requests, a second first grade class was established for young people 13 to 33 years old. The teacher herself had to develop a curriculum and to provide appropriate learning materials for these older but unschooled students. Her first priority was to teach signs and fingerspelling so the students could communicate with each other. After 2 years, they communicated well and acquired basic literacy skills. They read newspapers, watched signed news weekly on television, discussed their country and its political system, and were aware of local, national, and international events. The curriculum addressed math skills at a functional level, emphasizing the handling of money, budgeting, buying and selling, and other basic skills necessary for work and life. Some of the students were embarrassed because they attended a school with much younger children. However, the older students' motivation was high because they understood the need to acquire academic skills and because at school they met deaf friends and established comfortable social relationships.

Jargalsaihan was a student in the older class. The son of a nomadic herdsman, he contracted meningitis at age 3. After his recovery, Jargalsaihan's parents realized that he could no longer hear. When he was 7 years old, his grandfather took him all the way to the special school in Ulaanbaatar. But when his grandfather tried to leave Jargalsaihan at the school, the boy was so distraught that his grandfather decided he could not leave him. After that, Jargalsaihan stayed home with his family and received no formal education. Although his sister went to school in the aimag center (living with their mother in a small house built by the family for this purpose), Jargalsaihan stayed with his father in the isolation of the countryside. As a boy, he participated successfully in traditional horse racing with other children from the area. He learned to be a good herdsman and deal skillfully with the family's herd of horses, camels, sheep, and goats.

Despite these achievements, Jargalsaihan's family worried about him. He was not able to communicate freely with other people and spent most of his time alone with the animals on the vast steppes. His parents wanted him to be able to read, write, and communicate with others, but they did not know how to teach him or where to send him for an education. Therefore, Jargalsaihan's family responded eagerly to the announcement about the new classes for deaf students in the town where his sister was in school.

Jargalsaihan now lived in the town with his mother and sister and went to school. His mother and sister attended the family sign language courses and learned to communicate better with him, although he still seemed isolated in family discussions. His sister was quite skillful in use of signs and fingerspelling. She was considerate and tried to interpret conversations. His parents were able to communicate only simple things concerning the animals or household in the ger, the round tent made of felt that was the family's home in the countryside. There was no doubt that the whole family loved this young man and was deeply concerned for his future. During a visit I made recently to the family's ger, his father said solemnly,

> I am getting gray hairs. I am concerned about my son. I want him to learn to take care of himself, get some vocational training, and be employed. It is easier for him in town. It is very difficult to be a herdsman when you are disabled. People are greedy and will try to take advantage of you.

Jargalsaihan's father went on to explain how grateful he and his family were for the young man's recent chance for an education.

After only one year in school, Jargalsaihan was able to communicate freely with his classmates. He, too, expressed gratitude for his education and showed a continuing eagerness to learn. Jargalsaihan could read the newspaper, follow subtitles on television, and understand the weekly televised news with sign language interpretation. He decided to move from the countryside to town because he had made many deaf friends.

Jargalsaihan wanted to develop his talent for drawing and become an artist or a designer. His next educational step had already been planned. After 2 years in school, he obtained academic skills sufficient for acceptance in a carpentry training program in Ulaanbaatar.

Jargalsaihan's rapid acquisition of sign language and functional literacy skills at such a late age is quite amazing. The opportunity to learn signs and to attend school resulted in a radical change in his opportunities for social interaction and in his occupational future. Thus, the educational changes put in motion by the Danish-Mongolian partnership and by Tulga's family had positive effects far beyond the town in which they began.

CONTINUING ISSUES AND CHALLENGES

Developments in the education of deaf children in Mongolia radically altered the life expectations for many children. In the two classrooms described above, students appear to be learning at a rapid rate, certainly faster than most children attending the traditional special school in Ulaanbaatar. The apparently fast development of language and academic skills after relatively late introduction to the new programs gives reason to question whether our expectations are generally too low for such children and young adults. Jargalsaihan's rapid development of language and emerging literacy skills is particularly impressive and suggests that, at least in some cases, potential for significant academic development continues far beyond the ages typically considered to be critical for these skills (Lenneberg, 1967).

The initial reports presented here must be considered tentative because the pilot program operated for a brief time and because conclusions are based on observations, parents' reports, and teachers' records. The pattern of achievement of the students in the two special pilot classes and of additional students in similar situations needs intensive longitudinal study. It is possible that early signs of rapid achievement are misleading and that this learning rate will not be maintained. Children in the pilot could have shown an initial burst of achievement as they acquired the ability to express in language concepts that were developed previously. However, there are a number of factors that may support their academic skills more effectively than has been typical for students in the separate special school.

The most obvious difference between the education provided in the local pilot program and that in the special school is that signs are used in the local classrooms. The special school traditionally used spoken language only and discouraged the use of signs. Many hours are spent in auditory and speech training. Only recently has signing been allowed in classes—and then only with students in the 8th and higher grades. As in other residential schools for deaf children, the children sign among themselves, but the sign language seems undeveloped for use in the educational environment. There is as yet no official sign language in Mongolia. For example, one of the local classroom teachers has a deaf son who attended the special school for 10 years. He returned home and helps frequently with the younger students. However, his own sign skills are quite limited because he had no skilled signing models, and the signs used in the residential school dorms are to a large degree homemade.

A second difference in the two school environments is teachers' training and, perhaps, their expectations for the students' academic progress. Although the teachers in the special school have a number of years of training in defectology to prepare them to work with deaf students, that training may have resulted in unrealistically low expectations for their students. Unlike the local pilot classes for younger students, which follow the regular curriculum with younger deaf students, the special school uses a modified, simplified curriculum. Deaf adults complained about the low achievement levels of graduates from the special school because the school does not manage to teach the children well enough so they may graduate at an appropriate level even though they spend 2 extra years in school. Most of the graduates of the school lack sufficient scores on examinations to be accepted at vocational schools and lack skills that would help them find employment.

In contrast with the teachers at the special school, those in the local pilot classes have little training specific to deaf children. Instead, their special training focused on the use of signs and fingerspelling. Perhaps because their training did not emphasize the limitations generally expected for deaf learners, these teachers did not assume that their younger deaf students would be unable to keep up with the regular curriculum. Earlier research (e.g., Rosenthal & Jacobson, 1968) showed the impact of teachers' expectations on children's school performance, and such an effect may be operating in the school environments in Mongolia.

Another advantage for the local pilot program is that parents are involved and support the program to a much greater extent than is typical for education in general in Mongolia. Parents of children in the two local classrooms support the classes by helping the teachers get materials for teaching aids and by providing special equipment for the rooms, such as plants and curtains. The parents also provide tea and a snack for the children daily. In addition, these parents formed an advocacy organization and are working to raise awareness and support in the community for all deaf and hard of hearing children and adults.

OBSERVATIONS FROM NEPAL

Nepal is also situated in Asia between China and India. Although it covers a small area (about the size of the state of Arkansas), its terrain includes the greatest range of altitudes found in any country on earth, from the low lands to Mount Everest, the world's highest mountain. Its population of more than 20 million people includes a dizzying array of cultural, linguistic, and religious groups. Taylor (1997) provided a poignant and indepth description of these cultural variations and their impacts on attitudes about and experiences of deaf persons in Nepal. She reported that deaf persons face particularly strong barriers in some of these Nepalese cultural groups because the deafness is considered a sign of lack of intellect and even "low moral worth" (p. 40).

Nepal is one of the poorest countries in the world, with minimal health services for persons living outside the capital city of Kathmandu and low literacy rates even for hearing people. Infant mortality and mortality for children under 5 years of age is very high. Life expectancy is 53 years (UNICEF, 1996). It is not surprising, therefore, that the incidence of hearing loss and deafness is also high. A survey of the prevalence of deafness and ear disease in Napal conducted by the Britain-Nepal Otology Services (BRINOS; 1991) revealed that 16.6% of the population over the age of 5 had some degree of hearing loss. More than 50% of the cases of hearing loss in school-age children were due to chronic severe otitis media (thus were conductive in nature and potentially preventable). Between 1.7% and 3% of the people are believed to be profoundly deaf (Kathmandu Association of the Deaf, 1990, cited in Taylor, 1997).

Special education began in Nepal in the 1960s with a few special schools and programs run by nongovernmental organizations (NGOs). The first school for deaf children was started in 1967 by the Welfare Society for the Hearing Impaired, and Mrs. Indira Shrestha. She trained in the United States at Smith College and the Clark School for the Deaf, using oral methods. This is the approach she introduced in Nepal. Some years later, Mrs. Shrestha returned to the United States and spent time at Gallaudet University, making contacts with educational programs using sign language in educational settings. On her return to Nepal, she taught sign language to the teachers in her school and introduced total or simultaneous communication. Some of the best students at the school helped to teach the faculty and other students Nepali Sign Language and developed the first Nepalese sign language dictionary. Encouraged by attendance at an international conference about culturally sensitive approaches to deaf education, Mrs. Shrestha is now considering introducing a bilingual/bicultural approach.

There are now a number of schools for deaf students in Nepal, both government and NGO sponsored. Most are using signing for educational purposes and provide a residential setting for their students. However, a limited number of students can be accommodated. Every year, for example, Mrs. Shrestha's school is faced with being unable to accept all children who apply. Many families decline to send their children to these schools because of transportation problems and the expense of getting the children to and from school at holidays and other breaks in the school year. Finally, as Taylor (1997) pointed out, some families find the cultural differences that develop between themselves and their children (who may be learning spoken dialects different from those at home, as well as learning Nepali Sign Language) cause problems in their relationship.

As part of its support to development of basic and primary education, the Danish government agreed in 1993 to support the development of an inclusive special needs education program. In the first phase of the program, support was granted for 65 resource classes for deaf students with an enrollment of about 650 children. Limited in-service training was given to selected teachers in primary and secondary schools in order to provide services to these children. Based on current applications, development of 70 additional classes is planned. Even with these classes in regular schools, however, a hostel system had to be established for many of the children because of the distances they must travel. The Nepalese government has realized that, when funding from DANIDA ends, this system may be too expensive for the country to support. Therefore, a new DANIDA-sponsored program aims to develop classes in local community schools. Because educators recognize that deaf children need to be with other deaf children, however, the goal is to develop educational units with two or more classes to establish a more comfortable learning environment for the deaf children in local schools.

I had the opportunity of visiting some of the DANIDA-sponsored classes when they first began and again after one and two years of service. As in Mongolia, the Nepalese deaf children began school with limited communication and social skills. From the first day, it seemed that the children liked to be in school and at the hostel because of the new deaf friends they made. However, the teachers and children had problems communicating. Fortunately, students and teachers (who were hearing) had the benefit of a special program developed by the National Association of the Deaf (NAD) that trained a group of young deaf men in using and teaching sign language. These young men were placed as teachers' aides in the classrooms. In addition to assisting the teacher and supporting sign language development, they also provided models for the children and involved them in after-school activities with other deaf adults.

Within 2 years, the respective roles of the teachers, aides, and students were well established. The teachers, who had been regular school primary teachers for many years, reported that they were teaching their deaf students the same skills and subjects they had taught other classes at the same level. They were able to communicate with their students using sign language and fingerspelling. The children had learned to communicate in a common sign language with each other, other deaf adults, and their teachers. The teachers report that the children learned to read and write and do arithmetic at an impressive rate. A few students passed the examination for first grade after one year in school and others followed. The young deaf men who were classroom aides continued their role supporting the children's development. The young men themselves benefited from what was typically their first employment experience. Unfortunately, because of salary issues, the young men's positions were eliminated after some time.

The deaf students seemed well adjusted to school. They were eager to show their work, their friends, and their hostels. Hearing children at the school interacted with the deaf students, and many hearing children began to learn some sign language. Some of the teachers of hearing children also acquired basic sign language skills. When it became known that deaf children were going to schools and were learning, many more parents began to bring their children to the school. Soon there was a long waiting list for the special classes.

Clearly, it will be a long time before all deaf and hard of hearing children in Nepal have access to education, although it is the ultimate goal of the program. However, attitudes toward deaf persons are changing as they demonstrate their ability to develop and learn. The Nepal Association of Deaf and Hard of Hearing People is currently working to support existing associations of deaf people all over the country and to develop new ones. A strong parent organization has been formed. Deaf persons are working to expand acceptance of Nepali Sign Language and develop a common language of signs across the country. They provide courses for deaf adults who never had the opportunity to learn sign language. A mobile ear care clinic, funded by DANIDA and the Nepal Ear Foundation, is providing medical services and hearing aids to children and adults. Audiological services are being strengthened at the Tribhuvan University Teaching Hospital in Kathmandu.

ISSUES AND NEEDS: COMPARISON WITH MONGOLIA

At this point, there has been no formal follow-up or assessment of the learning and developmental achievements of the deaf students in the new classes in either of these two countries. The observations I report here, as well as reports from parents and teachers, can provide only subjective evidence of progress. However, in Nepal as in Mongolia, students appear to be progressing much faster than expected. A major factor is the formal use of sign language in the classrooms. Also, the issue of teacher expectations should be raised again. The newly trained Nepalese teachers, unlike the teachers in the older special schools, seem unaware of assumptions that deaf children need much special preparation and slow introduction to language and literacy. Thus, the new teachers simply proceeded to use the regular curriculum and expected typical rates of progress. Informal observations indicate that many students are subsequently progressing at a rate expected for hearing children.

The extent to which classes in local community schools can provide deaf children with the academic and social experiences they need remains to be seen. Initial reports from Mongolia are positive and suggest benefits from parents' interactions with schools and their children on a daily basis. It may be that relative benefits from local (mainstreamed) versus special (residential) schools are culture specific and that cultural expectations will be involved in the relative efficacy and acceptance of the two settings.

It is obvious, however, that systematic research should be done on the process of educational change and the progress of deaf and hard of hearing children in these and other developing countries as they are provided increased educational access. It appears that the children I observed are profiting from changes in their educational system that are based on experiences of more developed countries. However, professionals in countries with longer experience in deaf education may also learn by observing these emerging systems. Might we find that our expectations for academic performance of deaf and hard of hearing children are lower than they need be? Might we discover that limitations related to age of language acquisition are more theoretical than real and that, in fact, the opportunity for significant effects from intervention is never lost? Might we find new insights about relations between communication modes and literacy as we watch the development of children from cultures (and with languages) very different from our own? Systematic documentation and study can provide the answer to these questions and enrich our knowledge.

REFERENCES

Britain-Nepal Otology Service. (1991). *Survey of the prevalence of deafness and ear disease in Nepal.* Kathmandu, Nepal: Author.

Danish International Development Assistance. (1994). *A developing world. Strategy for Danish development policy towards the year 2000.* Copenhagen, Denmark: Ministry of Foreign Affairs.

Danish International Development Assistance. (1997). *Denmark's development assistance 1996.* Copenhagen, Denmark: Ministry of Foreign Affairs.

Lenneberg, E. (1967). *Biological foundations of language.* New York: Wiley.

Rosenthal, R., & Jacobson, L. (1968). *Pygmalion in the classroom: Teachers' expectations and pupils' intellectual development.* New York: Holt, Rinehart, & Winston.

Swedish International Development Authority. (1995). *Poverty and disability: A position paper.* Stockholm, Sweden: SIDA.

Taylor, I. (1997). *Buddhas in disguise. Deaf people of Nepal.* San Diego: Dawn Sign Press.

United Nations. (1989). *Convention on the rights of the child.* New York: Author.

United Nations. (1994). *The standard rules on the equalization of opportunities for persons with disabilities.* New York: Author.

United Nations. (1995, March). *The Copenhagen declaration and programme of action.* Copenhagen, Denmark: The World United Nations Social Summit for Social Development.

United Nations Children's Fund. (1990). *World declaration on education for all and framework for action to meet basic learning needs.* Jomtien: The Inter-Agency Commission.

United Nations Children's Fund. (1996). *The state of the world's children.* New York: Oxford University Press.

United Nations Educational, Scientific and Cultural Organization. (1994). *The Salamanca statement and framework for action on special needs education.* Paris, France.

Nature Versus Nurture
in the Development
of Cognition in Deaf People

C. Tane Akamatsu
Toronto District School Board
Carol Musselman
University of Toronto
with Avraham Zwiebel[1]

The notion of a "psychology of deafness" has been examined in the litera-ture for many centuries. Moores (1987) stated that, in the 20th century alone, three major perspectives have emerged: (a) deaf as deficient (Pintner & Patterson, 1917), (b) deaf as concrete (Mykelbust, 1964), and (c) deaf as equivalent but different (Furth, 1964). More recently, a fourth perspective has become increasingly used for studying cognitive develop-ment, particularly with regard to the role of education. This theory, broadly defined as social construction, states that the origins of cognitive develop-ment in individuals are found in social interaction, particularly in the inter-

[1]The initial work on this paper was conducted in collaboration with Avraham Zwiebel, prior to his untimely death in 1994. His last affiliation was Bar-Ilan University, Ramat Gan, Israel.

actions that are mediated through the use of meaningful symbols, primarily language (Vygotsky, 1978). Thus, the origins of cognition and cognitive development are viewed as interpersonal rather than intrapersonal. Therefore, although the potential for higher level thinking resides within the individual, its actual development is triggered and mediated by symbolic interaction.

Social constructivist theory claims that it is through the use of language by more capable others (typically parents and teachers, although peers may be included) that the individual comes to create his or her internal symbolic system to be used in thinking. From this perspective, language both enables and empowers intelligence. Language and intelligence are seen as intimately intertwined, such that language development drives intellectual development as much as intellectual development drives language development.

In their review of these ideas, Bonkowski, Gavelek, and Akamatsu (1991) offered several applications to the study of deaf children's learning. Indeed, most deaf children begin school with a limited language and knowledge base, because the interpersonal communication necessary for normal intellectual development (particularly through language) has been virtually inaccessible to them (see Marschark, chap. 16, this volume). A few deaf children are born into situations where a natural and complete signed language is available, but these students constitute a small minority. Education is necessary in today's society, rather than merely facilitative, for the development of young minds. Bonkowski et al. (1991) noted that "the advent of schooling, with its emphasis on explicit teaching and literacy, could be expected to significantly influence not only *what* we think but *how* we think" (p. 187). Therefore, the lack of fully accessible and mutually comprehensible language has profound consequences for the developing child (Akamatsu, Gavelek, & Bonkowski, 1990; Akamatsu & Stewart, 1992).

Vygotsky's (1985) social constructivist framework has a critical contribution to make to the study of cognitive development because it emphasizes the importance of environmental (as well as hereditary) effects, including the specific effects of schooling. The theory also suggests that it might be useful to compare the performance of individuals on different subsets of cognitive skills, rather than to consider cognition as a unitary skill. This stems directly from the role of semiotic mediation in learning and the notion of the zone of proximal development (ZPD). Semiotic mediation, or interpersonal communication through conventional signs (in the semiotic, not manual language, sense), allows the creation of intersubjectivity, which, in turn, makes it possible for teaching and learning to occur. Semiotic mediation makes thinking observable and thus creates the conditions for learning to occur. Eventually learners develop the ability to self-regulate their own thinking without constant interpersonal interaction. The degree of success varies as a function of teachers' and learners' inherent abilities and how well intersubjectivity can be established. This may vary across domains of knowledge and kinds of skills as well as on task specific dimensions (e.g., visual vs. nonvisual stimuli, sequential vs. simultaneous presentations of stimuli, verbal vs. nonverbal processing, and concrete vs. abstract stimuli).

ASSESSING COGNITIVE DEVELOPMENT: THE NATURE–NURTURE DEBATE

IQ tests generally assess an individual's cognitive functioning in a variety of domains. For deaf children, however, only performance tests or psychomotor subscales are typically used so that the estimate of intellectual functioning is not biased by the children's limited opportunity to develop language or the existence of communication difficulties between child and examiner. Although intelligence tests purport to measure broad intellectual functions such as reasoning and memory, content analysis of a variety of tests reveals them to be knowledge based and, in particular, school-knowledge based. Furthermore, performance on supposedly nonverbal subtests can be affected by the student's verbal knowledge. Sternberg (1997) and his colleagues found that test scores were higher when there was a match among natural propensity, teaching, and assessment, suggesting that the lack of such specific matching results in many students not being able to demonstrate maximal abilities. That is, the greater the match among what is taught, what is tested, and what the child naturally has a propensity for learning, the better the child does on a particular test. With respect to deaf students, for example, item analysis reveals that their performance on certain standardized intelligence tests differs from that of hearing students, even though their overall scores are similar (e.g., Maller, 1996, 1997). At least some of these differences may be attributable to the curriculum.

A body of research already exists on hereditary factors in intelligence (e.g., Sternberg & Grigorenko, 1997). To what extent is intelligence inherited, and what data can be brought to bear on this question? Although substantial correlations among the intelligence of family members have been replicated many times, with few exceptions, it has not be possible to establish direct causal links between heredity and intelligence. The relationship is perhaps best described as dialectical, with neither heredity nor environment being foreground or background but each being constitutive of that which makes up intelligence.

Researchers investigating the role of heredity accept Spearman's notion that overall performance on intelligence tests reflects a general factor of intelligence (g), and scores on particular tasks measure specific intellectual factors (s). What is debated is how g and s are measured, under what social conditions they are measured, and what kinds of models are used to explain the data. In their reliance on the overall IQ score, the design of heritability studies seems to imply that g is the only index of intellectual ability. However, an individual's general level of intelligence does not accurately reflect how smart he or she is when faced with specific tasks. A full scale IQ of 100 may reflect good verbal skills and rather poor nonverbal skills or vice versa. More to the point, this score may also be achieved by an individual with a particularly large vocabulary and talent in manipulating words who has a difficult time solving visual puzzles within a specified time limit and vice versa. Indeed an s factor, such as musical talent, which is not even tapped by IQ tests, may be extremely well developed in a person with otherwise poor cognitive abilities.

Despite these limitations in the measurement of intelligence, behavior–genetic theorists have taken the lead in devising specific tests of their hypotheses. For example, studies of the inheritability of intelligence have used differences among monozygotic (MZ) twins raised together versus those raised separately, dizygotic (DZ) twins, biological siblings, and adoptive siblings to disambiguate conflated environmental effects obtained when only one child per family is studied. In a detailed comparison of socialization and behavior–genetic theories, Scarr (1997) noted this fact and challenged socialization theories, such as social constructivism, to follow suit. She also suggested several ways that socialization theory can be modified to take genetic effects into account in a way that goes beyond merely restating that genetics and environment interact.

The most striking findings from the behavior–genetic corpus, which have been replicated many times, are that (a) the IQ scores of adoptive children correlate more highly with their birth mothers than with their adoptive parents, and (b) MZ twins have IQs that are more highly correlated than DZ pairs who, in turn, have more highly correlated IQs than ordinary siblings. In his review of a number of large scale studies, Bouchard (1997) suggested that, because a whole host of (mostly unknown) environmental factors interact with specific genotypes in nonspecific ways, the only plausible explanations for similarities in IQs in MZ twins raised apart in a western society continue to be genetically based. Methodological difficulties, however, make such an unqualified conclusion unwarranted. The samples in adoption studies, for example, have a restricted range of IQ scores. This suggests that the adoption process—from both the birth mother's and the adoptive families' perspectives—is selective, if not for IQ then for socioeconomic status (SES) (Loehlin, Horn, & Willerman, 1997). Consequently, the ability to tease out heredity from environmental effects is limited, because the samples are not drawn from the general population.

But what counts as environment? Wahlsten and Gottlieb (1997) pointed out that physical and chemical characteristics of amniotic fluid, which are biological in nature, serve as the environment for the developing fetus. Further, they note that genotypes interact unpredictably (or at least nonlinearly and nonadditively) with environment:

Thus, biological experimentation with laboratory animals has revealed that, while genes and environment are distinct entities, they do not act in isolation from one another; furthermore separate genes do not act separately, and development itself is not completely specified by an individual's heredity and environment. Consequently, it is misleading to claim that the influence of genetics and the environment can be separated statistically in a psychologically meaningful way. (p. 182)

Working from a philosophical standpoint, Bidell and Fischer (1997) proposed that intellectual development is the result of self-organization among different integrative systems, ranging from the smallest gene to the largest community of people. They took a systems approach, which was predicated on the interactive and interparticipatory character of systems; thus systems are seen as existing only in corelation with other systems with which they interact to create a whole. They suggested that, in addition to genes and environment, a randomness factor also plays a role, thus rendering it impossible to specify purely genetic and purely environmental effects. Citing several animal studies (e.g., Gartner, 1990; vom Saal, 1984; Wahlsten & Bulman-Fleming, 1987), they argued that, even when genetic and environmental facts are tightly controlled, differences in phenotype persist. In humans, where such controls cannot be applied, the randomness effect is likely even greater.

Biological substrates of intelligence and the effect of environment and instruction on the expression of these substrates have been investigated by several people (see reviews in Ceci, Rosenblum, de Bruyn, & Lee, 1997; Gardner, Hatch, & Torff, 1997; Miller, 1997). It is clear from these reviews of the genetic–environment interaction studies that so many factors enter into the ultimate phenotype of a given individual that biological constraints serve merely to set broad limits on human functioning rather than causally determining such functioning. Even when specific genetic and environmental factors can be found, researchers are dealing with probabilities rather than absolutes, as Wahlsten and Gottlieb (1997) also suggested. Furthermore, the abilities that can be measured and observed are a function not only of the specific genotype but of the interaction of that genotype with proximal processes (the individual's interactions with people, environment, symbols, tools) as well as more distal environmental resources (e.g., family SES, level of education, prevailing state of the economy, and such). The idea that g exists at all is called into question with findings that the same kinds of cognitive processes appear to be applied with greater or lesser efficiency depending on the specific task.

Using data from the MacArthur Longitudinal Twin Study, Resnick (1977) found that the link between language and intellectual development increases during the second year of life at the time that the "language explosion" typically occurs. Often with deaf children, this is the year during which the deafness is discovered (or confirmed) precisely because of the absence of this language explosion. He also found that some heredity effects may be further enhanced by environmental factors (e.g. maternal language). The heredity effects observed for expressive language included the sophistication of children's expressive vocabulary, processes that create a more or less talkative child, and the willingness of a child to talk to unfamiliar people (i.e., temperament: fearfulness, anxiety, shyness, etc.).

THE EFFECTS OF HEREDITY AND ENVIRONMENT
ON THE COGNITIVE DEVELOPMENT OF DEAF CHILDREN

Interest in the relative performance of deaf youth with inherited deafness compared to those deafened through disease or accident dates from Vernon and Koh's (1970) early work showing that deaf children of deaf parents (DC-DP) generally scored higher on linguistic and academic tasks than deaf children with hearing parents (DC-HP). Because both groups in the Vernon and Koh study were composed of children with evidence of inherited deafness, some investigators, including Vernon and Koh, claimed that the DP advantage normally derives from early exposure to manual communication; still others claimed that it reflects the greater specificity of inherited deafness compared to the more widespread insult to the organism that may accompany adventitious deafness. Subsequent studies confirmed the DP advantage and acknowledged the ambiguity surrounding it. Evidence for environmental influences comes from a study by Zwiebel and Mertens (1985), which used a factor analytic approach to investigate the intellectual structure of deaf and hearing students. These investigators found differences between the two groups that disappeared over time and speculated that they reflected early experiential and language deficits.

Our interest in comparing children with inherited and acquired deafness derives from a social interactionist point of view: In addition to the effects of heredity, families who have experience with deafness should be better able to adapt to the communication and social needs of deaf children, resulting in an IQ advantage. Such an advantage might not be general but might reflect the specific adaptations made by families. Thus our position differs from both the communication and insult hypotheses. Like the former, it posits an interactional, rather than a biological, mechanism. Like the latter, it does not posit that differences result solely from communication mode. As we have seen, however, cognitive differences may reflect both heredity and environmental influences. Thus, it is difficult to make specific predictions, and this study is designed to be exploratory.

To investigate these questions, we compared performance on tests of intelligence and communication in a sample of deaf students that could be divided into two groups: those with evidence of hereditary deafness (hereditary) and those without (adventitious). For some comparisons, the hereditary group was further divided into two subgroups: a small group of children with two deaf parents (deaf parents) and a larger group of children who, although they did not have deaf parents, did have a number of deaf relatives suggestive of a hereditary connection (familial). Most previous studies that compared DC-DP with DC-HP were unable to disentangle the effects of heredity from language and culture. The composition of this sample provides a unique opportunity to investigate the nature–nurture question as it applies to deafness with more precision.

Previously, Zwiebel (1987) conducted a study in Israel using similarly constituted groups. Although education in Israel at that time was oral, Zwiebel found some use of manual communication among the familial group and, not surprisingly, consistent use by those with deaf parents. Using the Snijders-Oomen Nonverbal Intelligence Test, he found a clear advantage for the deaf parent group. Children in the familial group had similar scores to those with adventitious deafness; however, because the SES of the former group was lower, Zwiebel argued that they benefited from their partial use of manual communication. That this advantage reflected environment rather than heredity rested on the fact that it was not general but specific to particular subtests, specifically those emphasizing information and comprehension as opposed to perceptual-motor skills. The present study was an opportunity to replicate these findings with a sample that had wider access to manual communication, using both verbal and nonverbal measures of intelligence, as well as measures of communicative competence.

THE ONTARIO DEAF STUDY

We have been involved in a longitudinal study of deaf children that allowed us to investigate the impact of nature and nurture over time. The Ontario Deaf Study followed a group of children over a 14-year period. The original sample was drawn from across the province of Ontario, Canada, and included 153 deaf children (85 boys, 67 girls), some 80% of the children in the province who met the criteria of age (3 to 5 years), hearing threshold level (70 dB or greater), and participation in a program for deaf children. The mean hearing threshold level was 98.7 dB, and 97% of the sample was deaf prelingually.

The early childhood phase of the study spanned the ages of 3 to 7 years, with participants tested at three points in time: preschool ($M = 4;4$ years), early childhood ($M = 5;2$ years), and primary years ($M = 7;10$ years). The study investigated the linguistic, academic, and psychosocial outcomes associated with various child characteristics, social background variables, and educational experiences (e.g., Lindsay, Shapiro, Musselman, & Wilson, 1988; Musselman, Lindsay, & Wilson, 1988).

A further follow-up was conducted in adolescence (Musselman, Mackay, Trehub, & Eagle, 1996; Musselman, Mootilal, & Mackay, 1996) and included all those from the original sample who could be located and who agreed to participate (*n* = 76; 27 males, 49 females). Their average age was 16;4 years. Except for gender (more teenage females agreed to participate), the adolescent and early childhood samples were similar on important variables (i.e., hearing loss, performance IQ).

Students were administered a test of intelligence at three points in time. During the preschool round, participants were given the *Leiter International Performance Scale* (LIPS). This measure was chosen because it is language free and easily administered to very young children. During the primary years, performance IQ was again assessed. In most cases, the appropriate *Wechsler* scale was used (i.e., the *WPPSI* or the *WISC-R*) depending on age. This test was selected because it provides a more comprehensive view of intellectual abilities. In adolescence, students were given the appropriate *Wechsler* scale (either the *WISC-III* or the *WAIS*). In adolescence the verbal scales were also administered, either in speech, simultaneous communication, or ASL, taking into account students' observed skills and expressed preferences. Details of the ASL translation and test procedures are described elsewhere (Nizzero, Musselman, MacKay, & Trehub, in preparation). These tests were selected so as to minimize the knowledge and language biases inherent in other tests.

IQ Levels

Test results revealed normal levels of performance IQ. The sample averaged 114.9 (*SD* = 20.3) on the *LIPS* in the preschool round; on the *Wechsler PIQ,* the sample averaged 108.2 (*SD* = 18.3) in the primary round and 98.3 (*SD* = 13.5) in adolescence. This is consistent with previous studies of intellectual functioning in deaf children (e.g., Vernon, 1967) and confirms the now conventional understanding that general intelligence can develop in the absence of age-appropriate language and communication skills. The higher than expected scores in the early years may reflect the nature of the test items or the fact that deaf children begin formal education at an earlier age than hearing children, an advantage that dissipates once their peers also begin attending school.

Turning to verbal IQ scores in adolescence, it is not surprising to find that the deaf students scored lower (*M* = 78.5, *SD* = 11.4). This is roughly 1.4 standard deviations below the mean for the test, which places the deaf sample at the seventh percentile. Thus, even when tested in their strongest communication mode, only a few deaf students were able to achieve a verbal score within the normal range.

The Effects of Heredity and Environment on Intelligence

As mentioned previously, students were assigned to one of three groups: *adventitious* (no significant evidence of hereditary deafness), *familial* (family history indicative of hereditary involvement, i.e., one deaf parent, grandparent, or sibling, or three more distant, deaf relatives), *deaf parents* (two deaf parents). The early childhood sample had sufficient numbers of children in each group for purposes of analysis. The smaller sample in adolescence restricted the analysis to only two groups: adventitious and hereditary (i.e., familial plus deaf parents).

The composition of the groups presents an almost ideal situation for comparison as they showed no differences on a number of important background characteristics: unaided and aided hearing threshold levels (unaided PTA: $M = 98.7$; aided PTA: $M = 45.2$), socioeconomic status ($M = 47.2$; Blishen & Roberts, 1976), and mothers' and fathers' years of education (mothers: $M = 12.1$; fathers: $M = 12.8$). The average age of the group was 4;4 in the preschool round, with the deaf parent group averaging 8 months older than the other two, $F(2, 146) = 4.94, p = .008$. Any differences in age, of course, do not present a difficulty for analysis, as IQ scores are corrected for age.

Table 15.1 presents the mean scores on the *LIPS* and *WISC-III* from the preschool and primary rounds for each of the three groups. The presence of group differences was tested using an analysis of variance (ANOVA) on each subtest or summary score. Although running multiple ANOVAs at the .05 level of significance increases the risk of a Type I error, we felt it was more important to minimize Type II errors in this exploratory analysis.

Inspection of Table 15.1 shows that the familial group had the highest mean score on all measures, followed by the deaf parents and the adventitious group. Group differences, however, were not significant for the *LIPS* and were significant on the *WISC-III* only for picture arrangement. A series

TABLE 15.1

Mean IQ Scores by Group (Preschool and Primary Rounds)

					WISC-III				
Group	*n*	*LIPS*	*PIQ*	*PA[a]*	*PC*	*OA*	*BD*	*MAZE*	*COD*
Adventitious	125	113.9	107.2	7.6[b]	9.1	9.2	9.4	7.0	8.2
Hereditary									
Familial	17	120.8	114.6	11.6	10.5	10.7	11.2	8.3	10.3
Deaf-par	13	117.8	109.5	10.7	10.3	9.7	11.9	10.6	9.6
Total	155	114.9	108.2	8.2	9.2	9.3	9.7	7.4	8.5

Note. The table uses the following abbreviations: LIPS (Leiter International Performance Scale), PIQ (Performance IQ), PA (Picture Arrangement Scale), PC (Picture Completion Scale), OA (Object Assembly), BD (Block Design), MAZE (Mazes), COD (Coding).
[a]ANOVA is significant, $F(2,141) = 5.63, p = .004$.
[b]Helmert contrast between the adventitious and the two hereditary groups is significant, $F(1,141) = 3.27, p = .001$.

of Helmert contrasts on the means for picture arrangement showed that the two hereditary groups scored significantly higher than the adventitious group, but the contrast between the familial and deaf parent groups was not significant.

Table 15.2 presents the IQ data from the adolescent round. There is again a discernible trend for the hereditary group to score higher than the adventitious group. Analyses of variance were conducted to compare groups on the full scale, performance IQ and verbal IQ scores. Differences on the full scale score were significant. Analysis of the performance subscales found a significant group difference on object assembly. Among the verbal subscales, a significant difference was obtained for comprehension.

Thus the data provide some support for the hypothesis of an IQ advantage for the hereditary groups. The fact that children with deaf parents did not score higher than those in the familial group (either statistically or visually) suggests that this advantage does not reflect early exposure to ASL or the deaf community. It can reflect either a neurological or an environmental advantage, that is, an enhanced ability by parents who have experience with deafness (whether hearing or deaf themselves) to respond to the needs of deaf children.

The data are ambiguous with respect to whether the hereditary advantage is general or specific. On the one hand, visual inspection shows that the hereditary groups tended to score higher on all measures in all rounds; furthermore, this difference was significant on the full scale score in adolescence. On the other hand, the additional three significant differences involved subtest scores. The failure to find additional significant differences may reflect the small size of the hereditary groups. It is interesting to note, however, that the subtests on which significant differences were observed—picture arrangement, object assembly, and verbal comprehension—seem to involve cultural knowledge, in contrast to other subtests that depend more heavily on perceptual skills (e.g., block design, mazes). Here again, however, the familial and deaf parents groups did not differ, making it difficult to side with either a biological or an environmental hypothesis.

Heredity and Communication Mode

Considerations of deafness nearly always devolve around issues of communication, and it might be expected that any group differences would ultimately be evident in communication practices and performance. Previous analysis of the sample indicated a tendency for increased use of sign communication over time (Musselman, Wilson, & Lindsay, 1989). In line with practices of the period, 93% of the sample had first been enrolled in auditory/oral (A/O) programs, either segregated classes or integrated settings. By the preschool round, only 67% was still educated orally, a fig-

TABLE 15.2

Mean IQ Scores by Group (Adolescence)

| Group | n | Summary Scores | | | Performance Scales | | | | | | Verbal Scales | | | |
		FSIQ[a]	PIQ	VIQ	PC	COD	PA	BD	OA[b]	SS	INF	SIM	ARI	VOC	COM[b]
Adven	55	84.5	96.4	77.4	8.3	9.6	8.9	9.6	9.5	9.7	5.4	6.4	5.9	4.3	5.4
Hered	22	90.0	102.8	81.1	9.1	9.9	10.1	10.8	11.4	10.9	6.4	6.8	7.0	4.3	7.0
Total	77	86.3	98.3	78.5	8.6	9.7	9.3	10.0	10.0	10.1	5.7	6.5	6.3	4.3	5.8

Note. The table uses the following abbreviations: FSIQ (Full Scale IQ), PIQ (Performance IQ), VIQ (Verbal IQ), PC (Picture Completion), COD (Coding), PA (Picture Arrangement), BD (Block Design), OA (Object Assembly), SS (Symbol Search), INF (Information), SIM (Similarities), ARI (Arithmetic), VOC (Vocabulary), COM (Comprehension).

[a]ANOVA is significant, $F(1,75) = 4.23$, $p = .043$.
[b]ANOVA is significant, $F(1,75) = 4.58$, $p = .038$.

265

ure that further declined to 58% by the primary round and 31% in adolescence. This change mainly reflects the flow of students into total communication programs (TC) as academic demands increase, although it is possible we were somewhat less successful in locating A/O students who were mainstreamed.

Given this overall trend, people might expect that families experienced with deafness would make this transition more quickly. Indeed, there is evidence of differences among the three groups. Table 15.3 presents the percentage of students in each group in A/O and TC programs for each round. Using a contingency coefficient, these differences were found to be significant in the preschool and primary years. The difference in adolescence did not attain significance, likely because so few children in either group remained in A/O programs. However, it is evident that these differences reflect the more rapid movement of students with deaf parents into TC programs, with little difference between the adventitious and familial groups. Thus parents' educational decisions—which can be predicted from their hearing status—reflect their own educational and social experiences.

Effects of Heredity and Environment on Communicative Competence

In addition to differences in intelligence, group membership might be associated with differences in communicative competence. The study included a number of measures of communicative competence. The screening test of the Language Assessment Battery (LAB) was used to assess children's comprehension of English grammar (Musselman [Reich], Keeton, & Lindsay, 1981). In this test, words and sentences are presented in the modality used in the child's school, either speech alone or simultaneous communication (SimCom). Children demonstrate comprehension by manipulating objects in a doll's house. There are two subtests, each

TABLE 15.3
Communication Mode by Group by Round

Group	Preschool[a]		Primary[b]		Adolescence	
	Oral	Manual	Oral	Manual	Oral	Manual
Adventitious	71%	29%	60%	40%	31%	69%
Hereditary						
Familial	69	31	53	47	23	77
Deaf-par	31	69	23	77	0	100

[a]$\chi^2 = 8.44; p = .01.$
[b]$\chi^2 = 6.61; p = .04.$

yielding a separate score. The first assesses knowledge of 52 high frequency content words (i.e., nouns, verbs, adjectives, adverbs). The second subtest assesses comprehension of 36 English sentences. The first item on this subtest is an agent-action construction: The dog is walking. The test progresses to sentences that include more semantic roles (e.g., Mother gives the baby a cookie), inflectional morphemes (e.g., The boy pulls the dog's foot), and compound and complex structures (e.g., The dog was pulled by the girl).

An assessment of mother–child communication was derived from a videotape of the dyad engaged in a series of structured tasks, with participants free to use any mode or combination of modes they chose. The expressive task required the child to name 24 objects presented by the mother. A receptive measure (42 items) was derived from a series of communication tasks of increasing difficulty: identifying a set of objects named by the mother (single words), identifying pictures described by the mother (short phrases), and sequencing pictures to represent a story told by the mother (connected discourse). In the primary round, spoken language was assessed by analyzing a language sample elicited via picture story cards. Full details of the scoring method plus detailed analysis of the results are presented in Musselman, Lindsay, and Wilson (1988) and Musselman (1990).

Deaf adolescents were assessed using an adaptation of the *Sign Communication Proficiency Interview* (SCPI), developed by Caccamise and Newell at the National Technical Institute for the Deaf (Newell, Caccamise, Boardman, & Holcomb, 1983). The SCPI assesses language proficiency within a conversational format. Skilled mature language users engage the testee in a face-to-face conversation using a flexible but highly structured protocol. Two previous studies adapted the SCPI to an adolescent deaf population, asking students to complete three interviews: one with a hearing person using speech alone, one with a hearing person simultaneously speaking and signing, and one with a deaf person using ASL (Geers & Moog, 1989; Moores et al., 1987). For further information about this measure and adolescents' overall skills, see Musselman and Akamatsu (in press).

The communication scores from the preschool and primary rounds are presented in Table 15.4. Looking at the LAB and mother–child communication scores, it can be seen that the deaf parent group consistently had the highest scores, with no consistent pattern evident between the familial and adventitious groups. An ANOVA on LAB words in the preschool round obtained a significant main effect for group and a significant Helmert contrast showing that the two hereditary groups scored higher than the adventitious group; the second contrast, between the familial and deaf parent groups, was not significant. There was also a significant group effect on the mother–child receptive score in the preschool round, together with a significant contrast between the two hereditary groups and the adventitious

TABLE 15.4
Communicative Competence by Group (Preschool and Primary Rounds)

Group	Preschool				Primary					
	LAB		Mom/Chd		LAB		Mom/Chd		Speech	
	Wrds[a]	Sents	Exp	Rec[b]	Wrds	Sent	Exp	Rec	Wrds	Sents[c]
Adventitious	15.5[d]	4.2	9.8	17.0[e]	37.2	16.1	22.0	35.3	38.6	4.0
Hereditary										
Familial	18.3	5.6	9.4	18.6	39.5	10.1	22.3	37.5	60.3	8.1[f]
Deaf-par	24.6	7.1	11.8	23.9	44.8	21.6	22.5	38.0	13.2	2.5

Note. Analysis of group differences included age as a covariate, and entries are adjusted means. The table uses the following abbreviations: LAB (Language Assessment Battery), Wrds (number of words), Sents (number of sentences), Mom/Chd (mother–child communication), Exp (expressive score), Rec (receptive score).
[a]Univariate test is significant, $F(2,145) = 3.40, p = .036$.
[b]Univariate test is significant, $F(2,127) = 3.18, p = .045$.
[c]Univariate test is significant, $F(2,136) = 3.25, p = .04$.
[d]Helmert contrast between the Aventitious and two Hereditary groups is significant, $t = -2.36, p = .02$.
[e]Helmert contrast is significant, $t = -2.24, p = .03$.
[f]Helmert contrast between the Familial and Deaf-parent group is significant, $t = 2.54, p = .01$.

group. The lack of significant differences between the familial and deaf parent groups may reflect their small size. None of the group differences in the primary round were significant. Thus, the statistical findings reveal an advantage associated with hereditary deafness. If taken at face value, however, the pattern of communication scores mirrors the extent of manual communication use among groups, as the children of deaf parents had the highest absolute scores. Not only did deaf parents enroll their children earlier in TC programs, but they exposed them to sign communication from infancy at home.

A different pattern is evident on the two measures of spoken language that were obtained in the primary round. Here the deaf parent group had the lowest average scores. On number of intelligible sentences, the main effect for group was significant; the contrast between the adventitious and hereditary groups was not significant, but the familial group scored significantly higher than the deaf parent group. The difference between the familial and deaf parent groups likely reflects the greater use of speech by the familial group. The better spoken language of the familial compared to the adventitious group (a difference that could not be tested statistically due to the nature of Helmert contrasts) most likely reflects the effects of heredity, as there is no reason to expect differences in the families' use of spoken language. Thus, in the superiority of the familial group over the other two groups is seen the operation of both heredity and environment.

Table 15.5 presents the communication scores from adolescence. Here group differences are no longer evident, either by visual inspection or statistical analysis.

DISCUSSION

The data presented here on the development of intelligence and communication skills are consistent with previous findings that favor individuals with inherited deafness, which was operationalized in those studies as being a deaf child of deaf parents. Earlier explanations tended to draw on the fact that deaf parents were able to provide a complete language to their deaf children from birth, as well as emotional and social acceptance of the deafness, two environmental factors that hearing parents, caught unaware by the diagnosis of deafness, were typically unable to do. The present study extends the inquiry by including both hereditary and adventitiously deaf groups of children with hearing parents and differentiating them from a hereditary group with deaf parents, thus providing an exploration of the interaction of heredity and environment.

Furthermore, we were able to study the performance of children of hearing parents to whom signing programs were available from early childhood (whether their parents took advantage of such programs). Therefore, by the time the children were adolescents, most had been able to develop a mode of communication that was generally sufficient for both educational and social purposes, regardless of parents' initial program choices.

Taken together, the results of this study once again show the interrelationships between heredity and environmental factors when studying development. On the one hand, we found heredity effects for early manifestations of intelligence (particularly as measured by standardized IQ tests). Despite important sociocultural differences between hearing and deaf families with children having hereditary deafness, we found these two groups to be more like each other and consistently different from the adventitious group.

On the other hand, we found evidence of environmental effects for communication mode. Hearing parents, regardless of their prior knowledge of or experience with deafness, made different communication choices for their children than did deaf parents. Finally, we demonstrated

TABLE 15.5
Communicative Competence by Group (Adolescence)

Group	SimCom	ASL	Speech
Adventitious	4.1	3.5	3.6
Hereditary	4.2	3.8	3.4

that communication skills reflected the effects of heredity as well as the interaction of heredity and environment: heredity leading to higher language skills in both the familial and deaf-parent groups compared to the adventitious group, and an heredity–environment interaction leading to enhanced spoken language among children with familial deafness compared to both other groups.

However, the data on intelligence do not support a hereditary explanation unambiguously. In addition to sharing a genetic etiology, both hereditary groups came from families that had some experience with deafness, experience that might have better prepared them to respond to and mediate their deaf child's early learning. This caution is reinforced by the fact that both Zwiebel's (1987) earlier study as well as the present investigation found the hereditary advantage to be most evident on subtests measuring information and comprehension (rather than perceptual-motor skills), areas in which social mediation would be expected to play a more critical role. Thus the mechanism behind the hereditary advantage remains unclear.

The contrast of our findings regarding intelligence with those of Zwiebel (1987) further suggests the action of environment: Zwiebel found higher scores in the deaf parent than the familial group. The latter group, however, did not have access to manual communication in school. It is possible that the availability of manual communication in Ontario at the time of this study allowed the familial group to actualize the potential benefits conveyed by heredity.

Miller (1997) argued in favor of viewing cultural factors as influences on intelligence that vary independently of ecological constraints. She noted that "attention to cultural meanings and practices mediate the impact of hereditary and environmental factors" (p. 269). Her work, which was conducted in many different cultures and in many different languages, using both original and modified Piagetian tasks, found that local adaptations to the tasks that made them more culturally meaningful changed the performance of the individuals tested (e.g., Cole, Gay, Glick, & Sharp, 1971; Cole & Scribner, 1974; Dasen, 1972, 1977; Irvine, 1978). Cole (1996) suggested that there exists "a universal [intellectual] potential, perhaps linked with species-wide maturation of the nervous system in some sort of species-average 'range of reaction'" (p. 92). In addition, he suggested both domain-specific and context-specific variation resulting from differential experience, which is driven by differing patterns of cultural practices and values. The data from the present study, derived from standardized tests but modified to suit the students' mode of communication, are consistent with this explanation.

But to study intelligence in this way is to assume that the child is a passive receiver of genes, environment, and upbringing. The point of social constructivist theory is that individuals play an active role in their own development. As Bidell and Fischer (1997) stated,

The role of the human agent in development is to continually create new relationships between multiple levels of biological and environmental systems through a unique capacity to integrate skills and capacities whose roots extend down through organismic systems to the heredity level and whose branches extend out into systems of socially patterned activity. (p. 194)

Thus, it would seem that hereditary factors initially play a role in delimiting the range of possible reactions, regardless of the environment into which the individual is born. Obviously, reaction to environment or, more accurately, the ability to access mediation to make sense of the environment, is determined both by hereditary factors as well as the nature of the environment itself. A deaf child born into a deaf family typically has immediate access to signed language and more knowledgeable others who can mediate a world from a deaf point of view. This knowledge and ability should provide the conditions for a maximal interactive response from the child. Our data on children from hearing families with hereditary deafness also suggests that such families are not completely unsuspecting of deafness and may not be surprised when a deaf child is born. Furthermore, such families, by dint of being somewhat familiar with deafness, are better positioned than unsuspecting families to mobilize resources for their deaf children. By having access to both the deaf and the hearing worlds, these deaf children may not only have the heredity advantage of a cleaner deafness but also mediated accessibility to both the deaf and the hearing worlds. At least for some tasks (e.g., learning spoken English), this provides an advantage that deaf parents are typically less able to provide.[2]

Thus, the interaction of hereditary and environmental factors is complex. The data suggest that both sets of factors impose constraints on development. Heredity operates by raising or lowering the range of possible responses to the environment. Heredity, as in the case of children with deaf parents, may also influence the character of the environment into which the developing child is cast. The environment, consequently, has its own effect on outcomes. Thus developmental outcomes reflect heredity, environment, as well as heredity–environment interactions.

What does this say for educators interested in maximizing the potential of all deaf children? One perhaps unfortunate conclusion is that educational manipulations—which represent part of the environment—are unlikely to completely override the influences of heredity and home. The findings also show that different environments facilitate different outcomes, with hearing families maximizing the child's potential for spoken language and deaf families maximizing the child's potential for signed language. This suggests that one educational strategy might be to comple-

---

[2]The reasons and remedies for this social disadvantage are beyond the scope of this paper and touch on political, historical, and social conditions that this study does not address.

ment the child's home environment, attempting to offer opportunities that the family is least able to provide. Thus educational decisions need to take into account what is known about the benefits and limitations of the child's previous environments. Moreover, children are not merely passive recipients of environmental input but active cocreators of the environment, including the manner in which people interact with them and the decisions they make concerning their welfare. Deafness imposes a set of constraints on how individuals are able to interact with their environment. Although parents and educators operate on the basis of their own values and concerns, it is, ultimately, the child's deafness that takes the front seat and constrains the decisions that are made and the developmental outcomes that ensue.

REFERENCES

Akamatsu, C. T., Gavelek, J., & Bonkowski, N. (1990, August). *Acquisition of word meaning in social contexts.* Paper presented at the International Congress on Education of the Deaf, Rochester, NY.

Akamatsu, C. T., & Stewart, D. (1992). Socially constructing language use for cognitive empowerment in deaf children. *Curriculum and Teaching: International Review of Curriculum and Instruction, 7*(2), 1–12.

Bidell, T. R., & Fischer, K. W. (1997). Between nature and nurture: The role of human agency in the epigenesis of intelligence. In R. J. Sternberg & E. Grigorenko (Eds.), *Intelligence, heredity, and environment* (pp. 193–242). Cambridge, England: Cambridge University Press.

Blishen, B. T., & Roberts, H. A. (1976). A revised socioeconomic index for occupations in Canada. *Canadian Review of Sociology and Anthropology, 13,* 5–15.

Bonkowski, N., Gavelek, J., & Akamatsu, C. T. (1991). Education and the social construction of mind: Vygotskian perspectives on the cognitive development of deaf children. In D. Martin (Ed.), *Advances in cognition, education, and deafness* (pp. 185–194). Washington, DC: Gallaudet University Press.

Bouchard, T. J. (1997). IQ similarity in twins reared apart: Findings and responses to critics. In R. J. Sternberg & E. Grigorenko (Eds.), *Intelligence, heredity, and environment* (pp. 126–160). Cambridge, England: Cambridge University Press.

Ceci, S. J., Rosenblum, T. E., de Bruyn, E., & Lee, D. Y. (1997). A bio-ecological model of intellectual development: Moving beyond h^2. In R. J. Sternberg & E. Grigorenko (Eds.), *Intelligence, heredity, and environment* (pp. 303–322). Cambridge, England: Cambridge University Press.

Cole, M. (1996). *Cultural psychology: A once and future discipline.* Cambridge, MA: Harvard University Press.

Cole, M., Gay, J., Glick, J. A., & Sharp, D. W. (1971). *The cultural context of learning and thinking.* New York: Basic Books.

Cole, M., & Scribner, S. (1974). *Culture and thought.* New York: Wiley.

Dasen, P. R. (1972). Cross-cultural Piagetian research: A summary. *Journal of Cross-Cultural Psychology, 3,* 29–39.

Dasen, P. R. (1977). *Piagetican psychology: Cross-cultural contributions.* New York: Gardner.

Furth, H. (1964). Research with the deaf: Implications for language and cognition. *Psychological Bulletin, 62,* 145–162.

Gardner, H., Hatch, T., & Torff, B. (1997). The third perspective: The symbol systems approach. In R. J. Sternberg & E. Grigorenko (Eds.), *Intelligence, heredity, and environment* (pp. 243–268). Cambridge, England: Cambridge University Press.

Gartner, K. (1990). A third component causing random variation beside environment and genotype: A reason for the limited success of a 30 year long effort to standardize laboratory animals. *Laboratory Animals, 24,* 71–77.

Geers, A., & Moog, J. (1989). Factors predictive of the development of literacy in profoundly hearing-impaired adolescents. *The Volta Review, 91,* 69–86.

Irvine, J. (1978). Wolof magical thinking: Cultural and conservation revisited. *Journal of Cross-Cultural Psychology, 9,* 300–310.

Lindsay, P. H., Shapiro, A., Musselman, C., & Wilson, A. K. (1988). Predicting language development in hearing impaired children using the Leiter International Performance Scale. *Canadian Journal of Psychology, 42,* 144–162.

Loehlin, J. C., Horn, J. M., & Willerman, L. (1997). Heredity, environment, and IQ in the Texas Adoption Project. In R. J. Sternberg & E. Grigorenko (Eds.), *Intelligence, heredity, and environment* (pp. 105–125). Cambridge, England: Cambridge University Press.

Maller, S. J. (1996). WISC-III verbal item invariance across samples of deaf and hearing children of similar measured ability. *Journal of Psychoeducational Assessment, 14,* 152–165.

Maller, S. J. (1997). Deafness and WISC-III item difficulty: Invariance and fit. *Journal of School Psychology, 35,* 299–314.

Miller, J. (1997). A cultural-psychology perspective on intelligence. In R. J. Sternberg & E. Grigorenko (Eds.), *Intelligence, heredity, and environment* (pp. 269–302). Cambridge, England: Cambridge University Press.

Moores, D. (1987). *Educating the deaf: Psychology, principles and practices* (3rd ed.). Boston, MA: Houghton Mifflin.

Moores, D., Kluwin, T., Johnson, R., Cox, P., Blennerhassett, L., Kelly, L., Sweet, C., & Fields, L. (1987). *Factors predictive of literacy in deaf adolescents in total communication programs.* Washington, DC: Gallaudet Research Institute.

Musselman, C. (1990). The relationship between measures of hearing loss and speech intelligibility in young deaf children. *Journal of Childhood Communication Disorders, 13,* 193–205.

Musselman, C., & Akamatsu, T. (in press). The interpersonal communication skills of deaf adolescents and their relationship to communication history. *Journal of Deaf Studies and Deaf Education.*

Musselman [Reich], C., Keeton, A., & Lindsay, P. H. (1981). The Language Assessment Battery for hearing-impaired children. *The Journal of the Association of Canadian Educators of the Hearing Impaired, 7,* 155–163.

Musselman, C., Lindsay, P. H., & Wilson, A. K. (1988). An evaluation of recent trends in preschool programming for deaf children. *Journal of Speech and Hearing Disorders, 53,* 71–88.

Musselman, C., Lindsay, P. H., & Wilson, A. K. (1989). Factors affecting the placement of preschool-aged deaf children. *American Annals of the Deaf, 134,* 9–14.

Musselman, C., MacKay, S., Trehub, S. E., & Eagle, R. S. (1996). Communicative competence and psychosocial development in deaf children and adolescents. In J. H. Beitchman, N. J. Cohen, M. M. Konstantareas, & R. Tannock (Eds.), *Language, learning, and behavior disorders* (pp. 355–370). New York: Cambridge University Press.

Musselman, C., Mootilal, A., & MacKay, S. (1996). The social adjustment of deaf adolescents in segregated, partially integrated and mainstreamed settings. *Journal of Deaf Studies and Deaf Education, 1,* 52–63.

Myklebust, H. (1964). *The psychology of deafness.* New York: Grune & Stratton.

Newell, W., Caccamise, F., Boardman, K., & Holcomb, B. R. (1983). Adaptation of the Language Proficiency interview for assessing sign communicative competence. *Sign Language Studies, 41,* 311–351.

Nizzero, I., Musselman, C., MacKay, S., & Trehub, S. E. (in preparation). The measurement of verbal and non-verbal intelligence in deaf adolescents.

Pintner, R., & Patterson, D. (1917). A comparison of deaf and hearing children in visual memory span for digits. *Journal of Experimental Psychology, 2,* 76–88.

Resnick, J. S. (1997). Intelligence, language, nature, and nurture in young twins. In R. J. Sternberg & E. Grigorenko (Eds.), *Intelligence, heredity, and environment* (pp. 483–504). Cambridge, England: Cambridge University Press.

Scarr, S. (1997). Behavior-genetic and socialization theories of intelligence: Truce and reconsiliation. In R. J. Sternberg & E. Grigorenko (Eds.), *Intelligence, heredity, and environment* (pp. 3–41). Cambridge, England: Cambridge University Press.

Sternberg, R. J. (1997). Educating intelligence: Infusing the Triarchic Theory into school instruction. In R. J. Sternberg & E. Grigorenko (Eds.), *Intelligence, heredity, and environment* (pp. 343–362). Cambridge, England: Cambridge University Press.

Sternberg, R. J., & Grigorenko, E. (Eds.). (1997). *Intelligence, heredity, and environment.* Cambridge, England: Cambridge University Press.

Vernon, M. (1967). Relationship of language to the thinking process. *Archives of General Psychiatry, 16,* 325–333.

Vernon, M., & Koh, S. (1970). Effects of manual communication on deaf children's educational achievement, linguistic competence, oral skills and psychological development. *American Annals of the Deaf, 115,* 527–536.

vom Saal, F. S. (1984). The intrauterine position phenomenon: Effects on physiology, aggressive behavior, and population dynamics in house mice. In K. J. Flennelly, R. J. Blanchard, & D. C. Blanchard (Eds.), *Progress in clinical and biological research: Vol. 169. Biological perspectives on aggression* (pp. 135–179). New York: Liss.

Vygotsky, L. S. (1978). *Mind in society: The development of higher psychological processes.* Cambridge, MA: Harvard University Press.

Vygotsky, L. S. (1985). *Thought and language.* Cambridge, MA: Harvard University Press.

Wahlsten, D., & Bulman-Fleming, B. (1987). The magniture of litter size and sex effects on brain growth in BALB/c mice. *Growth, 51,* 240–248.

Wahlsten, D., & Gottlieb, G. (1997). The invalid separation of effects of nature and nurture: Lessons from animal experimentation. In R. J. Sternberg & E. Grigorenko (Eds.), *Intelligence, heredity, and environment* (pp. 163–192). Cambridge, England: Cambridge University Press.

Zwiebel, A. (1987). More on the effects of early manual communication on the cognitive development of deaf children. *American Annals of the Deaf, 132,* 16–20.

Zwiebel, A., & Mertens, D. M. (1985). A comparison of intellectual structure in deaf and hearing children. *American Annals of the Deaf, 130,* 27–31.

Education and Development
of Deaf Children—or Is It
Development and Education?

Marc Marschark
National Technical Institute for the Deaf,
Rochester Institute of Technology

The purpose of this chapter is to examine some of the relations between development and education, with particular regard to children who are deaf. The various chapters in this book, as well as other books about deaf children, hearing children, or just plain old children, make it clear that there are a variety of perspectives and approaches to each of these domains. This broad issue has been addressed by several theorists (e.g., Piaget, Montessori, Nelson, Vygotsky), but few investigators have written in any detail about the complex linkage between education and child development, even when the two domains are discussed in the same context (but see Schlesinger & Meadow, 1972).

UNDERSTANDING THE PSYCHOLOGY AND EDUCATION OF DEAF CHILDREN

Many educators and developmentalists interested in deaf children appear to believe that there is, or should be, some unitary, correct approach to educating deaf children.[1] In this view, each of us should hold and adhere to a particular theory of instruction or development and, as a senior colleague once told me, "it is essential that we stay theoretically consistent." As it relates to deaf students, this orientation most often emerges with regard to the primary mode of educational communication, but it also surfaces in the educational process itself. Alternatives to the particular approach of choice (at the moment) are often criticized or ignored by such unity-seeking individuals, particularly when suggested by nonteachers. Often included in the nonteacher category are university faculty who study child development and instructors who are also researchers but who admittedly sometimes do not practice what they teach. For the record, I therefore, identify myself as an educator-researcher-administrator. I freely admit that I do not teach in a K–12 classroom, but I may have something to offer those who do.

In contrast to those seeking pedagogical uniformity, other educators (i.e., K–12 personnel) and developmental investigators (e.g., university personnel) often see education-teaching-learning as more of an eclectic endeavor, precisely what my senior colleague was warning me against. In this mode, we seek to increase our knowledge and improve teaching methods, and we do whatever works. Theory is secondary, if not forgotten. Individuals with this orientation thus like to think that they are not bound by a theoretical perspective but can embrace new ideas that come from someone else's theoretical backyard (after a thorough, skeptical, examination, of course). Certainly, when we look at unitary educational approaches in the field of deaf education, we have to admit that the majority have not been very successful.

Now if you ask us, nearly everyone will claim to be part of this second group, and we think of ourselves as the antithesis of rigid! After all, what we want is what is best for children—in this case, deaf children—and we will do whatever is necessary to enhance their educations and opportunities. If you watch what we do, however, the picture may appear rather different. We often are channeled by how and where we were trained, by our pet theory, model, or framework, or by our academic self-images. We may not be rigid, but we often do not appear to recognize the value of alternative possibilities. This is not to argue that holding a particular theoretical orientation with regard to deaf education is a bad thing. All too often, a focus only on the practicalities of "what works" results in the teaching of isolated facts or skills, leaving students without sufficient flexibility to adapt to novel concepts and tasks (Marschark, 1993a; Marschark & Everhart, 1995). An underlying understanding of the nature of learning and development is an important, if not essential, component to teaching children how to learn, and it does not matter if they are deaf or hearing.

---

[1] This feeling of narrowness seems as though it is more common in the field of deaf education than in education at-large, but the feeling may only be a reflection of my own biases and lack of breadth.

Looking at the educational process itself, there appear to be two broad styles characterizing the practical aspects of education—and within them the consistency–eclecticism distinction described above.[2] One of these styles has been termed the *hydraulic model* of education (Neal, 1998). According to Neal, the hydraulic model views information and knowledge like a fluid that has to be transferred from the head of the instructor to the head of the child. The good news is that because all children's heads are about the same, when we fill them, the fluid will conform to any minor differences in shape. The hard part is figuring out the most effective way to transfer the fluid, especially to deaf children. Do we try to pour it in as quickly as possible or a bit at a time (e.g., massed or spaced practice)? Do we warm it up first (e.g., simplify it) so that it feels more comfortable? What is the best container or pouring system (i.e., language) to use? How can we be sure it fills up all the little nooks and crannies without leaving gaps?

Instructors who like the hydraulic model appear to believe that more information is better, leading Neal (1998) to suggest that this is why so many educators and academic administrators like the Internet so much: It provides immediate access to an enormous quantity of information. Researchers who implicitly or explicitly accept the hydraulic notion tend to view development at-large in the same way as they view education: the process of effectively transferring knowledge and skill from the environment and from others through teaching, trial and error learning, and by experimentation.[3] Maturation provides increasing capacity for processing and retention in this model; thus we see cognitive development, language development, and social development proceeding at much the same rate for most children across cultures and contexts (see Marschark & Everhart, 1997). Consistent with this view, several investigators (e.g., Bebko & Metcalfe-Haggert, 1997; Case, 1992; Ceci, 1990; Johnson, Fabian, & Pascual-Leone, 1989) argued that many of the changes observed in cognitive development derive more from changes in processing mechanisms than from increasing knowledge. As young children develop greater capacities for attention and memory, they are better able to deal with information of cognitive, linguistic, and social importance. That is, the shape of the learning container may change over time, but it does so in predictable, homogeneous ways.

In contrast to the capacity-oriented approach of the hydraulic model, other instructors adopt what looks like more of a *water park model* of education. In this view, there is no simple, unitary analogue for knowledge or knowledge acquisition. Information is out there in a variety of forms, it can be accessed in a variety of ways, and no two children will do exactly the

---

[2]I admit at the outset that this is somewhat of an oversimplification and is not based on any rigorous or exhaustive analysis.

[3]Notice that this description does not mean that I am advocating for a learning theory approach to education. Learning need not be continuous, quantitative, or mechanistic.

same things or react in exactly the same ways (e.g., Marschark, 1993a; Nelson, 1996). The water park model assumes that children all have individual learning styles and slightly different learning needs, at least for optimal learning. Such differences arise from differences in experiences, skills, and physiological/neurophysiological factors (e.g., sensory loss, neurological organization, etc.).

Viewed from the water park, deaf children are likely to have different and more variable learning styles and learning needs than hearing children. Both the between-group (deaf–hearing) differences and the within-group (deaf) heterogeneity derive primarily from differences in early environments, a topic to be considered at length later. Adding to the normal background variability among deaf children, however, will be additional heterogeneity related to the physiological causes of their hearing loss and much greater variability in early experience relative to hearing peers. From the teacher–researcher point of view, all of this makes life difficult. Not only do we have to find the most effective way to facilitate knowledge acquisition in children, but each child may learn differently and at different rates. For the most part, such differences may be irrelevant (or impossible) in a classroom. Sometimes, for some children, they will be critical.

As a member of the water park crowd (or at least a wanna-be), I believe that much, but not all, of learning and development need to be seen as problem solving activities. Whether talking about language, cognitive, or social domains, much of what children learn comes from encountering new information, assimilating it with what is already known, considering it, and playing with it. Not all problem solving is necessarily active or conscious, but learning requires dynamic interaction with an accessible environment even when the learning component is relatively passive (e.g., what a child learns about number from playing with marbles). Piaget (1952) described this process with regard to cognitive development as *logico-mathematical reasoning,* and I have suggested that a similar process, *psycho-linguistic reasoning* (Marschark, 1993b), operates in language learning. Implicit in the latter process (I cannot speak for Piaget) is the recognition that deaf and hearing children may have different knowledge bases, different strategies, and even different brain organizations that can affect learning in subtle and not-so-subtle ways. I believe there is abundant evidence to support this view (see Bebko & McKinnon, 1997; Marschark 1993b; Marschark & Mayer, 1998; Siple, 1997), and it should not be a provocative position. Even in cases of remarkable similarity in deaf children's knowledge, there may be sufficient differences to influence the quality or the quantity of what is learned (McEvoy, Marschark, & Nelson, 1999; Tweney, Hoemann, & Andrews, 1975). Understanding of the education and development in deaf children, like education per se, therefore, requires far greater individualization and flexibility than assumed thus far. That brings us to the key issue of the ways in which children interact with and learn from the world.

THE NATURE OF THE CHILD–WORLD INTERFACE

I have argued in several venues that there are three primary factors that have preeminent importance in understanding deaf children's educational and psychological interactions with the world: (a) early access to language, (b) early social interactions, and (c) diversity in both object- and person-oriented experience (e.g., Marschark, 1993a, 1993b, 1997; Vaccari & Marschark, 1997). In order to gain a full understanding of the complex mosaic of education and development, it is necessary to consider all three of these factors as well as their interactions.

Implications of Early Access (or Lack of Access) to Language

Of the three aforementioned factors, perhaps the most important is early language experience. Language acquisition begins at birth, with both passive exposure to language input and reciprocal and synchronous, dynamic interactions around parental language. Functionally important communication by the infant occurs very early, if not immediately after birth (Marschark, 1993b), even if true language output has to wait another 6 months or so.

Given this very early language-learning scenario, it should be apparent that the language environment and language accessibility for children in the first few months is crucial. Hart and Risley (1995) demonstrated this fact most clearly, showing a striking disparity in hearing children's language development as a function of the amount of language experience they receive. Given the well documented paucity of effective language access available to young deaf children, it is worthwhile to diverge slightly to describe their findings.

Hart and Risley (1995) studied the language development of 42 hearing children, drawn from professional, working-class, and welfare families, from the time they started saying their first words until they were about 3 years old. Most importantly for this and the next section, Hart and Risley examined both the quantity and quality of interactions with family members that formed the contexts for the children's language development. They found that regardless of ethnicity, gender, birth order, or socioeconomic status, all children had essentially the same kinds of daily language experiences. Children from higher socioeconomic status homes, however, had a greater frequency of language interaction with their parents (number of parental words per hour was a particularly potent predictor of language growth), and interactions were more likely to occur in the context of several high-quality characteristics like parents "just talking" with their children for the purpose of engaging them and being social, not to achieve any specific end. These quality features of parents' language, which represent the "incidental teaching of language," were found to have a direct and ever-expanding influence in their children's language and cognitive development (the latter is more my generalization than Hart & Risley's). Their analyses indicated that "what parents said and did with their children in the first 3 years of language learning had an enormous impact" (p. 159) on language growth and significantly influenced reading and vocabulary test performance when children reached the third grade.

Hart and Risley found numerous instances in which children's language experience accounted for 25% to 50% of the variance in their language abilities by age. Furthermore, across the 42 children, 86% to 98% of the words found in each child's vocabulary consisted of words also found in their parents' vocabularies. Such findings clearly indicate the importance of early language experience for children's language development. More centrally, they confirm the long-held intuition of many investigators that deaf children who do not have effective access to language in the family are likely to be at a decided disadvantage. That disadvantage will increase through the school years if not somehow remedied. The provision of interpreters or other support services within the school environment cannot overcome existing lags if children do not have the linguistic and cognitive tools to utilize them effectively.

Hart and Risley's primary finding was that children who had slower rates of vocabulary development were also those who had fewer language experiences in interactions with their parents (Nelson, 1973), a situation faced by the vast majority of deaf children. Furthermore, the gap in vocabulary size between children with stronger and weaker language skills, a difference strongly related to rates of cognitive growth, increased with age. This finding is similar to findings with regard to deaf children of hearing parents, who enter school with a language disadvantage relative to hearing peers that typically increases over time (see Marschark, 1993b).

At first blush, it may seem trite to suggest that, regardless of the mode of early language, normal development for both deaf and hearing children requires effective early communication with those around them. Nonetheless, probably everyone reading this book has encountered deaf children who are not provided with effective early communication, even if some kind of exposure to language was attempted. The need for effective linguistic communication goes beyond day-to-day practicalities and academic instruction, however. Those deaf children who appear most likely to be competent in all domains of childhood endeavor tend to be those who actively participate in linguistic interactions with their parents from an early age. From those interactions, they not only gain social knowledge, they gain cognitive and social problem solving strategies, information about self and others, and a sense of being part of the environment (Hart & Risley, 1995; Marschark, 1993a). Such belongingness leads to self-esteem, an internal locus of control, and motivation (Vaccari & Marschark, 1997), which, in turn, influence educational achievement.

From a more practical perspective, Winston (1994) pointed out that providing deaf children with interpreters in educational settings cannot provide access to information unless those children already have suffi-cient linguistic competence to be able to understand what is going on. Otherwise, she suggested, it is like a hearing person trying to learn com-puter technology that is being taught in a foreign language: "'Including' deaf students who are not yet competent in either ASL or English is equally unfair and exclusionary, yet educators and parents alike tend to accept the myth that children can somehow accomplish this arduous, if not impossi-ble, task"[4] (p. 54). Simply put, lack of full access to information and a rela-tive lack of communication skill, or both, will prevent deaf children from reaching their potentials (Johnson, Liddell, & Erting, 1989).

Even when the early communication is effective, deaf children may still face barriers to literacy acquisition if there is a fundamental difference in a language they have been using to communicate and the language needed for literacy. For example, suppose a deaf child uses ASL more or less effec-tively in communication with parents and peers. Some theorists (e.g., R. E. Johnson et al., 1989) argue that this fluency is transferable to, or at least supports, literacy skills in English. Mayer and Akamatsu (1999; see also, Mayer & Wells, 1996), however, argued convincingly that this is not the case. They pointed out that, generally, there is essentially no empirical evi-dence to indicate that speaking ability in one (first) language is related to the ability to read and write in another (second) language. Investigators have shown a strong correlation between the ability to read and write in one language and acquisition of the same skills in another language. Mayer and Akamatsu noted, however, that even this relation becomes ten-uous when the orthographies of the two languages are dissimilar. Accord-ingly, they argued that because sign languages generally "do not have widely accepted written forms, deaf students cannot acquire these liter-acy skills in their first language to transfer to the written form of a second spoken language" (p. 2). Mayer and Akamatsu therefore concluded that there is no reason to expect "linguistic transfer" between the ability to sign one language (e.g., ASL) and to read and write in another (e.g., English).[5]

Implications of Early Access (or Lack of Access) to Social Interaction

Education involves acquiring the roles, rules, and values of an individual's society. Both parental and peer relationships are thus essential to social development. Promoting the growth of such relationships is not a simple matter, however, if effective communication is impeded. A complete dis-cussion of this issue requires more space than is available here, and other chapters in this book provide a host of relevant information. Brief over-

---

[4]Educators familiar with deaf children may be aware of this situation, but most teachers in mainstream settings are not (Ramsey, 1997).

[5]Mayer and Wells (1996) emphasized the importance of ASL in the teaching and socializa-tion of deaf students. The point is simply that fluency in sign language does not transfer to reading and writing.

views of linguistic and cognitive concomitants of parent–child and child–child relationships thus are sufficient for present purposes.

A variety of investigations described the communicative interactions of hearing parent–deaf child dyads (see Gregory, 1998, Marschark 1993b, for reviews). Greenberg and Marvin (1979), for example, reported that, on average, high-communication dyads showed more mature attachment relationships than low-communication dyads, regardless of the mode of their communication. Evidence from studies with preschool and early school age children reveals that relative to mothers in either hearing or deaf dyads, hearing mothers of deaf children are more likely to be controlling in their verbal and nonverbal interactions (e.g., Meadow, Greenberg, Erting, & Carmichael, 1981; Musselman & Churchill, 1991); hearing mothers who have not had the benefit of early, communication-based intervention programs tend to be more controlling of deaf children's behavior compared to those mothers who have had such training (Greenberg, Calderon, & Kusché, 1984; Lederberg, 1993). I (Marschark, 1993b) suggested that this pattern of maternal control likely has its basis in earlier interactions where mothers often feel inadequate and helpless in dealing with their young deaf children. Mothers who establish an effective channel of communication with their deaf children presumably have less need for such control and especially physical control (Erting, Prezioso, & Hynes, 1990; Lederberg, 1993; Rea, Bonvillian, & Richards, 1988). In short, poor mother–child communication can have "rapidly compounding and debilitating effects on the cognitive, social, and emotional development of deaf children" (Calderon & Greenberg, 1997, p. 472).

Hart and Risley (1995) noted that children's experiences with language really cannot be separated from their experiences with social interaction, because parent–child language interactions are "saturated with affect" (p. 101). As children get older, linguistic interaction becomes even more important for social and emotional development, as parents communicate social norms, behavioral rules, and the reasons for observed and imminent socioemotional events. Effective parent–child communication provides for more effective and efficient transmission of social information, facilitating the extension of social interactions outside the family and into peer relationships. The establishment of effective parent–child communication strategies thus should not only help promote better early interactions but should have long-term beneficial effects in language and cognitive development. These gains, in turn, should increase success in academic areas during the school years. What is not clear is whether these gains are in direct proportion to the effectiveness of parent–child communication or whether the system can tolerate a significant amount of variability as long as some threshold level of communication has been achieved.

For hearing parents, effective communication with their deaf children tends to result in more satisfying interactions and the lesser use of physical control and punishment. Desselle (1994), for example, found that parent–child communication involving deaf teenagers was positively related to self-esteem and academic success (see also Gregory, 1998). Kluwin and Gaustad (1994) further found that families using signed communication demonstrated significantly greater emotional bonding among family members. Such findings do not necessarily mean that any particular mode of communication is better for social development, but they do reemphasize the need for effective parent–child communication.

Turning now to child–child relationships, advocates of mainstreaming and inclusion suggest that deaf children benefit both linguistically and socially from being surrounded by hearing peers. Studies by Antia (1982), Lederberg, Ryan, and Robbins (1986), and Minnett, Clark, and Wilson (1994), however, have shown this assumption largely to be without merit. Although young deaf children do communicate with hearing peers, especially in play situations, they clearly prefer to play and communicate with children who share the same hearing status, even if they demonstrate similar social behaviors across both contexts (e.g., Minnett et al., 1994). Degree of hearing loss clearly affects the likelihood that deaf children will engage in social interaction with hearing children, but the feeling appears to be mutual on the part of their hearing peers (Lederberg et al., 1986; Vandell & George, 1981). Further, a variety of studies by Meadow-Orlans, Spencer, Lederberg and others have shown that play interactions are related to communication fluency (see Spencer & Hafer, 1998), just as studies by Mohay, Calderon, Greenberg and others have shown that mother–child interactions are related to their communication fluencies.

Social interaction among deaf children and between deaf and hearing children is not just an issue of having friends or socializing at school. The consequences of such interactions—or the lack thereof—are far reaching in both social and cognitive domains. Students with positive social interactions in school tend to have higher academic achievement, better mental health, and are more likely to succeed in their careers (see Marschark, 1997, for a summary). For example, deaf children's relationships with peers frequently have been described as impulsive and superficial. Those deaf children with deaf parents and those whose hearing parents are involved in early intervention programs, however, show relatively normal patterns of social interaction with peers (Calderon & Greenberg, 1997). Although there is considerable variability in this domain, Lederberg (1991) found that within the preschool setting, deaf children who were higher in language ability were more likely than children with poorer language abilities to play with multiple peers at one time, to interact with teachers, and to use and receive more language from their play partners (see also, Cornelius & Hornett, 1990; Lederberg, Ryan, & Robbins, 1986; Spencer, Koester, & Meadow-Orlans, 1993). Deaf children were more likely to use linguistic and nonlinguistic visual communication with deaf than hearing peers, and such interactions tended to be less object centered than those between deaf and hearing playmates. Spencer and Deyo (1993) similarly noted that observed differences between deaf and hearing children's play behaviors appear to be largely the consequence of differences in language ability, and they found that deafness without delayed language development did not result in lower levels of play behavior.

Beyond the educational benefits of peer interactions, children use such relationships to identify with others that are like them and to obtain instrumental and emotional support (Marschark, 1993a). Social relationships thus make children part of peer and cultural groups and promote academic achievement (Gregory, 1998). Children who are denied such opportunities early in life, for whatever reason, cannot benefit optimally from other aspects of experience. The available data thus indicate that social interactions provide deaf children with a variety of linguistic and nonlinguistic opportunities for learning that would not be otherwise available. Diverse social, linguistic, and cognitive experiences appear to enhance the flexibility of deaf children in dealing with later social interactions and the necessity of growing up in a largely hearing world.

Implications of Early Access (or Lack of Access) to Experiential Diversity

A third essential ingredient of normal development is exposure to diverse experiences. In the context of deaf children, the issue of *experiential diversity* has a long but sullied history, so it is important that I first explain exactly what I mean by the term. In 1993 (Marschark, 1993b), I tried to provide a perspective on how the language and cognitive abilities of deaf children, together with social interaction and the environment at large, come together to guide development. Everhart and I (Marschark & Everhart, 1997) later expanded this discussion and did so more explicitly, with regard to relations of language and thought.

The gist of that argument was that it is through active exploration of the environment, experience with people, things, and language that children acquire knowledge—including metalinguistic knowledge, metacognitive knowledge, and learning to learn. The strategies by which children go about such learning are unlikely to be innate, at least beyond the basics of discrimination, generalization, and the related mechanisms of simple conditioning (see the "operating principles" described in Marschark, 1993b, chap. 12). Rather, most of the building blocks of learning are acquired from the application of basic perceptual, learning, and memory processes (which are more likely to have innate components) as a result of experience. With sufficient resources, learning becomes a self-motivating and self-sustaining pursuit, whereas in the absence of diversity, there are no problems to solve, no need for flexibility. I concluded by arguing that in our attempts to ensure that deaf children have the necessities for academic and practical pursuits, we sometimes oversimplify and focus too much on the concrete and literal. We forget that the basic elements must fit into the larger picture of life-long learning and the whole child.

This position has occasionally been misinterpreted as suggesting that deaf children are in some way deprived of experience relative to hearing children. In terms of their being awake roughly the same number of hours in a day, an individual certainly could not argue that hearing children of hearing parents have any more experience, per se, than deaf children of deaf parents. It may be, however, that deaf and hearing children have qualitatively different experiences.[6] Some such differences prove to be positive, some prove to be negative, but the vast majority are neutral with regard to anything we might want to refer to as educational success. To the extent that there are individual differences—personal, cultural, or otherwise—between deaf and hearing people, this is not surprising. Nor is there anything (nor should there be anything) terrible about talking about them (cf. Hoffmeister & Harvey, 1996). Indeed, the whole point of this chapter is that by ignoring such differences we may be denying deaf children optimal educational opportunities and, at worst, we may be doing them educational harm.

In the case of deaf children with hearing parents, the situation may be somewhat different than it is for hearing children of hearing parents or deaf children of deaf parents. Now, the quantity of linguistic experience becomes an issue (Hart & Risley, 1995). The previous two sections of this chapter clearly point to the fact that not having full access to academic and social environments negatively impacts children. In particular, lack of effective communication reduces the diversity of potentially educational experiences. This is the sense in which I want to discuss differences in the diversity of experience, a distinction that derives directly from a discussion provided by Liben (1978).[7]

Liben's emphasis was on the observed heterogeneity among deaf children and the need to better understand individual differences and their interaction with the various environments of the child. Consistent with arguments of Piaget (1952), Liben argued that experience with objects and individuals are essential to normal development. "In the case of deaf children, the reliance on visual processing rather than auditory processing makes for qualitative differences in experience, and the early sensory deprivation of deafness may lead to indirect restrictions on the child environment because of reduced organismic exploration. ... [Further,] the

---

[6]In the case of deaf children of deaf parents, if there are any such qualitative differences, they do not not appear to have any obvious, long-term consequences on development.

[7]The issue of diversity of experience also relates to Kant's distinction between analytic and synthetic concepts. For Kant (1781/1976), analytic propositions relate to logical truths, which can be known regardless of experience (e.g., that a spilled coffee cup is still coffee). Synthetic propositions depend on experience and their truths cannot be determined in the absence of experience (e.g., there is coffee in cup). Deaf and hearing individuals, a priori, may have similar analytic abilities but differing synthetic abilities. Both of these assertions, however, remain to be tested (see Marschark, 1993b, Chapter 7).

environment may be reduced for the deaf child [of hearing parents] as a consequence of caretaking practices. Within the family setting, parents are likely to overprotect their deaf children, thus reducing the range of experiences and objects available for manipulation" (p. 202). Both Furth (1966) and Watts (1979) made similar arguments in explaining the consistent lags in deaf children's performance on conservation and problem solving tasks relative to hearing peers.

The importance of all of this, at least in the present context, is not to make judgments about the quality of any particular educational system or the generic abilities of deaf children. Understanding deaf children's knowledge about the world and their theories about the way it works has to be one of the highest priorities for developmental and educational researchers, as well as educators and teachers of educators. Only through better elucidation of the basic teaching and learning processes can researchers and teachers know how deaf children's abilities and individual differences interact with learning situations. Rather than continuing to draw general conclusions about the effects of hearing loss and sign language use on development and academic success, it would behoove us to develop a better model of how deaf children learn, with special attention to within-group heterogeneity. Only then can we distinguish possible effects on achievement of differences in content knowledge and learning strategies from differences due to the mode of communication or language fluencies. In other words, we have to understand the structure of deaf children's knowledge so that we can mold our educational methods appropriately. To the extent that knowledge, strategy use, and problem solving are significantly different for deaf and hearing children, the application of "hearing" educational methods may be inappropriate. Flexibility and adaptability in teaching methods are the key, because the deaf students in any particular class may approach the same material in a variety of different ways (viz., water park model reprise).

This conclusion has two implications beyond those already discussed. One of them concerns the education and content knowledge of teachers of deaf children. Teachers of deaf children (i.e., teachers trained to teach deaf children) who are unfamiliar with the content of the courses they are teaching (e.g., English teachers teaching science) are themselves lacking the conceptual structures necessary for coherent communication of academic material in alternative ways. Similarly, teachers of hearing children (i.e., teachers not trained to teach deaf children) are lacking the essential understanding of how deaf children learn (Ramsey, 1997). Either situation can be remedied, but they first have to be recognized and accepted.

The experiential differences of deaf students as compared to hearing students, particularly with regard to formal and informal learning situations, also might make for differences in motivation or their approaches to learning situations. In this case, the effects on learning of relative differences in the quality or diversity of experience are indirect, contrasting with the direct impact of experience or lack of experience. Not all cultures, or even subcultures within a particular society, have identical values. Those goals that are seen as worth achieving therefore vary to a greater or lesser extent across cultural and ethnic groups as well as within those groups. The differences in values and attitudes between deaf and hearing populations or, more likely, between deaf children of hearing parents and children who share the same hearing status as their parents, might result in their having somewhat different academic goals than hearing peers. Differences between deaf and hearing children in both parent–child interactions (e.g., the communication of family values) and child–child interactions (e.g., the communication of peer group values) also might contribute to their having some distinctive, achievement-related ambitions.

In trying to identify the loci of differences in academic performance of deaf and hearing children, therefore, it seems important to consider differences in values and standards as well as differences in experiences in the academic environment. Academic success is multifaceted and is not predictable from any single variable or combination of variables. Certainly, the complexity of this situation creates headaches for the parent, teacher, researcher, or metaeducator interested in the development and education of deaf children. Daunting though it may be, it is time to develop a better model of the deaf learner.

SUMMARY: LIVING IN THE REAL WORLD

Undoubtedly, portions of this chapter seem obvious to various readers. Hopefully, however, different readers find different parts obvious. It should be fairly evident, by this point, that a full understanding of the teaching–learning process for deaf children requires a fairly sophisticated understanding of the processes and contents of language, cognitive, and social development. This is not to downplay the importance of understanding the communication, experiential, and family histories of individual deaf children in order to optimize their educational opportunities (hence the importance of individualized education plans, IEPs[8]). Nevertheless, I believe that a better understanding of the mechanisms of development can facilitate parents' providing of stimulating (implicit or explicit) educational experiences for their deaf children. Many deaf parents will not need such assistance, as their intuitive parenting skills (Koester, 1992), based on their own experiences, will be sufficient. Most hearing parents, however, as well as some deaf parents who themselves had hearing parents, tell us that they are in need of information and advice.

---

[8]An educational psychologist friend recently noted that developing IEPs and implementing IEPs are two very different matters, and that, unfortunately, the latter often does not follow the extensive work that went into the former.

Most developmental psychologists would be sympathetic with the thesis that we have to understand the whole child to fully understand development. In general, European researchers appear to apply more of a whole-child, organismic approach to development than their more reductionistic American counterparts. Neither of these approaches, alone, is likely to be fully successful, but their integration rather than their opposition will go a long way toward providing a better development-learning-teaching model for deaf children. The hard sell seems to be convincing "basic" researchers of the importance of linking the major findings from developmental research to the practical needs of teachers, parents, and other professionals. We all recognize the potential implications of our own work, but few of us write at an appropriate level or publish in the appropriate places for nonacademic audiences to take advantage of that work.

Lest this argument appear only intended for the soapbox, it is important to note that parents and teachers can provide a wealth of important information for the developmental investigator. Particularly with regard to deaf children, where the heterogeneity is likely to be greater than in the case of hearing children (Marschark, 1993b), such information can support or contradict attempts at generalization from specific research findings. In the domain of infant research, such investigator–parent collaboration happens frequently, due to the need to have a parent involved in most research paradigms. With older children, typically tested in schools or preschools, face-to-face, investigator–parent interactions are rare, and both teachers and researchers typically have neither the time nor the inclination to discuss the larger but seemingly irrelevant issues. Recognizing the practical constraints under which most of us work, new attempts at such interactions seem well worth the effort. Given the nature of recent changes in the public's perception of academicians and research and in the government's emphasis on accountability, there are indirect as well as direct gains to be made here.

As one investigator who habitually was fairly remote from parents and teachers but is now seeking greater interaction, I fully recognize the potential problems as well as the potential benefits in advocating for this kind of approach. Beyond the potential contribution of important information to my research, however, reaching out to teachers and parents increases the probability that someone will actually make use of my research findings, outside of the laboratory. Not only does all of this enhance the quality of my research, it provides me with a moral satisfaction that enhances the quality of my research life.

ACKNOWLEDGMENTS

The author wishes to thank Jennifer Lukomski, Patricia Spencer, and Rosemarie Seewagen for helpful comments on an earlier draft of this chapter.

REFERENCES

Antia, S. D. (1982). Social interaction of partially mainstream hearing impaired children. *American Annals of the Deaf, 127,* 18–25.

Bebko, J. M., & McKinnon, E. E. (1990). The language experience of deaf children: Its relation to spontaneous rehearsal in a memory task. *Child Development, 61,* 1744–1752.

Bebko, J. M., & Metcalfe-Haggert, A. (1997). Deafness, language skills, and rehearsal: A model for the development of a memory strategy. *Journal of Deaf Studies and Deaf Education, 2,* 133–141.

Calderon, R., & Greenberg, M. (1997). The effectiveness of early intervention for deaf children and children with hearing loss. In M. J. Guralnik (Ed.), *The effectiveness of early intervention* (pp. 455–482). Baltimore: Brookes.

Case, R. (1992). *The mind's staircase.* Hillsdale, NJ: Lawrence Erlbaum Associates.

Ceci, S. J. (1990). *On intelligence—more or less: A bio- ecological treatise on intellectual development.* Englewood Cliffs, NJ: Prentice-Hall.

Cornelius, G., & Hornett, D. (1990). The play behavior of hearing-impaired kindergarten children. *American Annals of the Deaf, 135,* 316–321.

Desselle, D. D. (1994). Self-esteem, family climate, and communication patterns in relation to deafness. *American Annals of the Deaf, 139,* 322–328.

Erting, C., Prezioso, C., & Hynes, M. (1990). The interactional context of deaf mother–infant interaction. In V. Volterra & C. Erting (Eds.), *From gesture to language in hearing and deaf children* (pp. 97–106). Heidelberg, Germany: Springer-Verlag.

Furth, H. G. (1966). *Thinking without language.* New York: The Free Press.

Greenberg, M., Calderon, R., & Kusché, C. (1984). Early intervention using simultaneous communication with deaf infants: The effect on communication development. *Child Development, 55,* 607–616.

Greenberg, M. T., & Marvin, R. S. (1979). Attachment patterns in profoundly deaf preschool children. *Merrill-Palmer Quarterly, 25,* 265–279.

Gregory, S. (1998). Deaf young people: Aspects of family and social life. In M. Marschark & M. D. Clark, (Eds.), *Psychological perspectives on deafness* (Vol. 2, pp. 153–170). Mahwah, NJ: Lawrence Erlbaum Associates.

Hart, T. R., & Risley, B. (1995). *Meaningful differences in the everyday experience of young American children.* Baltimore: Paul H. Brookes.

Hoffmeister, R., & Harvey, M. A. (1996). Is there a psychology of the hearing? In N. S. Glickman & M. A. Harvey (Eds.), *Culturally affirmative psychotherapy with deaf persons* (pp. 78–98). Mahwah, NJ: Lawrence Erlbaum Associates.

Johnson, J., Fabian, V., & Pascual-Leone, J. (1989). Quantitative hardware stages that constrain language development. *Human Development, 32,* 245–271.

Johnson, R. E., Liddell, S. K., & Erting, C. J. (1989). *Unlocking the curriculum: Principles for achieving access in deaf education* (Gallaudet Research Institute Working Paper 89-3). Washington, DC: Gallaudet University.

Kant, I. (1976). *Critique of pure reason.* London: Macmillan. (Original work published 1781)

Kluwin, T. N., & Gaustad, M. G. (1994). The role of adaptability and communication in fostering cohesion in families with deaf adolescents. *American Annals of the Deaf, 139,* 329–335.

Koester, L. S. (1992). Intuitive parenting as a model for understanding parent–infant interactions when one partner is deaf. *American Annals of the Deaf, 137,* 362–369.

Lederberg, A. R. (1991). Social interaction among deaf preschoolers: The effects of language ability and age. *American Annals of the Deaf, 136,* 35–59.

Lederberg, A. R. (1993). The impact of deafness on mother–child and peer relationships. In M. Marschark & M. D. Clark (Eds.), *Psychological perspectives on deafness* (pp. 93–119). Hillsdale, NJ: Lawrence Erlbaum Associates.

Lederberg, A. R., Ryan, H. B., & Robbins, B. L. (1986). Peer interaction in young deaf children: The effect of partner hearing status and familiarity. *Developmental Psychology, 22,* 691–700.

Liben, L. S. (1978). Developmental perspectives on experiential deficiencies of deaf children. In L. Liben (Ed.), *Deaf children: Developmental perspectives* (pp. 195–215). New York: Academic Press.

Marschark, M. (1993a). Origins and interactions in language, cognitive, and social development of deaf children. In M. Marschark & D. Clark (Eds.), *Psychological perspectives on deafness* (pp. 7–26). Hillsdale, NJ: Lawrence Erlbaum Associates.

Marschark, M. (1993b). *Psychological development of deaf children.* New York: Oxford University Press.

Marschark, M. (1997). *Raising and educating a deaf child.* New York: Oxford University Press.

Marschark, M., & Everhart, V. S. (1995). Understanding problem solving by deaf children. In T. Helstrup, G. Kaufmann, & K. H. Teigen (Eds.), *Problem solving and cognitive processes* (pp. 315–338). Bergen, Norway: Fagbokforlaget.

Marschark, M., & Everhart, V. S. (1997). Relations of language and cognition: What do deaf children tell us? In M. Marschark, P. Siple, D. Lillo-Martin, R. Campbell, & V. S. Everhart (Eds.), *Relations of language and thought: The view from sign language and deaf children* (pp. 3–23). New York: Oxford University Press.

Marschark, M., & Mayer, T. (1998). Mental representation and memory in deaf adults and children. In M. Marschark & M. D. Clark (Eds.), *Psychological perspectives on deafness* (vol. 2, pp. 53–77). Mahwah, NJ: Lawrence Erlbaum Associates.

Mayer, C., & Akamatsu, T. (1999). Bilingual-bicultural models of literacy education for deaf students: Considering the claims. *Journal of Deaf Studies and Deaf Education, 4,* 1–8.

Mayer, C., & Wells, G. (1996). Can the linguistic interdependence theory support a bilingual-bicultural model of literacy education for deaf students? *Journal of Deaf Studies and Deaf Education, 1,* 93–107.

McEvoy, C., Marschark, M., & Nelson, D. L. (1999). Comparing the mental lexicons of deaf and hearing individuals. *Journal of Educational Psychology, 91,* 1–9.

Meadow, K. P., Greenberg, M. T., Erting, C., & Carmichael, H. (1981). Interactions of deaf mothers and deaf preschool children: Comparisons with three other groups of deaf and hearing dyads. *American Annals of the Deaf, 126,* 454–468.

Minnett, A., Clark, K., & Wilson, G. (1994). Play behavior and communication between deaf and hard of hearing children and their hearing peers in an integrated preschool. *American Annals of the Deaf, 139,* 420–429.

Musselman, C., & Churchill, A. (1991). Conversational control in mother–child dyads. *American Annals of the Deaf, 136,* 99–117.

Neal, E. (1998). Using technology in teaching: We need to exercise healthy skepticism. *Chronicle of Higher Education,* June 19, 1998, B4–B5.

Nelson, K. (1973). Structure and strategy in learning to talk. *Monograph of the Society for Research and Child Development, 38,* (149).

Nelson, K. (1996). *Language in cognitive development.* New York: Cambridge University Press.

Piaget, J. (1952). *The origins of intelligence in children.* New York: Basic Books.

Ramsey, C. L. (1997). *Deaf children in public schools.* Washington, DC: Gallaudet University Press.

Rea, C. A., Bonvillian, J. D., & Richards, H. C. (1988). Mother–infant interactive behaviors: Impact of maternal deafness. *American Annals of the Deaf, 133,* 317–324.

Schlesinger, H. S., & Meadow, K. P. (1972). *Sound and sign: Childhood deafness and mental health.* Berkeley: University of California Press.

Siple, P. (1997). Universals, generalizability, and the acquisition of signed language. In M. Marschark, P. Siple, D. Lillo-Martin, R. Campbell, & V. S. Everhart (Eds.), *Relations of language and thought: The view from sign language and deaf children* (pp. 24–61). New York: Oxford University Press.

Spencer, P. E., & Deyo, D. A. (1993). Cognitive and social aspects of deaf children's play. In M. Marschark & D. Clark (Eds.), *Psychological perspectives on deafness* (pp. 65–92). Hillsdale, NJ: Lawrence Erlbaum Associates.

Spencer, P. E., & Hafer, J. C. (1998). Play as "window" and "room": Assessing and supporting the cognitive and linguistic development of deaf infants and young children. In M. Marschark & D. Clark (Eds.), *Psychological perspectives on deafness* (Vol. 2, pp. 131–152). Mahwah, NJ: Lawrence Erlbaum Associates.

Spencer, P., Koester, L., & Meadow-Orlans, K. P. (1993). Communicative interactions of deaf and hearing children in a day-care center: An exploratory study. *American Annals of the Deaf, 139,* 512–518.

Tweney, R. D., Hoemann, H. W., & Andrews, C. E. (1975). Semantic organization in deaf and hearing subjects. *Journal of Psycholinguistic Research, 4,* 61–73.

Vaccari, C., & Marschark, M. (1997). Communication between parents and deaf children: Implications for social-emotional development. *Journal of Child Psychology and Psychiatry, 38,* 793–802.

Vandell, D. L., & George, L. B. (1981). Social interaction in hearing and deaf preschoolers: Successes and failures in initiations. *Child Development, 52,* 627–635.

Watts, W. J. (1979). The influence of language on the development of quantitative, spatial, and social thinking in deaf children. *American Annals of the Deaf, 12,* 45–56.

Winston, E. A. (1994). An interpreted education: Inclusion or exclusion? In R. C. Johnson & O. P. Cohen (Eds.), *Implications and complications for deaf students of the full inclusion movement* (Gallaudet Research Institute Occasional Paper 94-2, pp. 55–62). Washington, DC: Gallaudet University.

Afterword

Deafness and Social Change: Ruminations of a Retiring Researcher

Kathryn P. Meadow-Orlans
Gallaudet University

The breadth, depth, and richness of the chapters in this book reflect the progress in theory and research with deaf children that has been made since my first hesitant steps were taken on a career path in 1965. Many of my oldest and most treasured friends and colleagues are represented in these pages, and the presence of some newer names and faces reflects the vitality and centrality of the field. This compilation illustrates the increasing sophistication of research methods since the 1960s. Quantitative research has moved from means and standard deviations to MANOVAs and regression equations. Qualitative research has become more acceptable to members of the general research establishment (gatekeepers for the most widely circulated journals), and ethnographic procedures have become more rigorous and standardized. I have always believed that cross-disciplinary collaboration provides fresh insights to any research question, thus was delighted to see represented those who have been trained in anthropology, education, communication science, linguistics,

293

developmental and cognitive psychology, psychiatry, sociology, and social work.

Compared to yesteryear there are more Deaf researchers and those who have native or near-native signing skills (e.g., Erting, Prezioso, & Benedict; Sheridan; Stone). Greater importance is given to involving participants as research partners and to incorporating the views of parents and the Deaf community. Computer and video technologies opened new ways to analyze data collected by naturalistic as well as experimental methods. Research is reported for deaf infants as young as 6 and 9 months of age (see Koester, Papoušek, & Smith-Gray; Swisher). This is a result of progress in identification and diagnostic procedures plus growing recognition of the importance of early intervention. All these trends are reflected in the preceding pages, auguring well for the future while exhibiting differences from the past. The chapters place in clear relief the changes that occurred for deaf children, their families, and their schools since the 1960s and provide a backdrop for thinking about research that might contribute to future gains for deaf children and their families. In the following pages, I present a model that may help to explain the mechanisms of the dramatic social changes in the education of deaf children and the status of deaf adults that in 30 years swept away patterns that had been in place for a century. After looking at the past, I offer some proposals for future research that might fruitfully be conducted.

REVIEWING THE PAST: 1970–1999

Perhaps the most astonishing change in this period concerns the use of sign language with deaf children in the home and at school. Before 1970, virtually all deaf children below age 12 were taught by auditory/oral methods. By 1975, two thirds of younger children and three fourths of high school age students were taught by total communication. In 1992, these overall figures remained about the same, although there were variations by degree of hearing loss, school placement, and age. Sign only (bilingual–bicultural education conducted in ASL) was reported by no more than 5% of schools (Moores, 1996) but has many passionate proponents and has evoked much discussion and debate.

This shift is even more astonishing when the strength of the opposition to sign language is recalled. Traditional oral educators could not bear to see a young child signing. Tales of signing hands tied together or whacked sharply with teachers' rulers are common. Parents were advised never to gesture to a deaf child and to ignore requests made through nonspeech modalities. The specter of deaf beggars peddling sign alphabet cards was used to frighten those who might be tempted to slip into a home sign vernacular.

How can this philosophical and pedagogical shift be explained? Complex social changes can never be attributed to a single influence or even to several but result from multiple factors all of which may interact with each other to speed or retard the rate of change. Research findings were certainly one factor spurring change in deaf education and communication.

Stokoe's linguistic studies (1960) and the Dictionary of American Sign Language (Stokoe, Casterline, & Croneberg, 1965) were a critical force driving this engine of change. The linguistic stamp of approval on a language formerly denigrated as an inferior form of English or a "pidgin language" helped to remove a stigma from the Deaf community and led to heightened respect for and among community members. It led eventually to sign language instructional programs all over the country, to interpreter training programs, to the acceptance of ASL in fulfillment of language requirements for advanced academic degrees, and to generally increased visibility of sign interpreting. A sign language interpreter was seen on nationwide television for the first time when Jimmy Carter accepted the Democratic presidential nomination in 1976. In the late 1990s, televised signing appears regularly.

Another stream of research influencing the shift to signing was a series of studies comparing the achievement, self-esteem, social adjustment, speech, and speechreading prowess of deaf children with deaf and with hearing parents (Meadow, 1967, 1968, 1969; Stuckless & Birch, 1966; Vernon & Koh, 1970). Because deaf parents (almost) uniformly used sign language with their children whereas hearing parents used oral-only communication, these two groups created, in effect, a natural experiment. In each of the studies, deaf children of deaf parents were found to perform or to be rated at higher levels than their peers with hearing parents. Vernon and Koh's study was especially persuasive. They compared deaf children with deaf parents to deaf children with hearing parents who had deaf relatives. Thus the deafness of both groups was most likely caused by heredity rather than a noxious virus or illness that could also influence cognitive functioning thereby depressing educational achievement. Although critics of the use of sign language had warned of its detrimental effects, cumulative results from these studies supported the idea that, at the minimum, the use of sign did not retard achievement.

Research at the University of California, San Francisco, in this early period suggested that interaction of mothers and deaf children was more positive when signs were incorporated in the communication schema (Schlesinger & Meadow, 1972). These several threads of behavioral research supported the general position that the social and educational difficulties of deaf children (90% of whom had hearing parents) were related not to their deafness per se but to social isolation resulting from the absence of early communication.

Research is only one part of the explanation of this particular change and perhaps only a minor one. Social change can best be seen as an interactive, push-pull, chain-linked affair in which progress or regress in one area is felt in many other areas. Thus, legal or legislative changes lead to improved access to education for deaf people, improving their occupational status, causing more positive attitudes toward deafness and sign language, more linguistic and educational research, convincing more hearing parents to learn sign language, creating new advocates inside and outside the Deaf community who press for additional legislation renewing the cycle. This can be viewed as a circular model that may be entered at any point. Legislation or research need not be the initial stimulus for change. Any force exerted on one link in the chain can stimulate movement on a neighboring or distant link.

Legislative changes in this period include Public Law 94-142, enacted in 1975, mandating free appropriate public education for all children with disabilities, ages 5 to 18, plus nondiscriminatory testing, individualized education plans, and schooling in the least restrictive environment. The most recent reauthorization of this law, Public Law 101-476, the Individuals With Disabilities Education Act of 1990, provides services from the time a disability is identified to age 21 and replaces the individualized education plan with an individual family service plan (Moores, 1996). The mandated least restrictive environment served to increase the trend toward local public school or mainstreamed enrollment and away from residential school placements for deaf children. In 1974, 40% of deaf children were enrolled in residential schools and 44% in local public schools. In 1994, 22% were in residential and 69% were in local schools (Moores, 1996).

The Americans With Disabilities Act of 1990 generated far-reaching changes for deaf people, notably in the provision of interpreters. This, in turn, led to an increase in interpreter-training programs. Although much of the program content is focused on legal and medical interpreting, educational interpreting is increasing as deaf students attend classes with hearing students. In 1995, at least 500 educational programs utilized sign interpreters.

Improvements in the educational and occupational status of deaf people have been documented by Barnartt and Christiansen (1996). The status of deaf people, especially deaf women, improved a great deal from the 1970s to the 1990s. In the 1970s, 61% of hearing women but only 37% of deaf women had white collar jobs. In the 1990s, 71% of hearing women and 66% of deaf women had such jobs.

These changes by and for deaf people in the United States are astonishing, and most of them demonstrate progress. However, no one concerned for the futures of deaf children can be complacent. Academic achievement levels are below what educators and parents would like. Early identification of hearing loss is not yet assured for all infants. Options for informed educational placement are too few for too many. Services for hard of hearing children, those with mental or physical health problems, and those in minority groups need improvement. It is important to think ahead and to identify some research priorities for the 21st century.

THE 21ST CENTURY

Planning Research for the Future

Material in several chapters suggests that researchers should look at subgroups of children and families to gain additional insight into the variations in deaf children's behaviors and achievements. The importance of socioeconomic status has perhaps been neglected. One author named social class "the dirty little secret of deafness" (Benderly, 1980), meaning that historically there has been a significant gap between the special services and opportunities available to deaf children with affluent, highly educated parents and those whose impoverished parents have little education. As Nash (chap. 12, this volume) pointed out, this differential is at odds with American egalitarian philosophy and therefore may be difficult to accept or to admit.

Lederberg and Prezbindowski (chap. 5, this volume) reanalyzed their previously published data comparing interactions of mothers with deaf children and those with hearing children. This is in an imaginative effort to explain why other studies reported significant differences in the quality of interactions favoring mothers with hearing children whereas their data did not. They proposed that one reason may lie in previous failures to match educational levels of experimental and control subjects. This is an important consideration in the design of future research. The significant relationship of positive hearing mother–deaf child interaction and amount of support received reported by the Gallaudet study (Meadow-Orlans & Steinberg, 1993) suggests that college-educated mothers may be more successful in obtaining supportive services. Perhaps those mothers have more experience negotiating bureaucracies and dealing with professionals to obtain the information and the services they need. These questions are significant for service providers.

A group of deaf children who can fruitfully be studied, and too often fall between the cracks, are those with behavioral problems or who are at risk for abuse. There have been consistent reports of a high prevalence of emotional problems among deaf children. These studies have been criticized by advocates for the Deaf community as somehow denigrating the capacities of deaf people. The result is a suppression or weakening of mental health services for a needy group. Calderon and Greenberg (chap. 10, this volume) documented the importance of socioemotional competence and programming for deaf children. Carefully designed studies to compare the mental health status and needs of deaf and hearing children could be undertaken. Drawing on her broad clinical experience, Steinberg (chap. 6, this volume) illustrated what sometimes happens to children whose emotional distress is neglected.

Cochlear Implantation

Cochlear implantation for deaf children is increasing at a phenomenal rate. In a national survey of support services, 11% of 404 responding parents of deaf and hard of hearing six- and seven-year-olds reported that their children had received cochlear implants (Meadow-Orlans, Mertens, Sass-Lehrer, & Scott-Olson, 1997). Some observers predict that 50% of eligible 10-year-old children will have had implant surgery by the year 2010. As Spencer (chap. 7, this volume) reported, response to an implant varies enormously, and the psychological, auditory, and linguistic consequences have received little research attention. This is a major area for research.

Mainstreaming

Mainstreaming, much debated, has received some research attention. However, additional information is needed about the kinds of students who benefit and those for whom residential placement might be the least restrictive environment. Stinson and Foster (chap. 11, this volume) provided a great deal of guidance for research about mainstreaming, pointing to an absence of adequate information about interpreters in mainstream settings and about effects of mainstreaming on self-esteem and socialization to Deaf culture. They concluded that "prolonged and close study of how support services are implemented ... is critical to our understanding ... of these services" for mainstreamed deaf students. The excerpts from student interviews included in the Stinson and Foster chapter demonstrate the value of the qualitative approach. Sheridan's (chap. 1, this volume) interviews with 7- to 10-year-old children provide wonderful insights to questions of deafness and identity, coupled with a compelling rationale for naturalistic inquiry.

Intervention and Curriculum

Programmatic or evaluation research on intervention techniques and curriculum innovations is proposed in several chapters. Mohay (chap. 9, this volume) points to the need to examine the Australian program of deaf-mother tutoring with larger groups of hearing mothers with deaf babies. Mertens, Sass-Lehrer, and Scott-Olson (chap. 8, this volume) demonstrate the importance of research on early family intervention programs. Stone's (chap. 13, this volume) plea for deaf-centered curricula for school-age deaf children could lead to an ambitious research program to evaluate the impact of various deaf studies curricula on the achievement, socioemotional adjustment, and self-image of deaf students. As Marschark (chap. 16, this volume) illustrated, it is critical to involve school personnel—teachers, administrators, and support staff—as partners in every phase of such research programs.

Dyssegaard's (chap. 14, this volume) work emphasized the importance of research evaluating the educational practices in developing countries and showed how this would be of value not only for those countries but to educators in other parts of the world informing them about the influence of teachers' and parents' expectations on students' achievements.

Parents' Belief Systems

Swisher (chap. 2, this volume) proposed new areas for research about deaf mothers' attention-gaining and turn-taking strategies with their deaf toddlers. A fascinating research area suggested by her work is an investigation of the influence of mothers' beliefs about children's cognitive and linguistic abilities on their childrearing practices. Which of parents' practices and strategies are intuitive, as explored by Koester, Papoušek, and Smith-Gray (chap. 4, this volume), and which are a result of their conscious ideas and deliberate plans? The impact of childhood deafness on a parent's world view of the nature of development is an area yet to be explored. A rich but underexploited source of information is parents' explanations of their own interactive strategies. In pilot studies for our Gallaudet Infancy Project, Erting and Prezioso explored this technique, viewing videotapes of mother–infant interaction with the mother participants. Unfortunately, time limitations curtailed that effort. The Erting, Prezioso, and Benedict (chap. 3, this volume) chapter is an extension of this approach and demonstrates its value.

Another area for investigation might hinge on the concept of good-enough parenting and good-enough language. Swisher (chap. 2, this volume) documented the wide variety of deaf mothers' early interactive strategies, all of which lead to positive child turn-taking abilities. One group of researchers is currently investigating deaf children's abilities to acquire complex sign language structures from less-than-fluent nonnative signers. This important question has broad implications. Perhaps professionals have been too demanding of hearing parents, expecting them to be more than good enough in both their social and linguistic interactions with their deaf children. Spencer's (chap. 7, this volume) poignant case study, based on interviews with hearing parents of a deaf child, showed that professionals may hinder rather than help families with mixed hearing status by expecting more than parents can reasonably do.

Deaf Children and the Life Span

A recurrent theme in many of my presentations to parents and teachers since the late 1960s has been the importance of viewing deaf children in the context of the life span. This view was bolstered by Schlesinger's insightful essay applying Erikson's developmental model of the eight age-stages to deafness (Schlesinger & Meadow, 1972). It seems possible that many of the early oral–manual controversies were based in part on the separation of professionals serving deaf children and those serving deaf adults. Teachers of young deaf children had little or no contact with deaf adults, and those serving deaf adults were unfamiliar with the concerns and decisions confronting hearing parents of deaf children. However, to do justice to a life span perspective would require longitudinal research following a heterogeneous cohort of deaf children from birth to maturity, like the studies conducted by the Institute of Human Development at the University of California, Berkeley (Clausen, 1993). For example, it would be extremely useful if Akamatsu and Musselman (chap. 15, this volume) were to extend their longitudinal study of children's cognitive and language skills by collecting additional data at both younger and older ages. Very little is known about how deaf children's educational performance relates to their occupational and social performance in adulthood.

This ambitious vision may be an impossible dream because it requires a firm institutional and financial support base and a team of dedicated researchers. Perhaps researchers need to work toward some impossible dreams if future deaf children are to move ahead in tomorrow's world.

A PERSONAL CONCLUSION

As I write this concluding chapter, I can do no better than to acknowledge all those who have contributed to my work. They include hundreds of parents and children who have participated in many different studies, some extending over 5 or more years, with multiple contacts for longitudinal data collection. They include dozens of teachers who provided assessments of students, reports of classroom performance, and insights from their daily observations, plus school administrators who welcomed me and my teammates into their schools despite the disruption and additional work. Colleagues have become friends as well as collaborators, those who are deaf always tolerant of my less-than-native signing skills.

My 8 years at the University of California, San Francisco, with Dr. Hilde S. Schlesinger at Mental Health Services for the Deaf were exhilarating and productive. Gallaudet University provided a supportive base from 1976 to 1995, and since the late 1980s Dr. Donald F. Moores was a consistently helpful director and colleague in the Center for Studies in Education and Human Development. Finally, members of the broader deaf education community have continued to be wonderful consumers—readers, users, and constructive critics of circulated research reports. The sense that they were ready to contribute to the research process and to utilize research results led me to continue in this field after the completion of my initial project and has been a constant source of personal and professional satisfaction. To all of these, and to my friends who contributed to this book, I send a thousand thanks.

REFERENCES

Barnartt, S. N., & Christiansen, J. B. (1996). The educational and occupational attainment of prevocationally deaf adults: 1972–1991. In P. C. Higgins & J. E. Nash (Eds.), *Understanding deafness socially, Continuities in research and theory* (2nd ed., pp. 60–70). Springfield, IL: Thomas.

Benderly, B. L. (1980). *Dancing without music.* Garden City, NY: Doubleday.

Clausen, J. A. (1993). *American lives, Looking back at the children of the Great Depression.* New York: The Free Press.

Meadow, K. P. (1967). *The effect of early manual communication and family climate on the deaf child's development.* Unpublished doctoral dissertation, University of California, Berkeley.

Meadow, K. P. (1968). Early manual communication in relation to the deaf child's intellectual, social, and communicative functioning. *American Annals of the Deaf, 113,* 29–41.

Meadow, K. P. (1969). Self-image, family climate, and deafness. *Social Forces, 47,* 428–438.

Meadow-Orlans, K. P., Mertens, D. M., Sass-Lehrer, M. A., & Scott-Olson, K. (1997). Support services for parents and their children who are deaf or hard of hearing. *American Annals of the Deaf, 142,* 278–293.

Meadow-Orlans, K. P., & Steinberg, A. G. (1993). Effects of infant hearing loss and maternal support on mother–infant interactions at 18 months. *Journal of Applied Developmental Psychology, 14,* 407–426.

Moores, D. F. (1996). *Educating the deaf, psychology, principles, and practices* (4th ed.). Boston: Houghton Mifflin.

Schlesinger, H. S., & Meadow, K. P. (1972). *Sound and sign: Childhood deafness and mental health.* Berkeley: University of California Press.

Stokoe, W. C., Jr. (1960). *Sign language structure: An outline of the visual communication systems of the American Deaf.* Studies in linguistics, occasional papers, 8, Department of Anthropology and Linguistics, University of Buffalo, New York.

Stokoe, W. C., Jr., Casterline, D. C., & Croneberg, C. G. (1965). *A dictionary of American Sign Language on linguistic principles.* Washington, DC: Gallaudet College Press.

Stuckless, E. R., & Birch, J. W. (1966). The influence of early manual communication on the linguistic development of deaf children. *American Annals of the Deaf, 111,* 452–460, 499–504.

Vernon, M., & Koh, S. D. (1970). Early manual communication and deaf children's achievement. *American Annals of the Deaf, 115,* 527–536.

Author Index

Subject Index

A

ADHD (attention deficit hyperactivity disorder), 11
Adult Child Language (ACL), 47
Affect, definition, 66
Affective tone, 66–67
African American culture, 231
Alienation, 12–14, 16–17, *see also* Isolation
American Sign Language (ASL)
  English literacy and, 41–42, 120–121, 281
  historical rise, 295
  initialized signs, 44
  linking signs and fingerspelling, 49–51
  metaphor in, 105
  in residential schools, 197
Americans With Disabilities Act (ADA), 213, 221, 296
Amplification technology, 122, 173–174, 198, *see also* Cochlear implants
Analytic propositions, 285
Anger, 97–98, 121
ASL, *see* American Sign Language
Attachment
  diagnosis of deafness and, 134
  domesticated others, 9–12, 16

maternal responsiveness and, 83
security of, 76–79, 90
sense of self, 77
Attention deficit disabilities, 11, 141
Attention deficit hyperactivity disorder (ADHD), 11
Attention getting, *see also* Joint attention; Turn taking
  breaking the line of gaze, 155, 157
  children's responses to, 29–30
  deaf mothers-deaf infants, 24–26, 28–34
  descriptive study of, 26–28
  divided attention, 156–157
  frequency of, 28–29
  in hearing parents, 58
  infant age and, 33–34
  observations of, 30–32, 118–119
  pointing, 155–156
  tapping, 25, 28, 31–32, 34–35
  touch and, 61, 155
  toys in, 31, 36
Autism, 141

B

Behavior problems
  diagnosis of deafness by, 134, 147
  mainstreaming and, 224–225
  need for communication and, 143